D1616062

INDIANS IN MALAYA

INDIANS IN
MALAYA

SOME ASPECTS OF
THEIR IMMIGRATION AND
SETTLEMENT (1786–1957)

KERNIAL SINGH SANDHU

CAMBRIDGE
AT THE UNIVERSITY PRESS
1969

Published by the Syndics of the Cambridge University Press
Bentley House, 200 Euston Road, London N.W.1
American Branch: 32 East 57th Street, New York, N.Y.10022

Library of Congress Catalogue Card Number: 69-10271

Standard Book Number: 521 07274 3

Printed in Great Britain
at the University Printing House, Cambridge
(Brooke Crutchley, University Printer)

CONTENTS

Contents

ILLUSTRATIONS

List of illustrations

TABLES

ix

List of tables

PREFACE

The full story of the Indians in Malaya has yet to be told. Here an attempt has been made to assemble the information relating to some aspects of their immigration and settlement, with special reference to the period of British rule (1786–1957).

The study is divided into three parts: the research setting of the work is discussed in the Aide-mémoire while Part 1 is devoted to the origins and characteristics of the Indian migration to Malaya during the period of British hegemony.

In this study, migration is defined as the essentially peaceful movement of individuals, from one country to another, with the intention of effecting a temporary or lasting change in residence. Migration so defined has a twofold aspect; it covers both 'immigration' and 'emigration', the movement into and out of a particular country, respectively. The term 'emigrants', as used here, applies to all persons leaving a country either temporarily or permanently, including both nationals and aliens. 'Immigrants' will be understood to mean persons moving either permanently or temporarily into a country, irrespective of whether they are nationals of that country or aliens. These definitions refer only to international movements, the movement of people within the boundaries of Malaya or the Indian subcontinent being termed 'internal migration'.

Part 2 follows up the modern Indian migration and discusses the growth, from the foundation of Penang, of the Indian population in Malaya, together with its changing composition, distribution and settlement patterns. Incidentally, it should be stated that the term 'settlement' is used here in the everyday parlance of the word, and denotes both the processes of occupying pioneer areas and the settlement ensembles themselves, that is the groupings, morphology and characteristics of individual features, *per se*.[1]

The bases of livelihood of the Indians and their role in the total Malayan economy are discussed in Part 3 while the study is rounded off in the Epilogue, which attempts to recapitulate the past, capture the present (1957) and discuss future developments and trends in the Indian community of Malaya.

The text has been supplemented and illustrated by a considerable

---

[1] P. E. James and C. F. Jones (eds.), *American geography: Inventory and prospects* (Syracuse, 1954), pp. 125–6; United Nations, *Multilingual demographic dictionary: English Section* (New York, 1958), p. 18.

number of maps and statistical tables. Generally speaking, the statistical data for the Indian and other population maps of Malaya have been processed on the basis of *mukims*, that is the smallest administrative units of the country. In certain instances, however, where the depiction of distribution patterns on the above basis was not possible, district boundaries have been used as areal units. But, for cartographic convenience, neither *mukim* nor district linear boundaries are shown in these maps. Consequently, there is no intended or strict correlation between administrative boundaries and isopleths shown on the final population maps.

A word is needed here also, on certain conventions employed in the text. No single system of transliteration or spelling of Indian or Malayan words has been followed. In the case of place-names, for convenience and because they occur so frequently in the quotations, the forms current during the period of British suzerainty have been retained; for example 'Tinnevelly' and not 'Tirunelveli', and, 'Malacca' and not 'Melaka' or 'Malaka'. For other South Asian and Malayan terms generally the local modern forms used by the Malayans and the peoples of the Subcontinent themselves have been adopted. These are italicized, except in such cases as names of castes, coins and communities, which are treated as other proper names or technical terms as the case may be. It should however be noted that it was not thought necessary to provide diacritical marks or etymologies for the various Asian and other foreign terms in the text, except where such indications were imperative for a proper understanding of, or were relevant to, the discussion.

Unless otherwise stated all dollar rates and data in the text are in Malayan or Straits dollars.[1] One Malayan (or Straits) dollar is taken as being equal to 2s. 4d. sterling,[2] U.S. $0.33 and Indian rupees (rps.) 1.55. The Indo-Malayan rate of exchange given here and in the subsequent pages is that which was prevailing prior to the devaluation of the Indian rupee in 1966.

Most of the research on which this volume is based was originally undertaken in the preparation of a thesis submitted for the degree of Doctor of Philosophy in the University of London. During the preparation, which included archival and field work in Malaya, India, Pakistan,

[1] Since 12 June 1967 Singapore and Malaysia have been issuing separate currencies —Singapore and Malaysian dollars respectively. These new currencies are, however, of equal value and fully interchangeable with each other. When these different currencies were established the two governments also agreed to treat the old joint currency (the Malayan dollar) on par with the new currencies. Malaysia and Singapore did not devalue when sterling devalued in November 1967, except for the old Malayan dollars still in circulation, which now became worth 85·7 Malaysian or Singapore cents.
[2] This Anglo-Malayan rate of exchange is that which prevailed before the devaluation of the pound in 1967.

Preface

Ceylon and Britain between 1960 and 1966, of the doctoral dissertation and its subsequent revision for publication I received unstinted support from innumerable individuals and institutions, and I wish to place on record my indebtedness to these anonymous helpers. I am also indebted to my colleagues of the University of Singapore and University College London for their encouragement and assistance, to Mr T. Allen, Mr J. Bryant, Mr C. Cromarty, Miss I. Loh, Mr P. K. Poon, Mr G. Riddle, Miss K. L. Tan, Mr W. Tan, Mr A. Wong, Miss J. Yeo and Mr M. Young for the skill and patience with which they helped with the maps and typing, to Professor C. A. Fisher for his valuable suggestions, to the Office of the High Commissioner for the United Kingdom in Malaya for its grant of the Merdeka (formerly the Queen's) Scholarship to study in Britain, and to the University of Singapore for allowing me a generous period of leave from official duties. But the largest measure of my thanks must be reserved for Professors H. C. Darby and Paul Wheatley for their advice and support in almost all stages of this work. Finally, it is fitting that I should also record my gratitude to the constant helpfulness and tolerance of the officials and staff of the National Archives of Malaysia, the Ministry of Labour, Malaysia, the National Library of Singapore, the University of Singapore Library, the Trade Commissioner for Pakistan in Singapore, the National Library of India, the Madras Record Office, the National Archives of India, the Public Record Office, the India Office Library, the Colonial Office Library, the British Museum and the Royal Commonwealth Society Library.

K.S.S.

Singapore
23 July 1967

ACKNOWLEDGEMENTS

For permission to use official and other copyright maps as bases for four of my maps, I am indebted to the Departments of Geography of the Universities of Malaya and Singapore for figs. 31*f* and 43 from Hodder (1953, p. 31) and Ooi (1959, p. 16), respectively, and the Surveyor-General, Survey Department, Malaysia, for figs. 38, 39*b* and 43.

ABBREVIATIONS

The following contractions are used in the footnotes below.

ABP	*Amrita Bazar Patrika* (Calcutta), followed by date.
ARAGIBM	*Annual Report of the Agent of the Government of India in British Malaya* (Calcutta, New Delhi), followed by year and page.
ARICCS	*Annual Report of the Indian Chamber of Commerce, Singapore* (Singapore), followed by year and page.
ARLDCS	*Annual Report of the Labour Department of the Colony [State] of Singapore* (Singapore), followed by year and page.
ARLDFM	*Annual Report of the Labour Department of the Federation of Malaya* (Kuala Lumpur), followed by year and page.
ARLDM	*Annual Report of the Labour Department of Malaya* (Kuala Lumpur), followed by year and page.
ARLDS	*Unpublished Annual Report of the Labour Department of Singapore for the year 1965*, followed by number of table and page.
ARPSDM	*Annual Report on the Postal Services Department, Malaya* (Singapore), followed by year and page.
ARSILFB	*Annual Report of the South Indian Labour Fund Board* (Kuala Lumpur), followed by year and page.
BM	*British Malaya [Malaya]* (London), followed by month, year and page.
BM:BP	*British Museum: Broughton Papers*, followed by category, folio page and date of document.
BP	*Birch Papers*, followed by category and date of document.
CARWIEA	*Consolidated Annual Report on the Working of the Indian Emigration Act, 1922* (New Delhi), followed by year and page.
CIAMMM	*Central Indian Association of Malaya: Minutes of Meetings*, followed by date of minutes.
C.O.273	*The Colonial Office's (London) Straits Settlements original correspondence*, followed by number of volume, year and date of correspondence or, as in the case of the Colonial Office Minute Papers, by number of Minute Paper.
COR	*Conference of Residents, Federated Malay States: Abstract of proceedings*, followed by date of proceedings.
CPMS	*Correspondence relating to the Protected Malay States*, followed by year, serial number and page of correspondence.
CSAR	*Colony [State] of Singapore Annual Report* (Singapore), followed by year and page.

Abbreviations

CSSMRCA	*Chinese Secretariat, Singapore, 'Monthly Review of Chinese Affairs, June, 1938'*, followed by page.
DCSI	*Debates of the Council of State of India* (New Delhi), followed by year, volume and page.
DLAI	*Debates of the Legislative Assembly of India* (New Delhi), followed by year, volume and page.
DOPD:CISF	*District Office, Port Dickson: Chuah Indian Settlement File*, followed by number, details and date of correspondence.
EICOS	O. W. Wolters, *Early Indonesian Commerce and the Origin of Sri Vijaya*, an unpublished thesis submitted for the degree of Doctor of Philosophy, University of London, 1960, followed by page.
ES	*The Eastern Sun* (Singapore), followed by date.
FFRB	*Father Fée's Record Book on the founding of St. Joseph's Tamil Settlement, Bagan Serai.*
FLDAAR	*Federal Land Development Authority Annual Report* (Kuala Lumpur), followed by year and page.
FMAR	*Federation of Malaya Annual Report* (Kuala Lumpur), followed by year and page.
FMG	*Federation of Malaya Government Gazette* (Kuala Lumpur), followed by year and page.
FMOYB	*Federation of Malaya [Malaysia] Official Year Book* (Kuala Lumpur), followed by year and page.
FMSAR	*Federated Malay States Annual Report* (Kuala Lumpur), followed by year and page.
FMSPAR	*Federated Malay States Police Annual Report* (Kuala Lumpur), followed by year and page.
FMSPD	*Federated Malay States: Proceedings of Durbars held in 1897, 1903 and 1927*, followed by page.
FMSRRCC 1930	*Federated Malay States: Report of the Rice Cultivation Committee, 1930* (Kuala Lumpur), followed by number of volume and page.
FNMERMP 1910	*The Financial News Map of the Estates of the Rubber plantation companies in the Malay Peninsula, 1910* (London).
F.O.	*Foreign Office (London) correspondence*, followed by number and date of correspondence.
GMPPD	*Government of Madras Proceedings in the Public Department*, followed by year, number and date of proceedings or Government Order.
GMPPWLD	*Government of Madras Proceedings in the Public Works and Labour Department*, followed by year, number and date of proceedings or Government Order. Some of the Government Order numbers are followed by the letter 'L', which denotes 'Labour'.
GRAPM	*General Report on the Administration of the Province [Presidency] of Madras* (Madras), followed by year and page.

Abbreviations

GRN	*Grenier's Rubber News* (Kuala Lumpur), followed by year, volume, number and page.
H	*The Hindu* (Madras), followed by date.
HCIOL	*The Hamilton Collection of the India Office Library* (London), followed by category and date of document.
HCOF	*The High Commissioner's [including the Secretary to High Commissioner's] Office Files of Kuala Lumpur*, followed by year, number and date of correspondence.
HD	*Hansard's Official Report of the [British] Parliamentary Debates* (London), followed by date.
HT	*The Hindustan Times* (New Delhi), followed by date.
I	*The Indian* (Singapore), followed by number of volume, year and page.
IDM	*The Indian Daily Mail* (Singapore), followed by date.
IE	*The Indian Emigrant* (Madras), followed by year, volume, number and page.
IICMM	*The Indian Immigration Committee: Minutes of Meetings*, followed by date of minutes.
IMR	*The Indo-Malayan Review* (Ipoh), followed by number of volume, year and page.
IO:EL	*India Office: Emigration Letters from India and Bengal*, followed by number of volume, year and page or number and date of proceedings.
IO:EP	*India Office: Emigration Proceedings of the Government of India*, followed by number of volume, year and page or number and date of proceedings.
IO:FP	*India Office: Foreign Proceedings of the Government of India*, followed by number of volume, year and date.
IO:HC	*India Office: Home Correspondence [Public Department]*, followed by number of volume, year and date of correspondence.
IO:IPPEL	*India Office: India: Public, Post Office and Ecclesiastical Letters*, followed by number of volume, year and date.
IO:JP	*India Office: Judicial Proceedings of the Government of India*, followed by number of volume, year and page or number and date of proceedings.
IO:PDI	*India Office: Public Despatches to India*, followed by number of volume, year, number and date of despatch.
IO:PPC	*India Office: Parliamentary Papers [Parliamentary branch] Collection*, followed by number of volume, year, title and date or page of report/correspondence.
IO:RJCMP	*India Office: Revenue, Judicial and Legislative Committee: Miscellaneous Papers*, followed by number of volume, year and date of document.
JAR	*Johore Annual Report* (Singapore, Johore Bahru), followed by year and page.
JIA	*Journal of the Indian Archipelago and Eastern Asia* (Singapore), followed by number of volume, year and page.

Abbreviations

JSSF	*Johore State Secretariat Files*, followed by category, number and year of file.
KAR	*Kelantan [annual] Administrative Report* (Kota Bharu), followed by year and page.
KGB	*Kew Gardens Bulletin* (London), followed by year and page.
MAJ	*The Malayan Agricultural Journal* (Kuala Lumpur), followed by number of volume, year and page.
MAREI	*Madras Annual Report on Emigration and Immigration* (Madras), followed by year and page.
MCECLFMS	W. L. Blythe, *Methods and Conditions of Employment of Chinese Labour in the Federated Malay States*, followed by page.
MCPFLC	*Minutes and Council Papers of the Federal Legislative Council* (Kuala Lumpur), followed by year and number of paper.
MDS	*Monthly Digest of Statistics* (Singapore), followed by month, year and page or number of table.
MM	*The Malay Mail* (Kuala Lumpur), followed by date.
MMECSS	*Minutes of Meetings of the Executive Council of the Straits Settlements*, followed by date of minutes.
MP	*Maxwell Papers*, followed by category and date of document.
MPM	*The Malayan Police Magazine* (Kuala Lumpur), followed by number of volume, year and page.
MRM	*Monthly Record of Migration* (Geneva), followed by number of volume, year and page.
MSB	*Monthly Statistical Bulletin of the Federation [States] of Malaya*, followed by month, year and page or number of table.
MSFMS	*Manual of Statistics relating to the Federated Malay States* (Kuala Lumpur), followed by year and page.
MSGAR	*Malay States Guides Annual Report* (Kuala Lumpur), followed by year and page.
MUAR	*Malayan Union Annual Report* (Kuala Lumpur), followed by year and page.
MUARLD	*Malayan Union Annual Report of the Labour Department* (Kuala Lumpur), followed by year and page.
MYB	*The Malayan Year Book* (Singapore), followed by year and page.
NAI:CEBHD	*National Archives of India: Consultations of the Emigration Branch of the Home Department*, followed by number and year of box and date and number of consultations.
NAI:EP	*National Archives of India: Emigration Proceedings of the Government of India*, followed by month (wherever applicable) year, category and number or date of file or proceedings. Some file numbers of these proceedings include the abbreviations 'L & O' or 'Os', which stand for 'Lands and Overseas' and 'Overseas' respectively.

Abbreviations

NAI:FPP	*National Archives of India: Foreign Political Proceedings of the Government of India*, followed by month, year, category, number and date of proceedings or consultations.
NAI:HDPP	*National Archives of India: Home Department Political Proceedings*, followed by month, year, category and number or date of file or proceedings.
NAI:RAD(S)P	*National Archives of India: Revenue and Agriculture Department [Survey] Proceedings of the Government of India*, followed by month, year and number of proceedings.
NAM:COHC	*National Archives of Malaysia: Original correspondence between the Colonial Office (London) and the High Commissioner for the Malay States*, followed by year, number and date of correspondence.
NHGMP	P. Wheatley, *Notes on the Historical Geography of the Malay Peninsula (mainly before 1900), prepared at the Centre for Southeast Asian Studies, University of California, Berkeley, for the Regional Conference of Southeast Asian geographers, Kuala Lumpur, Malaya, 2–23 April, 1962,* (Mimeo., Berkeley, California, 1962), followed by page.
OGMSG	Abdul Karim Bagoo, *Origin and Growth of the Malay States Guides*, unpublished Academic Exercise, History Department, University of Malaya, Singapore, 1956, followed by page.
P	*The Planter* (Kuala Lumpur), followed by year, volume, number and page.
PAMAR	*[United] Planters' Association of Malaya Annual Report* (Kuala Lumpur), followed by year and page.
PAMC	*[United] Planters' Association of Malaya Circulars,* followed by year, number and page of circular.
PAMMM	*[United] Planters' Association of Malaya: Minutes of Meetings,* followed by date of minutes.
PAR	*Perak Annual Report* (Taiping, Kuala Lumpur, Ipoh), followed by year and page.
1957 PCFM	*1957 Population Census of the Federation of Malaya* (Kuala Lumpur), followed by number of report and table or page.
PCGGI	*Proceedings of the Council of the Governor-General of India* (Calcutta, New Delhi), followed by year, volume and page.
PFC	*Proceedings of the Federal Council* (Kuala Lumpur), followed by year and page.
PG	*The Penang Gazette* (Penang), followed by date.
PGG	*Perak Government Gazette* (Taiping, Kuala Lumpur), followed by year and page.
PINC	*Papers of the Indian National Congress*, followed by category of document, year and page or date.

Abbreviations

PLCSS	*Proceedings of the Legislative Council of the Straits Settlements* (Singapore), followed by year, number of paper (where necessary) and page.
PMBR	*Proceedings of the Government of Madras Board of Revenue*, followed by date.
PMOJMCCEL	*Principal Medical Officer, Johore, 'Memorandum on the Collection by Cess from Employers of Labour of dues for hospital treatment, 1938,'* followed by page.
PP	*Parliamentary Papers* (London), followed by volume, year, part of volume or number of paper and page.
PPSE	*Papers of Penang Sugar Estate*, followed by number of volume, year and date of document.
PWIG	*Prince of Wales Island Gazette* (Penang), followed by date.
RCHE 1924	*Report of the Commission appointed to enquire into certain matters affecting the Health of Estates in the Federated Malay States, 1924* (Singapore), followed by page.
RIIFMS	*Report on the proceedings of a commission appointed to consider the question of the encouragement of Indian Immigration to the Federated Malay States*, followed by page.
RLC 1890	*Report of the commissioners appointed to enquire into the state of labour in the Straits Settlements and Protected Native States, 1890* (Singapore), followed by page.
RLC 1896	*Report of the commissioners appointed to enquire into the question of Indian immigration, 1896* (Singapore), followed by page.
RSB	*The Rubber Statistical Bulletin* (London), followed by year, volume, number and page or table.
RSE 1957	*Report of the committee set up to enquire and investigate into the causes, extent and results of the Sub-division of Estates in the Federation of Malaya, 1957* (Kuala Lumpur), followed by page or number of table.
SABI	*Statistical Abstracts for British India* (Calcutta, New Delhi, London), followed by year and page.
SAR	*Selangor Annual Report* (Kuala Lumpur), followed by year and page.
SB	*The Straits Budget* (Singapore), followed by date.
SDT	*Singapore Daily Times* (Singapore), followed by date.
SEMMPI	*Statement Exhibiting the Moral and Material Progress and condition of India* (Calcutta, New Delhi, London), followed by year and page.
SFP	*Singapore Free Press* (Singapore), followed by date.
SGG	*Selangor Government Gazette* (Kuala Lumpur), followed by year and page.
SI	*The Servant of India* (Poona), followed by year, volume, number and page.
SJ	*The Selangor Journal* (Kuala Lumpur), followed by number of volume, year and page.

Abbreviations

SM	*The Sunday Mail* (Kuala Lumpur), followed by date.
SNL:COGSS	*Singapore National Library: Original correspondence between the Colonial Office (London) and the Governor of the Straits Settlements*, followed by year, number and date of despatch.
SNVFM	*Statistical information concerning New Villages in the Federation of Malaya, 1952* (Kuala Lumpur).
SSAR	*Straits Settlements Annual Report* (Calcutta, Singapore), followed by year and page.
SSARID	*State of Singapore Annual Report of the Immigration Department* (Singapore), followed by year and page.
SSBB	*Straits Settlements Blue Book* (Singapore), followed by year and page.
SSFR	*Straits Settlements Factory Records*, followed by number of volume, year and date of proceedings, consultations or document.
SSG	*Straits Settlements Government Gazette* (Singapore), followed by year and page.
SSR	*Straits Settlements Records*, followed by category, year and number of item.
SSSF	*Selangor State Secretariat Files*, followed by year and number of file.
ST	*The Straits Times* (Singapore), followed by date.
SYB	*Singapore Year Book* (Singapore), followed by year and page.
T	*The Times* (London), followed by date.
YRSK	*Yearly [annual] Report on the State of Kedah* (Penang, Alor Star), followed by year and page.

To minimize the already heavy burden of footnotes only abbreviated notes are given for all other material. The system of footnote citation adopted for this material is that of the name of the author followed by the year of publication and page number. All these and other citations are included in full in the select bibliography (see p. 318), except for those illustrating some minor point for which a full reference is included in the footnotes.

The select bibliography is divided into unpublished and published sources. The former are listed alphabetically by title and the latter by author or, where this is not available, by title. The section on published sources is further subdivided into two parts: the first includes books, part(s) of book(s), pamphlets, articles and maps, and the second newspapers and periodicals.

A GLOSSARY OF INDIAN, MALAY AND OTHER LOCAL TERMS USED IN THE TEXT

adat: Malay, local custom; common or customary law in general.

adimai: Tamil, slave, bondsman.

āśrama: Sanskrit, hermitage; resting-place; abode of an ascetic.

atap: Malay, roofing thatch. Customarily manufactured from fronds of the nipa palm (*Nipa fruticans*, Wurmb.). *Ataps* from the bertam palm (*Eugeissona tristis*, Griff.) are also common but considered of inferior quality.

bagi-dua: Malay, a system of renting land, literally implying division of costs, profits and losses on an equal-share basis, but in practice may involve other arrangements with regard to the actual sharing.

bahara: Malay, a local measure of weight approximately equal to 400 lb., but which has historically varied with time, place and commodity.

bangsal: Malay, shed; temporary structure of wood or *atap* for use as a booth, stable, labour-line, or any similar purpose.

baniya: both Hindi and Punjabi, Hindu trader or shopkeeper-cum-moneylender.

belukar: Malay, secondary forest consisting predominantly of shrubs, herbs and young trees.

bendahara: Malay, chief minister in an old Malay state (but with other meanings in Java and Sumatra).

Benggali: Malay, native of Bengal; Northern Indian.

bigha: both Hindi and Punjabi, a North Indian measure of area approximately equal to half an acre.

brāhmaṇa: Sanskrit, member of the highest or priestly caste of the original four castes in the Indian social structure.

burra sahib: both Hindi and Punjabi, a man of some position, especially a European.

calôrmi: Sanskrit, moving or agitated waves.

caṅkam: Tamil, guild, corporation, association or party.

Ceṭṭinaaṭu: Tamil, the Chettiar homeland.

chaiwalla: Hindi, tea-seller.

cinna kangani: Tamil, minor or deputy *kangani*.

cuvarkam: Tamil, heaven.

dar al-Islam: Malay, the world of Islam as contrasted with the *dar al-barab*, the territories of the infidels.

darwan: both Urdu and Punjabi, gate or door-keeper.

Dharmaśāstra: Sanskrit, Sacred Laws of the Hindus.

dhuk: both Hindi and Punjabi, sufferings, pain, sorrow or difficulties.

doodwalla: Hindi, milkman or dairy-keeper.

duli: Malay, dust. In Malay honorifics signifies dust under the foot of royalty.

Glossary of terms

Feringgi: Malay, a European, especially a Portuguese.

gula melaka: Malay, palm sugar; jaggery.
gurdwara: Punjabi, Sikh temple.
Gurmukhi: Punjabi, the written language of the Sikhs.

haji: Malay, a man who has made the pilgrimage to Mecca.
hulu (ulu): Malay, upper part, especially the headstreams of a river, and then by extension the interior of a territory.

izzat: both Urdu and Punjabi, honour; self-respect.

jaga: Malay, watchman; caretaker.
jajahan: Malay, district.
janmi: Malayalam, superior landholder (landlord) of Malabar.

kajang: Malay, waterproof matting.
kale pani: both Hindi and Punjabi, black waters; Andaman Islands.
kaḷḷu: Tamil, toddy.
kaḷḷukkaṭai: Tamil, toddy shop.
kaḻutai: Tamil, donkey; ass.
kampong: Malay, rural settlement.
kaṇakkapiḷḷai: Tamil, foreman or headman.
kangani (kangany): Tamil, foreman or labourer of some standing; labour recruiter.
karang: Malay, ore-bearing stratum.
kathi: Malay, a registrar of Muslim marriages and divorces who also has some judicial powers.
kati: Malayo-Javanese, a measure of weight which has varied considerably from time to time and place to place but which is now fixed at approximately equal to 1⅓ lb.
katti: Tamil, knife.
kedai: Malay, shop.

Keling (Kling): Malay, native of Madras; Southern Indian.
kepala: Malay, headman.
kerah: Malay, corvée.
kerani: Malay, clerk.
kongsi: Hokkien (also Cantonese, Hakka and Teochiu), partnership or association of any sort. Primarily used of Chinese guilds and secret societies, but also of syndicates in general. In popular speech in Malaya often used as an abbreviation of *rumah kongsi* (Malay) = labourers' communal dwelling.
kṣatriya: Sanskrit, member of the second highest or warrior caste of the original four castes in the Indian social structure.
kuttee: both Hindi and Punjabi, hermitage; resting-place.

lalang: Malay, tall coarse grass, *Imperata cylindrica*, Beauv.
lebai: Malay, a pious village elder; a mosque official.

mahamulia: Malay, most illustrious; a Malay honorific applied only to royalty.
maistry: Hindi, foreman; labour recruiter.
mandur: Malay, overseer.
mantra: Sanskrit, a Vedic hymn; a mystical verse or magical formula; incantation.
maṇveṭṭi (mumṭi): Tamil, hoe.
masok Melayu: Malay, assimilation into the Malay community through conversion or intermarriage.
maulana: Malay, my lord; my master; a term used when addressing learned doctors of law.
mentri: Malay, minister; official.
merdeka: Malay, freedom or independence.
mirasi (districts): Tamil, the Tamil districts of hereditary land tenure.

mirasdar: Tamil, a hereditary land-lord.

mleccha: Sanskrit, foreigners; non-Āryan.

mukim: Malay, territory sharing a common mosque; territorial sub-division for purposes of land revenue and administration.

mulada: Canarese (Kanarese), heredi-tary farm servant; labourer.

mulla: both Urdu and Punjabi, a learned man; a Muslim preacher or teacher.

Mungkali kwai: Cantonese, literally 'Bengali' devil, but in popular speech used to denote all North Indians and especially Sikhs.

munsif: Urdu, village headman or official.

musafirkhana: both Urdu and Pun-jabi, rest-house or hospice.

mutalaaḷi: Tamil, man of some wealth, such as a rich shopkeeper or land-lord.

nāgara: Sanskrit, city, town or city-state.

Nan-yang: Mandarin, South Seas, in the sense of Southeast Asia.

narakam: Tamil, hell.

orlong: Malay, a measure of area approximately equal to $1\frac{1}{3}$ acres.

padang: Malay, treeless waste land; an expanse of grass; in colonial times applied to playing fields and small parkland lawns.

padi: Malay, rice (i) as a plant; (ii) in the ear; (iii) as unhusked grain.

padiyal: Tamil, a hereditary farm servant; tenant; labourer.

paduka: Malay, a Malay honorific meaning 'royal'.

paisa: both Hindi and Punjabi, money.

paṇḍitá: Sanskrit, one learned in Sanskrit lore; today the term is used occasionally as an honorific and bestowed on distinguished Hindus.

pankhawalla: both Hindi and Pun-jabi, fan attendant.

pannaiyal: Tamil, hereditary farm servant; tenant; labourer.

pardesi: both Hindi and Punjabi, foreigner; foreign (land).

pelas (palas) tikus: Malay, a small palm, *Licuala acutifida*, Mart.

pikul: Malay, a measure of weight approximately equal to $133\frac{1}{3}$ lb.

pukka nawkri: both Hindi and Pun-jabi, a permanent pensionable em-ployment or job.

purdah: Urdu (also Hindi and Pun-jabi), veil; curtain, particularly one serving to screen women from sight of strangers, especially men; figuratively, Indian system of secluding women of rank.

puthal-surat: a composite Tamil and Malay term meaning new im-migrant or bearer letter, that is a note or certificate promising em-ployment in Malaya.

Ramasamy: a common paternalistic or derisive name, the specific meaning depending on the circum-stances of application; used princi-pally by Europeans, especially planters, to denote *all* South Indian labourers in Malaya.

sabha: Hindi, guild, corporation, association or party.

samseng: Hokkien, ruffian, gangster or thug.

samudra-yātrā: Sanskrit, sea travel.

sekolah ugama: Malay, religious school.

sewa: both Hindi and Punjabi, service; aid.

shahbandar: Malay, harbour super-intendent; municipal-cum-port officer.

shahukar: Punjabi, merchant or trader.

silara (*cillarai*) *kangani:* Tamil, minor or deputy *kangani.*

sinkeh: both Hokkien and Teochiu, new arrival or 'greenhorn' in *Nan-yang.*

sirdar (*sardar*): both Urdu and Hindi, chief; foreman; labour recruiter.

sireh: Malay, betel-vine; the leaf of this vine in which are wrapped parings of areca nut and morsels of gambier and lime, the whole of which forming the betel quid. When chewed this quid has a mildly stimulating effect.

śloka: Sanskrit, distich; stanza.

surau: Malay, a private mosque in contradistinction to a mosque of general assembly.

tāla: Sanskrit, Palmyra palm (*Borassus flabellifera*, Linn.).

Tamilnaatu: Tamil, the Tamil homeland.

tantal: Tamil, overseer; foreman.

tar: Hindi, Palmyra palm (*Borassus flabellifera*, Linn.).

taraṅga: Sanskrit, wave; section of a book.

tari: both Hindi and Punjabi, toddy.

thitti-surat: A composite Tamil and Malay term denoting a leave of absence letter or a certificate of identity or current employment in Malaya.

tongkang: Malay, a lighter or large, shallow-draft, sea-going barge.

tooni: Tamil, a South Indian boat.

towkay: Hokkien, head of family or business; used colloquially to denote owner of property or wealth.

tuan (*tuan besar*): Malay, man of some position, especially a European.

vaikuntam: Tamil, heaven.

wayang kulit: Malay, shadow-play.

zamin: both Urdu and Punjabi, land.

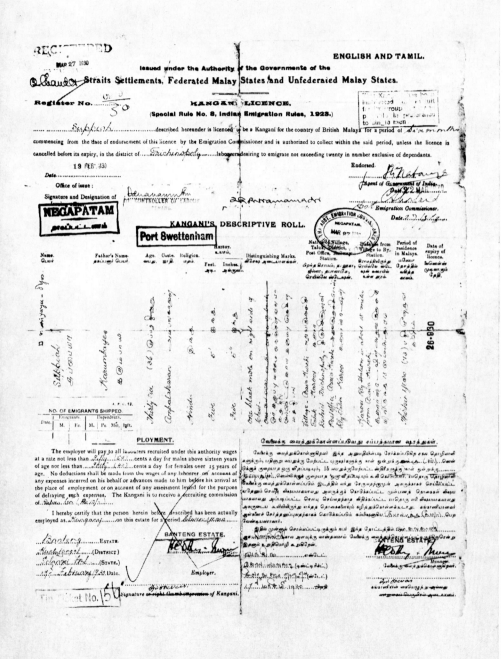

Fig. 1 (a) Front side.

A *kangani* licence

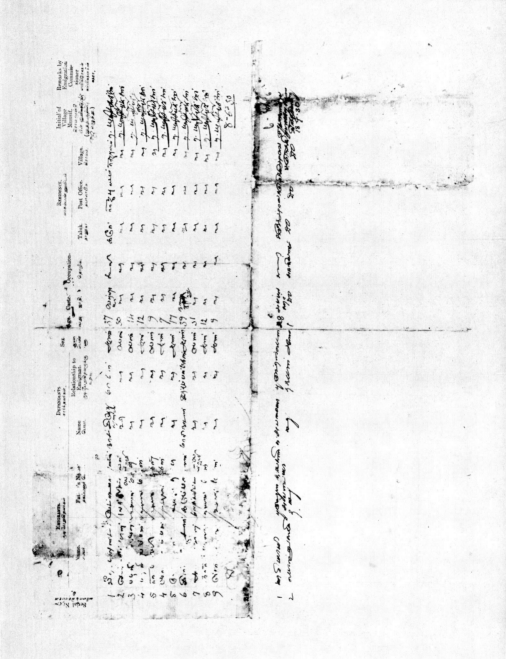

Fig. 1 (b) Reverse side.

AIDE-MEMOIRE

Malaya[1] occupies the southern half of the long narrow peninsula that projects from the Southeast Asian[2] landmass far southwards into the Indonesian Archipelago. Singapore Island, at the peninsula's southern tip, is now joined to the mainland by a causeway across the Johore Strait. Lying interposed between the Indian and Pacific Oceans, Malaya, in the first place, occupies a focal position in relation to the rest of Southeast Asia. Not only is it the meeting ground between the continental and insular parts of the region but its physical and human ties with Indonesia, particularly Sumatra, are characteristically close, while on its northern margins continental influences are, and have been, equally significant. Secondly, situated as it was almost exactly half-way between its two great neighbours, India[3] and China, it was, in the days of the sailing ship, an unavoidable coastline, for mariners sailing east or west through the Southeast Asian seas, to be negotiated only by a lengthy circuitous coastal voyage or by transpeninsular portage. The role of an unavoidable landfall was emphasized by the monsoonal nature of the winds over the Indian Ocean and the China Sea.[4] The advent of steam navigation introduced some modifications but Malaya continued to border on the shortest sea-route between India and China. Thirdly, the Straits of Malacca and the Straits of Singapore occupy key positions for all shipping between the Pacific and the Indian Ocean ports. The pattern of Southeast Asian seas makes them a natural convergence area for seaborne trade not only for the island world but also for international shipping lines, which are of necessity and convenience funnelled through these Straits, making Singapore, and before it Malacca, the 'Gibraltar of the East' (fig. 2).

The pivotal position of Malaya has from ancient times made it an arena

[1] Unless otherwise stated, the term 'Malaya' or 'British Malaya', as it was called before independence, is used throughout the text to include both the Federation or the present-day States (West Malaysia) of Malaya and the State or Republic of Singapore. Although separated politically from each other, these two territories have nevertheless traditionally functioned together.

[2] For present purposes 'Southeast Asia' comprises Burma, Thailand, Cambodia, Laos, North and South Vietnam, Singapore, Malaysia, Brunei, Indonesia, Portuguese Timor and the Philippines.

[3] Unless otherwise stated, the terms 'India' and 'Indian subcontinent' include both the present-day Union of India (Bharat) and Pakistan; 'Indian' denotes all persons of Indian origin, including Pakistanis.

[4] Dale, 1956, pp. 1–31.

of conflicting foreign interests; and these have markedly influenced its history. Indian influences established the earlier pattern while the expansion of Europe into Asia marks the later stages.

The Indian era of Malayan history (up to A.D. 1511) was the period when Indianized[1] kingdoms flourished in Malaya and elsewhere in Southeast Asia, either as semi-independent city-states or under the hegemony of some controlling power, also Indianized and generally based outside Malaya. It falls into two broad divisions, which can be conveniently described as the age of the city-states (up to c. A.D. 1400), when the focus of attention was the isthmian tract of the Siamo-Malay peninsula,[2] and the period of the Malacca Sultanate (c. A.D. 1400–1511), when the centre of attention was the Straits of Malacca.

Archaeological discoveries in Malaya indicate the presence of man in the area at some time between the ninth and the third millennium B.C.,[3] but it was only as a result of the diffusion of Indian cultural traits in the region in the early centuries of the Christian era that there developed *nāgaras* based on Indian concepts and cults of royalty and court-life. During the next millennium the fortunes of these city-states waxed and waned; either they enjoyed brief periods of precarious independence or they were under the aegis of some outside power, finally becoming absorbed into the Thai or Malaccan kingdoms in the fourteenth century. After this the focus shifted to the Straits of Malacca region with the rise of the Sultanate of Malacca.

Malacca, from a struggling 'thieves' market' in the first years of the fifteenth century, gradually developed into the greatest emporium of the Muslim world of Southeast Asia. Its prosperity and strategic position drew the attention of the Portuguese, who conquered it in 1511 as part of their plan to gain a monopoly of the valuable spice trade. But their dream of monopoly was never completely fulfilled as they lacked the necessary resources for such an ambitious undertaking. The Portuguese were both traders and crusaders and their proselytizing zeal won few friends but many enemies amongst the newly Islamized countries of Southeast Asia. Furthermore, their continued monopolistic trade policy,

[1] 'Indianized' and 'Indianization' are terms associated with the process which established a cross-cultural link between India and Southeast Asia and by means of which Indian, particularly Hindu and Buddhist, cultural traits were transferred from the Subcontinent to Southeast Asia.
[2] The term 'Siamo-Malay peninsula' or 'Peninsula' is used in the text to denote the club-shaped territory jutting out from the Southeast Asian landmass from about 15°N. latitude to the island of Singapore (fig. 2). This is to distinguish it from the ambivalent and ambiguously used term, 'Malay Peninsula', which from henceforth will be used only to denote the Federation or States of Malaya, unless otherwise stated and explained.
[3] Tweedie, 1953, pp. 9–78.

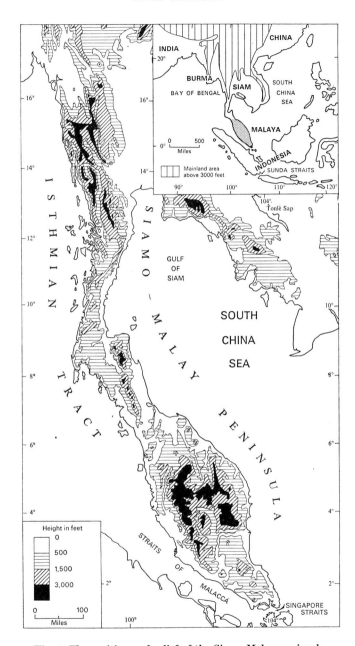

Fig. 2. The position and relief of the Siamo-Malay peninsula.
Inset: The position of Malaya.

although ineffectively implemented, led a number of merchants to avoid or desert Malacca for the other parts of Southeast Asia. Despite these reverses, Malacca appears to have retained its pre-eminence for some time during the Portuguese hegemony, but then entered upon a period of prolonged decline. Its capture, in 1641, by the Dutch, who had followed the Portuguese in quest of the same trade, accelerated this process. The Dutch capture of Malacca was, like that of the Portuguese, part of an overall plan to secure control of such contemporary Southeast Asian trade staples as spices and tin, and to eliminate all unfriendly foreign interests, including Indians. For the next century and a half they endeavoured to maintain an economic monopoly along the coasts of Malaya, while the interior of the country was racked by Thai, Achehnese and Minangkabau invaders attempting to carve out territorial niches for themselves. The constricting effects of the Vereenigde Oostindische Compagnie's monopolistic trade policy ensured Malacca's continued decline.

The foundation of Penang by the British in 1786, as an entrepôt and a base, was a virtual death blow to Malacca and to Dutch power in Malaya. Within a few years Malacca's trade almost ceased and the moribund town was itself occupied by British forces in 1795, only to be returned to the Dutch in 1818. However, with the conclusion of the Anglo-Dutch treaty of 1824 the town and its environs permanently came under British rule. Meanwhile, in 1819, Singapore had been founded and was already showing unmistakable portents of its future prosperity. Together with Province Wellesley, the strip of land opposite the island of Penang, and the Dindings, near the mouth of the Perak river, which were acquired by the East India Company in 1800 and 1826 respectively, the three territories were in 1826 amalgamated to form the Straits Settlements, with Singapore as its capital from 1832. When the Company's rule was abolished in 1858, control over the Straits Settlements was transferred to the India Office and thence, following agitation by local British interests, to the Colonial Office in 1867.

In 1874 the Colonial Office reversed its policy of non-intervention in the affairs of the Malay States[1] and accordingly occupied Perak, Selangor and Sungei Ujong (a part of the State of Negri Sembilan) in that year and appointed a British Resident in each to manage its administration. Pahang and the remainder of Negri Sembilan were later incorporated in this system. To co-ordinate policy and practice, especially in respect of road and railway construction, land alienation and immigration, these four states were consolidated into a single federation—the Federated

[1] This term is employed to include both the Federated and Unfederated Malay States of the country (fig. 3).

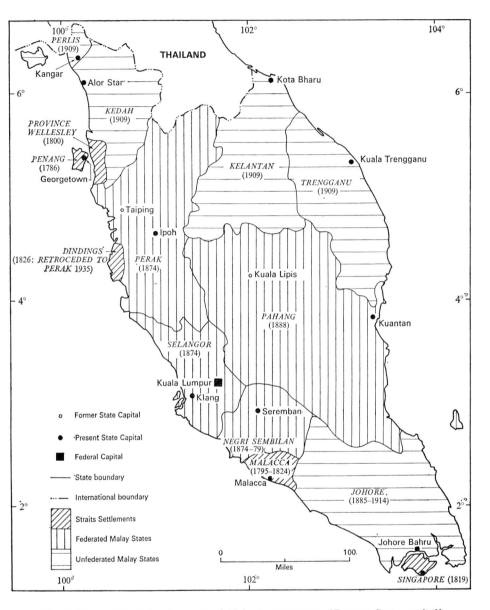

Fig. 3. The political development of Malaya, 1786–1941. 'Present State capital' refers to the position in 1967.

Malay States—in 1896 and Kuala Lumpur was chosen as capital. In 1909 the states of Kedah, Perlis, Kelantan and Trengganu came under British rule as protected states. Finally in 1914, Johore, which as early as 1885 had already become a British sphere of influence, also came under British control. These five states were collectively called the Unfederated Malay States, and each one of them was allotted a British Adviser, who in practice had virtually the same role as the Residents in the Federated Malay States. Therefore, although there have been internal changes since then, the present territorial limits of Malaya can be said to date from 1914 (fig. 3).

Malaya remained under British control till 1942 when it was occupied by the Japanese, who held it till their defeat in 1945. With the return of the British to Malaya the Straits Settlements possessions of Penang and Malacca,[1] together with the 'hotch-potch' of Federated Malay States and Unfederated Malay States, were all amalgamated to form a single political unit—the Malayan Union—in 1946, as a step towards streamlining administration and political control. Singapore was left out of this Union, as a separate British Crown Colony. In 1948, following agitation by Malay nationalists for special privileges, the Malayan Union, which granted equal economic and citizenship opportunity to all races domiciled in Malaya, was scrapped and replaced with the Federation of Malaya, which guaranteed primacy of the Malays in such matters as land, government employment and political franchise. *Merdeka* was granted in 1957, when Persekutuan Tanah Melayu, or the Federation of Malaya, was formally inaugurated as a sovereign state. Singapore soon followed to become the internally self-governing State of Singapore in 1959. In 1963 these two units together with the Borneo territories of Sabah (British North Borneo) and Sarawak were linked together into a new independent Federation—the Federation of Malaysia. Kuala Lumpur, the capital of the Federation of Malaya, was retained as capital of the new Federation too. However, this new arrangement lasted for less than two years, and in August 1965 Singapore was once again on its own, this time as a fully independent republican state.

The smallest administrative unit in the Malayan political hierarchy is the *mukim*, roughly the equivalent of the English parish, which forms part of a district or *jajahan*. The *jajahans* in turn are grouped to form states (figs. 4, 5).[2] Each state has its own legislature, administrative

---

[1] The Dindings were separated from the Straits Settlements and returned to Perak State in 1935 (fig. 3).

[2] Though there have been several alterations, such as some larger units being subdivided and some smaller units being grouped to form larger units, there does not seem to have been any significant change in the overall framework of *mukim* and district boundaries in the Straits Settlements since the 1890s and in the Malay

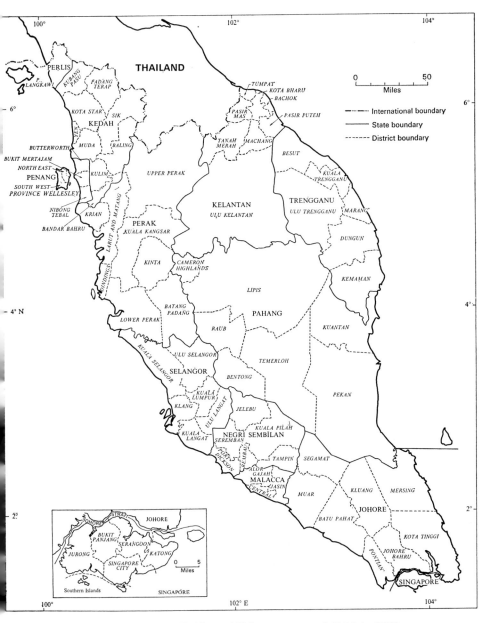

Fig. 4. The political divisions of Malaya: states and districts, 1957.

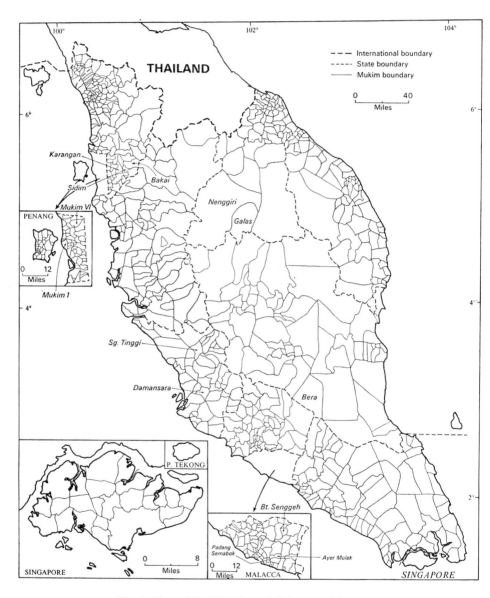

Fig. 5. The political divisions of Malaya: *mukims*, 1957.

service and such other governmental paraphernalia, in addition to the Federal equivalent. Indeed until after the Second World War, although overall policy was decided by the Colonial Office through the Governor of the Straits Settlements who was also the High Commissioner for the Malay States, the Straits Settlements and the Malay States engaged their junior governmental personnel quite separately. This to some extent also applied to the individual states forming the Straits Settlements and the Federated and Unfederated Malay States.[1] For the sake of administrative convenience, private enterprise, too, tended to follow the political divisions. Such factors often militated against and reduced inter-state migration.[2]

Modern Malaya has traditionally been separated into western and eastern Malaya, on the basis of economic development and population patterns. Western Malaya, consisting of the states of Kedah, Perlis, Penang, Perak, Selangor, Negri Sembilan, Malacca, Johore and Singapore, with its inherent advantages and the benefit of the momentum of an earlier start in economic development, is the dominant partner, containing most of the tin mines, rubber plantations, towns, major ports, roads and railways, in addition to more than 80 per cent of the total population of the country and about an equal proportion of the Chinese and Indian populations. Eastern Malaya, comprising Pahang, Kelantan and Trengganu States, has been developed comparatively little but it has great potentialities as it contains much of the country's remaining arable land and also large deposits of iron-ore, which have only recently been mined on an extensive scale.[3]

A century and a half ago Malaya had an estimated population of less than 500,000, predominantly Malays.[4] The settled parts of the country consisted of a few clearings around the coast and along the rivers and isolated patches in the forest and swamps. Production was limited very largely to foodstuffs, small quantities of some exotic crops and jungle items. Yet today it contains more than 10,000,000 people including

States since the 1930s. In the case of Singapore *mukims* ceased to be used for census purposes in 1957, being replaced by the 1956 Legislative Assembly electoral divisions and polling districts. However, the boundaries of the latter divisions are not totally alien to their *mukim* predecessors; in most cases it merely meant the division of a single *mukim* into a number of electoral or polling units. In these circumstances, though some adjustments are necessary, comparison with the previous *mukim* divisions is still possible. There is very little uniformity in size between *mukims* within the individual states or the country as a whole. In 1957, for example, they ranged from 1,611 (Nenggiri, Kelantan) to 0·04 (Padang Semabok, Malacca) square miles in area (fig. 5).

[1] Tilman, 1964, pp. 82–101 *et seq.*
[2] See Part 2 below.   [3] See Parts 2 and 3 below.
[4] Anderson, 1824, pp. 30 ff.; Newbold, 1839, vol. 1, 54–5, 136–7, 283, 418–19; Crawfurd, 1856, p. 259.

not only some 4,500,000 Malays and significant numbers of Europeans, mainly British, Eurasians, Arabs, Jews, Thais and Ceylonese, but also the biggest Chinese population outside the two Chinas and, with the possible exception of Ceylon,[1] the largest overseas Indian concentration. Moreover, although covering an area of only 50,824 square miles, Malaya is the source of about a third of the world's supply of rubber and tin,[2] as well as large quantities of palm oil, copra and pineapples.[3] The port and bastion of Singapore commands a pivotal location in east–west communication lines and trade routes.

In this remarkable transformation of Malaya from forest and swamp into one of the richest and best developed countries in Asia, the Malay took little active part, modern Malaya being mainly the joint creation of British, Chinese and Indian capital, enterprise and labour. The Malay had until quite recently remained largely tied to his traditional, highly localized, *kampong* agricultural economy, based on tiny landholdings eked out with a little fishing and hunting.

A number of books and articles have been written on modern Malaya and its people and their economy.[4] The Malays[5] have been the subject of several of them while the characteristics and contributions of the British and Chinese communities in Malaya have also received considerable attention.[6] In the building of present-day Malaya the role and contribution of the Indians has also earned, often extravagant, acknowledgement. Three examples must suffice.

[1] Enquiries at government offices in Colombo and New Delhi in 1962 revealed no conclusive evidence relating to the total number of Indians in Ceylon then. The estimates of the Ceylonese officials ranged from 800,000 to 1,000,000 persons while those of their Indian counterparts in New Delhi were of the order of 700,000 to 850,000.

[2] International Bank for Reconstruction and Development, 1955, pp. 9, 34, 244; Fisher, 1964, pp. 610–15.

[3] See Part 3 below.

[4] The writer has in mind the works of such authors as Smith, 1952; Ginsburg and Roberts, 1958; Hodder, 1959, and Ooi, 1963.

[5] R. J. Wilkinson, *History of the Peninsular Malays* (Singapore, 1920); R. Firth, *Malay fishermen: Their peasant economy* (London, 1946); L. R. Wheeler, *The modern Malay* (London, 1928); J. M. Gullick, *Indigenous political systems of Western Malaya* (London, 1958); E. H. G. Dobby, 'Padi landscapes of Malaya', *The Malayan journal of tropical geography* (Singapore), vi (1955), 1–78, and x (1957), 3–139; Federated Malay States, *Papers on Malay subjects* (Kuala Lumpur, 1907–11); Abdul Majid, *The Malays in Malaya* (Singapore, 1928), and Winstedt, 1947, are some examples.

[6] See, for example, F. A. Swettenham, *British Malaya: An account of the origin and progress of British influence in Malaya* (London, 1948); Clodd, 1948; C. E. Wurtzburg, *Raffles of the eastern seas* (London, 1954); Mills, 1942; Purcell, 1948; Freedman, 1957; S. O. Ong, *One hundred years' history of the Chinese in Singapore: A chronological record of the contributions of the Chinese community to the development of Singapore from 1819 to 1919* (London, 1923); L. F. Comber, *Chinese secret societies in Malaya* (New York, 1959), and Blythe, 1947.

Aide-mémoire

... With little exaggeration it has been said of Europe that it owes its theology, its literature, its science and its arts to Greece: with no greater exaggeration it may be said of the Malayan[1] races that till the nineteenth century they owed everything to India: religions, a political system, medieval astrology and medicine, literature, arts and crafts . . .

    . . . India found the Malay a peasant of the late stone age . . . and left him a citizen of the world.[2]

Few people have bothered about the subject sufficiently to realize what the people of India and Ceylon did in the early days of the country. When British officers came into the country they numbered four or five in one State and perhaps three or four in another, but they had devoted staffs mainly composed of the people of India and Ceylon.

    . . . The people from India and Ceylon . . . did not know the customs of the people of the country, but they were sent out to the wilds to do their work and they did it . . . and everyone would always be grateful to the people of India and Ceylon for being the pioneers of the work of those days.[3]

. . . The Indian Labourers were the creators of Malaya's . . . rubber wealth and were called 'the life blood of the colony' . . .[4]

Yet, except for numerous scattered references in publications dealing with India or Malaya or Southeast Asia,[5] as a whole, and a few books and articles, mostly politically biased, on certain aspects of the community,[6] there has, to the writer's knowledge, so far been no detailed

[1] In present-day local parlance the term 'Malayan' is not restricted to Malays, but denotes anyone who has made Malaya his or her home.

[2] Winstedt, 1944, pp. 183, 195.

[3] Sir George Maxwell, former Chief Secretary of the Federated Malay States, cited by Krishnan, 1936, p. 21.

[4] J. Mitchell, a member of the Straits Settlements Legislative Council, cited by Krishnan, 1936, p. 21.

[5] Sundaram, 1930; Dobby, 1950; Kondapi, 1951; Smith, 1952; Ginsburg and Roberts, 1958; Hodder, 1959; Parmer, 1960; Wheatley, 1961; Ooi, 1963, and Fisher, 1964, are some examples of such works.

[6] Almost all this literature has been by Indians themselves, either sojourners or temporarily or permanently domiciled in Malaya. Until academics began to interest themselves in Indian problems in Malaya, nearly all of these writers were journalists or leaders of the Indian community or some other such persons, and as noted above their accounts more often than not had a definite political bias. For the most part their writings have been panegyrics of Indian achievements in Malaya and condemnations of the Indians' poor treatment by the British Malayan government and *tuans*. The majority of them appear to have had the same singular motive: to eulogize and publicize the position of the Indians as a whole, or their particular sector of interest or achievement, probably in the hope of improving their status. In these circumstances, these works, although they contain useful information—some of the comments and descriptions being by keen observers—are of limited research value. Practical considerations forbid me itemizing all examples of the foregoing genre of writings but K. A. Neelakandha Aiyer's *Indian problems in Malaya* (Kuala Lumpur, 1938), V. G. Nair's *Swami Satyananda and cultural relations between India and Malaya* (Kuala Lumpur, 1960), and G. Netto's *Indians*

study of any kind, and much less a geographical one, covering the whole of the long period of Indian arrival and settlement in Malaya.

It is the aim of this work to make a study of some aspects of Indian overseas[1] migration to, and settlement in, modern Malaya from its beginnings, with the establishment of the East India Company station at Penang in 1786 to 1957, the year of Malaya's independence from British rule.[2] It was decided to confine the study to this period partly for practical reasons partly on account of there being little significant continuity between the earlier Indian contacts with Malaya and those which were developed under British rule, and not least because 1957 marks the end of one era—the colonial—and the beginning of another— independence—in Malaya's history and development. Furthermore, 1957 also serves as a bench-mark for comparative purposes, as it was also the year of the latest population census in the Federation (States of Malaya)

in *Malaya: Historical facts and figures* (Singapore, 1961) are three fairly representative samples. Neelakandha Aiyer was secretary of the politically militant Central Indian Association of Malaya during the time of the preparation and publication of his book. Its aim was to acquaint the people of 'the mother country' with something about Malaya and of the Indians who lived there (p. v.) and particularly, it would appear, of their various disabilities in the field of employment and political representation. This work was so critical of the Malayan government that it was banned immediately upon its publication. V. G. Nair's volume is a rambling panegyric of twentieth-century Indian missionary activity, particularly that of the Malayan Shuddha Samajam or Pure Life Society and its founder Swami Satyananda who, in the words of the author (preface), 'in the midst of turmoils and calamities, carried high the banner of the Indian Rishis which proclaimed the transcendental philosophy of universalism that united mankind with the unbreakable bonds of compassion and love'. Based mainly on secondary sources, Netto's work purports to set out the 'historical facts and figures' relating to Indians in Malaya (preface). However, this aim is scarcely achieved. There are many errors of which the following are examples. On p. 9, we find '...there is...evidence that India had contacts with Malaya six or seven centuries before Christ'. There is no such evidence. Then on p. 33 he says, '...every estate was a *virtual concentration camp* with forced labour' (italics mine). It is true that the lot of the Indian labourers was indescribably hard on some estates but this hardly constitutes a ground for such wild exaggeration as the above. Again (p. 55) he informs us that 'over 10,000 Sikhs had been employed as watchmen in Malaya' and there were '10,000 Sikh moneylenders'. It is not certain which year he has in mind but it appears to be 1947. If his figures are to be believed they would make *every* gainfully occupied Sikh in Malaya in 1947 a 'watchman' and a 'moneylender'—a ridiculous misrepresentation. Finally (p. 63), he states that '*all* the Indians who took part in the Indian Independence League and the Indian National Army were interned by the British Military Administration on treason charge (*sic*)'—italics mine. Only some of the leaders were interned (cf. Chettur, 1948, pp. 13 *et seq.*).

[1] With the exception of a few Indians who are known to have made their way overland by way of Burma and Thailand, and a small number who travelled by air, all migration between the Subcontinent and British Malaya was by sea.

[2] In Malaya, the year 1957 is generally taken to mark the end of British rule for the country as a whole, notwithstanding the fact that Singapore did not formally become fully self-governing till 1959.

and Singapore. Finally, more than 95 per cent of the Indian immigrants entering Malaya over the last 2,000 years appear to have come into the country between 1786 and 1957.

The sources of information available included whole series of official and private manuscript and printed confidential and published records of the Malayan, Indian and British governments and of individuals, organizations and groups located in the archives, libraries and private depositories in Malaya, India and Britain. To this vast collection must be added the numerous books, articles, periodicals, newspapers and maps containing information relating to the Indians in Malaya. Finally, as indicated above in the Preface, there was the field work: in addition, the writer having travelled extensively in Malaya and India since his childhood, he undertook planned field work in Malaya during the vacations of the 1960–1, 1961–2 and 1965–6 sessions and in India and Pakistan in July–September 1962 and February–March 1965 to supplement and illustrate the source materials described above.

The foregoing sources of information represent a mass of material, in fact an embarrassing amount of material in terms of quantity and variety. For example, the *Straits Settlements factory records* for the years 1786 to 1830 alone run into nearly 200 volumes, each volume in turn consisting of hundreds of closely hand-written folio pages. But the quality and usefulness as source materials, for our purposes, of these and the rest of the records and other material is another matter. Indeed, one of the major and constant problems was not one of selection but of resolving the uneven coverage and emphasis, inaccuracy, unreliability, discontinuity and the fragmentary, obscure and contradictory character of some of the source materials available. Typical though this is of most sources of information it is especially applicable to the material in Malaya. For instance, no one place in Malaya possesses a complete set of even such basic published records as the federal and state *Annual Reports* and the population census reports. Similarly, many of the unpublished records and the memoranda and other material printed for restricted circulation also show wide gaps. For example, records of the pre-war[1] Residents' conferences are non-existent, except for the *Abstract of the proceedings of Residents' conferences, 1922–31* and *Index of decisions of Residents' conferences, 1897–1928* preserved in the National Library, Singapore. Likewise, the original correspondence between the Residents and the Advisers and between them and the High Commissioner (also the Governor of the Straits Settlements) for the Malay States,

---

[1] Unless otherwise stated the terms 'pre-war' and 'post-war' refer to the period before and after, respectively, the Japanese occupation of Malaya (1942–5).

and the minutes, memoranda and letters that went into the formation of the High Commissioner's (and the Governor's) despatches to the Colonial Office, have been lost for ever.

Much material was lost during the Malayan campaign, following the Japanese invasion, through destruction or removal by retreating British officialdom, and as a result of bombing, fire, looting and general vandalism. The small federal museum at Kuala Lumpur, for example, was bombed and much of the material there never recovered.

The Japanese soldiers showed little respect for things British and in many places they made huge bonfires with government files, records and books in addition to urging the people to discard all books in the English language.[1]

The British Military Administration, which replaced the Japanese upon the latter's surrender in 1945 and ruled Malaya till the re-establishment of civil government in 1946, did little to salvage the old records. In fact, in some cases more destruction was done during this short period of time than during the whole of the Japanese occupation.[2]

Finally, some of the materials that survived or were saved or salvaged by some conscientious civil servant have since been misplaced or lost through neglect or are unavailable through maladministration.[3]

[1] Many people destroyed their libraries for fear of Japanese reprisals. The more enterprising ones not only sold their own collections as paperweight to shopkeepers, junk-dealers and vendors but also the old government records and files in the offices where they worked. It was not an uncommon sight during and immediately after the Japanese occupation to see food-pedlars serving their peanuts, fried bananas, curry-puffs and other similar delicacies on memoranda of Residents and Advisers or on sheets from the files of the Labour Department or the *Proceedings of the Federal Council* or some other such records.

[2] Pilfering of and black-marketing in government property was a profitable business during the British military administration period while many valuable materials found their way out of the country in the possession of officials and other individuals as private property, perhaps to adorn family or *alma mater* libraries or become collectors' items.

[3] Until a few years ago, when the post of 'Keeper of Public Records' was created, there was no central depository for the reception or storage of public records. They were to be found dumped in places like Public Works Department garages, Education Department store-rooms and the basement of the State Secretariat Buildings in Kuala Lumpur. Even as late as 1960, though some progress had been made to locate and collect the surviving records, little had been done to catalogue or arrange them, and most of them continued to rot in crates adorning the steps and the ground floors of the Dewan Tunku Abdul Rahman and the old Telecommunication Building, Kuala Lumpur, in which were located, then, the offices of the Keeper of Public Records-cum-Director of the National Museum. In Singapore, the situation was somewhat better, the available records being housed in the (Raffles) National Museum and Library. But even here the organization was chaotic and what older records were salvaged have only recently been saved from complete destruction, through mould, by the installation of an air-conditioning unit. Then, here, too, full-scale documentation of what has survived is still in progress and is beset with handicaps, not the least of which is the dearth of qualified workers.

14

Aide-mémoire

The loss of source material in Malaya would have been even more serious were it not for the fact that much of the published material on Malaya and also the Governor's (and High Commissioner's) despatches to the Colonial Office survive in London, which is easily the best centre in the world for codified material on Malaya. Then there is also the survival of the Malayan immigration and other correspondence with India in Madras, New Delhi and the India Office library in London. However, most of the documentary materials which have survived, and are available in Malaya and in these various centres, have a political flavour. Again, many of them are not directly concerned with the Indians but contain reference to them.

Much that follows has been culled from such widely located and fragmentary source materials as those discussed in the preceding paragraphs. In these circumstances problems of modification and verification were ever present and pressing, and some uneven coverage and omissions in the text unavoidable.

The text has been illustrated and amplified by numerous statistics. In addition, since statistics about the Indians in Malaya are not to be found in any one place or source and some of these are even in danger of gradually becoming inaccessible for one reason or another, it was felt that the inclusion of as many of these statistics as possible in the text would not only reinforce the narrative but also collect and preserve these statistics in one source for future research and reference.

The inclusion of these statistics in the text in a coherent and intelligible form, however, posed a number of problems. In the first place, though Indian immigration into Malaya dates from the very first day of the foundation of Penang, bodies like the Emigration and Immigration Department, Madras, the Indian Immigration Department, Straits Settlements, the Indian Immigration Committee, Malaya, and the Agent of the Government of India in British Malaya, which were all at one time or other concerned with collecting data on Indian migration, did not come into existence till 1875, 1879, 1907 and 1923 respectively.[1] Then, too, not all of them functioned continuously and still fewer collected migration data. Similarly the first Malaya-wide population census was not taken till 1921.

It appears that this lack of adequate statistics is not just a peculiarity of the earlier phases of Indian settlement in British Malaya, but rather a recurrent malady. There is little accurate information on the large shifts and dispersals of population that took place during the Japanese occupation. The same can almost be said of the changes that took place in the distribution of the Indian population after the proclamation of

[1] See Part 1 below.

the Emergency[1] in 1948, and the consequent resettlement of rural peoples: despite a plethora of state and district War Executive Committees and Resettlement Officers, no comprehensive up-to-date information is available on the actual (new) locations, provenance, numbers and composition of the total population affected by the resettlement programme.[2]

More important than just the availability of sufficient figures is, perhaps, the fact that several of them do not lend themselves to meaningful interpretation because they either lack uniformity and continuity or are inaccurate and unreliable. For example, reviewing the situation up to date, *The Penang Gazette* in its issue of 2 October 1852 was led to remark, 'only the entries about the arrival and departure of square rigged vessels were accurate. The rest (of the statistics)', it continued, 'were not statistics but lying figures...Surely', it went on, 'there is enough real work in this world to save men of being set such a spinning of sand and weaving of moon beams such as the attempt to manufacture facts by the multiplication of errors must prove.' This warning about the unreliability of statistical data was echoed, although in a different context, half a century later by the superintendent of the 1901 population census of the Federated Malay States: '...the Census returns... in 1891 are...unreliable...'[3] Neither are the later population censuses free from discrepancies.[4]

Again, too, although migration was a major factor in the population growth of pre-war Malaya, a proper system of recording, compiling and publishing migration statistics has never been established. Before the last war, data relating to migration referred almost entirely to the records of Chinese and Indian sea-passengers embarking and disembarking at the ports. For the most part they are concerned with only

[1] A state of emergency, popularly referred to as 'The Emergency', was proclaimed in Malaya on 16 June 1948, following the outbreak of an armed Communist revolt. The Emergency ended twelve years later, on 31 July 1960.

[2] Sandhu, 1964, pp. 157 ff.

[3] Hare, 1902, p. 2.

[4] For instance, the *Census of British Malaya, 1921* (Nathan, 1922, p. 148) enumerated 32,456 Indians in Singapore on 24 April 1921, but its 1947 counterpart (del Tufo, 1949, p. 588) gives a figure of 33,028 Indians in Singapore for the same date. Similarly, the total number of Indians in Malaya on the night of 1 April 1931 is given as 624,009 in the 1931 census (Vlieland, 1932, p. 121) but as 621,847 in the 1947 census (del Tufo, 1949, p. 78) for the same date. No explanation is given in any of the census reports for the changing figures. Then a simple check—inter-census change should be numerically equal to the sum of the natural increase and net immigration—applied to the 1947–57 inter-census period reveals an undercount of some 200,000 persons in the total population of Malaya in 1957 (United Nations, 1962, pp. 28–41). Indeed, this undercount was probably higher when we take into account that the registration of births is incomplete, under-registration in the remoter states like Kelantan and Trengganu being as high as 20 per cent in the 1947–57 period (Saw, 1964, pp. 45–6).

those travelling as deck-passengers. In the case of the Indians this was further limited, until 1929, to only South Indians,[1] no record being maintained of North Indian passengers until that date. Moreover, the migration data, until 1954, do not separate the permanent migrants, temporary migrants, residents, visitors and transit passengers. From 1954 more detailed information is available in respect of immigrants as a result of the rather strict immigration regulations.[2] For example, the annual arrivals are now divided into two broad categories of persons, those coming in for residence and those coming in for visits (including transit).[3] However, without corresponding statistics on emigrants, it is not possible to obtain an accurate picture of net migration, in the sense of permanent or temporary residence.

Then, migration statistics for Indians were collected simultaneously by the Labour Department (which succeeded the Indian Immigration Department, Straits Settlement),[4] Malaya, the Madras Government, the Indian Immigration Committee, Malaya, and the Agent of the Government of India in British Malaya, but their totals seldom agreed.[5]

An additional problem is that the arrival and departure figures of the Indians from 1946 onwards include all such persons entering or leaving Malaya irrespective of which country they were travelling to or from. Furthermore, these data and those for the preceding years, too, are mainly for Malaya as a whole, and there is little possibility of separating the movements to and from the individual Malayan states and India.

Finally, there is the problem that little information is available of inter-state, let alone inter-district and inter-*mukim*, population movements, the only information being from Malayan birthplace and identity-card[6] statistics. But until after the war more than three-quarters of the Indians in Malaya were born outside Malaya. With regard to identity cards, these have been issued only from 1948. Any change of address had to be notified. In the case of movement from the Federation (States) of Malaya to Singapore and vice versa, this involved the surrendering of the existing identity-card for one of the territory of the new address.

---

[1] For our purposes 'South (Southern) India' comprises the present-day Indian states of Andhra Pradesh, Madras, Mysore and Kerala. The rest of mainland India and Pakistan comprises 'North (Northern) India' (figs. 9, 11).

[2] See Part 1 below.

[3] *SSARID*, 1960, pp. 2–8.

[4] See p. 15 above.

[5] For example, for the period 1925–30, for which comparable figures are available, the number of South Indian deck-passengers arriving in Malaya is given by the above bodies as 577,329 (*SSAR*, 1926–30), 451,786 (*GRAPM*, 1926/7–1931/2), 577,536 (*IICMM*, 1931) and 581,134 (*ARAGIBM*, 1926–30) respectively.

[6] All residents of Malaya twelve years and above in age were required to register for identity-cards under the *Emergency (Registration) Regulations, 1948*. Although the Emergency officially ended on 31 July 1960, identity-cards continue to be required.

Aide-mémoire

Records of persons notifying change of address and exchanging Federation (States) of Malaya cards for Singapore and vice versa would then constitute statistics of persons moving between one *mukim*, district and state and between the Federation (States) of Malaya and Singapore. Unfortunately, the record of persons changing addresses within the Federation (States) of Malaya has never been published, or for that matter, never compiled or collected either on a chronological or territorial basis. Records of persons exchanging Federation (States) of Malaya identity-cards for Singapore and vice versa have, however, been published from 1955 onwards. However identity-card statistics, even if all changes recorded were available, do not, and cannot, in any way represent a complete picture of internal migration because they exclude children below twelve years of age, and in many cases persons do not trouble to change identity-cards or notify change of address, on the pretext that they are planning to return to their old address. Such shortcomings in the statistical data often make comparative analysis difficult.

In view of the foregoing limitations, especially in statistical data, it may appear that a study of Indian immigration and settlement in Malaya—involving as it does considerable reliance on statistical material —can be little more than an exercise in imagination. But the effort is not all that quixotic. When the statistical data, despite their deficiencies, are combined with all the other available information it is possible to build up a tolerably detailed and composite picture of the Indian arrival and settlement in Malaya. In any case, in a new and emerging country with a peculiar developmental history and problems there is a great need for a broad understanding; for preliminary data and analysis rather than for mathematical manipulation and complex polemics. Doubtless in the future a greater emphasis on finer detail and statistical ingenuity will be in order, but in the meantime if the present study serves to fill in some of the gaps in the vast subject of Indian overseas migration, settlement, impact and assimilation in Malaya, and provides a basis from which future work may be initiated then it will have fulfilled its purpose.

PART 1

INDIAN IMMIGRATION INTO
BRITISH MALAYA: ORIGINS
AND TRENDS

1

INDIANS IN PRE-BRITISH MALAYA

In a dim distant unrecorded age
we had met, thou and I, —
When my speech became tangled in thine
and my life in thy life.

The East Wind had carried thy beckoning call
through an unseen path of the air
to a distant sun-lit shore
fanned by the coconut leaves.
It blended with the conch-shell sound
that rose in worship at the shrines
by the sacred waters of the Ganges.

The great God-Vishnu spoke to me
and spoke Uma, the ten-armed Goddess:
'Make ready thy boat, carry the rites of our worship
across the unknown sea.'
The Ganges stretched her arm to the eastern ocean
in a flow of majestic gesture.
From the heavens spoke to me two mighty voices—
the one that had sung of Rama's glory of sorrow
and the other Arjuna's triumphant arm—
urging me to bear along the waves
their epic lines to the eastern islands,
and the heart of my land murmured to me its hope
that it might build its nest of love
in a far-away land of its dream...

(Rabindranath Tagore)[1]

India's contacts with Malaya probably go back to pre-Christian times.[2] The full implications of the wealth of the region, however, do not appear to have been realized till about the early centuries A.D.[3] Since then,

---

[1] These stanzas, and those that follow on p. 31 below, comprise a poem entitled 'To Java', translated from his own Bengali original, 'Sri-Vijaya-lakshmi', written at Batavia on 21 Aug. 1927 and now forming part (pp. 40–2) of his *Jabha-Yatrir patra* or *Letters of a pilgrim to Java* (Thakura Rabrindranatha Centenary edition, Calcutta, 1961). 'To Java' is included in Durairajasingam, 1954, p. 14.

[2] Nilakanta Sastri, 1938, pp. 380–7; Chang, 1934, pp. 1–3; Hall, 1955, p. 23.

[3] Coedès, 1948, pp. 41–5; 1962, pp. 54 ff.; Wheatley, 1961, pp. 184–9; Lohizen-de Leeuw, 1954, pp. 44–5; Majumdar, 1937, p. 61.

for more than a thousand years, there was a frequent movement of Hindu and Buddhist traders, and, to a lesser extent, adventurers, priests, *panditás* and such like to the veritable El Dorados of Malaya and other Southeast Asian areas—the *Suvarnabhūmi* or Land of Gold beyond the *calôrmi* or moving waves. This flow was in all likelihood parallelled by the movement of Southeast Asian, especially Malaysian,[1] traders and others across the Bay of Bengal. This two-way traffic, through inter-marriage and cultural assimilation, witnessed the Indianization of the local way of life, the emergence of a number of city-states and the flowering of civilization throughout the more favoured coastal plains and riverine tracts of the strategic Siamo-Malay peninsula, particularly in its isthmian sector. The organization of these minutial kingdoms was based on Hindu or Buddhist concepts and cults of state, royalty and court life. The arts, religions and customs practised, at least by the aristocracy, were also Indian; Sanskrit was the sacred language and the means of literary expression. The mythology of ancient Indian classical writings such as the *Vedas* and *Purānas* and the Epics and the observance of the *Dharmaśāstra* also played important roles, while the nobility and the rulers were either Indians or Indianized local chiefs.[2] Several of these Indianized *nāgaras* prospered and featured prominently in Southeast Asian affairs, during, and to some extent also just after, the first millennium A.D.[3] This isthmian age, or age of the city-states,[4] probably represented the apogee of Indian influence in Malaya. Subsequently, although Indians did feature prominently in Malayan affairs now and then, as for example during the Malacca Sultanate (c. A.D. 1400–1511), they never recovered their former commanding position. Though some of them lingered on, the majority of the city-states, too, tended to decline and, with the founding of Temasik (the forerunner of modern Singapore) towards the end of the thirteenth century and the establishment of Malacca about 1400, the focus of attention in the Peninsula

---

[1] Used here in its wider sense of people of the Malay world—the region comprising southern Thailand, Malaysia, Singapore, Indonesia, Brunei, Portuguese Timor and the Philippines.

[2] Nilakanta Sastri, 1959, p. 68; Hall, 1955, p. 13; 1964, pp. 17–18; Braddell, 1956, p. 4; Wheatley, 1961, pp. 182–5; Leur, 1955, pp. 92–9; Ferrand, 1919, pp. 201–2; *EICOS*, pp. 120 ff.; *Jātakamālā*, No. xiv, *śloka* 15; (N. G.) Majumdar, 1926, pp. 5–6; Majumdar, 1927, pt. ii, pp. 25–95; 1937, p. 37 n. 3; Chaudhari, 1952, p. 205; *Kathāsaritsāgara, Taranga* 13, *ślokas* 73 ff.; Tawney, 1925, i, 156 ff.; Sastri, 1924, pp. 312–13; Subrahmanya Aiyar, 1934, p. 222; Das, 1893, pp. 8–9; Puri, 1956, pp. 89–92; Chhabra, 1935, p. 63; Bosch, 1952, pp. 1–25.

[3] The characteristics and fortunes of these early kingdoms are treated at length in several publications, notably Braddell, 1935 *et seq.*; Wheatley, 1961, 1964*b*; Tibbetts, 1956; Luce, 1925; Pelliot, 1903; Groeneveldt, 1876; Wales, 1935 *et seq.*; Briggs, 1951, and Devahuti, 1965.

[4] Wheatley, 1961, pp. 282 ff.

shifted from the north to the region of the Straits of Malacca.[1] Following this the isthmian tract rapidly became insignificant.

The depression in the fortunes of the isthmian states coincided with the gradual degeneration of Hindu and Buddhist influence in India. Ancient Indian society had been noted for its pragmatism and spirit of tolerance and for its ability to absorb new elements. It promoted trade and international contacts. All this, however, changed following the stagnation and decline of Hinduism from about the eighth and ninth centuries and the subsequent introversion aud degeneration of Indian society into narrow, exclusive and parochial groups of people. The transformation appears to have been brought about by the rise in the power of the *brāhmaṇas* and the decline of Buddhism. Beginning from about the fourth or fifth century A.D., this prophetic and liberal doctrine of early India slowly degenerated into passive, hierocratic and hierarchical rigidity. It became a vehicle of religious dignitaries and a magical and ritualistic exploitation of the masses by groups of monks and hermits. Before the close of the twelfth century it had virtually disappeared in India, having become increasingly less significant.

In the meantime *brāhmaṇa* power had grown at the expense of *kṣatriya* power. *Brāhmaṇas* had become the king-makers. They not only interpreted and made their own laws but also enforced them much more rigorously than hithertofore as is indicated in the thirteenth-century compilation, *Caturvargacintāmani*, by Hemādri. They prohibited commensalism and intermarriage between different groups and slowly but surely forced society into the rigid strait-jacket-like mould of the caste system. This had disastrous effects on Hindu society. Intellectual pursuits and the spread of learning among the ordinary folk were checked while the arts and crafts were degraded to a position of inferiority. Growth of trade was also arrested through increasingly vehement emphasis on the ceremonials of purity and condemnation of *samudra-yātrās* and traffic with foreigners and foreign countries. Concurrent with degradation of Hindu society was the erosion of Hindu political power through the incursions of Muslim invaders and merchants and also through conversion.[2] It reached its nadir with the establishment of Mughal authority in 1526 and the disastrous defeat of the Hindu Vijayanagar kingdom of South India in 1565.

All this meant the drying up of an important source of influence and inspiration for the Indianized states of the Peninsula and the rest of

---

[1] Nilakanta Sastri, 1954, p. 14; 1955, pp. 209–20; *EICOS*, pp. 542–5; Hultzch, 1891–1929, II, 105–9; Wheatley, 1961, pp. 300–5; *Sĕjarah Mĕlayu*, pp. 60 ff.; Brown, 1952, pp. 30 ff.

[2] Chanda, 1922, p. 122; R. C. Majumdar, *Ancient India* (Benares, 1952), pp. 499–508; 1951–60, VI, 547 ff.

23

Southeast Asia. Owing to the nature of the available records it is difficult to point to specific examples proving a link between the changes in India and the diminution of Hindu and Buddhist influence in the Peninsula, but it is not impossible that these changes in the Indian homeland would have contributed to the decline and eventual demise of the Indianized kingdoms of the region and the rise of Islam in Southeast Asia.

With the conversion of Malacca early in the fifteenth century, Hinduism and Buddhism were finally supplanted by Islam. Before this proselytizing faith Hindu and Buddhist beliefs were suppressed and, what is more disastrous for the student trying to reconstruct the story of early Malaya, the wealth of Indian statuary which marked the sites of the ancient settlements was almost wholly destroyed.[1] Yet not all of what India had contributed directly or indirectly to Malay life was lost, for as the Malay saying goes:

> *Hutang emas dapat di-bayar*
> *Hutang budi di-bawa mati.*
> (Debts in gold may be settled by payment;
> debts in knowledge are only absolvable in death.)

Many words of Indian origin still remain in the Malay language, mainly those relating to ritual, law and court ceremony, but also including others such as book, lion, herald, mango, nutmeg, pleasure, time, punishment, loyalty, religion, fasting, property, vase, intellect, independence and sin. And the gods of the Hindu pantheon, although excluded from the new religion, persisted as infidel genies summoned to the aid of the lover, the warrior or the sick man. The guardian genies of the modern state of Perak include not only Solomon and Ali, the Prophet's son-in-law, but also the Hindu Brahma and Viṣnu, while on the accession of a Perak sultan, his chief herald reads the following formula in Sanskrit: 'Fortunate great king, smiter of rivals, valorous, whose crown jewels ravish the three worlds, whose touch dispels suffering, protector, pilot over the ocean of battle, confuter of opponents, fortunate supreme overlord Raja Parameswara.' Then this same herald whispers in the ear of the new ruler the Hindu name of the demigod from whom Perak royalty are supposedly descended. Again at his installation a Malay sultan must sit motionless, thus exhibiting his divinity according to Indian ideas, and in present-day Negri Sembilan the herald who proclaims the election of a new ruler must stand on one leg with the sole of his right foot resting on his left knee, in the same way that *brāhmaṇa* sun-worshippers stand on one foot with the other placed against the ankle. And still many

---

[1] Low, 1908, pp. 172 ff.; Winstedt, 1958, p. 27.

titles of the Malay aristocracy incorporate Sanskrit honorifics such as *duli, mahamulia* and *paduka*.[1]

Malay magic is richly impregnated with Indian lore and Malay charms which patently reflect the influence of Indian *mantras*, while an elaborate Hindu ritual precedes episodes from the Vedic epic *Rāmāyaṇa* enacted in the *wayang kulit* (shadow play), the Malay equivalent of the Punch and Judy Show, of Kelantan.

These are but a few of the many legacies left to the modern Malay by the process of Indianization begun some 2,000 years ago. Numerous others can be found in the late Sir Richard Winstedt's two books, *The Malays: A cultural history*[2] and *Shaman, Saiva and Sufi: A study of the evolution of Malay magic*.[3] Although it is difficult to subscribe *in toto* to all the conclusions drawn by this erudite Malay scholar from the few and casual historical data available to him, there appears, however, to be little reason to quarrel with his final summation of the effects of Indian influence on Malay life, which is that 'though he is (or may be) unconscious of it, from the cradle to the grave the Malay is surrounded by survivals of Indian culture'.[4]

There is little agreement among scholars either on the origins and progress of Islam in Southeast Asia or the circumstances surrounding the foundation and development of the Malacca Sultanate. What appears to be generally accepted, however, is that Indians and their associates played a significant, often dominant, role both in the rise of Malacca as a mighty mart, the premier Muslim Malay port-city of the region, and in the planting of the new faith in the Eastern Lands.[5]

The men who brought Islam across the Bay of Bengal were probably members of a mercantile community. Islam is an expansive religion and imposes on all the faithful the duty of Muslim teachings, including the furtherance of *dar al-Islam* or the world of Islam. In this context, unlike their Hindu and Buddhist predecessors, Muslim merchants, besides being traders, were also knights of the spirit. To help them in their proselytizing activities they seem to have brought along with them *mullas*, Ṣūfī mystics and other preachers 'learned in the sect of Mohammed—chiefly Arabs',[6] who were esteemed in these parts for their knowledge of the new faith. It appears that it was principally the efforts of these small groups

---

[1] Winstedt, 1944, pp. 186–96. [2] Winstedt, 1958.
[3] Winstedt, 1925. [4] Winstedt, 1944, p. 195.
[5] Hill, 1961, pp. 1–8; Marrison, 1951, pp. 28–37; Hall, 1955, pp. 177–85; Winstedt, 1942, pp. 211 *et seq.*; Schrieke, 1955–7, part I, p. 237; part II, pp. 230 ff.; Majumdar, 1951–60, VI, 651–2; Dames, 1918–21, II, 148–210; Meilink-Roelofsz, 1962, pp. 61 ff.; Cortesão, 1944, I, 142–3; II, pp. 229 ff.; Fatimi, 1963, pp. 12 ff.; Johns, 1957, pp. 8–11; Wheatley, 1964*b*, pp. 119–76; Harrison, 1963, pp. 43–52.
[6] Cortesão, 1944, II, 240.

of scribes, mystics and missionaries, and, to a lesser degree, their mercantile patrons, coupled with the political and economic ambitions of local rulers, that set Islam on the march across the Malay world.[1]

As noted above, before the proselytizing zeal of Islam not only were all visible signs of Hinduism and Buddhism wiped out, but the traditional and the Indianized concepts upon which Malay life was based were either undermined or modified. Ever since these early times Islam has fashioned the *mores* of Malay life and has been a powerful factor in the moulding of the cultural landscape of their homeland. To every *kampong* and town it brought a mosque or *surau* while into nearly every holding it introduced a potential for subdivision—a process checked only by legislation in some states during this century. In addition, it introduced the Malay to the Perso-Arabic alphabet, which the latter adopted as his own together with a number of Muslim religious prefixes and honorifics such as *Lebai*, *Haji* and *Maulana*.

Information on the economic pursuits of the Indians in Malaya during the periods of the Malacca Sultanate and the Portuguese and Dutch control of the Straits is obscure but we may surmise that with one possible new development these would in all probability have been very much like those of the preceding years, that is trade, crafts, provision of services and such like. The exception appears to be that by the seventeenth century some Indians had settled to cultivating crops as a means of livelihood. They do not seem to have been very successful, however, partly because they were not 'inclined thereto (towards agriculture)'.[2] Apparently trade, especially in commodities of low bulk but of high value such as spices, pepper, precious metals and textiles, was still the Indian's forte. But here the Muslim merchants had slowly but certainly supplanted their Hindu and Buddhist countrymen and by the seventeenth century, if not earlier, had become the dominant element. Indeed among the Indian carriers of goods in the Straits and across the Bay of Bengal the Hindus seem to have been virtually eclipsed by the Muslims. Such at least is the impression from the contemporary accounts of Southeast Asian commerce written by Europeans; when discussing Indian traders, they mainly mention Muslim merchants and shipping.[3]

The factors which were responsible for this further and final slump in the status and role of the Hindu merchants *vis-à-vis* their Muslim

[1] Johns, 1957, pp. 8–11; 1961, pp. 4–14; Fatimi, 1963, pp. 71–100; al-Attas, 1963, pp. 21–2; Schrieke, 1955–7, part I, pp. 7–79; part II, pp. 308–9.
[2] Bremmer, 1927, p. 51.
[3] Moreland, 1920a, pp. 198–9, 245; 1920b, pp. 517–33; Schrieke, 1955–7, part I, pp. 12 ff.; part II, pp. 232 ff.; Leur, 1955, p. 112; Majumdar, 1951–60, VI, 648 ff.; Cortesão, 1944, I, 41–2, 82; II, 240 ff.; Major, 1857, part II, p. 5; part III, p. 19; part IV, p. 9; Appadorai, 1936, II, 444 ff.; Meilink-Roelofsz, 1962, pp. 34 ff.; Dames, 1918–21, II, 75 ff.; Bowrey, 1905, p. 24; Bassett, 1964, pp. 114–22.

brethren in Malaya and elsewhere in Southeast Asia are obscure. But any hypothesis that might be mooted would have to take the growth of the Muslim influence, at the expense of its Hindu counterpart, in India into consideration. Through further conquests and conversions more and more Hindu shipping passed into Muslim hands in the centuries following the firm establishment of the new faith in the northern tracts of the Subcontinent in the thirteenth century. Coupled with this was the stagnation, or possibly even further degradation, of the Hindu society which, despite the presence of the democratic social organization of the Muslims in its midst, continued to combine what Majundar trenchantly denounces as 'catholicity in religious outlook with bigotry in social ethics'.[1] In this setting overseas travel, difficult enough for Hindus in former times owing to religious sanctions against the crossing of the ocean, became even more difficult, as embarkation on a Muslim ship would have meant certain contamination through contact. With the gradual loss of their own shipping and their inhibitions against travelling on Muslim ships, Hindu merchants were increasingly bound to the land. In Gujarat, and possibly in Bengal too, this changeover had already taken place in the early years of the sixteenth century, by which time the role of the Hindu merchants of that area in the overseas trade was limited to brokerage, sale and supply of goods, money and services in their home ports.[2]

This reduced the Hindu carriers of sea-borne cargo to virtually those from South India, particularly the Coromandel coast, where shipping was still partially in Hindu hands, partly because of the relatively late establishment of Muslim power in this region. But this state of affairs did not last and it was only a matter of time before this remaining Hindu shipping also passed into Muslim or other hands. For example, large parts of Vijayanagar, the last of the great Hindu kingdoms of South India, passed into Muslim control in 1565. This meant, one suspects, that there was a further diminution in Hindu-owned or Hindu-controlled shipping, besides the virtual end of effective Hindu secular power throughout India until the second half of the seventeenth century. The Madras area, the home of the Hindu Tamil (*Keling*) merchants—the principal non-Muslim Indian traders of contemporary Malaya—was again in turmoil in the seventeenth century, following the incursions of the Mahrattas, Mughals, Dutch, French and English into peninsular India. Probably, besides decimating the remaining Hindu shipping further, these incursions also interfered both with their markets and sources of supply, thereby reducing their efficiency.

[1] Majumdar, 1951–60, vi, 616–17 *et seq.*
[2] Dames, 1918–21, i, 109 ff.; Meilink-Roelofsz, 1962, pp. 63–4.

Immigration: origins and trends

In Malaya itself, the collaboration of Tamil Hindu merchants with the Portuguese seems to have soured their relations with many of the Muslim Malay rulers, thereby hampering trade.[1] Furthermore, attacks on Portuguese shipping in Malacca by the Malays and Dutch would in all probability have entailed the loss of some Hindu ships too among others. While all this was going on in Malacca, the Muslims were generally consolidating their position in the Archipelago.

Although Hindu merchants of South India were still prominent, their Muslim brethren, particularly the Gujaratis and Tamils, appear already to have become the most influential in the Malacca court before the end of the fifteenth century.[2] Through diplomatic marriages, erection of mosques, presents and general goodwill these Muslims became 'great favourites with the King and obtained whatever they wanted'.[3] Gradually they became not only prominent in the commerce of the port but also a powerful force in the royal court intrigues of Malacca, and were in a position to make or mar kings and *mentris* (ministers), as, for instance, their success in appointing the 'full-blooded Tamil trader' Raja Kasim as *mentri* in Malacca in the fifteenth century. In this way the Muslim Indian merchants probably exerted a tremendous influence over Malacca's commercial and foreign policy. For example, it appears that it was largely they, together with the *mullas*, *kathis* and Arabs, who managed to persuade the Sultan to take strong action against the Portuguese when the latter appeared in Malaccan waters as trade and political rivals.[4] They had heard alarming reports of the Portuguese political and missionary activities in the Indian Ocean and their interference in the Indian Ocean trade, and urged the Sultan to have no truck with the *Feringgis* but instead to prepare to wage a jihad 'for as India was already in the hands of the Portuguese, Malacca should not pass to the infidels'.[5]

---

[1] In contrast to their Muslim brethren who opposed the newcomers, many of the Hindu merchants either remained neutral or actively aided the Portuguese during and after the capture of Malacca, presumably largely because of strong religious prejudices against militant Islam and also because of commercial rivalry between them and the Muslim traders. Such divergent stands of the Muslims and Hindus did not go unnoticed by the Portuguese. For example, while Timuta Raja, the chief of the Muslim merchants, was executed, Naina Chetu, a Tamil Hindu trader who had succoured Portuguese prisoners kept at Malacca between 1509 and 1511, was rewarded by the grant to him of the 'governorship' of the *Kelings* with the office of *bendahara*. Needless to say, if anything, such Portuguese approbations of their acts made the Hindu traders all the more unpopular with the Muslim Malays (de Gray Birch, 1875–84, III, 118; Macgregor, 1955, p. 5; Winstedt, 1935, p. 62; Cardon, 1934, p. 13; Cortesão, 1944, II, 258, 281).

[2] Cortesão, 1944, II, 265–73; Winstedt, 1935, p. 45.

[3] Cortesão, 1944, II, 241.

[4] de Gray Birch, 1875–84, III, 69; Winstedt, 1935, pp. 54–62.

[5] Cortesão, 1944, II, 280.

Indians in pre-British Malaya

The failure of the Sultan and his Indian and other Muslim allies to thwart the Portuguese at Malacca appears to have given added stimulus to the spread of Islam elsewhere, with the result that by the end of the seventeenth century it had firmly established itself over much of the Malay world. In this setting the co-religionist Indian Muslim merchants enjoyed tremendous advantage over their Hindu countrymen in the Muslim Malay ports. They gradually emerged as the sole Indian shippers of the Archipelago, aided, no doubt, too by the fact that the Dutch had no violent religious feud with them, fearing them mainly as trade rivals. With the collapse of the Portuguese stronghold of Malacca the Muslims also appear to have strengthened their position among the Indian merchants in the Peninsula. In all probability the Hindus here would have found it extremely difficult to compete with their better placed Muslim colleagues, especially in the traffic with the Muslim Malay ports. It would seem therefore that at least economic expediency, if nothing else, would have compelled the Hindus to sell or rent their remaining shipping or otherwise leave the port-to-port conveyance of goods in Muslim or other similarly well placed hands, and confine themselves to transactions on land on the same lines as their Gujarati compatriots at home, that is, to brokerage and other services and supplying goods and money. The same sort of changeover would probably also have taken place in the Tamil Hindu Coromandel coast homeland.

The cumulative effect of these reverses on the Hindu community of Malaya appears to have been that this once generally prosperous body of people declined in status and wealth. Indeed, some of its members even sank into abject poverty, as is illustrated by the case of one Nachodar Giantij of Malacca, who had to have his debt cancelled because he died 'without any estate'.[1] Neither did the Muslims come out too well from the prolonged conflict and disturbed conditions in India and Malaya. It is true that they were now virtually the only Indian shippers but it is equally true that while they were cornering the Hindu shipping, their vessels, as also some of the Hindu ones, in turn were passing into European control, and they were steadily being edged out by the Europeans as the principal suppliers and carriers of goods across the Bay of Bengal. The comparatively smaller and scattered business and agency houses of the Indians found competition increasingly difficult with the larger resources and centralized administration of the Portuguese crown and the Dutch and English East India Companies. There was also the growing strength of the 'country' or private European traders, owners or agents of ships, who were already showing unmistakable signs of their future omnipotence in the Bay of Bengal and other Asian commerce.

[1] Bremmer, 1927, p. 123.

Immigration: origins and trends

Finally, with the establishment of European rule in Southeast Asia and India the Indian merchants also lost control of their trade staples—spices and textiles—as well as their principal markets and sources of supply.

The Indian intermediary, formerly so important, was of little or no significance in the spice trade by the second half of the eighteenth century, or even earlier. He had been gradually squeezed out of this profitable trade by the northern Europeans, particularly the Dutch, through a combination of restrictive trade practices and political conquests. Similarly in the textile trade the Europeans began to cut out the Indian middleman. First of all they placed their orders directly with the producers and finally established their own factories in India employing Indian workmen.[1]

The decline in Mughal power and governmental machinery from the seventeenth century onwards was also a serious blow to Indian commerce. Accompanying the disturbed conditions that followed the disintegration of the once mighty Mughal Empire into small states was the tendency for local princes and mintmasters to debase the coinage. The confusing multitude of rupee types that emerged from these operations, each based on the particular standards adopted by the local mints, resulted in a loss of confidence in business circles and consequently a further slump in Indian commercial activity.[2]

The conquest of India and Malaya, especially the former, was the final nail in the coffin of Indian maritime enterprise of any significance in the eastern seas. As a result Indian influence declined in Malaya as well and except for a few Indians who continued to feature prominently in the affairs of the Malay states until they fell into British hands,[3] the Indians in Malaya generally ceased to be of any significance in terms of economic or political consequence until the early decades of the present century. Even then, despite some who succeeded in amassing huge fortunes, the Indians never recovered their former importance, for, as will be seen shortly, the newcomers who now flocked in large numbers to Malaya were generally quite a different class of people. Moreover, the circumstances in which they came were almost entirely different from those of their predecessors.

---

[1] Glamann, 1958, pp. 139–41; Meilink-Roelofsz, 1962, pp. 191, 210, 222–68; Leur, 1955, pp. 127–32, 211–14, 371–2; Raychaudhuri, 1962, pp. 16 ff.

[2] Battacharya, 1954, p. 106; Glamann, 1958, p. 66.

[3] Bassett, 1964, pp. 121–2.

2

CAUSES OF INDIAN IMMIGRATION INTO BRITISH MALAYA

Thy call reaches me once again
  across hundreds of speechless years.
I come to thee, look into thine eyes,
  and seem to see there the light of the wonder
  at our first meeting in the forest glade,
  of the gladness of a promise
When we tied golden threads of kinship
  round each other's wrists.

That ancient token, grown pale,
  had not yet slipped off thy right arm,
And our wayfaring path of old
  lies strewn with the remnants of my speech.
They help me to retrace my way to the inner chambers of thy life
  where still the light is burning that we kindled together
  on the forgotten evening of our union.
Remember me, even as I remember thy face,
  and recognise in me as thine own,
  the old that has been lost, to be regained and made new.

(Rabindranath Tagore)

Despite the great antiquity of the Indian overseas migration to Malaya outlined in the foregoing pages and the debt of Malay culture to ancient India, there were seldom large numbers of Indians in Malaya in the pre-British period; and nearly all the approximately 1,100,000 Indians at present in Malaya are either themselves immigrants or descendants of recent immigrants. The period of modern Indian immigration into Malaya dates from the foundation of Penang in 1786, but it became a significant feature in Malayan demography only in the latter half of the nineteenth century, following the establishment of British paramountcy in India and the consolidation of British power in Malaya. Furthermore, whereas the earlier immigrants were primarily financiers and traders in rare commodities or purveyors of a superior organization and civilization, the modern Indian migrant, until the Indian government's ban on assisted labour emigration in 1938, was chiefly an unlettered labourer coming into the country to work for a pittance on some plantation or government project. Again, unlike the earlier phase, the modern migration was not so much a spontaneous flow but more a regulated and arranged movement, induced to a considerable extent by governmental action and the persuasions of prospective employers and their agents. Finally, whereas the earlier movement was small in volume, the later migration was on a large scale. The causes for this metamorphosis were mainly political and economic changes in India and Malaya.[1]

Conditions in India

Beginning essentially as commercial ventures, the seventeenth-century English 'factories' in India willy-nilly blossomed out into subahs and finally into an empire. By about the mid-nineteenth century almost the whole of India had come under British political and economic control. This subjugation in practical terms meant that thenceforth, until India's independence in 1947, India's interests were in general subordinated to the needs of the paramount power and among other innovations India was to be an economically vassal state.

The evidence for this economic vassalage has already been extensively, though by no means satisfactorily, documented.[2] In any case, it is a topic outside the scope of the present study. For our purposes, therefore, it suffices to say that the political economy of England appears to have demanded, especially after the Industrial Revolution, the conversion of India from an exporter of manufactured goods to that of a supplier of raw materials to the British industrial complex and a market for the consumption of the products of those machines. To this end rival Indian commercial and industrial competition in India seems to have been curbed by the British.[3] For example, shipbuilding, which was still an important industry in India in the early years of the nineteenth century,[4]

---

[1] Some social factors like the problems of caste, prejudice against crossing of seas, *purdah* and the joint-family system also tended to discourage emigration, until very recent times, among the upper and cultured classes of Indian society, but they were comparatively of little or minor significance (Nair, 1937, pp. 1, 40).

[2] See, for example, V. Anstey, *The economic development of India* (London, 1929); R. Dutt, *The economic history of India, 1757–1900* (New Delhi, 1960); D. H. Buchanan, *The development of capitalist enterprise in India* (New York, 1940); Gadgil, 1942; Brown, 1963; Sovani, 1954a, 1954b; Morris, 1963, 1966; Lamb, 1955 and J. Strachey, *The end of empire* (London, 1961).

[3] Dutt, 1950, pp. 256–67; Lamb, 1955, pp. 464 ff.; Brown, 1963, pp. 38–107; Sovani, 1954a, pp. 87–104; cf. Morris, 1963, pp. 606–16.

[4] Between 1801 and 1821, 237 ships, weighing a total of 105,693 tons with an estimated value of some 20,000,000 rupees, were built on the Hooghly alone. In almost every respect these ships were apparently the equals, if not superiors, of the similar types constructed in contemporary Britain or elsewhere in Europe (Mookerji, 1957, pp. 180–1; Law, 1877, II, 4).

was discouraged through arbitrary tariffs or restrictive legislative measures. The arrival in London of Indian-owned, Indian-captained and Indian-manned ships aroused much hostility on the part of the British shipping interests. They feared ruin through the competition of these eastern 'intruders'. The British government's response to pressures to safeguard and encourage British shipping was a resort to arbitrary legislation. On 25 July 1814 an Act (54. George III, c. 134) was passed by Parliament severely restricting Indian shipping and ships employing Indian sailors.[1] The Act stipulated that ships entering English waters whose crews were not at least 75 per cent British were liable to forfeiture, while the captain in all cases had to be a white Briton. Finally, even the use of Indian-built ships was prohibited in the Indo-British trade from 1814 onwards, although this was evaded for many years afterwards. In India itself local shipping was also discouraged by discriminatory tariffs. In the Madras Presidency, for instance, the general import duty on goods brought in by Indian ships was raised to 15 per cent in 1872 compared with $7\frac{1}{2}$ per cent in the case of British ships. Even other foreign ships were given preference over local ships. These measures dealt an effective blow to the Indian shipping industry and, combined with the technical progress of Western shipping, reduced it to insignificance by 1840, after which date no large ships appear to have been built in India until comparatively recent times.[2] A corollary to these changes was the fact that Indians ceased to play any major role in the external sea-borne trade of India. This role had already considerably declined in the days of the (British) East India Company's monopoly; the eclipse of Indian ocean shipping simply served to effect the *coup de grâce*.[3]

The decline of Indian ocean shipping and industrial, commercial and financial enterprise in India meant that the Indian entrepreneurial classes lost their principal and traditional sources of income and investment. The 'intelligentsia', too, seems to have suffered, for the decline of Indian economic enterprise meant that the 'most paying of the honourable means of livelihood' were now closed. Perhaps even more fundamental and far-reaching than the actual loss of *paisa* was the impact of these economic reverses on the spirit and attitudes of Indian enterprise.

Ejected from their former pre-eminence the mercantile classes ap-

[1] *IO:PPC*, 55 (1808–12), Fourth Report, app. 47, pp. 23–4; Digby, 1901, pp. 101–3; Raju, 1941, pp. 222–3.
[2] Raju, 1941, pp. 222–3; Mookerji, 1957, p. 182; Raghavaiyangar, 1892, p. 56; *C.O.273*, 327 (1907), 30.4.1907; Macalister, 1803, p. 25; Datta, 1961, p. 110; Sovani, 1954*b*, p. 875.
[3] Bannarjea, 1951, pp. 436 ff.; Raju, 1941, pp. 203–7.

peared to grow shy, inward looking and less adventurous in the field of investment and enterprise. Rather than running the risk of arousing the antagonism or earning the displeasure of British officialdom or the power-ful 'nabobs', many of them now contented themselves with the sub-servient roles of underlings of British enterprise. Others just simply hoarded whatever they managed to salvage or turned to such safe investments as government stocks, foreign companies' shares or land, especially the last.[1] Agricultural land had practically no market value in almost the whole of India until the advent of British rule.[2] However, with the introduction of the new concept of landlordism, modelled on the British pattern, and the institution of revenue and survey settle-ments, recording of property rights and the establishment of civil courts, it became a moderately free transferable asset. Furthermore, with ever increasing pressure on it,[3] it acquired an increasing market value[4] in most parts of the country. Acquisition of land by the capitalist classes also had official blessing, and again the analogy of the landed gentry of the United Kingdom made land-ownership a new status symbol. Thus it is not surprising that about the beginning of the nineteenth century one of the dual ambitions of many Indians was to become a substantial zamindar, the other was to become a government pensioner. The latter, at least until the full flowering of the nationalist movement in the present century, appealed to the intelligentsia, for with the virtual closure of their former avenues of employment, only service under the state promised profitable careers for talent. With the growth of the nationalist movement in India, especially during the early part of the present century, another powerful factor was added to those already inhibiting the emigration of men of talent and leadership. Not only did

---

[1] Sinha, 1946, pp. 29–30; Sovani, 1954b, pp. 873–4; Datta, 1961, pp. 47–78; Thorner, 1955, pp. 126–7; 1962, pp. 51–9; Lamb, 1955, pp. 467 ff. Cf. H. G. Aubrey, 'Industrial investment decisions: A comparative analysis', *The journal of economic history* (London), xv, no. 4 (December 1955), pp. 335–59.

[2] Bhatia, 1963, pp. 18–19; Thorburn, 1886, p. 49.

[3] See pp. 37–8 below.

[4] The increasing value of land in India is amply borne out by the following examples:

	Punjab		Tanjore (Madras)	
	Price per acre in rupees			
Year	All land	Cultivated land		
			Year	Price per acre of wet land
1896/7	43	78	1823/4	Rs. 12
1906/7	58	103	1852/3	Rs. 39
1916/17	111	227	1878	Rs. 245
1925/6	285	477	1903	Rs. 458 (?)

(Punjab, 1930, i, 377; cf. Raghavaiyanger, 1892, p. lxxxv; Kumar, 1965, p. 142.)

the nationalist movement attract to itself many of the élite of India but also that of the Indian overseas. In short then, with the passing of Indian ocean shipping and the decline and change in the patterns of Indian enterprise and investment, the fountainhead that had in the past nourished the already declining stream of emigrants representing the higher strata of Indian society and culture now virtually dried up. The groups that were now most pressured or tempted to move out of India were of quite a different social and economic background.

Concurrent with the change in the fortunes of the entrepreneurial and other such groups was the increasing distress of the poorer classes of India's population. Information regarding levels of living in those days is extremely scanty and imprecise, but early India seems to have evolved a socio-economic structure which appeared quite capable of maintaining some kind of static equilibrium. The sheet anchor of this stability was the village economic system, largely based on general self-sufficiency, limited outside contacts, mainly on account of poor communications and transport, and a corporate life centred on the cultivation of communal land for food and other needs. This primary activity was integrated with and supplemented by the products of local handicraft; there seemed to be a ready sale for this outside and also for any agricultural surplus that there might have been. Population growth was normally slow, pressure on land limited, and agriculture had settled down to a customary routine. The standard of life was probably by no means high or comfortable; but neither does it appear to have been too unsatisfactory or uncertain.[1]

How long this agrarian structure would have survived if British rule had not supervened is difficult to say, though signs of disintegration and impoverishment, that included a significant number of peasants without land or in debt, were already beginning to appear well before the arrival of the British.[2] The evidence for this is far from conclusive, but on the whole the arrival of the British appears to have accelerated and accentuated this process, as the old order based on such features as corporate life, custom and barter was generally supplanted by a highly centralized administration, contract and a cash nexus.

[1] *C.O.273*, 111 (1881), 18.11.1881; Nanavati, 1944, pp. 74–5; Gadgil, 1950, pp. 8–29; Raju, 1941, pp. 15–25; Raghavaiyangar, 1892, pp. 1–11; Davis, 1951, pp. 23–6; Kumar, 1965, pp. 29–30, 107; Srinivas and Shah, 1960, pp. 1375–8; Majumdar, 1951–60, III, 561–641; VI, 601–60; Sovani, 1954b, pp. 857–63; S. M. Ikram, *Muslim civilization in India* (New York, 1964), pp. 107–12 *et seq.* Cf. Morris, 1963, pp. 608 ff.; 1966, pp. 207–8.
[2] Moreland and Geyl, 1925, pp. 30, 60 *et seq.*; Misra, 1932, p. 4; Raghavaiyangar, 1892, pp. 1–11; Morris, 1963, pp. 607–11; 1966, p. 207; E. Thompson and G. T. Garratt, *Rise and fulfilment of British rule in India* (London, 1934), pp. 422–35.

Immigration: origins and trends

This transformation and the related developments have been dealt with in both official and unofficial literature.[1] The utter subjection coupled with the greater and often increasing poverty of the common people forms an integral part of the economic vassalage of India to Britain.[2] It, too, is outside the purview of our study and no more than a brief summary of its relevant aspects is necessary here.

In the earlier pages we have noted the curbing and consequent decline of indigenous industry. This meant not only the decline of many of the industrialists but also the loss of customary means of livelihood for large numbers of spinners, potters, millers, shoemakers, and such like. While some of them were undoubtedly absorbed by such new developments as railway, road and harbour construction, there were few with alternative means of survival open to them, that might be suitable to their traditional skills. Most of these appear to have had little choice but to leave the country or to fall back on the agriculturist—the very agriculturist who was increasingly in dire economic straits.[3]

With the introduction of the new concept of private ownership by the British, land seems to have become to the moneylender and the landlord a valuable avenue of investment and income, and to the cultivator a ready security against which he could borrow easily to meet his changing domestic and public requirements. The need for the cultivator to borrow mounted as he was steadily drawn into the monetary economy and for the most part burdened with new, usually inflexible and frequently heavy taxation, which had to be paid in cash.[4] But, with few exceptions, his agricultural activity was primarily for subsistence and he invariably cultivated a plot too small to make an income. Consequently he could accumulate little or no capital in advance. In these circumstances he had little choice but to borrow in order to discharge his obligations. Since his collateral, too, was invariably poor, he was forced to borrow from the

[1] In addition to the literature listed on p. 32 n. 2 above, see, for example, *IO:PPC*, 32 (1797); 220 (1881–91); 221 (1888); Digby, 1901, pp. 534 *et seq.*; Hunter, 1908, pp. 99 ff.

[2] It is generally agreed that the condition of the nineteenth-century and later Indian agriculturalist was grim, but whether this grimness was a direct creation of the impact of British rule or basically a continuation of a pre-existing position has been a matter of sharp debate, with the main protagonists the foreign and Indian academics, and it is unlikely that the last word has yet been said on the subject.

[3] Datta, 1961, pp. 79–120; Gadgil, 1942, pp. 31–58; Kumar, 1965, p. 181; Raman Rao, 1958, pp. 172–87.

[4] *IO:PPC*, 220 (1881–91), J. O. Miller, 'Report on the condition of the agricultural classes during the last decade, 1881/2–1891/2', pp. 26–7; Raghavaiyangar, 1892, p. 57; Thorner, 1955, pp. 124–8; Kumar, 1965, pp. 78–98, 171–2; Thomas and Natarajan, 1936–7, pp. 67–73; Natarajan, 1938–9, p. 186; Sovani, 1954*b*, p. 867.

Causes of migration in modern times

baniya, moneylender or landlord,[1] who more often than not charged him interest rates ranging from 9 to 300 per cent against the security of his land.[2] Accumulating year after year such a loan could rarely be repaid in full; either the farmer finally lost his land and was turned out or found himself bound to his landlord for life.

Sometimes the cultivator, although dispossessed, was allowed to remain as a tenant. In fact as more and more land passed into the hands of non-cultivating classes,[3] this form of landholding became common. In some parts of the country the majority of the cultivators were tenants. These tenants were at the mercy of the landlord who, as he had all the advantages of any litigation against a poor, illiterate unsophisticated peasant, was able to pursue various devices to increase his revenue from his tenants. Rackrenting increased, the landlord, in some areas, taking 40 to 60 per cent of the produce and at times even 80 per cent.[4] Tenants who showed resistance were summarily ousted, as there were always others waiting to take their place. This state of affairs became increasingly intolerable with the growth of the agricultural population and the intensification of the struggle to hold on to land at any cost.

India's population growth has been painstakingly analysed by Davis, and little more comment is required here than to say that after remaining

---

[1] Often all these three functions were combined in one and the same person.

[2] Intensive village surveys carried out in the late nineteenth and early twentieth centuries by a number of people in different parts of India have revealed that in some provinces between two-thirds and three-quarters of the agricultural population were in debt. In some areas, as, for example, in parts of Madras, the figure was at times as high as 90 per cent and the debts varied from Rs. 35 to Rs. 900 per family (*IO:PPC*, 220, 1881–91, J. O. Miller, 'Report on the condition of the agricultural classes during the last decade, 1881/2–1891/2', p. 26; Nehru, 1932, p. 106; Mukhtyar, 1930, pp. 247–54; Ramaswamy, 1946, pp. 132–6; Mukerjee, 1939–41, I, 169–70; Thomas, 1940, pp. 370–2; Punjab, 1930, I, 164–5; Sovani, 1954b, p. 870; 1954a, p. 89).

[3] While there was probably little or no mass dispossession of the peasantry by moneylenders and traders, there is little doubt that substantial numbers of cultivators were losing part, if not all, of their family plots to non-cultivators including absentee and other types of landlords. The 1927–8 Royal Commission on agriculture in India, for instance, found that in parts of the Punjab, the supposed stronghold of Jat owner-cultivators, the number of Jat owners increased by less than 3 per cent between 1885–6 and 1918–19. During the same period the number of non-cultivating owners increased by 500 per cent. The same sort of changes were also taking place in other parts of the country. In Madras, for example, much of the land had passed into non-cultivating hands even before the end of the nineteenth century. In 1891, for instance, cultivating ryots owned less than a quarter of the total cultivated land. Much of the remainder was apparently in the hands of landlords other than specifically moneylenders or traders (United Kingdom, 1927–8, III, 131–4; Raghavaiyangar, 1892, pp. 74–5. Cf. Kumar, 1965, pp. 168–79; Morris, 1966, pp. 192, 205–6).

[4] Misra, 1932, p. 64; *IO:PPC*, 221 (1888), Letter from govt. of Bengal to govt. of India, dated 30 June 1888; Madras, 1930, I, 14.

virtually static, or increasing extremely slowly, for centuries, it gathered momentum from about the middle of the nineteenth century and by 1941 had reached some 390,000,000 souls compared with the approximately 130,000,000 in 1845.[1] In other countries that experienced similar large increases in population but still managed to make great economic advances, a shift in occupational structure took place. An increasing proportion of the people found employment in such undertakings as manufacturing, services, transportation and merchandising. Consequently, despite the growth in population there was little or no increase in the pressure on farmlands in terms of supply of land per cultivator. In India, however, there was apparently little significant change in the overall pattern of employment. The few industries and other non-agricultural activities that the British allowed to develop were able to absorb only a small proportion of the enormous annual increase in population, and more than 85 per cent of the Indians continued to be in the countryside up to the beginning of the Second World War. In practical terms this meant that farming had to support a growing number of people.[2] At the same time—with the exception of some parts of the country which registered favourable progress, though mostly in the nineteenth century—there was no marked increase in the supply of farmland.[3] The increasing size of the agricultural population might not have become such an acute problem had there been a comparable rise in the productivity per acre, especially of food-crops. It is more than possible that with favourable developments such as the establishment of political stability, better irrigation and transport systems, increasing crop specialization and large domestic and foreign markets, the output per acre rose in several instances. On the whole however, labouring under such stresses as overcrowding, little or no attempt at conservation practices, low capitalization, poor techniques, indebtedness and problems of tenancy, productivity tended to remain comparatively low or static.[4] In such a situation where population growth was for the most part outstripping both availability of farmland and its productivity, underemployment and unemployment on a colossal scale became the common denominator in the countryside of twentieth-century India.[5]

[1] Davis, 1951, pp. 24–90.
[2] Das, 1931, p. 14; Sovani, 1954a, p. 89; Thorner, 1955, pp. 121–7; cf. Morris, 1963, pp. 611–17.
[3] Thorner, 1955, pp. 121–7; Subramaniam, 1945, pp. 7–9; Davis, 1951, p. 207; Sovani, 1954b, p. 868; 1954a, p. 88; Kumar, 1965, p. 192.
[4] Venkatasubbiah, 1920, pp. 85–9; Davis, 1951, pp. 206–12; Brown, 1944, pp. 152–6; Thorner, 1955, pp. 121–7. Cf. Morris, 1963, pp. 611–17; 1966, pp. 200, 205–9.
[5] United Kingdom, 1927–8, iii, 580–2; Davis, 1951, p. 210. Davis estimated that there were between 90,000,000 and 200,000,000 surplus people on farms by 1941.

Causes of migration in modern times

In fact, whatever the causes, even before the end of the nineteenth century it already presented 'a picture of poverty exceeded in few other civilized areas':[1]

> The conclusion to be drawn is that of the agricultural population, a large proportion, say 40 per cent.., are insufficiently fed, to say nothing of clothing and housing...They have to undergo long fasts, having for a considerable part of the year to satisfy themselves with one full meal in a day...[2]

Even this state of affairs referred to years of 'favourable agricultural conditions' which were by no means assured, dependent as they were on the vagaries of the monsoonal rains. Consequently, famines, usually followed by epidemics, were always round the corner, bringing death and desolation in their wake.[3] In many cases the only hope of survival was flight. The omnipresent caste structure and joint-family system, often severely limiting social and economic mobility, accentuated the pressure to escape.[4]

Typical though this was of the general mass of Indian peasantry, it was especially applicable to its labouring element. The ranks of these people were augmented by the influx of artisans leaving moribund handicraft industries, and the flow of such other elements as the dispossessed or displaced ryots; numbers were also constantly replenished by a large natural increase.[5] In 1891 there were 17,000,000 agricultural labourers

[1] *IO:PPC*, 220 (1881–91), 'Confidential reports on the conditions of the lower classes in India, 1881–1891'; 221 (1888), 'Confidential notes of proceedings of conference held at Delhi, Friday, 30th March, 1888, to discuss the relief of over-populated tracts'; Davis, 1951, p. 205; *C.O.273*, 111 (1881), 18.11.1881; Thorner, 1955, pp. 109–28; 1962, pp. 82–112; Hunter, 1908, pp. 99 ff. Cf. Morris, 1963, pp. 608–14; 1966, pp. 188–207. In the absence of any conclusive statistical data it is difficult to gauge *real* income in India, but it appears that if there was any rise in the level of living before the outbreak of World War II, it was niggardly, for in 1931–2 the *overall* average per capita income in India was officially given as less than £5 per year (1/22 that of the Americans, 1/15 that of the British, 1/5 of the Japanese and 1/3 that of the Malayans); in the case of the peasantry the incomes were even lower (Rao, 1944, p. 104; Davis, 1951, pp. 205–6; Ghosh, 1946, p. 29). Digby (1901, p. 534), on the other hand, is of the opinion that the incomes in fact declined from an average of 2*d.* per person per day in 1880 to ¾*d.* in 1900.
[2] *IO:PPC*, 221 (1888), Letter from govt. of Bengal to govt. of India, dated 30 June 1888.
[3] *IO:PPC*, 320 (1881–91), J. O. Miller, 'Report on the condition of the agricultural classes during the last decade 1881/2–1891/2', p. 1; Kumar, 1965, p. 104. Even as late as 1943 a famine in Bengal is reputed to have claimed 3,500,000 lives (Bhatia, 1963, pp. 7–8, 324, 343).
[4] United Kingdom, 1931, pp. 14–17; Kumar, 1965, p. 142; Sovani, 1954*a*, pp. 101–2; Hutton, 1961, pp. 46 ff.; Gore, 1963, pp. 178–218. For a provocative new slant on the Indian joint-family system from the pen of an alien see P. Munz, 'The Marabar caves revisited', *Pacific viewpoint* (Wellington, New Zealand), vii (1966), 131–50.
[5] Bhatia, 1963, pp. 17–18; Davis, 1951, pp. 73–5; Kumar, 1965, pp. 78–101, 191–3; Gadgil, 1942, pp. 31–58; Raman Rao, 1958, pp. 172–87.

in India, in 1901 35,000,000 and a decade later 41,000,000.[1] Being almost totally illiterate and possessing few marketable skills, they were mostly fit only for manual work. Being primarily outcastes or low castes their disabilities under the caste system were particularly burdensome; and vested interests made certain that they never forgot their position. They had, therefore, virtually no other hope of escaping this tyranny except possibly through emigration.

There was little notable variance in the plight of these classes from one province of India to another and the example of Madras must suffice. There was a substantial increase in the number of farm labourers here, especially from about the second half of the nineteenth century, and by 1921 they made up about 20 per cent of the total rural population.[2] These labourers consisted of farm servants (those employed on a yearly or more permanent basis), mainly 'hereditary', and ordinary field labourers (those engaged by day or month or season) or journeymen. The farm servants were principally Adi-dravidas or Untouchables. In 1891, there were about 500,000 to 1,000,000 such *padiyals*, *pannaiyals*, *muladas* or *adimais*, as the farm servants used to be variously called,[3] in Madras Presidency.[4] By 1921 there were about 3,000,000.[5] They were virtual serfs of the landlords and usually got into that state through taking a loan and having to work it off while being maintained by the landlord. If they were valuable the landlords took care that their debt was not worked off and thus a man was attached to his master for life. His children, too, were similarly bound until the debt was paid, which could only mean worked off. If a farm was sold these 'hereditary' labourers were sold with it, together with the debt.[6] Their only way of escaping from this form of servitude was by emigrating.[7]

The information on this point is fragmentary and obscure but, for whatever it is worth, it tends to give the impression that, with one or

---

[1] Das, 1931, p. 14; Patel, 1952, p. 14. Patel (pp. 9–20), in fact, feels that the total numbers of agricultural labourers in pre-World War II India were even higher than those given here. For example, his estimated totals for 1891 and 1901 are 25,000,000 and 52,000,000 respectively. However, both his data and methods are of doubtful accuracy and have been much criticized. (See, for example, Morris, 1965, p. 41; 1966, pp. 191 ff.).

[2] United Kingdom, 1927–8, III, 313; Kumar, 1965, pp. 180–3. Cf. Morris, 1966, p. 196.

[3] Although it is possible that originally each one of these terms may have had specific meanings, as for example, *pannaiyal* denoting a bonded permanent farm servant and *adimais* a slave, in practice these differences between the various terms appear to have become blurred by the nineteenth century, if not earlier, and frequently tended to be used interchangeably. (Cf. Kumar, 1965, p. 41 *et seq.*)

[4] Raghavaiyangar, 1892, p. 76; Kumar, 1965, pp. 14–48, 75–6, 180–3; Raju, 1941, p. 39.

[5] United Kingdom, 1927–8, III, 313.

[6] Hutton, 1961, p. 222; Kumar, 1965, pp. 14–48, 75–91.

[7] United Kingdom, 1927–8, III, 313–14.

Causes of migration in modern times

two exceptions, there was little significant difference in the overall
wretchedness of these people from place to place, irrespective of their
type of agrestic servitude. The exceptions to the general pattern appear
to have been places like the *janmi* parts of Malabar and such *mirasi*
districts as Tinnevelly, Chingleput, South Arcot, Tanjore and Trichinopoly (fig. 9). In these areas the position of the farm servants was
reputedly worse. Here a few high-caste landlords, called *janmis* and
mirasdars, respectively, frequently claimed to have a prior right over
all land in the village, including the villagers' home sites and unoccupied
land too. The outcaste or low-caste labourer here had little or no chance
of ever acquiring any land and was invariably at the complete mercy of
his lord and master, being liable to be expelled from the only land available for the hut sites if he should offend the *mirasdar* or *janmi*, as the
case may be. With increasing monetization the demands of the landlord
on his *pannaiyals* became even more oppressive. In some of the *mirasi*
domains, for example, the *pannaiyal* was forced to work from sunrise to
sunset,[1] and if he was ever dilatory in the discharge of his bond he was
'confined without victuals and beaten with rods...'[2]

The position of the field or wage labourers or journeymen, the majority
of whom were also from the outcaste groups, was even more deplorable.[3]
At least the farm servant had a hope of some food even in a bad season;
in the case of the wage labourer even this was uncertain. Employment
was possible for only four to eight months of the year, and even then by
no means assured.[4] Wages were extremely low and seldom kept pace
with the rising cost of living. For example, wages of a day male labourer
increased from 2d. to 4d. in the 1890s, to 4d. to 6d. per day in the 1920s;[5]
but at the same time the purchasing power of the rupee in India fell by
about 50 per cent.[6] The vast majority of them led a hand-to-mouth
existence in a chronic state of semi-starvation,[7] or, to use a Gandhian
hyperbole, in 'perpetual fast'. Life for them was not so much a question
of degree of discomfiture but more a ceaseless struggle just to hang on to
the very breath of life. Difficult enough in favourable conditions, this
became extremely difficult in times of economic stress for they were the
first to be paid off.

[1] United Kingdom, 1927–8, III, 314–15; Hutton, 1961, pp. 205–6; Dennery, 1931,
pp. 196–211.
[2] *IO:PPC*, 32 (1797), 'Minute by Lord Hobart (Deputy Secretary to the Court of
Directors) on the deplorable state of Carnatic and Tanjore owing to usurious loans'.
[3] United Kingdom, 1927–8, III, 315; Kumar, 1965, pp. 150–1, 192.
[4] Strachey, 1937, p. 417; United Kingdom, 1880–5, I, 175; Kumar, 1965, p. 192;
Dennery, 1931, pp. 196 ff.
[5] United Kingdom, 1927–8, III, 336–9; Kumar, 1965, pp. 162–7.
[6] *SEMMPI*, 1921–2, pp. 194–5; Kumar, 1965, p. 167.
[7] Raghavaiyangar, 1892, p. 97.

41

Immigration: origins and trends

They had precious little to fall back on and were often reduced to the level of animals.[1] In such circumstances they, also, had no choice but to emigrate or face slow death through starvation.

Pari passu with the impoverishment of the peasantry, the lot of the babu or clerical and other such salaried classes also took a turn for the worse from about the latter half of the nineteenth century.

The economic development of India did not keep pace with the educational progress of the people. An ever-growing number of youths with a knowledge of English were leaving schools and universities. Most of them hankered for government jobs, but fresh avenues in this field were limited and not easy to come by, at least from about the 1900s if not earlier. Jobs in private commercial and industrial concerns were not popular. In any case opportunities of employment in these agencies were not numerous as there were not many such concerns in India then, it being largely an agricultural country still. Again, custom and institutions were still strong enough to deter many members of these classes from adopting pursuits in which manual labour was necessary or which were considered socially degrading, such as farming.[2]

Even in the case of those who managed to secure the right jobs, wages seldom kept pace with the rise in costs. For instance, while the price of staple foodstuffs in Madras rose by 80–100 per cent between 1888 and 1908, the wages of the government clerks in the area showed an increase of only 30–50 per cent during the same period.[3] The position of the English-educated was further complicated by the fact that as speakers of the language of the *burra sahibs* they felt compelled by their social status to keep up appearances. Finally, quite apart from their own immediate families, most of which were large enough, the joint-family system of the area placed an additional burden on the heads of the earning members. Therefore, in the face of inadequate wages, large commitments, rising prices, the decreasing purchasing power of the rupee and keener competition for a limited number of jobs, the English-educated babu found it increasingly difficult to maintain his home or position in the existing conditions in the area.[4] Consequently, it is

[1] 'The description in "The Siege of Corinth" of dogs gnawing human skulls is mild compared with the scenes of horror we are daily forced to witness in our morning and evening rides...It is dreadful to see what revolting food human beings may be driven to partake of. Dead dogs and horses are greedily devoured by these starving wretches; and the other day an unfortunate donkey having strayed from the fort, they fell upon him like a pack of wolves, tore him limb from limb and devoured him on the spot...' (An eyewitness account by Capt. W. Campbell, during the famine of 1833–4, known as the Guntur famine, cited in Raghavaiyangar, 1892, p. 15.)
[2] *SEMMPI*, 1911–12, pp. 164, 377–8; O'Malley, 1941, pp. 138–87, 645–69; Sovani, 1954b, pp. 877–82; 1954a, p. 98.
[3] *SEMMPI*, 1911–12, pp. 368–9.   [4] *Ibid.*

not surprising that more and more English-speaking Indians began to look elsewhere than their own mother country to make a better living.

Concurrent with these developments in India, political and economic changes in Malaya, too, tended to inhibit the immigration of such Indian elements as entrepreneurs of substantial means or literati of any note, while encouraging the influx of labourers and clerical classes, particularly the former.

CONDITIONS IN MALAYA

It will be remembered that beginning with the acquisition of Penang Island in 1786, Britain gradually extended her influence into the mainland and finally by 1914 was in actual control of the whole of Malaya; and that the early Indian community in Malaya was already on the wane as an economic, political and social force well before the arrival of the British at Penang. This eclipse, however, was not total and, as evidenced by contemporary accounts, at the time of the British advance into Malaya there were still some Indians remaining in positions of considerable influence in the Malay courts as the sultans' merchants, general advisers and financiers.[1]

Francis Light, the founder of Penang, in fact regarded them as a serious obstacle to the extension of British commerce in the Malay ports: ' I have kept my ground here (Kedah) notwithstanding the opposition of the Choolias (South Indians), Danes and Dutch. The former seem resolved if possible to exclude the English from any connection in the places where they trade... '[2] The subjugation of the Malay States by the British, however, finally ended the era of Indian influence at Malay courts, for not only did the Indians lose their former positions but steps were taken to prevent any return to these positions in the future.[3] The subservience of the Malay courts meant that the Indians lost a significant avenue of investment, income and prestige.

Concurrent with the extension of the British hegemony over Malaya was the cornering of the country's major financial, shipping and commercial activities by European agency houses and banking interests.[4]

---

[1] *SSFR*, 1 (1769–95), 1.9.1787; 2 (1786–7), 13.12.1786; Anderson, 1824, p. 52; Winstedt, 1923, p. 121; 1932, pp. 39–41; Clodd, 1948, p. 9; W. Marsden, *A grammar of the Malay language* (London, 1812), pp. 137–8; *C.O.273*, 1 (1838–58), 24.4.1842; 110 (1881), 31.12.1881; 226 (1897), 6.7.1897; 311 (1905), 25.1.1905; *SDT*, 30.12.1881; Bassett, 1964, pp. 121–2; Tregonning, 1965a, pp. 12–18; Nathan, 1922, p. 85; Krishnan, 1936, pp. 12–14.

[2] Clodd, 1948, p. 9.

[3] *C.O.273*, 110 (1881), 31.12.1881; 134 (1885), Colonial Office, minute no. 18779; 226 (1897), 6.7.1897; 311 (1905), 25.1.1905.

[4] Puthucheary, 1960, pp. xiii–xix, 23–59.

This, coupled with the rise of the Chinese as the principal middlemen and shopkeepers in Malaya, considerably reduced the scope for any large-scale Indian capital investment. Similarly investment in land on any substantial scale was also limited, owing to a land policy favouring Malay or European ownership.[1]

Opportunities in Malaya for the intellectual and adventurous elements in Indian society were none the more attractive. In the religious field the Gujarati gurus had been superseded by those from the Hadramaut, and the Sayyid now were the 'most esteemed priests' of Islam in Malaya.[2] The Malayan Civil Service, the upper echelon of the Malayan administration, remained reserved for Europeans and, subsequently, Malays only until after World War II. This meant that no matter how qualified an Indian might be he could not attain anything better than a subordinate post. In the business firms, too, he could hope for little more than an assistantship.[3]

Lawyers and such like appear to have found difficulty in acquiring registration to practise,[4] while opportunities for gaining political influence too were severely limited. There was no political enfranchisement in Malaya until after the Japanese occupation; there were only legislative councils consisting of official and nominated members. Unlike the Chinese and Malays, Indians were excluded, through what appears to have been little more than a discriminatory race policy, even from these bodies until the 1920s,[5] when an Indian was first nominated.[6] Even then, too, the government gave the impression of taking away with one hand what it had given with the other: as Indian intellectuals in Malaya began to interest themselves actively, especially after World War I, with the nationalist cause in India, the problem of Indian labour in Malaya became involved with the whole question of the political and economic

[1] *SSSF*, 1882, 362/82; 1884, 617/84, 1598/84, 1697/84; 1885, 543/85, 1286/85; 1909, 4209/1909; 1920, 2438/1920; *JSSF*, G.A. 350/1939; *SAR*, 1905, pp. 3–4; Tan, 1963, pp. 15–16; *FMSRRCC 1930*, II, 72; Weld, 1883–4, pp. 268, 288; *PFC*, 1923, p. B 113; *PFC*, 1933, p. C 293; *SB*, 10.7.1894.

[2] Winstedt, 1923, p. 49.

[3] *C.O.273*, 300 (1904), 17.8.1904; 17.9.1904; Colonial Office minute, no. 29635; 391 (1912), Colonial Office, minute nos. 5675, 6261, 7201, 7202, 7593, 8504, 10041; *MP*, Maxwell to Bracken, 22.9.1942; Maxwell, 1945, pp. 283–4; *I*, v (1932), 11; *HD*, 29.2.1912; 13.3.1912; 14.3.1912; 27.3.1912; 1.5.1912; *ST*, 27.1.1912; Neelakandha Aiyer, 1938, pp. 50 ff.; Tilman, 1964, pp. 45–9, 102–4 *et seq.*

[4] *C.O.273*, 273 (1906), 28.2.1906; Nair, 1937, p. 41; *NAI:EP*, 1940, file no. 51–10/1940 Os.

[5] *C.O.273*, 376 (1911), Colonial Office, minute no. 24942; 378 (1911), 25.10.1911, Colonial Office, minute no. 33284; *BP*, E. W. Birch, 'Memorandum on the Malay race in the Federated Malay States, dated Taiping, 28th May, 1906'; *MP*, Jones to Maxwell, 20.1.1943; Neelakandha Aiyer, 1938, pp. 92–4.

[6] An Indian was first nominated to the Straits Settlements Legislative Council in 1922 and to the Federal Council of the Federated Malay States in 1928.

status of the Indian community in Malaya. As this problem began to attract the attention of public opinion both in India and Malaya, the Malayan government, apparently growing apprehensive lest the politically conscious Indians inspire some feeling amongst the local peoples, especially the Indian labourers, thereby disturbing the *status quo*, began to submit the Indian intelligentsia to the closest scrutiny. Partly, it appears, for this purpose a governmental political organization, the Special Branch, was created in 1919 and two Indians from the Indian police force were seconded to it as supernumerary officers.[1] One of the functions of this organization was to keep a 'local suspect list' of 'subversive' Indians—that is Indians who evinced an interest in such matters as conditions of labour or political questions in general—and harass them if necessary. These 'suspects' were mostly professional people. Most of the membership of the Central Indian Association of Malaya,[2] for example, is believed to have at one time or the other appeared on the list. Perhaps even more drastic steps were taken to prevent, as far as possible, the entry into Malaya, henceforth, of Indians capable of leadership or political agitation.[3]

To sum up, there was little in economic opportunity or governmental policy to encourage any large-scale immigration of Indian big business or professional élites into pre-war Malaya. In fact, if anything, there was in the case of the latter, at least, an actual discouragement, certainly from the beginning of the 1920s. On the other hand, immigration of Indian labour was not only welcomed but openly solicited. This posture of the Malayan government was not unique but reflected a general attitude of British colonial governments towards the whole question of Indian

[1] *C.O.273*, 408 (1914), 7.12.1914; 14.12.1914; 24.12.1914; Colonial Office, minute no. 48606; 420 (1915), 17.2.1915; 17.6.1915; 424 (1915), 14.1.1915; 429 (1915), 10.8.1915; Colonial Office, minute nos. 38661, 49231; 432 (1915), 17.11.1915; 441 (1916), 4.5.1916; 15.6.1916; 450 (1916), 16.3.1916, Raghavan, 1954, pp. 63–9; Onraet, 1947, p. 81. The Indian Government's interest in the political activities of the Indians in Malaya was motivated not so much by what they were doing in Malaya but more by what bearing their activities had on the Nationalist movement in India. This was especially so during and after World War I, when it was revealed that Indian intellectuals in Malaya were actively involved in fostering the downfall of the British Raj in their homeland.

[2] See p. 110 below.

[3] Personal interviews with Mr N. Raghavan and Mr A. K. Sen, former President and General Secretary of the Central Indian Association of Malaya, respectively, and Mufti Nisar Ahmad Khan Sahib, retired Indian supernumerary officer, Malayan police force; Parmer, 1960, pp. 65–6; *NAI:EP*, 1935, file no. 330/35—L & O. The membership of the Central Indian Association of Malaya principally consisted of professional and business people. The association championed the cause of the Indian labourers in particular and the community in general. It came into being in 1936, merged into the wartime Malayan branch of the Indian Independence League and was disbanded after the Japanese occupation.

immigration.[1] They welcomed, or were prepared to tolerate, as the case may be, Indians as a labouring or a subordinate class, but not as that which might one day conceivably compete with European interests, or, perhaps even more important, upset or undermine the Raj.[2]

In Malaya, although not a declared policy, this bias or discrimination nevertheless appears to have been frequently practised surreptitiously, if not openly.[3] This attitude of the Malayan government coupled with the political and economic changes in India largely explains the lack of any substantial numbers of big business, highly qualified professional and other such classes in the stream of modern Indian migration to the country.

Labour migration[4]

There is some variance in the published literature as to precisely when the first Indian labourer arrived in British Malaya. The report of the commissioners appointed to enquire into the state of labour in the Straits Settlements and Protected Native States (Malaya) in 1890 postulates the first entries to the 'commencement of the present (nineteenth) century'.[5]

J. Geoghegan, Under-Secretary to the government of India in the Department of Agriculture, Revenue and Commerce and who was closely associated with the administration of Indian emigration, on the other hand, talks of a Tamil exodus, including domestic servants and agricultural labourers, to the Straits Settlements from the 'end of the eighteenth century'.[6] The Department of Labour and the South Indian Labour Fund Board, Malaya, prefer to settle for 'the late eighteenth century'.[7]

Examination of the contemporary *Straits Settlements factory records* has, however, produced conclusive evidence that Indian labour immigra-

---

[1] In its extreme form this attitude took the form succinctly summarized in the late South African statesman, Sir Thomas Hyslop's oft-quoted phrase: 'We want Indians as indentured labourers but not as free men' (Kondapi, 1951, p. 7).

[2] Gangulee, 1947, pp. 8–11; Sanderson, 1910, part I, p. 4; Kondapi, 1951, p. 7.

[3] *C.O.273*, 40 (1870), 22.10.1870; 300 (1904), 17.9.1904; Colonial Office, minute no. 29625; 317 (1906), 28.2.1906; *MM*, 18.8.1910; *ST*, 14.5.1933; 19.5.1933; *IMR*, I (1933), pp. 16–19; Jenks, 1920, p. 73; *NAI:EP*, April 1917, B proc. 26–41; June 1919, B proc. 1–131; May 1920, B proc. 13; 1933, file no. 84–2/33—L & O; 1936, file no. 91/36—L & O 1936 B.

[4] To avoid confusion, unless otherwise stated, the term 'labourer' is used in this study in the same sense as its employment in the pre-World War II Malayan and Indian documents, namely as including every artificer, miner, servant in husbandry, and every other person employed for the purpose of personally performing any manual labour or of recruiting or supervising persons for, or in performance of, such labour. It includes dependants of a labourer (wife, father, mother and children and adopted children under the age of fourteen, as are living with and dependent on him). It excludes camp-followers and personal domestic servants *not* performing or under contract to perform any work for any other person for payment or reward.

[5] *RLC 1890*, p. 36. [6] Geoghegan, 1873, p. 1.

[7] *ARSILFB*, 1959, p. 28.

tion into Malaya had certainly commenced by 1787, if not earlier. Only three months after his landing in Penang, Francis Light had requested the Governor-General in Council, India, to send him a 'supply of one hundred coolies, as the price of labour in Penang was enormous'. This request was not met but a similar request shortly after this for a supply of 'artificers' was granted and a group of twenty-five Bombay artificers landed in Penang in July 1787.[1]

Although they probably do not strictly come under the official category of labour migrants, it would not perhaps be out of place to record that the European officials and settlers proceeding to Penang with Francis Light appear to have taken Indian domestic servants along with them. Similarly the garrison-elect appears to have trailed its quota of Indian camp-followers.[2] This means that Indian domestic servants and camp-followers, quite apart from lascars and sepoys, were present from the very moment that Light and the European merchants stepped ashore at Tanjong Penaga, the site of present-day Georgetown, on 18 July 1786.[3] Judging from present-day experience it is not impossible that some of the camp-followers and domestic servants would not have been averse to engaging in part-time labour, outside their normal duties, for extra pocket money.

Other labourers were not far behind either, for by the early 1790s we are informed by no less an authority than Light himself, that there were already 'about one thousand' Indian shopkeepers and 'coolies' settled on the island, and vessels from the Coromandel coast were bringing 'annually 1,300 or 2,000 men who by traffic and various kinds of labour obtain a few dollars with which they return to their homes and are succeeded by others'.[4]

Once the spring had been tapped the stream of Indian labour immigration broadened in the ensuing years, especially following the acquisition of Province Wellesley by the Company in 1800, of Malacca in 1824 and the foundation of Singapore in 1819. But the demand, except during the periods of economic slump, for labour appears to have nearly always exceeded the supply. This shortage was partially offset through the employment of slaves[5] and, from about the end of the eighteenth century, especially of Indian convicts who had been sentenced to terms of transportation in the Straits Settlements. But this did not last, for slavery was abolished in the Company's territories in the Straits in the first decade of the nineteenth century,[6] and, as will be seen

[1] *SSFR*, 2 (1786–7), 13.12.1786; 17.9.1787.   [2] *SSFR*, 1 (1769–95), 1.9.1787.
[3] *JIA*, IV (1850), 629; Cullin, 1905, p. 4.   [4] *SSFR*, 6 (1794), 1.8.1794.
[5] *SSFR*, 2 (1786–7), 13.12.1786.
[6] *SSFR*, 185 (1805–30), 12.11.1805; 29.1.1808.

later on,[1] following continuous protests from the local British settlers against accepting 'expatriated villains from the jails of India', the Straits Settlements penal stations were also finally closed in 1873 and the convicts removed to the Andaman Islands. The abolition of slavery and the withdrawal of convict labour left a gap in the labour needs which became gradually more acute, especially with the onset of the tin rush in the latter half of the nineteenth century and the initiation by both planters and the government of ambitious programmes of economic development, towards the end of the nineteenth century, following the extension of British control over the Malay States.

Demand for Indian labour in Malaya

The Industrial Revolution and the development of large-scale production in Britain led to the exploitation of the colonies as sources of supply of raw materials for production and as markets for consumption of manufactured goods. Among the very first instructions of the Company to Light were that he should particularly 'attend to the raising of all kinds...(of) useful productions'.[2] Its vision appears to have been shared by its employees for they espoused the mercantilist policy of their employer with tremendous enthusiasm not only in their official but in their private capacities too.[3] In this they were also joined by the European merchants and other colonials. Not only was the country to be a strategic and commercial asset but it was also to yield exportable products wherewith to pay for its administration and protection. A number of the Europeans, at least the British ones, were of 'that class of lower English gentry accustomed to the management of land, and were familiar from their earliest days with such words as "improvement" and "agricultural geology"'.[4] Their thoughts thus turned, quite naturally, to the soil as an outlet for their surplus capital. Moreover, they were firmly convinced that the future of Malaya lay in the development of

---

[1] See pp. 132–40 below.

[2] *SSFR*, 1 (1769–95), 2.5.1786; 'Memoir on Prince of Wales Island considered politically and commercially' (undated).

[3] As early as 1790, Light had begun obtaining pepper, nutmegs and cloves from such places as Acheh, Amboina and Mauritius, while one of Raffles' first acts after the occupation of Singapore was to send a consignment of clove and nutmeg plants and seeds from Bencoolen, together with instructions, to the Resident, Singapore, requiring him to exert his 'utmost endeavours to establish the cultivation' under his 'immediate authority' (*SSFR*, 9, 1805–10, 17.4.1802; 5.7.1804; 30.9.1805; *JIA*, vɪɪɪ (1853), 320). Efforts of Straits officials had also resulted in the creation of a Board of Plantations, among the duties of which was the 'encouragement of agriculture', and, finally, the institution, in 1804, of a system of loans at moderate interest to help planters in 'time of stress or need' (*SSFR*, 6, 1794, 1.8.1794; 11, 1805, 4.10.1805).

[4] Wheatley, 1954, p. 64.

crops for export, for which it was eminently suited, awaiting only the investment of capital and the advent of labour to yield rich harvests of tropical crops.[1] Malaya to them and their latter-day compatriots was a country 'where nature had been prodigal of her richest gifts'.[2] Officials in Malaya appear to have anticipated Joseph Chamberlain's view of the Empire as an 'undeveloped estate'[3] and to this end regarded it as only proper that prospective capitalists should be given every encouragement[4] even to the extent of making 'gifts of land to pioneers'.[5] They fervently believed, and invariably acted on it, that a fundamental economic policy in Malaya should be the encouragement of commercial agriculture over other forms of enterprise.[6] In this they had the sympathy and support of the higher authorities too. Joseph Chamberlain, in the first days of his tenure as Secretary of State for the Colonies, echoing the views of his predecessor, wrote to the Governor of the Straits Settlements:

...The point of greatest importance appears to me...to be the encouragement of agriculture in order that the prosperity of these (Malay) States, which has hitherto depended so largely upon the plentiful supplies of tin, may still be assured, if, and when, their mineral sources in the course of years show signs of depletion...[7]

In such a favourable climate of goodwill and active encouragement considerable quantities of capital, especially European, both from within and outside the country, began to flow into commercial agriculture. And, beginning with the cultivation of such crops as spices and pepper

---

[1] Farquhar, Lt.-Governor of Prince of Wales Island, in 1805 reported that he was fully satisfied that agriculture in experienced hands required 'patience only to repay all its expenses and to reward munificently the labours of the industrious and persevering planter'. Further south, 'Agricola', writing thirty years later, enthused, 'The soil is good,...the climate fine,...the situation excellent,...and nought is wanting but the hand of man to bring abundance to our own doors.' Nor were their latter-day compatriots of the Malay States, the discovery and exploitation of the country's famous tin-fields notwithstanding, any the less enthusiastic or uncertain about Malaya's agricultural potential (*SSFR*, 9, 1805–10, 30.9.1805; *SFP*, 9.6.1836; *C.O.273*, 124; (1883), 27.4.1883).

[2] *C.O.273*, 124 (1883), 27.4.1883.

[3] J. Gallagher and R. Robinson, *Africa and the Victorians* (London, 1961), pp. 395–7.

[4] To give practical effect to these aims some of the early British Residents even opened up plantations and engaged in tin prospecting, later turning the properties over to European capitalists who were thus spared the initial risks of development (*SSSF*, 1882, 362/82; 1884, 617/84, 1598/84, 1622/84, 1697/84; 1885, 543/85, 1286/85; Parmer, 1960, p. 6).

[5] *C.O.273*, 105 (1880), 23.11.1880.

[6] *C.O.273*, 117 (1882), 14.12.1882; *SJ*, v (1897), 141–2; Swettenham, 1895–6, p. 291.

[7] This sentiment was reiterated by C. P. Lucas, Assistant Under-Secretary in the Colonial Office, two months later in a Colonial Office minute of 7 November 1895: '...On general policy...we must make every effort to provide for the time when tin shall be played out in the Malay Peninsula, by such means as encouraging... agriculturalists' (*C.O.273*, 207, 1895, Colonial Office, minute no. 20124; *PLCSS*, 1895, p. C 127).

in the 1790s, sugar in the 1830s and coffee in the 1870s, the mercantilist experiments reached their crescendo with the 'rubber rush' of the early years of the present century. Allured by the almost fabulous fortunes[1] promised by Raja Rubber, millions of pounds worth of money was poured into the Malayan countryside and thousands of acres of new and reclaimed land were snapped up by a horde of companies and individual planters, all thirsting after the 'white gold' (see Part 3).[2] Similarly motivated efforts were later extended to oil palm and tea. At about the same time, the Malayan government on its side of the battle to subdue 'the wildness to new civilization',[3] in addition to providing loans at low rates of interest,[4] easy terms in respect to alienation of land[5] and taxes on new enterprises[6] and promoting research and experimentation,[7] launched an ambitious programme of municipal, port, communication, drainage, road and railway construction to facilitate the economic development of the country in general and agriculture in particular.[8]

Malaya has an equatorial climate characterized by an abundant rain-

---

[1] For example, in 1910 the Pataling Rubber Estates Syndicate, floated in 1903, with an issued capital of £22,500 sold 320,000 lb. of rubber at a net average price of 6s. $2\frac{1}{2}d.$ per lb. against an all-in cost of production of $11\frac{1}{2}d.$ per lb. The company paid a dividend of 325 per cent in that year. Between 1905–6 and 1909–10 dividends paid by Cicely Estate, Selangor, rose from 10 to 130 per cent for preference and from 5 to 125 for ordinary shares. Rubber land values showed equally spectacular appreciations:

Age of tree (years)	Value per acre in 1905–6 (£ sterling)	Value per acre in 1909–10 (£ sterling)
1	15	55
2	35	110
3	60	200
4	120	500
6	140	700

(*GRN*, 1910, I, xi, p. 4; xii, p. 6; xiv, p. 6; II, ii, p. 7; *NHGMP*, p. 29.)

[2] By 1913, for example, British capital investment alone amounted to £40,000,000 (*C.O.273*, 403, 1913, 19.11.1913). A decade later it had increased to more than £100,000,000 (A. Phillipson, *The rubber position and government control*, Westminster, 1924, p. 6).

[3] *C.O.273*, 105 (1880), 23.11.1880.

[4] *PFC*, 1912, p. C 26; *SSSF*, 1908, 1486/1908.

[5] Any bona fide planter in the Malay States could obtain land in large blocks, for such crops as sugar, coffee, tea and rubber, on 999-year leases or in perpetuity virtually free for the first few years and thereafter at quit rent of only 10–20 cents per acre per year (*C.O.273*, 94, 1878, 11.7.1878; *SSSF*, 1879, 2701/79; 1884, 878/84; 1889, 325/89; I. Bird, *The Golden Chersonese*, London, 1883, p. 357).

[6] Export duty on the produce of the new enterprise was seldom above $2\frac{1}{2}$ per cent *ad valorem* (*C.O.273*, 94, 1878, 11.7.1878; State of Perak, 1894, pp. 121–51).

[7] The government had established the Botanical Gardens of Singapore in the second half of the nineteenth century. This was followed by the inauguration of the Department of Agriculture and the Rubber Research Institute in Kuala Lumpur in 1905 and 1926 respectively.

[8] *PLCSS*, 1900, p. C 117; Ferguson, 1911, pp. 114–15; Chai, 1964, pp. 19–36 *et seq.*

fall, high humidity and a uniformly high temperature. The soils are mostly of low inherent fertility but with a year-round growing season plant growth is rapid. Pioneering is both arduous and expensive and in the absence of adequate machinery and weed killers required a large labour input. In addition, large numbers of labourers were required for the constant battle to maintain security of tenure against rapid weed invasions of the patches already cleared.[1] Few labour-saving mechanical appliances were available or suited to local conditions in nineteenth and early twentieth century Malaya. In any case, much of the new work, on plantations at least, did not easily lend itself to mechanical methods, and, consisting in the main of simple repetitive tasks, called instead 'almost exclusively for unskilled workers'.[2] The case of rubber adequately illustrates this point. To draw the latex each tree has to be cut every morning or alternate mornings. The cut has to be just deep enough to tap the latex cells without penetrating or extending so far as to damage the general circulation of the tree. A cup has to be set to catch the latex which trickles from the cut bark. Each cup has to be emptied after every tapping and reset. The latex has to be gathered by a certain time lest it ferment or becomes adulterated with rainwater, and must then be taken to a central collecting place and finally to the factory where it has to be treated, coagulated and rolled prior to smoking and packing.[3]

These operations called for large numbers of workers. One tapper, quite apart from weeders, factory hands and such like, was needed for every 300–450 trees or four to five acres of productive rubber. Moreover, this high demand for labour remained quite constant throughout the year, there being little change in the general average amount of work to be done.[4] It was desirable, therefore, that the supply of labour should be

[1] This was fully appreciated by that shrewd judge of Malayan ecology, Captain James Low (1836, p. 10), who as early as 1836 remarked: 'There is no parallel in Europe to the labour attending the cultivation of a plantation here...In the course of a couple of months, the best cleared land, if left to itself, will be choked with a rank crop of tall weeds, and wiry reedy grass...*lalang* (*Imperata cyclindrica*, Beauv.). This has to be quickly eradicated or it will cost, when its roots have struck deep, twenty dollars per *orlong* (one and one-third acres) to destroy it in light soils and from forty to eighty dollars in clayey soils...No valuable exotic will thrive where its roots are invaded by this pest...It will kill spice trees, coffee plants and sugar cane, and interferes greatly with the growth of the hardier coconut tree...Having got rid of this bane...vigilance will be required to prevent new crops arising from seeds...brought by the winds...'
[2] International Labour Organisation, 1950, p. 25.
[3] Dobby (1950, p. 113) likens these labour needs of a rubber plantation to those of a dairy farm in that they involve the same relentless and monotonous routine of dealing with each productive unit (in this case the tree) or operation individually or separately.
[4] Although individual trees do have a rhythm in productiveness it varies from tree to tree and thus does not in any appreciable degree affect the normal requirements of a plantation.

4-2

constant. Furthermore, since it took about a year to train a labourer to be a reasonable worker in a specific job such as tapping or factory work, it was necessary that the labourer should be of a type that would stay on a plantation for at least a few years, if not for the rest of his life.

Other plantation crops like sugar, coffee, tea and oil palm were about equally demanding with regard to labour requirements, while every mile of railway track or road hacked through jungle, swamp or highland needed hundreds of labourers. In short, the extent and nature of the plantation and government undertakings in a difficult natural environment, coupled with the fact that nearly all the work had to be done by hand and cheaply enough to make the ventures competitive with older and more favourably established areas, meant that there soon grew up in Malaya a tremendous demand for workers in general and lowly paid, unskilled, manageable labour in particular.[1] This demand increased as the pace of economic development quickened, especially in the first two decades of the present century.

Several avenues were explored to meet the growing needs for cheap labour. The indigenous Malays appeared quite happy with their customary farms and fishing stakes and were not inclined to work fixed hours of labour day in and day out.[2] In any case being few and natives of the country and owners of the soil, they could obtain a living usually in a more congenial manner than by working for wages on some estate or other similar alien undertakings.[3] As such they could not be obtained in sufficient numbers to work regularly for wages.[4] Some British Residents even resorted to the traditional Malay feudal practice of *kerah* (corvée) in lieu of taxes. But this measure, too, achieved little, there being few means of enforcing the law in a country then virtually devoid of roads or railways, and was finally abandoned in 1891.[5] In such circumstances employers thus had of necessity to turn to immigrant labour.

[1] *SSSF*, 1884, 4809/84; 1894, 3886/94; *JSSF*, G.A. 51/1910; *RLC 1890*, app. A, p. 176; Jackson, 1961, p. 108; Low, 1836, pp. 10 ff.; Grist, 1936, pp. 73 ff.; Maxwell, 1891–2, pp. 26–7.

[2] *BP*, Harrison to Birch, undated; Birch to Resident-General, Federated Malay States, 28.5.1906.

[3] An amusing story is told that as one of the means to stimulate Malays to work, Capt. Light is said to have loaded one of the guns of the vessel attached to him with a bag of silver dollars and fired it into the jungle, leaving the Malays to pick them up, which they could not well do without at the same time clearing the ground of its underwood and jungle (*JIA*, IV (1850), 36). But even such ingenious and unorthodox tactics too did not have the desired long-term effect (*T*, 28.8.1884).

[4] Maxwell, 1891–2, p. 26; *SSSF*, 1884, 526/84.

[5] *SSG*, 1885, p. 871; Parmer, 1960, pp. 16–18; Chai, 1964, pp. 98–102. There was a radical shift in government policy regarding the employment of indigenous Malay labour on plantations from about the dawn of the present century, in the sense that it now no longer seemed to be keen to see Malays leaving their *kampongs* for estate work. This was certainly so in the case of the estates adjoining *padi* areas.

African slave labour, which had built up the plantations of the West Indies, was experimented with in a small way in the 1780's. But it was soon out of the question as the slave trade was prohibited in British territories in the first decade of the nineteenth century, and finally slavery was legally abolished with effect from 1 August 1838.[1] African voluntary labour was not available either, for with bitter memories of slavery behind them Africans were not anxious to embark even as free emigrants.[2]

White labour was not only expensive[3] but wellnigh impossible to recruit for plantation work in the tropics, which were then among the Europeans referred to as the 'white man's grave'.[4] Even if available there was the problem that they would insist on decent wage standards, on proper housing and such like, and, after the fashion at home, might form trade unions and compel employers to 'respect the force of organized labour'.[5] In any case, the very idea of a white man working as a common labourer among the 'natives' in a place where it was considered essential to keep up the prestige of the Europeans was anathema to the race-conscious Victorian *tuan besars*, the nabobs of the Indies.[6]

In Asia itself, attempts were made by rubber planters to recruit labour from Korea. These attempts, however, proved abortive, partly due to the opposition of the Korean government and partly due to the lack of support from both the Malayan authorities and the Colonial Office.[7]

Japan, too, was thought of as a possible source of labour,[8] but no positive action appears to have been taken in this direction by either the Malayan government or the European planters. In any case Japanese emigrants, protected by their government against exploitation while

In Kedah/Perlis in 1920, for example, applicants for rubber plantation land were prohibited from employing local Malay labour, and were required to satisfy the government that they were in a position to import sufficient immigrant labour for development and maintenance purposes before their applications could be approved (*HCOF*, 1920, Kedah 504/1920, 28.2.1920; Chief Secretary, 510/1920, 2.3.1920).

[1] *SSFR*, 2 (1786–7), 13.12.1786; 185 (1805–30), 12.11.1805; 29.1.1808; Harris, 1933, pp. 52–64.
[2] *PP*, XXIII (1847–8), part I, para. 13207.
[3] *PP*, XXXII (1831–2), paper no. 724, pp. 8–30; Cameron, 1865, pp. 181–2; Sinha, 1946, pp. 55–6; *SSFR*, 183 (1821–5), 18.9.1823.
[4] Mukerjee, 1936, pp. 53, 254; Ruhomon, 1939, p. 7; A. Grenfell Price, *White settlers in the tropics* (New York, 1939), pp. 30–2; Earl, 1846, p. 115; 1853, p. 43.
[5] The Fabian Society, 1942, pp. 2 ff.
[6] Cameron, 1865, pp. 281–2; Lovat, 1914, pp. 315–16; Weld, 1883–4, pp. 269 ff.; *BM*, May 1926, p. 6; Labour Research Department, 1926, p. 14; *PPSE*, 24 (1897–8), 21.1.1898.
[7] *C.O.273*, 359 (1910), 17.8.1910; 23.9.1910; 21.10.1910; 22.11.1910; 29.12.1910; Colonial Office, minute no. 29420.
[8] *RLC 1890*, p. 65; *PPSE*, 26 (1900), 25.5.1900; 26.6.1900.

abroad,[1] were not prepared to accept a low wage or standard of living in a tropical colony, and, if emigrating at all, they preferred to go to their own colonies or to the Americas.[2] The few Japanese labourers who did come to Malaya came on a short term basis to work exclusively on the Japanese-owned and operated mines or rubber estates in the country.[3] In such circumstances employers had no alternative but to confine their search for cheap labour to sources nearer home, principally China, Java and India.

Chinese immigrants were already present in substantial numbers in the Straits Settlements by the early years of the nineteenth century, while many of them had also by this time begun to penetrate into the Malay States in search of tin, gold and such like lucrative undertakings. The Chinese were generally considered the best workers,[4] being hard-working, skilful, adaptable people, able and willing to attempt whatever the situation called for, 'whether manual labour or crimping, mer-chandising, mining or prospecting, usury or piracy or gang robbery'.[5] But they were 'inclined to be disorderly, cost more in police and super-vision and (gave) more trouble'.[6] Almost all of them were suspected of being members, or under the influence, of secret societies, many of which, originally religious or benevolent 'self-help' associations, had by the nineteenth century degenerated into little more than 'Pirates and Robbers Co-operative Associations'.[7] This raised all kinds of doubts and fears of security amongst potential employers, especially on the many estates that were miles away from anywhere and invariably in the charge of one or two Europeans only.[8] Perhaps more, if not most, im-portant was the fact that the Chinese was an economic man *par excellence*. He left his homeland primarily to better himself financially, to become if possible a *towkay* in his own right. As such he was not

[1] Carr-Saunders, 1936, p. 267.

[2] Mukerjee, 1936, pp. 170–1; Dennery, 1931, pp. 61–7.

[3] *JAR*, 1911, pp. 19–20; Vlieland, 1932, p. 87; personal interview with officials of the Japanese Embassy, Singapore.

[4] This was generally agreed among employers as is amply illustrated by this outburst of 'six feet three of big-voiced British complacency' when a doubt was expressed as to the advisability of employing Chinese. 'Bosh!...bosh, utter fat-headed bosh! Why there isn't in the whole world a better worker than the (Chinese). You can't give him too much to do. He will take on double shifts for a few extra cents, and he has a head worth fifty Tamils and a score of Javanese...As for health, why you can feed him on stale cat-meat washed down with draughts of cholera and enteric germs, and you can breed mosquitoes to sing him to sleep—he will never turn a hair. Give him a pipe of opium occasionally, so that he can dream of the girl he left behind him, and you may forecast your output to an ounce' (A.W.S., 1910, p. 85).

[5] Hinton, 1929, p. 14.

[6] *RLC 1890*, p. 66; *SSFR*, 172 (1827), 29.6.1827; Hinton, 1929, p. 14.

[7] Purcell, 1948, pp. 155–6; Mills, 1960, pp. 239 ff.; L. F. Comber, *Chinese secret societies in Malaya* (Singapore, 1959), pp. 32 ff.
A.W.S., 1910, pp. 85–6.

prepared to remain in any employment of low income any longer than absolutely necessary. Finally, he considered that he was likely to prosper better under the employ of his own countrymen and consequently did not cherish the idea of serving under an alien employer. Whenever he did work for a 'foreign devil', he invariably did so on a 'contractor system', that is working through his own *kepala* (headman) or contractor for payments on an *output* basis. Employers in this system had, thus, contact only with the *kepalas* or contractors. This was even more so because few of these employers spoke or understood Chinese.[1] They were thus at the mercy of the *kepalas* or contractors, who were liable to leave whenever better opportunity beckoned elsewhere.

This state of affairs was linked up with the mode of importing Chinese labour. The majority of the *sinkehs* or newcomers were too poor to pay their passage from China to Malaya and consequently, until the 1930s, generally came under a system in which labour brokers in the ports of south China, working in conjunction with their counterparts in Singapore, paid the expenses of the voyage for batches of emigrants. On arrival in Malaya the *sinkehs* were sold to the highest bidder, for whom they had to work until their value was paid off.[2] This was a profitable business and became virtually a monopoly of Chinese 'coolie rings'. Attempts by planters to break or bypass this monopoly and recruit Chinese labour in China itself through their own agents proved fruitless partly due to the combined opposition of the Chinese government (which generally did not approve of emigration by its citizens) and the labour brokers, and partly through disunity in their own ranks. There was also lack of support both from the mining companies, one of the principal employers of Chinese labour, and the Malayan government, which appears to have regarded the whole move as unnecessary and liable to involve it in endless trouble with a foreign non-British government.[3]

Opinion among employers was divided regarding the suitability of Javanese as labourers. Some thought them intractable and lazy, many of them being sickly.[4] Others regarded them as good workers, certainly better than the Tamils, and there was nothing wrong with their physique or ability to work.[5] Moreover, being culturally and ethnically similar to the Malays they would assimilate more easily and thus make more suitable potential settlers than the Indians or Chinese.[6] But the crux of the

[1] *MCECLFMS*, pp. 5 ff.; Blythe, 1947, p. 70.
[2] Sandhu, 1961 *a*, pp. 10–11; Blythe, 1947, pp. 40 ff.
[3] *C.O.273*, 369 (1911), 13.3.1911; Colonial Office, minute no. 13123; 373 (1911), 28.3.1911; 374 (1911), 24.8.1911; Parmer, 1960, pp. 104–8.
[4] A.W.S., 1910, p. 85; Parr, 1910, p. 2; *RLC 1890*, app. A, p. 87.
[5] A.W.S., 1910, pp. 84–6; *RLC 1890*, p. 66; Parr, 1910, p. 5.
[6] *COR*, 20.9.1907; *FMSPD*, p. 54.

matter was that Javanese labour was on the whole difficult to import,[1] largely because of the emigration restrictions imposed by the Dutch government which, since 9 January 1887, permitted labour recruitment in Java only, and that too on contracts which had not only to be enforced but seen to be enforced.[2] Moreover the cost of importing such labour was almost prohibitive, being two or three times that of an Indian of the same category.[3] Efforts by planters to reduce the cost and streamline the cumbersome emigration procedure were in vain, partly because of lack of support from the British authorities[4] who, as one planter put it, were 'all of a tremble lest anything you do should cause an international incident'.[5] When the Malayan government did finally decide to champion the cause of the planter *vis-à-vis* the Dutch authorities in 1941,[6] its efforts were practically still-born owing to the imminence of the Japanese invasion. In these circumstances, where the Malay proved unmotivated or was otherwise unavailable, Negro and European labour alike impracticable, with the Chinese expecting more and finding other and more remunerative occupations, and the Javanese being both difficult and expensive to acquire, the Indian became indispensable.

Of the people of the Subcontinent the South Indian peasant, particularly the untouchable or low caste Madrasi, was considered the most satisfactory type of labourer, especially for light, simple repetitive tasks.[7] He was malleable, worked well under supervision and was easily manageable.[8] He was not as ambitious as most of his Northern Indian compatriots and certainly nothing like the Chinese. True, he had little of the self-reliance or the capacity of the Chinese,[9] or for that matter of many of his own countrymen from the other parts of the Subcontinent, but he was the most amenable to the comparatively lowly-paid and rather regimented life of estates and government departments. He had fewer qualms or religious susceptibilities, such as aversion to crossing the dreaded *kale pani* and food taboos, than his Northern fellows, and cost less in feeding and maintenance.[10]

Acclimatization to Malayan conditions was comparatively easier for

[1] Jenks, 1920, p. 63; Parr, 1910, pp. 1–5.
[2] As one irate British planter put it, 'The Dutch Government worries one to death with its regulations... You get about twice as many inspectors nosing round as if you had Tamils or Chinese, and Heaven help you if the medico has a liver when he calls' (A.W.S., 1910, pp. 84–5).   [3] Parr, 1910, pp. 2, 41.
[4] *C.O.273*, 360 (1910), 7.1.1910; 17.3.1910; Colonial Office, minute paper no. 2948; Parmer, 1960, pp. 109–12.   [5] A.W.S., 1910, p. 84.
[6] *PAMC*, 1941, 12, app. A; 1946, 7, pp. 5–6; Parmer, 1960, pp. 112–13; *PLCSS*, 1941, pp. 178–9.   [7] *NAI:EP*, Jan. 1884, B proc. 7–14.
[8] Figart, 1925, p. 174.   [9] Vlieland, 1934, p. 67.
[10] *SSFR*, 94 (1824), 15.4.1824; personal interviews with Mr T. P. Sundaram, former Assistant Controller of Labour, Federation of Malaya, and four European estate managers, in Perak and Johore, who wish to remain anonymous.

him as South India was not totally different from Malaya climatically. Moreover he was already adjusted to a low standard of living, was a British subject, accustomed to British rule and well-behaved and docile. Typical though these features were of South Indian workers in general, they were especially so in the case of the Adi-dravidas, or Untouchables, who formed the main labouring groups of South India.[1] The relegation of the outcastes to a sort of ghetto was carried, at least in the pre-war period, in South India to great lengths, the intolerance of the *brāhmaṇa* being particularly conspicuous.[2] Some *brāhmaṇas* considered themselves defiled if some such outcastes as the Pariahs and Pallas came within a distance of twenty-four, thirty-six or, as in some cases, even more feet. The relegation of these classes to the level of animals in a caste-ridden society naturally tended to deprive them of initiative and self-respect, and made them a cringingly servile group. These people had neither the skill nor the enterprise to rise above the level of manual labour. Primitive and ill-organized, they never appear to have known the art of collective bargaining. They were therefore also especially desirable as a 'black-leg' counterpoise to the more progressive labouring elements such as the Chinese who were liable to resort to the strike weapon quite readily.[3] Willing to accept low fixed wages, they enabled employers to keep wages depressed. All in all then these features of the South Indian Adi-dravidas made them almost the ideal labouring material for the furtherance of capitalist endeavours in Malaya.[4] Furthermore, many of the European planters, especially during the days of extensive coffee planting, came to Malaya from Ceylon, where they had been used to South Indian labour. They firmly believed that Madrasis 'must always be the mainstay of planters'. They were the best suited for such specific tasks as picking crops.[5] Similarly a number of senior government officials and contractors, particularly those in the public works and railways departments, also came from Ceylon where they too had handled Indian labour. They also preferred Madrasis 'for all work' on such projects as road and railway construction. The State Engineer, Selangor, for instance had no doubts that Madrasis were specially adapted for road making and were the 'best metal breakers'.[6] Finally, unlike the case of the Chinese, many of the early European

---

[1] T. W. Holderness, *Peoples and problems of India* (London, 1912), pp. 101 *et seq.*; Hutton, 1961, pp. 192–222; Kumar, 1965, pp. 49–59.
[2] Hutton, 1961, pp. 71–91; H. H. Risley, *The people of India* (Calcutta, 1908), pp. 135 *et seq.*
[3] *RLC 1890*, app. A, p. 103; *SJ*, IV (1896), 439; *HT*, 8.5.1938; *DLAI*, 1938, II, 1891; *C.O.273*, 145 (1887), Colonial Office, minute no. 11291.
[4] The Fabian Society, 1942, pp. 1–30.
[5] *RLC 1890*, app. A, p. 58; *RLC 1896*, pp. C 237–8.
[6] *RLC 1890*, app. A, pp. 22 *et seq.*; *RLC 1896*, p. C 241.

planters and government officials either themselves had some knowledge of the language of the Indian labourers or had English-speaking subordinates who did, thereby facilitating direct contact and control.

Apart from economic and administrative reasons, Indian immigration was also desirable as a political move, especially to counterbalance the growing numbers and influence of the Chinese.[1] This is best shown in the policy statements of Sir Frederick Weld, Governor of the Straits Settlements in 1887:

> I am...anxious for political reasons that the great preponderance of the Chinese over any other race in these Settlements, and to a less marked degree in some of the Native States under our administration, should be counterbalanced as much as possible by the influx of Indian and other nationalities...[2]

The Chinese were turbulent, and faction fights amongst them were not infrequent. They were enterprising and daily increasing in numbers and influence and at this rate of progress could one day conceivably oust the British from their privileged position. Both the British government and planters were, therefore, wary about the Chinese and considered it 'by no means desirable to let the Chinese obtain too exclusive a possession of the Peninsula'.[3] In short, it was imperative to take immediate measures to check Chinese influence and ensure the safety of British interests. The casting of the Indian in the role of a counterpoise to the Chinese was considered to be one such effective step. Finally, some of the early officials also felt that the introduction of Indian immigrants into the Malay States 'might possibly, to a certain degree, render obligatory a more permanent adoption of the Residential system' in those states 'than has as yet been decided upon, as it would not be possible to leave the immigrants under the uncontrollable rule of a Malay Sultan'[4] —shades of the Trojan Horse!

The Malayan government and employers were well aware of the economic and social stresses prevalent amongst the poorer classes of India and therefore, quite naturally, entertained sanguine hopes that there would be a veritable voluntary and uninhibited flood of Indian labour, especially from South India—the home of one of the largest concentrations of Chamars (Cherumans), Pariahs (Paraiyans), Pallas (Pallans) and other depressed 'lepers'[5] of Indian society. However, this expected mass movement of labour did not fully materialize until the

[1] *NAI:EP*, Sept. 1922, confidential B proc. 49–50.
[2] *C.O.273*, 145 (1887), 11.5.1887; 146 (1887), 24.9.1887.
[3] *C.O.273*, 2 (1858–9), 4.2.1858; 6 (1863–4), 2.9.1863; A.W.S., 1910, pp. 85–6 *et seq.*
[4] *SNL:COGSS*, 1878, 119, 25.4.1878; *PLCSS*, 1881, paper no. 18, para. 4.
[5] Untouchables, Depressed classes, Scheduled classes, Adi-dravidas, Exterior castes, Outcastes or Harijans, as these people were variously called, formed, on the average, about one-sixth of the total population of Madras Province in the nineteenth century and early decades of the present century. In terms of numbers,

early years of the present century and even then not quite in the manner initially expected. Although the extremely low and chancy level of living of the Indian peasant tended to push him out of his village hearth, several factors, at least until the early years of the present century, appear to have militated against his leaving. Centuries of isolated living in the traditional and familiar environment of virtually one and the same village seemed to have endowed the Indian peasant with more than the usual reluctance to move associated with his kind. Social customs and institutions militating strongly against overseas emigration to distant places further reinforced this. Except for a few notable exceptions, mainly in Northern India, he was generally not an 'economic man' in the sense of, say, his Chinese counterpart. Consequently he needed far stronger forces of propulsion and attraction than was normal in many other societies. Even under the most desperate conditions he seldom left immediately, preferring to hang on to the bare thread of life in his familiar milieu on the chance that his karma or kismet might change for the better. Then if he conquered his fears of the unknown, he seldom knew where to go, his horizon being normally limited to little beyond his home village or taluk. Perhaps most important of all, even if he knew the way to the nearest port, he rarely had the ready cash to pay for his trip from the village to the port, let alone the voyage beyond. Finally, in the event of his departure actually materializing, being invariably in debt or bonded to the landlord or moneylender, he had to run the gauntlet of their guards.[1]

Apart from these factors the attitude of the Indian government, too, impeded emigration to Malaya during the nineteenth century. The Indian government of this period often seemed to be uncertain about the benefits, both to itself and the individuals concerned, of emigration, particularly to distant colonies, involving, as it usually did, at least one or two years' absence from the mother country. Indeed, now and then, it expressed fears that emigration of able-bodied peasants might lower agricultural production, and consequently revenue, at home.[2] In the case of Malaya, it had other reservations also. It tended to regard Malaya as a distant colony. Moreover, it was still uncertain about conditions in Malaya and its own role in the movement of Indian labourers across the Bay of Bengal. Quite naturally, therefore (being uncertain about

there were some 7,000,000 of them in 1921 and 8,000,000 twenty years later (United Kingdom, 1927–8, III, 334; Krishnaswami, 1947, p. 26; Hutton, 1961, pp. 192–222; Kumar, 1965, pp. 49–59).

[1] *SEMMPI*, 1898–9, p. 705; Dennery, 1931, pp. 202 ff.; Sundaram, 1930, p. 4; *SSSF*, 1895, 4303/95; *PLCSS*, 1897, p. C 168.

[2] *PMBR*, 23.11.1843; 1.5.1847; 7.6.1847; 19.7.1847; 13.5.1850; 8.8.1850; Kumar, 1965, pp. 139–41.

conditions in Malaya and its own role in this traffic), it felt it politic, until such a time as these matters were mutually resolved, to take the safer line of restricting or controlling the emigration of labourers going out on hire.[1]

Then, in addition to the other colonies such as Fiji, West Indies and Mauritius which maintained an elaborate system of inducements and of recruitment, there were the next-door neighbours, Ceylon and Burma, both of which desired emigrants from India. They had the blessing of the Indian authorities and freedom from restrictive legislation. Furthermore, they offered generally higher wages, better conditions of service and a lower cost of living, than did Malaya. For example, the minimum wages of an Indian immigrant labourer in Burma in 1890 amounted to some Rs. 10 per mensem, compared with the approximately Rs. 4 to Rs. 5 per mensem paid in the Straits Settlements to such persons during the same period. Moreover, while every Indian in Burma and Ceylon landed a free man, many of his countrymen venturing to Malaya did so as indentured labourers (table 1).[2]

Again, service conditions in nineteenth-century Malaya were unattractive. Workers lived in dilapidated and filthy *bangsals* or labour lines and medical attention was poor or totally absent. Moreover, comparatively few Indians had heard about Malaya and those who had held the popular belief that it was a country covered with thick virgin jungle, where hyperendemic malaria and beri-beri took a heavy toll of human lives and where men worked until they dropped into their graves. In other words it was 'a death trap yawning to engulf the surplus population of India'.[3] Migrants, therefore, were not too anxious to come to Malaya until conditions improved.

Finally, traffic in human freight was a profitable business and a 'ring of local recruiters' virtually monopolized the labour movement from the Indian ports and in effect deliberately restricted the flow, to ensure constantly high commissions.[4]

But since a large supply of cheap labour was imperative for the development of Malaya, the government, in conjunction with the planters and other employers, from as early as the 1880s, set about overcoming the above obstacles and ensuring a constant copious flow of labour, especially from South India.

First, conditions of service were on the whole improved, as regards passage, accommodation, remuneration and such like. Indenture was abolished in 1910 and wages of free labourers were raised from 20 to

[1] *IO:EP*, 1502 (1880), pp. 77–172; 1862 (1882), pp. 35–63.
[2] *RLC 1890*, pp. 40–56.   [3] *SSSF*, 1894, 3886/94.
[4] *RLC 1890*, pp. 40–6; *RLC 1896*, p. C 223.

Causes of migration in modern times

Table 1: Comparative flow of Indian immigrants
into Burma, Ceylon and Malaya, 1880–1889

Burma		Ceylon		Malaya	
year	number of immigrants	year	number of immigrants	year	number of immigrants
1880–1881	6 682	1881	54 204	1881	6 648
1881–1882	8 020	1882	51 640	1882	9 728
1882–1883	22 075	1883	39 055	1883	10 429
1883–1884	12 659	1884	45 962	1884	15 904
1884–1885	5 993	1885	46 665	1885	21 461
1885–1886	7 616	1886	39 907	1886	20 308
1886–1887	24 642	1887	72 660	1887	16 892
1887–1888	38 956	1888	81 710	1888	20 496
1888–1889	38 014	1889	64 459	1889	18 032
TOTALS	164 657		496 262		139 898

Note: Ship fares
India–Malaya
    Before 1887.   Rs. 15 per single journey.
    1887–1890.   Rs. 8 per single journey.
India–Ceylon
    Before 1877.   25c (rupee cents) per single journey.
    1877–1890.   25c (rupee cents) per single journey.
India–Burma
    Before 1877.   Rs. 5 per single journey.
    1877–1890.   Rs. 5 per single journey.
Source: Compiled from *RLC 1890*, pp. 40–56.

30 cents per day in 1890 to 35 to 45 cents in the 1900s, generally putting them above those prevailing in contemporary Ceylon and Burma. These wages represented more than three times what labourers could earn in parts of India at that time.[1]

Secondly, a steamship subsidy was inaugurated to stimulate immigration. In 1887 the Straits Settlements, Perak, Selangor and Johore agreed to contribute towards an annual subsidy of $30,000 to reduce steamship fares between Negapatam and Penang. In consideration for this sum, a European shipping firm, Huttenbach, Liebert and Company, agreed to run a fortnightly service for all bona fide agricultural labourers at the reduced fare of Rs. 8 per head as compared with the earlier rate of Rs. 15. Subsequently the remaining Malay States also joined in the scheme and the annual subsidy was increased to $250,000 and a new agreement signed, this time with the British India Steamship Navigation

[1] *SEMMPI*, 1912–13, p. 124; *RLC 1890*, pp. 40–56; Parmer, 1960, table 8.

Company, which extended the service to the other South Indian and Malayan ports and at even more frequent intervals.[1]

Thirdly, a notification, the *Penang Circular*,[2] which limited the payment of commissions to only those agents who recruited indentured labour, was rescinded in 1897 and payment allowed thereafter to all agents irrespective of the class of labour recruited.[3]

Fourthly, on the government level, representation to the Indian government to look favourably on emigration to Malaya was stepped up by the Malayan government. The government of Malaya donated large sums of money in aid of famine relief in India, at the same time advising the Indian government that the best relief would be for the Indian government to encourage emigration.[4] Furthermore, it felt that as Malaya was a British possession its development would contribute to the larger and common good of the British Empire. These 'patriotic urgings of the Empire builders' together with the fact that the Indian government, having been favourably impressed by the report of its fact-finding mission to Malaya in 1883,[5] now felt satisfied with the treatment of Indian emigrants to Malaya, led to its withdrawing all restrictions on emigration on its side in 1897.[6] Finally in 1900, agreement was reached to facilitate the free flow of emigration to Malaya.[7] But this emigration was to be only from South India. The Indian government felt that labour emigration from North India could not be permitted on the same lines as from the South. North India was not the 'natural home' of emigration to Malaya. Unlike South Indians those from the north found Malaya a 'totally alien environment'. Consequently, special laws, on the same lines as those prevailing in the case of more distant colonies, would have to be promulgated to regulate their recruitment in India and treatment in Malaya. This would have to be specially so, too, because most of the distant colonies drew much of their labour from the Northern Indian provinces and it would be impolitic and administratively difficult to permit Malaya to secure labour

[1] *RLC 1890*, p. 40; *SSAR*, 1900, p. 182; *SSAR*, 1902, pp. 187–8; *SSAR*, 1907, pp. 15–16; *PLCSS*, 1901, pp. C 7–14; *SSSF*, 1905, 614/1905.
[2] Section (*b*) of the *Penang Circular* of 8 November 1887, stated: 'No agent or recruiter shall receive any commission on coolies not entered in the list of indentured coolies.' This was a measure calculated to benefit sugar planters, the principal employers of indentured labour, by forcing recruiters only to recruit indentured labour. It severely restricted the labour supply of coffee planters and others who relied mainly on free labour. This they could not obtain in sufficient numbers without paying adequate commissions to their agents (Carey, 1895, p. 409).
[3] *PLCSS*, 1896, pp. B 183–4; *IO:EP*, 4981 (1896), p. 1065.
[4] *PLCSS*, 1900, p. C 117.
[5] *IO:EP*, 2278 (1884), pp. 703–63.
[6] *IO:EP*, 5210 (1897), pp. 338–9.
[7] *IO:EP*, 5899 (1900), pp. 461–4; *PLCSS*, 1900, pp. C 119–20.

from these areas on any other terms than those pertaining in the case of those colonies.[1] Furthermore, although it did not say so specifically, it appeared that the Indian government was not particularly keen to allow Northern Indians, especially the sturdier ones like the Punjabis, Rajputs, Pathans and Mahrattas, as they were required for British interests in India itself, in such services as the armed and police forces. In any case, it felt that it had 'no reason to believe that the labour population of South India, which owing to the circumstances of climate and race is the natural source of supply' to the Malay States, 'is not ample to meet all requirements'.[2]

Fifthly, in 1907, a semi-official body known as the 'Indian Immigration Committee', consisting of official and private employers' representatives, was inaugurated with the desire to establish a central administrative machinery for the importation of Indian labour on a large scale and to create a system of registration of labourers to reduce crimping or the enticing of one employer's labourers by another employer or his agent through the offer of higher wages or better conditions of service. The Committee's work was embodied in the *Tamil Immigration Fund Ordinance*, enacted in the Straits Settlements in September 1907. Similar statutes were passed in the Malay States.[3] Under these legislations, all employers of Indian labour had to pay an assessment on the number of days worked by all Indian labourers in their employ. The funds thus accrued were to be used for the maintenance of the recruiting depots in India and the quarantine stations in Malaya, besides providing free passage and board to all bona fide Indian labour emigrants.[4] Amendments in 1908, 1909, 1911 and 1913 to the Ordinance made the work of the Committee more comprehensive and all recruitment of Indian labour was placed under its jurisdiction. Moreover, these amendments provided that, in addition to passage and board, all other legitimate expenses (including the agreed commission to agents) connected with the Indian labour emigrants from the time of their recruitment in India until their arrival at their place of employment in Malaya were to be met from the Fund, with effect from 1 May 1914.[5]

[1] *IO:EP*, 5899 (1900), p. 465; *PLCSS*, 1900, p. C 119; *NAI:EP*, 1934, confidential file no. 208/34—L & O.
[2] *PLCSS*, 1900, p. C 119; *C.O.273*, 315 (1905), 8.6.1905.
[3] *PAMAR*, 1923–4, app. A; *PLCSS*, 1907, pp. B 133–5.
[4] The fund, initially called the 'Tamil Immigration Fund', was later styled the 'Indian Immigration Fund' (*ARSILFB*, 1959, app. A).
[5] After this the only additional expenses that an employer had to meet were the 'extra' commission he was prone to pay his agents to induce greater flow of labour on to his premise and feeding charges in Malayan depots and quarantine camps for the days above the stipulated period that his labourers spent there (*IICMM*, 8.5.1914; *PAMAR*, 1913–14, p. 7).

Immigration: origins and trends

Malpractices and gross exploitation of labour were to be curtailed, while employers who failed to comply with the regulations of the Ordinance were to be penalized by heavy fines or have their licence to recruit Indian labour revoked. In other words, the Indian labourer was to be not only assured a free passage and board to place of employment but was also to be protected. Furthermore, he was to be landed entirely free from debt through advances or other similar charges. To see that these regulations were observed, a Department of Labour, under a Controller with a large staff, was established in 1912.[1]

Sixthly, beginning with a depot at Negapatam in 1890, several other depots capable of handling many hundreds of emigrants were established in such places in South India as Avadi, Papakovil and Melpakkam, as collecting and 'clearing houses' for Indian labour migrants. Government officers were posted to these depots to help, supervise and generally encourage the movement of Indian labour to Malaya.[2] On the Malayan side quarantine and immigration depot accommodation was enlarged at Penang and Singapore and a new depot created at Port Swettenham to facilitate the flow of Indian labour from these ports to the interior.[3]

Finally, it was well known among Malayan employers and considered 'hardly an exaggeration' that the South Indian labourer was 'highly gullible', even for his kind; that 'political economy' had virtually no meaning to him; and, perhaps most important of all, that an agent or recruiter could, if it was made worth his while, 'persuade' him 'to go anywhere'.[4] To this end then, propaganda, aimed at projecting a favourable image of Malaya in the minds of Indians in general and South Indian labour in particular, was stepped up both in India and Malaya by the Malayan government and planters. For example, E. V. Carey, Chairman of the Selangor Planters' Association, even went so far as to advocate the appointment by the Association 'of an experienced European well up in the dialects of Southern India, who should travel continuously with his bullock cart and tent through the labour districts, preaching the gospel of emigration to this country, distributing advertisements freely and recruiting coolies when opportunity offered'.[5] Although this suggestion of Carey was not taken up literally, there did evolve an elaborate system of recruitment which embodied the basic ingredients of the above suggestion.

Advertisements giving particulars about labourers' free passages to

---

[1] Marjoribanks and Marakkayar, 1917, pp. 32 *et seq.*; Parmer, 1960, pp. 43–4; *MM*, 22.4.1910; 18.8.1910; *C.O.273*, 341 (1908), 30.7.1908; Colonial Office, minute no. 30902; 363 (1910), 9.2.1910.

[2] Planters' Association of Malaya, 1919, pp. 1 ff.; *ARSILFB*, 1959, pp. 9–10, 28–9.

[3] *SSAR*, 1913, p. 34; *ARSILFB*, 1959, pp. 9–10, 28–9.

[4] *SSAR*, 1904, p. 97.   [5] Carey, 1895, pp. 409–12.

Malaya—'the land of opportunity and plenty'—were inserted in Tamil, Telugu and Malayali vernacular newspapers of Southern India. Labourers already in Malaya were urged to send letters to their friends and relatives in India telling them about conditions in Malaya. At times glamorous brochures outlining the facilities, including shops selling 'fresh...low cost' toddy, available on estates for labourers were also supplied by plantation managers for despatch along with the letters. Needless to say, it was seen to that these letters and brochures now depicted Malaya in general and estate life in particular in exceedingly favourable terms. Posters, bill-boards and literature were liberally distributed and posted in the South Indian villages and railway stations.[1] Lastly, agents with sufficient money to pay advances and make suitable presents were sent round to the prospective areas of supply. They spared few pains in painting highly glowing, often false, pictures of prospects and opportunities in Malaya. Furthermore, and more important, they offered the Indian labourer the means wherewith to make the journey to Malaya. This artificial pressure of recruitment and inducement,[2] applied at appropriate psychological moments in the context of the proverbial penury of the Indian peasantry, proved decisive. It substantially overcame the practically non-existent migratory mobility of the Indian peasantry, and large-scale Indian immigration into Malaya began about the beginning of the present century.

It was thus primarily the spectre of stark want, or actual starvation and suffering at home, coupled with the persuasions, promises and the provision of cash and other means of emigration by the Malayan government and private employers or their agents, and not so much a question of 'the call of the sea, the call of adventure, the thrills and uncertainties of Life, and even Death, in unknown lands',[3] that brought Indian labourers in large numbers to the shores of Malaya. Still less was it in response to an invitation to 'come (and) colonise...a land united with their own country by almost inseparable bonds of culture, tradition and association' or the call of duty to help the Malays to develop their country, as some Indians would have us believe.[4] This is not to claim that there were no immigrants who were inspired by such and other similar sentiments. There would in all probability have been some such cases, but their numbers must have been infinitesimal. The labour movement was predominantly an 'arranged' one, in that almost every stage of its movement from its home in India to its place of employment

---

[1] *C.O. 273*, 324 (1906), 31.1.1906; personal interview with Mr T. P. Sundaram, former Assistant Controller of Labour, Federation of Malaya; Arasaratnam, 1965–6, p. 87.
[2] Sundaram, 1930, p. 4.
[3] Raghavan, 1954, pp. 98–102.
[4] *IE*, 1915, ii, ii, pp. 39 *et seq.*; *I*, v (1929), 27 ff.

in Malaya was arranged and taken care of by someone else. Thus there was little or no spontaneity about it and much less a 'call of adventure' or service. All this talk of 'siren-like Malaya beckoned;...history compelled; and India's adventurous hearts found it difficult to resist...'[1] is understandable in the context of the Indian nationalists' striving for the greater glorification of India, but as a portrayal of an actual event it is little more than wishful thinking. This is confirmed not only by a mass of literary evidence[2] but also by the oral testimony of a number of labourers, government officials, labour leaders and recruiters (*kanganis*) interviewed by the writer both in India and Malaya. Almost every labourer who was questioned and who intimated that either he himself knew or had learnt through his father, mother, grandparents or by other means of his family's *raison d'être* for moving to Malaya, invariably included the recruiter or agent among his 'reasons' or 'excuses'. Most of them in fact put the whole 'blame' on friends, relatives or recruiters who, they maintained, promised them or their forebears easy money and living, a 'chance to change the *narakam* of the village hovel for the *cuvarkam* or *vaikuntam* of the Malayan plantation', and who provided them with the necessary money or means to make the journey hither. The testimony of the labour officers and leaders tends to confirm the important role that the recruiters and other similar agents played in inducing the labourer to make the initial move. This aspect was also admitted by some of the *kanganis* interviewed.[3] They themselves and others they believed, worked on the principle of the old Tamil proverb:

> If you scatter rice on the ground, will
> not the crows of the air gather to it?

One of them, a very elderly native of Trichinopoly, Madras, who had gone blind since the Japanese occupation, in fact appeared to be in no doubt that his blindness was heavenly retribution for his sins in inveigling unsuspecting labourers to Malaya through false promises!

But when the labourers were questioned on their own or their families' economic and social position in India as a factor in inducing emigration, they were, quite understandably, reticent. They tended to play this down, many of them actually insisting that they were well-off in India.

---

[1] Raghavan, 1954, pp. 101–2.

[2] See, for example, *IO:PPC*, 32 (1797); 220 (1881–91); 221 (1888); 222 (1888); *SEMMPI*, 1860/1–1934/5.

[3] Exactly how many of the pre-war labour-recruiting *kanganis* are still surviving in Malaya is unknown but in 1962 the Labour Department and the National Union of Plantation Workers in Malaya estimated the number to be less than a hundred. The numbers in India are unknown; the writer was able to locate only one of them, on the outskirts of Negapatam.

Causes of migration in modern times

When pressed further for any other reasons for emigrating besides the inducements of agents, they tended to bring such factors as family quarrels, caste, desire to earn money and free the family plot, repair or build a new house, pay off a debt, and so on, but not their utter poverty. A few of them did, however, stress their own or their families' poverty and starvation as an important factor in their emigration. One of them, an elderly retired labourer, who had come to Malaya from Coimbatore in the 1920s, repeatedly emphasized that he would not have left his village, *kangani* or no *kangani*, if he had not been literally starving. He expressed the same opinions about a relative, who died on the notorious wartime Siam–Burma railway project of the Japanese (see Part 2), who had been a debt-worker of a *mirasdar* and saw no end to his miserable existence except through death or flight. He chose the latter and ended up in Malaya.

The *kanganis*, and some of the labour officers too, were equally forthright about the depressed economic and social position of the labouring classes as an important factor in promoting their emigration to Malaya. The *kanganis* continuously stressed that their methods of persuasion were possible and to a considerable degree aided by the general ignorance, poverty and misery of the labouring classes. (*Kalutai*, donkey, was the expression most commonly used by them in describing the coolie emigrants.)

Non-labour immigration

Thus far we have been concerned only with labour immigrants but they were not the sole Indian migrants to modern Malaya. With the establishment of British rule in Malaya the day-to-day business of the government and commercial departments and agencies came to be conducted mainly, if not wholly, in English. But until the early years of the present century there was little progress in English education in the country, mainly it appears as a result of governmental parsimony, pusillanimity, ambivalence and lack of local staff. This attitude of the government, however, changed for the better towards the end of the last century and thenceforth it began to pay more attention to education, but this brought it face to face with the problem of staffing the new schools. In the meantime, despite the fact that a school teaching English had been established in Penang as early as 1816, there were only 9,000 students, and these mostly too in the lower classes, in all the English teaching schools in Malaya in 1900. Then too, they were not taught directly in English until the early years of this century. Teacher training was non-existent until 1907. A technical school was not opened until 1906 and it did not assume college status until 1942.

Adequately supervised and staffed trade and commercial schools were not started until the 1920s and the birth of a school of agriculture was even later, the first one being opened only in 1931. A medical school and an arts college, 'to train assistants', were opened only in 1904 and 1928 respectively, and did not reach university status until after the Japanese occupation.[1]

Consequently there were few local people with a competent knowledge of English, and fewer still with the necessary training, for work in the government services or the business world. Then again, of the few English-educated people, the majority were Chinese, many of whom preferred private enterprise. If they did venture into wage employment, it was mainly in the direction of the commercial world of their own countrymen rather than government service. There was, therefore, an acute shortage of trained or 'trainable' subordinates for administrative, clerical and technical functions, particularly in the governmental services. This became increasingly so following the political and administrative transfer of the Straits Settlements from the India to the Colonial Office in 1867,[2] and especially so after the establishment of British hegemony over the Malay States and the launching thereafter of ambitious programmes of administrative, economic and social development by the enthusiastic and hardworking British Residents, Advisers, engineers, contractors, planters, agency houses, bankers, miners, doctors, educationists and the like.[3]

In the absence of any adequate local means of meeting these imperative demands both the government and private employers had no alternative but to seek their necessary requirements of English-speaking junior staff from sources outside Malaya. Possible areas of supply were Britain, Australia, New Zealand, Ceylon and India, the last two having had the advantage of a comparatively earlier and wider diffusion of English, technical and scientific education than Malaya. Attempts to recruit subordinate staff in Britain, Australia and New Zealand were virtually in vain as the conditions of service and pay offered in Malaya were considered not sufficiently attractive to compensate for a stay in the tropics—the white man's grave![4]

In the case of the Indian and Ceylonese, however, the conditions *were* sufficiently attractive. For example, wages offered to clerks, teachers and technical assistants in late nineteenth-century Malaya were substantially higher than those prevailing in Ceylon and two, three and,

[1] *SSAR*, 1892, p. 383; *FMSAR*, 1901, p. 17; Cheeseman, 1955, pp. 30–47.
[2] Until this time, some of the shortage could always be made good through secondment from the Indian services. The transfer put a stop to this.
[3] *SSAR*, 1898, p. 388; Cheeseman, 1955, pp. 31–9; *SSSF*, 1892, 6/92.
[4] *SSAR*, 1900, pp. 163–9; *SSSF*, 1892, 6/92.

occasionally, four times as high as those in India.[1] Moreover, there was
the promise of a steady job in a not too distant country and, in the case
of government service, the prospect of a *pukka nawkri* and, on its
completion, a government pension. This was considered the ultimate in
success by many a contemporary Indian (and Ceylonese) as is exemplified by the following popular Tamil quotations:

> *Kooli meeyttaalum kampanikku meey*
> (Even if it means just tending fowls it
> is better to do so for the Company [that
> is the government]).

> *Araik kaacu veelaiyaanaalum aracaanka veelai ventum*
> (Even if it is work worth only half a cent it should
> be government work).

Then, again, we have seen that, *pari passu* with this development of a
tremendous demand for English-educated assistants in Malaya, there
was a glut in the Indian market itself for such talent and growing
distress amongst the salaried classes as a result of insufficient jobs,
rising costs and commitments.[2] The situation in Ceylon was very much
the same.[3] Consequently there came a substantial number of English-
educated Indians, especially from the South, and Jaffna Tamils from
northern Ceylon, initially it appears through Malayan government and
private recruitment, assistance or encouragement and later of their
own volition and under their own steam.[4] Here, at least until the
1920s (Part 3), they easily found employment in building roads and
railways, in surveying lands and in doing the work of clerks, dressers,
plantation and office assistants, teachers, technicians and so on. As
much of the labour force employed by the government and planters and
a number of other enterprises was from South India, the Tamil, Malayali
or Telugu speaking English-educated South Indians and Jaffna Tamils
were especially welcome. They were invaluable in dealing with this
labour and in acting as links between them and their generally British,
or English-speaking, employers.

Just as South Indians proved to be invaluable in the clerical and
technical services, similarly Northern Indians, particularly the tall,
sturdy Sikhs, were much sought after for such employment as soldiers,
policemen, watchmen and caretakers.

[1] Personal interview with Mr R. Thambipillay, retired schoolmaster, Victoria
Institution, Kuala Lumpur; *SSSF*, 1892, 950/92; *SEMMPI*, 1911–12, pp. 164–77.
[2] See pp. 42–3 above.
[3] Personal interview with Mr R. Thambipillay, retired schoolmaster, Victoria
Institution, Kuala Lumpur; *C.O.273*, 19 (1868), 27.6.1868.
[4] Coomaraswamy, 1946, p. 3; *SSSF*, 1892, 950/92.

Immigration: origins and trends

The problem of providing an adequate internal security, one of the essentials for the cherished economic development of the country, in early British Malaya appears to have been more difficult than that usually associated with such pioneer areas. The population was largely transitory, widely dispersed and extremely mixed, consisting of such elements as Muslim Malays and Indians, 'ancestor-worshipping' Chinese, Hindu Tamils, Christian Europeans and Eurasians and Buddhist Siamese and Sinhalese. The large number of Chinese with their secret societies were a special problem and a major source of disorders and crime. Quite apart from the difficulties of ordinary policing they were also regarded as a political threat, to the extent that if not controlled they might take possession of the country. These fears and the problem of controlling them increased with their growing numbers and the reduction in the Indian military garrison following the transfer of the Straits Settlements from Indian to Colonial Office control. The situation was further aggravated by the assumption of paramountcy in the Malay States by the British, for this not only vastly extended the area to be policed but also introduced a new problem of security in the form of dispossessed Malay chiefs who had to be watched, at least in the early stages of British hegemony. But as the early British administrators had no intention of handing over the country to the Chinese immigrants or letting it relapse into the control of the Malay rulers, and instead wanted to see it developed under their directions as a British asset, they set about taking the necessary measures to ensure this. One such obvious measure was the organization and maintenance of a modern efficient military and police force for internal law and order, external security being left to Britain.[1]

As in the case of securing the necessary labour supplies, several avenues were explored to meet the security needs. Malays, Javanese, Filipinos, Boyanese and Bugis were experimented with. There was, however, a general reluctance on their part to serve in these branches of government service. This was partly so, it appears, because of the general turbulence that marked the early phase of British rule, and partly because of the nature of police work, involving as it did considerable discipline and odd hours of work—rather irksome and alien concepts to their traditional mode of life. In any case, they could earn a reasonable, if not comparable, living in other and more amiable and safer occupations. Consequently it was difficult to get sufficient numbers of recruits from the local Malays, at least in the early days of the British administration. Then too, even if available, it was the con-

[1] *SSAR*, 1855–6, pp. 20–2; *C.O.273*, 2 (1858–9), 4.2.1858; 6 (1863–4), 29.7.1863; 10 (1867), 20.4.1867; 81 (1875), 4.11.1875; 85 (1876), 18.10.1876.

sidered opinion of British police officers that they would not be at all effective in dealing with the Chinese, who had little or no respect for the military or police capabilities of the Malays. Finally, recruits from amongst the people of the Malay world, especially indigenous Malays, were regarded as altogether 'too close' to the local populace. As such, although they could be usefully employed to some extent in ordinary police duties, the British government and Residents considered it generally 'objectionable' and 'undesirable' that any substantial security arrangements, and certainly not those of a 'decidedly military character', be left in Malay hands.[1]

Opinion on the employment of Jawi Pekans[2] and South Indians as policemen was also unfavourable, although for somewhat different reasons. They were tried in the Straits Settlements in the nineteenth century. They proved quite 'active and intelligent', but they did not have even 'the slightest confidence' of their officers or the general public, many of them being members of secret criminal societies. Moreover, the British officers and the Straits Settlements Police Commission of 1879, set up to observe and recommend improvements in the police force, considered them 'very corrupt, thoroughly untrustworthy' and totally unsuited for dealing with the troublesome Chinese, who appeared to pay only the scantiest attention to the South Indian and Jawi Pekan policemen.[3] There was constant agitation by officials and members of the public that the 'ranks of the force ought to be carefully weeded' of South Indian and Jawi Pekan policemen and this was finally achieved towards the end of the nineteenth century.[4]

Since most of the disorders and crimes were associated with the Chinese community it was also suggested that Chinese should be employed for police work. But other than as detectives the weight of opinion was almost wholly against their employment in police duties. No 'respectable' Chinese would consider becoming a constable, the social stigma attached to such work being a powerful deterrent. Anyway, more money could be made in other and more honourable undertakings. Only *samsengs* (gangsters) would be attracted and they were expected, by the Chinese community leaders themselves, to be 'ten times more corrupt than the Tamils or Malays'. Finally, most important

[1] *C.O.273*, 17 (1868), 26.2.1868; *SNL:COGSS*, 1876, 369, 18.10.1876; *PLCSS*, 1872, p. 18; *PLCSS*, 1876, app. 3, pp. ccii–cciv.
[2] See pp. 167–8 below. Jawi Bukans, Jadi Bukans or Jawi Pekans, as they have been variously called, are offsprings of Malay mothers and Indian, especially Tamil and Bengali, fathers.
[3] *PLCSS*, 1872, pp. 18–19; *PLCSS*, 1873, paper no. 27, p. 5; *PLCSS*, 1879, paper no. 32, pp. cclxxi–cclxxviii.
[4] *PLCSS*, 1879, paper no. 28, p. ccxliii; *SSAR*, 1894, p. 19; *SSAR*, 1899, p. 417.

of all, since much of the rationale for the organization of the police was the supervision and control of the Chinese community, especially its secret societies, it was feared that there might be collusion between it and the local Chinese constables.[1]

It was thought for a while, too, that perhaps the above objections would be overcome if instead of engaging local Chinese, recruits with no local connections were obtained from Hong Kong. This was attempted in 1891 when fifty men were thus engaged. But the experiment ended in total failure, the men proving thoroughly 'untrustworthy'. They were dismissed in 1894[2] and thenceforth, until after the Japanese occupation, no Chinese are known to have been employed in police work other than in such roles as detectives, officers and clerks.

Europeans too were thought of as constables and in fact a force of twenty-one trained British policemen was recruited in England. They arrived in Singapore in 1881. But they were soon dissatisfied with the conditions of service and pay. It became increasingly difficult to control them and they had finally to be shipped back a few years later.[3] Anyway, the whole idea of Britons working as common constables was considered impolitic, embarrassing and highly damaging to the prestige of the white man by the *tuan besars*, whose sentiments could not be lightly ignored.[4] The experiment was never attempted again.

In these circumstances where Malays, other Southeast Asians, Chinese, Jawi Pekans, South Indians and Europeans were unavailable, impracticable or unsuitable except for certain specific duties, the government had of necessity to turn to alternative possible sources of police and military recruits. It turned to the Northern Indian provinces, particularly the Punjab and Northwest Frontier (fig. 11). Amongst the inhabitants of these areas, the Sikhs were particularly sought after.

They were sufficiently mobile and poor at home and were quite prepared to migrate and work for three to five years for such low wages as $9–15 per month, in the hope of living frugally and saving enough to return home to buy new land or redeem the mortgaged family plot. If promised steady increments of about $1 a year, with the prospects of a pension thrown in and suitable leave arrangements enabling them to visit their homes periodically, they could be persuaded to serve for much longer periods. Being wholly reliable, 'fairly uncorruptible', conscientious and generally quick to learn, they were considered fairly suitable for all branches of the security services, but especially so for

[1] *PLCSS*, 1872, pp. 18–33; *PLCSS*, 1873, paper no. 27, pp. 1–3.
[2] *SSAR*, 1890, pp. 570–1; *SSAR*, 1891, p. 142; *SSAR*, 1894, p. 19.
[3] *SSG*, 1882, p. 365; *SSAR*, 1890, pp. 570–1; Onraet, 1947, pp. 82–3.
[4] Labour Research Department, 1926, p. 14; *BM*, May 1926, p. 6; Cameron, 1865, pp. 281–2.

armed police work or for military and para-military duties, where their stature, bearing and martial traditions and reliability were invaluable.[1] They had been tried in police work by the British in Hong Kong as early as 1867, and had worked exceedingly well amongst the Chinese population.[2] The Chinese appeared to have a healthy respect and fear of the capabilities of the *Mungkali kwai* ('Bengali (Sikh) devils'). Thus in these circumstances they appeared to be just the right 'means of fully over-awing' the Chinese population in Malaya too. Moreover, they had little connection with the rest of the people and were, therefore, equally suitable for dealing with them. Finally, they appeared to have the confidence of the European and other community leaders who had by this time apparently heard of the exploits of the Sikhs in Hong Kong and elsewhere.[3]

The Straits Settlements received their first batch of Sikh policemen in 1881. The fame of these men and of their colleagues as effective security guards in Perak and other parts of the country spread rapidly. As a result they were also eagerly sought after by private employers for such duties as caretakers, watchmen, guards and dunners.[4]

Besides the clerical and potential security-force immigrants there was also a continuous stream of petty Indian enterpreneurs, business-men, moneylenders, merchants, traders and such like, who found

[1] *SSG*, 1880, p. 496; *SSG*, 1881, p. 422; *SSG*, 1882, p. 365; *SSG*, 1883, pp. 1097–8; *SSAR*, 1888, p. 69; *PLCSS*, 1879, paper no. 28, p. ccxliii; paper no. 32, p. cclxxviii.
[2] G. B. Endacott, *A history of Hongkong* (London, 1958), p. 153; *PLCSS*, 1879, paper no. 32, p. cclxxviii.
[3] In fact, while the government was still debating on the pros and cons of the different ethnic groups as police and military material, a Malay chief, Ngah Ibrahim, the Orang Kaya Mantri of Larut, Perak, commissioned one Capt. Speedy, former Superintendent of Police, Penang, to go to Northern India and enlist a force of fighting men to help him to save his tin mines from the depredations of Chinese insurgents. Speedy returned with ninety-five men, mainly Sikhs, Pathans and Punjabi Muslims, and on 29 September 1873 proceeded to Larut to put down the disorders caused by feuding Chinese clans. At about the same time, the British intervened and took control of the affairs of Perak and also Selangor and Sungei Ujong (Negri Sembilan). Speedy was appointed Assistant Resident of Perak and instructed to re-enlist as many of the Mantri's force as would be possible as 'Residency Guard', the nucleus of the proposed Perak police. This was done and the Residency Guard and a number of other Northern Indians who followed in the wake of their relatives and friends in this force were subsequently absorbed into the Perak Armed Police. Others found employment in the police forces of the other Malay States and in the Malay States Guides, a military regiment created in 1896 (*C.O.273*, 85, 1876, 18.10.1876; Colonial Office, minute no. 13901; 196, 1894, 24.7.1894; 213, 1896, 5.3.1896; *KAR*, 1909, pp. 8–10; *JAR*, 1913, pp. 14 ff.; *YRSK*, 1905–6, p. 13; *T*, 19.1.1902; *IO:FP*, 770, 1873, 16.9.1873; 3.10.1873; 771, 1873, 16.9.1873; 25.9.1873; Gullick, 1953, p. 34; Wilkinson, 1908, p. 124).
[4] *SSG*, 1882, p. 365; *FMSAR*, 1915, p. 8; Harrison, 1929, p. 57; *MPM*, I (1928), 17–525; III (1930), 160; *NAI:EP*, Dec. 1904, Secret memorandum by Swettenham dated 12.8.1903; *NAI:EP*, Oct. 1915, secret file no. 154, serial no. 1.

increasing scope in Malaya, catering for the special needs of their countrymen and in many other fields. They in turn imported, assisted or encouraged a host of assistants and underlings to come to Malaya to help them in their undertakings. The rapidly expanding economy of Malaya also witnessed an influx of such other people as tradesmen and hawkers, who arrived either under their own steam or through the assistance of some other person or agency.[1]

With a growing horde of graduates being turned out by the several colleges and universities in India, the English-educated Indian, like his lesser qualified clerical brethren, also began to find it extremely difficult to get into the cherished, but comparatively limited and highly competitive, government services or other such desirable *pukka nawkris*. Prospects in Malaya for such classes of Indians were by no means rosy, being limited until World War II to subordinate roles in a European-dominated government and professional world. But even such opportunities were apparently, in some cases at least, sufficiently attractive compared with those in India, for a small number of professional Indians such as doctors, lawyers and teachers were also seen to be following in the wake of their labour, commercial and other countrymen.[2]

Then, too, part of the military garrison in Malaya, until the Indian independence, tended to be drawn from units of the British Indian Army. Quite apart from some of the militiamen remaining in Malaya after their demobilization, these garrison units trailed a substantial number of camp-followers. Some of these, too, appear to have branched off into other undertakings, either on the departure of their unit or at times even while it was still stationed in Malaya.[3]

Finally the Malayan government occasionally toyed with the idea of introducing Indian farmers as colonists, who would not only help to develop the resources of the country but also help the growth of a permanent labour force, since they were expected to settle permanently in Malaya.

---

[1] *SSFR*, 4 (1789–91), 10.4.1789; 5 (1792–3), 5.4.1793; 6 (1794), 1.8.1794; Marjoribanks and Marakkayar, 1917, p. 42; Nanjudan, 1950, pp. 34-8.

[2] *SEMMPI*, 1911–12, pp. 377–8; *C.O.273*, 40 (1870), 22.10.1870; 300 (1904), 17.9.1904; Nair, 1937, p. 40; Moothedan, 1932, pp. 40–1.

[3] *SSFR*, 1 (1769–1795), 'Memoir on Prince of Wales Island considered politically and commercially', undated; 2 (1786–7), 20.3.1786; personal interview with Mufti Nisar Ahmad Khan Sahib, former Indian supernumerary officer, Malayan police force.

3

TYPES OF MIGRANTS AND
RECRUITMENT OR MOVEMENT

Labour immigration formed the bulk of the movement of Indians into British Malaya until about the outbreak of World War II. However, several distinctions must be made not only within this labour movement but also between it and other forms of immigration. For example, there is the distinction between assisted and unassisted migration of labour. Within the assisted category, however, there were four different types: the first consisted of those assisted on the basis of an indenture contract; then there were the so-called 'free' or 'independent' and *kangani* labourers. All these three types were recruited. The fourth category was that which consisted of non-recruited labourers, who were also assisted to emigrate. Finally, there is the distinction between labour migration of all types and the non-labour movement of such classes as professional and commercial people and clerks and technicians.

ASSISTED LABOUR MIGRATION

Indentured immigration
Indenture like slavery was peculiarly adapted to the recruitment of labour through migration. It enabled business enterprises to transfer labour to newly developing areas and yet restrained that labour from immediately taking up holdings of its own in these new areas. Less satisfactory than slavery because less permanent it nevertheless was the most convenient alternative substitute. Indentured emigration from India came into its own in the nineteenth century,[1] receiving its

---

[1] Precisely when the British government first allowed indentured emigration out of India is uncertain. Capt. Birch, Commissioner of Police, Calcutta, in his evidence before the Calcutta Emigration Committee of 1838, when talking about Mauritius and Bourbon, appeared to suggest 1819 as the year of the first such movement to the above places; Dr Mouat, a Bengal civil servant, thought it was 1826. However, Geoghegan, Under-Secretary to the government of India, who made a special study of labour emigration from India up to 1873, found no evidence in the official records to support a date earlier than 1830, when a French merchant, Joseph Argaud, carried some 130 Indians on five-year contracts to Bourbon with the permission of the Indian government. This was followed by a shipment of 'about forty' to Mauritius in 1834 (Geoghegan, 1873, pp. 1–2; *NAI:CEBHD*, 1, 1830–40, 5.10.1830, consultations 1–5).

75

'first great impetus from the abolition of slavery' in the British territories in 1833–4, when colonial planters and governments turned to India to fill the gap in the supply created by the emancipation of slaves.

The system reached its perfection in the relatively more distant sugar colonies, such as Mauritius, Fiji and West Indies. Indenture supposedly originated with a contract, usually written and voluntarily assumed, but it was an unusual contract, because it bargained away the labourer's personal freedom for an extended period. Often, in addition, emigration under this system was the result of ignorance on the part of the labourer and coercion or fraud on the part of the employer or his agents. It was therefore often not a true contract at all, but merely a fictional one.

Presumably the contract led to the status of free labour at the end of the indenture period, but it could also lead to re-indenture or a return to India. Naturally many an employer undertook to maintain his workers at as small a cost as possible, to work them as hard as possible, and to keep them on the job as regularly as possible. At the end of the indenture he tried to renew the agreement for another stretch if the worker was still productive, or to get rid of him if he was not.[1] In short, indenture was, as a former Chief Justice (1863–8) of British Guiana, J. Beaumont, described it, 'a monstrous rotten system, rooted upon slavery, grown in its stale soil, emulating its worst abuses and only the more dangerous because it presented itself under false colours, whereas slavery (had) the brand of infamy written upon its forehead'.[2]

The system in Malaya differed from that in the sugar colonies but mainly in detail and less so in spirit, the labourer in Malaya, if anything, being 'far less liberally treated'.[3] For example, once the procedure of indentured recruitment had been systematized, labourers in the other British colonies were recruited by their respective governments and made available to employers of indentured labour. In Malaya, however, recruitment was by speculators or employers themselves or through their own or private agents in India. The Malayan government's function was merely to watch over the fulfilment of the contract between the individual employer and the immigrant. In practice even this was seldom done. The approved period of contract in Malaya varied between one and three years compared with the five years in the sugar colonies; but whereas the emigrant to these colonies did not have to pay for his

---

[1] McNeil and Lal, 1915, part i, pp. 4–80; Cumpston, 1953, pp. 9 ff.; Gillion, 1962, pp. 103–29; *PCGGI*, 1911–12, l, 363–97; Dev, 1940, p. 14.
[2] Ruhomon, 1939, p. 47. [3] *SSG*, 1882, p. 490.

recruitment or passage expenses, his compatriot in Malaya had to pay back all advances received and the cost of his passage. Finally, unlike the movement to the distant colonies which was strictly regulated almost from its inception, the migration to Malaya was entirely free of any regulations, other than those introduced in 1857 and 1859 to control overcrowding on ships, until the 1870s.[1]

There is some variance in official and unofficial dating of the arrival in Malaya of the first indentured labourers from India. As early as 1823 we find Raffles enacting an ordinance to protect labourers who were 'brought from China and *elsewhere*' (my italics) 'as passengers who have no means of paying for their passage, and under expectation that individuals resident in Singapore will advance the amount of it on condition of receiving the services of the parties for a limited period in compensation thereof...'[2] It is not impossible, but by no means certain, that elsewhere included Java and India.

C. Kondapi, in his post-war study of the general position of Indians overseas, appears to imply that 1833 was the year when Tamil and Telegu workers were first brought into Malaya to work on plantations.[3] He does not, however, indicate the source of his information. Neither is there any other way of verifying this information, as Kondapi informs the writer that he lost all his notes during a rainstorm and cannot remember where he received the information. In any case, this date is by no means unquestionable. Captain Low, who made an on the spot survey of the soils and agriculture of the Straits Settlements in the early 1830s, makes no mention of indentured Indian labour on plantations there.[4] Neither does J. Balestier, the American Consul in Singapore and a pioneer sugar planter of the 1830s.[5]

The contemporary records of both the Straits and Indian governments, too, appear to be silent on this point. Later records of these two governments appear to settle for 1857 as the year which inaugurated the system of 'assisted' labour migration between the two territories. In 1857, and again in 1859, acts were passed by the Indian government to prevent overcrowding on non-European passenger ships plying the Bay of Bengal. The effect of these legislations was to increase the expense of the voyage and lessen the number of emigrants. To meet the change, they maintain, 'there sprang up a system of assisted (indentured) migration'.[6] But against this we have the evidence of J. M. Vermont, member of the Straits Settlements Legislative Council and a veteran sugar planter of many years standing in Province Wellesley,

[1] Geoghegan, 1873, pp. 63–4; *SSAR*, 1922, pp. 505–8.   [2] Blythe, 1947, p. 68.
[3] Kondapi, 1951, p. 41.   [4] Low, 1836.
[5] *JIA*, II (1848), 139–50.   [6] *RLC 1890*, pp. 36–7.

and C. W. S. Kynnersley, a magistrate in which capacity he was associated with Indian labour for more than thirty years in the latter half of the nineteenth century. Vermont, writing in 1866, records that Malayan employers were already in the habit, prior to 1857, of paying the passage costs of the Indian labourers on their arrival in Malaya.[1] Although he does not state this, one may surmise that this was done on the understanding that, like the Chinese *sinkehs*, these labourers were expected to serve the employer advancing the money for a certain period as compensation thereof or until the 'loan' was paid off.

The testimony of Kynnersley is more specific. Commenting, in his role as rapporteur, on a paper delivered by A. W. S. O'Sullivan, Indian Immigration Agent and later Assistant Colonial Secretary, Straits Settlements, on 'The relations between South India and the Straits Settlements' before the Straits Philosophical Society, Singapore, on 13 October 1900, he says that a batch of ninety-seven Indian labourers were brought into Malaya from Calcutta in 1844. This was in the nature of 'an experiment' and was necessitated by the expansion of sugar cultivation in Province Wellesley by European planters, especially in the 1840s, and the consequent rise in the demand for suitable labour.[2]

To sum up, on the basis of this evidence indentured labour migration from India to Malaya could possibly predate 1823 and certainly was not as late as 1857. The experiment had already been tried in 1844.

Although used to some extent in road, railway and other projects, by government and private contractors, it was with the sugar plantations that the indentured Indian labour migration to Malaya was chiefly associated. The labour requirements for sugar-cane cultivation were constantly fairly heavy, 'at least one unit of Indian labour per acre', compared with the work on coffee, pepper and gambier estates. The sugar planters therefore required a steady and large labour force.[3] Several of the Malayan planters had served their apprenticeships in such areas as the West Indies and Mauritius, and felt that such a labour supply could only be ensured by binding it to long-term contracts. Moreover, in view of the long-established rival sugar industries of the older colonies, it was necessary that this labour should be as cheap as possible to keep the Malayan ventures sufficiently competitive. They were, therefore, not prepared to enter into free competition with other Malayan employers of Indian labour in the market, preferring to get theirs through indentured recruitment.[4]

This recruitment generally consisted of two types, that conducted or

[1] Vermont, 1888, pp. 4–5.   [2] O'Sullivan, 1913, pp. 185–6.
[3] Low, 1836, pp. 49–52; Jackson, 1961, p. 5.
[4] O'Sullivan, 1913, pp. 185–6; *PPSE*, 24 (1897), 6.8.1897.

inspired by speculators and that similarly initiated by the employers themselves. The system operated by speculators in the 1870s was described by H. J. Stokes, Acting Sub-Collector, Tanjore, as follows:

...A shipowner advances money to a head maistry (recruiting agent) who employs under him several subordinate maistries. These latter have to go about to villages and persuade coolies to emigrate. This they do by representing, in bright colours, prospects of enrichment and advance. The ignorant coolies believe easily and while some volunteer to go to try their fortune, many are persuaded. The maistries...get ten rupees a head for every adult cooly they bring, all contingent expenses being paid. A lower price is given for boys who are not in such demand, and a somewhat higher rate for young and good-looking women.

The coolies thus obtained are kept in godowns (or depots) in Negapatam (or other ports) until a sufficient number is collected. They are then shipped on the shipowner's vessel and accompanied by the head maistry to the port of destination. There they are sold under contract to serve for certain periods. Each man fetches about five pounds; and all expenses of maintenance, passage money, etc., are discharged by the purchaser. The shipowner and head maistry divide the profits...[1]

Since the traffic was so profitable, *maistries* were concerned mainly with securing as large a supply of labourers as needed, often, if need be, resorting to kidnapping. This applied not only to males but females and boys as well:

...Women...who have a passing quarrel with their husbands or parents are seduced away by females employed for the purpose, who bring them on board ship before they know what they have done. Boys are carried off suddenly from their village and are lost to their parents...[2]

Neither were these neo-slave-traders too particular about the manner of conveying their human merchandise to the Straits ports, crowding as many as possible into whatever space was available.[3] The Indian Passenger Acts of 1857 and 1859, designed to check overcrowding, do not appear to have totally eliminated this abuse, as is apparent from this extract from the diary of an assistant superintendent of police, Madras, published in the *Police Weekly Circular* (Madras), dated 4 February 1865:

...This morning I accompanied the Master Attendant on board one of those cooly traders...waiting...to start for the Straits. It was a beastly sight, coolies crowded together like beasts...[4]

The recruitment and 'sale' of labourers by speculators was contrary to the Indian law, as Act XIII of 1864 made it illegal to assist any native of

[1] *GMPPD*, 1870, 40–4 of 13.9.1870; *NAI:EP*, Sept. 1870, proc. 1–15.
[2] *Ibid.*
[3] *GMPPD*, 1885, 510–12 of 15.5.1888.
[4] *GMPPD*, 1870, 40–4 of 13.9.1870; *NAI:EP*, Sept. 1870, proc. 1–15.

Immigration: origins and trends

India in emigrating except in conformity with the Act and only to those countries approved by the government. Malaya was not one of them.[1] Even later on when agreement was reached between Malaya and India to allow migration of labour, the 'speculator' traffic, apart from the enactments applying to overcrowding on passenger vessels in general, still remained outside the pale of the law, which in fact specifically debarred it. But while it was well known that this 'coolie trade' was a flourishing business, it was found extremely difficult to procure sufficient evidence to convict the speculators. In any case, when the Madras police did get more than usually troublesome, it was only necessary to switch this traffic to the French ports where it appears to have been a relatively simple matter to pass the labourers off as passengers, or for that matter, if need be, as French subjects, and thus outside the pale of the British emigration laws pertaining to Malaya. In fact, after 1872, when labour migration in general to Malaya was legally permitted and regulated for the first time, the coolie trade appears to have been centred mainly at such French ports as Karikal and Pondicherry rather than its former strongholds of Negapatam, Nagore and Cuddalore (fig. 11).[2]

Employer recruiting was done primarily through two Negapatam commercial firms, Messrs. Adamson, McTaggart and Company and Ganapathi Pillai and Company, and to a lesser extent through the Madura Company of the same place and of Madras, on a commission basis. Employers in need of labour either approached these firms in person or, as was more usual, wrote to them. These firms sent out their subagents, who in turn employed professional recruiters to do the actual recruiting. Until 1872, this traffic, apart from the Passenger Acts of 1857 and 1859, was also unregulated, and in fact illegal since the Indian Act XIII of 1864 excluded Malaya from its permissive list of countries allowed to recruit labour in India. After this date, however, following the passing of the Indian Act of 1877, and its Malayan complementary *Ordinance I of 1876*, an Emigration Agent, appointed by the Straits Settlements government, was stationed in Negapatam. At the same time the Madras government appointed a Protector of Emigrants. Depots were to be subject to inspection and approval by the Protector. Recruiting of labour was to be restricted to persons licensed as recruiters by the Protector and to districts specified in such licences. Every recruit was to be taken before a magistrate who registered particulars and ascertained that the emigrant was willing to emigrate. But in practice beyond licensing of the recruiters, virtually no super-

[1] Geoghegan, 1873, pp. 63–4.
[2] *IO:EP*, 694 (1875), pp. 23–66; 2526 (1885), pp. 965–7; 4358 (1893), pp. 1767–9; *GMPPD*, 1873, 82–4 of 18.3.1873; 99–102 of 31.12.1873; 1875, 89–90 of 30.3.1875; 1880, 43–5 of 14.6.1880.

80

vision was exercised over the actual process although the Indian government insisted that recruiting be controlled and licensed.

The recruiters were generally the riff-raff of the country and owing 'to their peculiar profession, were an eager, callous and, too often, an utterly unscrupulous race of men'. They generally cared little as to how they got their man as long as they got him and the commission. Furthermore, unlike their speculator counterparts who had at least to worry about the sale potential of their merchandise, these recruiters had no such qualms, being merely fulfilling an order for x number of men for an employer, who was usually in any case in Malaya and therefore in no position to check the quality of his labour immigrants until their arrival there. Then it was too late. Consequently, until the medical examination of such emigrants was more vigorously imposed towards the end of the nineteenth century, many of the men recruited were unhealthy and debilitated labourers. Often they came from the non-agricultural classes, for example, weavers, washermen and cooks, and usually broke down when put to work, deteriorating into 'hospital birds' and swelling the already high mortality rate.[1]

It is impossible to gauge exactly how many Indians entered Malaya as indentured labourers from the inception of the system to its abolition in 1910. Statistical data are available only from 1866. From this year until the abolition, 122,000 indentureds came into Malaya, an average of 2,700 per annum. If we were to take 1844 as the beginning of the indenture system and apply the average annual flow of the above years retrospectively to the period 1844–65—not totally unreasonable since the flow in the early 1860s at least is said to have averaged about 4,000 per annum[2]—we get a total of more than 181,000 entries for the period 1844–1910. To this should be added an estimated 1,700 entries per year for the period 1870–1910 representing the verbal contract indentureds arriving as so-called passengers. On the basis of such totals it would appear that some 250,000 indentured Indian labourers entered Malaya between 1844 and 1910. Needless to say, if we were to see the inception of the system earlier, say in the 1820s, the total would be even higher. Anyhow, even on the basis of the above total, the indentured migration formed some 13 per cent of the assisted labour, 9 per cent of the total labour and nearly 6 per cent of the whole Indian immigration into Malaya up to 1957—a much more significant portion in all three streams than has been the custom hitherto to acknowledge (table 2; Appendix 3).[3]

[1] *RLC 1890*, pp. 36–45, app. L; *RLC 1896*, pp. C 230–1; *SSAR*, 1922, pp. 506–9.
[2] *GMPPD*, 1870, 40–4 of 13.9.1870; *NAI:EP*, Sept. 1870, proc. 1–15.
[3] *ARSILFB*, 1959, pp. 28–34.

Immigration: origins and trends

The average annual number of arrivals given above hardly tells the whole tale of the annual movement of the Indian indentureds into Malaya, there being considerable fluctuation from year to year (Appendix 2). On the basis of the available figures it appears that 1900 was the year with the highest number of arrivals, 8,615. The annual volume of movement towards Malaya appears to have been influenced more by such factors as bad harvests and catastrophes in India, rather than the conditions or demand in Malaya.[1]

Another significant feature of this movement was that it consisted predominantly of adult males, generally between the ages of fifteen and forty-five, the proportion of women and children in the total stream being seldom above, although frequently below, 20 and 10 per cent respectively. This was partly because, unlike in the case of the other and more distant colonies where the government of India, anxious to promote normal family life and minimize the evils associated with a large disproportion of the sexes, insisted on 25–50 per cent of the emigrants being females,[2] there was no such stipulation in the case of Malaya. Partly, this was due to the fact that the migration was not a family movement by any means, consisting primarily of single or married males, unaccompanied by their womenfolk or children.

More than a third of the indentureds, both legal and illegal, were not agricultural labourers at all, being mainly weavers, oil-millers and such like.[3]

The indentured migration to Malaya was essentially a South Indian phenomenon, the others being only a few hundred recruits from the Bengal area of the Ganges valley. This appears to have been partly because a number of the North Indians who were tried as indentured labourers proved 'troublesome', complaining of the conditions of service and refusing to work. Then, more important, there was the fact that the Indian government refused to sanction indentured emigration from any part of India, other than Madras. Within this province the emigrants, at least those leaving under government supervision, were mainly drawn from the districts of Tanjore, Trichinopoly, Madras and occasionally Salem and Coimbatore. This was so mainly because the recruiters limited their area of recruitment close to Negapatam, the principal and frequently the sole port for all *regulated* indentured emigration. The other port occasionally handling such traffic was Madras. In contrast, the unregulated and illegal speculator coolie trade appears to have made up its cargo of human beings from such other ports, too, as Karikal, Pondicherry, Cuddalore, Porto Novo and Nagore

[1] *RLC 1890*, app. A; *IO:EP*, 1862 (1882), pp. 31–5; 4358 (1893), pp. 463–4.
[2] Gillion, 1962, pp. 55–6.   [3] *RLC 1890*, app. A.

(fig. 11).[1] Until the 1870s much of the coolie trade appears to have been carried on by Indians themselves employing Indian-owned sailing ships. With increasing government supervision, however, the general supplanting of sail by steam and the decline and final disappearance of Indian shipping, this traffic passed to European shipping, which already handled the rest of the indentured migration.[2]

On the Malayan side, almost all, and certainly all the legal, indentured Indian labourers disembarked at Penang, whence, after the usual port formalities such as quarantine, they were distributed to their employers, mainly in Province Wellesley and Perak. These two areas absorbed 60 and 20 per cent, respectively, of all those legally indentured by written contracts, the rest going mainly to Negri Sembilan. Similar details for those illegally indentured by verbal contracts alone are unavailable but it appears that they too apparently followed the same pattern of distribution.[3] Province Wellesley and the adjoining State of Perak, particularly the former, were the principal sugar areas of the country and, as stated above, it was with sugar cultivation that Indian indentured immigration was chiefly associated.

The lot of the Indian indentured labourers varied from employer to employer, but it was generally hard, often indescribably so. We have already noted how many of the employers appear to have worked on the principle of maintaining their workers at as small a cost as possible, of working them as hard as possible and of keeping them on the job as regularly as possible, if need be by force or flogging. Nine to ten hours per day, six days a week was the normal load of work. Those who had signed legal contracts were bound to these conditions for varying periods ranging from 313 to 940 days of work. In practice these were liable to be extended for an indefinite period. For one thing, through illness mainly, it was seldom that the Indian labourer was able to work for more than twenty days a month. For another, he had to make up lost time for days spent attending court, in prison, absence without permission and absence through sickness, in excess of thirty days per year. He was also under obligation to continue to work until any sums due to the employer in repayment of advances and so on were paid. Finally, until 1862 when it was abolished a 'joint and several' contract appears to have been customary; under this all the labourers of a gang signed a contract rendering each of them liable for the default of any of

---

[1] O'Sullivan, 1913, pp. 185–6; *SSAR*, 1891, p. 161; *SSAR*, 1901, pp. 116–17; *SSAR*, 1902, p. 192; *IO:EP*, 1862 (1882), pp. 55–81.

[2] *GMPPD*, 1870, 40–4 of 13.9.1870; *NAI:EP*, Sept. 1870, proc. 1–15; *SSAR*, 1886, p. 313; *SSAR*, 1897, pp. 167–8; *SSAR*, 1898, p. 101; *IO:EP*, 1862 (1882), pp. 55–81.

[3] *SSAR*, 1891, p. 159; *SSAR*, 1906, p. 20.

the others—even to the extent of making 'one man in a hundred work out the defaults of ninety-nine absconders'. In short, employers had considerable means of extending the labourer's period of indenture, and many of them appear to have exercised these. It was seldom that such a labourer secured his release at the end of three years. Then, too, there was the possibility of the employer trying to reindenture or renew the agreement for another stretch if the worker was still productive.

Wages were exceedingly low, being only 9 cents ($2d.-3d.$) per day in the 1860s and 16–18 cents in the 1900s. Furthermore, these wages were fixed for the period of the contract and paid only for the days actually worked and those approved as holidays. The paltry earnings were further denuded by deductions for loans, advances on passage costs and fines. Much of the remainder, too, was often, as the Principal Medical Officer, Straits Settlements, discovered on his visit to sugar estates of Province Wellesley in 1879, 'frisked' off him by his other creditors—the *kedai mutalaaḷi*, *taṇṭal* and the older hands on the estate, who victimized him right and left. Often the newcomer had insufficient left to purchase such staples as rice, let alone extras. In such cases he was reduced to eat all the rubbish he could lay his hands on, 'unripe fruit, sugar-cane, garbage and offal of all descriptions'. This affected his health and thence in turn his ability to work regularly. Irregular attendance diminished his earnings and thereby his means, even further, to purchase sufficient food. This in its turn meant greater emaciation—a vicious cycle broken only through flight or death. This demoralization, as the Colonial Secretary, Straits Settlements, had occasion to remark in the Legislative Council at its 14 November 1892 meeting, was conceivably aggravated by the arrival of the labourer in new surroundings and finding things 'not quite as he expected' and seeing before him 'apparently no end', falling into 'a despairing state of mind', which 'often end(ed) in sickness and death'. Then, too, this despairing state of mind was 'materially added' to by the fact that he saw 'all round him men of his own kindred and country earning very much higher wages (as free labourers)'.

The problem of the verbal-contract indentured was even more serious as his wages and work were not even specified. He was expected to serve his employer until he had paid off his debt, which seldom bore any resemblance to the actual amount received or expended on him. Then, too, his debt was often augmented with such additions as fines and contributions. His chances of settling such debts were very slim indeed, and he could thus be held as long as needed. He was, therefore, often in a condition which, if not amounting to actual slavery, was not far removed from it. Under such circumstances it is not then surprising that the individual labourer often deserted or 'lost all interest in life' and waited for death to terminate his misery.[1]

Indenture in Malaya, like its counterparts in the other colonies, was altogether an obnoxious device of recruitment and exploitation of cheap labour and could well form the subject of a full-scale separate study. One of its worst features, quite apart from those discussed above, was that it imposed on the labourers, at least in the case of those with written contracts, a criminal liability for the most trivial breaches of the contracts in place of the civil liability which usually attached to such lapses. They could thus be liable to imprisonment with hard labour, 'not only for fraud, not only for deception, but for negligence, for carelessness and...for even an impertinent word or gesture to the manager or his overseers'.[2]

The labourers, quite understandably, resented their conditions of employment and their labour output on the whole appears to have been unsatisfactory. Desertions were frequent, in spite of severe penalties if caught. For example, there were no less than 610 desertions out of a labour force of 1,026 indentured immigrants on Gula estate, Perak, alone in 1895.[3] More serious was the shockingly high mortality rate among the indentureds, who appear to have literally died like flies; the death rate among the newcomers in some areas appears to have been as high as 80–90 per cent.[4]

As tales of such suffering in Malaya filtered back to India, there to join others of a similar nature from the other indentured labour importing colonies, the system became increasingly unpopular in India, especially following the development of Indian nationalism. Indians attacked it not only on moral grounds but also as an affront to the national *izzat* of the country, indenture being regarded as an insult to India and inconsistent with the sentiment of national self-respect.[5] This stand was ably, albeit hyperbolically, summed up in the Council of the Governor-General of India in 1910 by Mazharul Haque. The people of India, he stated, 'are disgraced by it abroad' and that

...the whole system of indentured labour is vicious in principle; it brutalises the employer; it demoralises the employed. It perpetrates the worst form of slavery in the guise of legal contract; it is bad in its inception, inhuman in its working and mischievous in its results, and ought to be done away with without any further delay.[6]

---

[1] *IO:EP*, 694 (1875), pp. 1 ff.; 2057 (1883), pp. 732–45; *RLC 1890*, pp. 35–54; *PLCSS*, 1879, paper no. 41; paper no. 42; *PLCSS*, 1892, pp. C 234–44; *C.O.273*, 75 (1874), Colonial Office, minute no. 3860; Jackson, 1961, pp. 57–69.
[2] *PCGGI*, 1911–12, L, 363–4.   [3] *SSAR*, 1889, p. 521; *SSAR*, 1895, p. 452.
[4] See pp. 169–71 below.   [5] *PCGGI*, 1911–12, L, 365–70.
[6] *PCGGI*, 1911–12, L, 378; *IO:EP*, 9021 (1912), pp. 369 ff.

Opposition to the system in Malaya, too, was mounting steadily, although confined largely to coffee and rubber planters. They appear to have been motivated mainly by economic expediency. With few exceptions they were used to, and employed, non-indentured labour only. They felt that the sugar planters were hampering the flow of labour from India by giving Malaya a bad name in that country through their indentured system.[1] The sugar planters themselves, who had constantly championed the indentured system, also began to waiver, especially as other sources of labour began increasingly to be available from the beginning of the present century. A few of them were already turning solely to *kangani* labour by the early 1900s.[2] In any case, the sugar industry of Malaya was already tottering at this time following the growth and competition of bounty-fed European sugar and the establishment of the industry on modern lines in Java in 1905. By 1906 there were no buyers for sugar estates and the last sugar factory in Malaya ceased operations in 1913.[3]

The final seal on the demise of indentured Indian immigration into Malaya was not set in that country or India but in England. Here organizations like the Anti-Slavery Society had waged an unceasing war on the system as a whole.[4] In the case of Malaya their efforts finally bore fruit in 1910 when a furore was caused in the House of Commons as a private member released the high mortality rates prevailing amongst the indentured labourers in Malaya and asked the Colonial Office for an explanation of the 'deplorable conditions'. This august body was itself shocked by this revelation; it mumbled a somewhat incoherent reply to the effect that it was making the necessary inquiries. With regard to its Malayan subordinates, however, it was more specific. Having examined the prevailing labour situation in Malaya, it saw no justification for the continuance of indentured recruitment from India and issued instructions that it should cease forthwith. This was complied with, with effect from 30 June 1910.[5] The existing contracts were allowed to run their course, the last one expiring in 1913.[6] Indenture was succeeded by another system of recruitment that had already developed, a system freer but not completely free, the 'free' and *kangani* system of obtaining labourers.

[1] *RLC 1896*, p. C 254.
[2] *SSAR*, 1902, pp. 188–9.
[3] Grist, 1936, pp. 10–11.
[4] J. H. Harris, *Coolie Labour in the British Crown Colonies and Protectorates* (London, 1910), pp. 3–24; 1933, pp. 52–73.
[5] *C.O.273*, 360 (1910), 7.1.1910; Colonial Office, minute no. 2947; 25.2.1910; 16.3.1910.
[6] *SSAR*, 1913, p. 189.

Types of migrants

'*Free*' recruited immigration

The indentured labour migration, consisting as it did of only a few thousand entries per year, was insufficient to meet all the labour needs of the sugar planters, let alone the large and growing demand for Indian labour within the government departments and the rest of the private sector, particularly the nascent but rapidly expanding rubber plantations. Moreover, most of these non-sugar employers preferred 'free' labour to indentured, considering the latter comparatively less efficient and more expensive.[1] To meet such needs there developed a system of recruiting free labour in India. It functioned side by side but quite apart from the indentured stream. It consisted of the *kangani* and non-*kangani* or so-called 'free' systems of labour recruitment.

The non-*kangani* system really consisted of two types, promissory-note and non-promissory-note labourers. The former was further sub-divided into three basic types: (i) those imported by the Malayan government and distributed to private employers and also to its own departments; (ii) those imported by the Malay Peninsula Agricultural Association, which served the interests of the sugar industry and maintained agents in India to facilitate the flow of such emigrants; and (iii) those introduced by the employers themselves. Actual recruitment of all three types was usually done through professional labour-recruiting agencies and their agents in India, acting on the instructions of the Malayan authorities.[2]

The labourers so recruited appear to have found employment mainly in the government service, especially in the Public Works Department and railway construction, and in the sugar industry where they supplemented its indentured supplies.[3] It appears to have been the general practice that each such labourer, either before leaving India or on arrival in Malaya, be required to sign a promissory-note for a sum which purported to be the amount expended on his behalf in the course of his recruitment and passage to Malaya. It was usually a sum 'much larger than true'. They were told that they would have to serve their employer for one year before the loan could be considered as paid in full. They could, however, rescind the promissory-note at any time by the payment in full of the amount stipulated therein. Failing to do this they had to work the statutory one year before they were free to leave. In practice, with the exception of those employed by the government,

---

[1] *RLC 1890*, p. 47; app. A, pp. 200–4; *RLC 1896*, pp. C 237–54.
[2] *RLC 1890*, app. A, pp. 200–4; *SSAR*, 1896, pp. 103–4; *SSAR*, 1899, pp. 77–82; *SSAR*, 1902, pp. 188–94; *SSAR*, 1903, pp. 270–86.
[3] *SSAR*, 1903, p. 285.

it was seldom that these labourers, like many of their indentured compatriots, were able to leave at the end of the stipulated period, employers being usually able to find some excuse for retaining them longer than the customary one year.[1] But unlike the indentureds, the wages of these labourers were those prevailing in the free market at the time of the signing of the agreement. Moreover, generally no deductions were made from these wages. Then again, these labourers were recruited from a far wider field than their indentured colleagues: Sikh and Rajput plate-layers, from the Punjab and Rajputana respectively, Mahrattas from the Bombay Province, Oriyas from Hyderabad State and Bengalis from the Ganges valley being also included in this stream besides the ubiquitous Madrasis.[2] However, recruitment of non-South Indian labour was not in the emigration agreement between Malaya and India and contrary to Indian law.[3] Consequently, with the exception of a few hundred Northern Indians whom the recruiters succeeded in getting out of India in the early 1900s, emigration of free labour, in terms of numbers, was also predominantly a South Indian affair. Moreover, the Northern Indian recruits were by no means an unqualified success as agricultural labourers, being quarrelsome and difficult to manage. The Sikh and Rajput plate-layers were satisfactory but they were brought in to do a special job—construction of the railway line between Negri Sembilan and Johore—under an engineer known to them. They were shipped back to India on completion of the task.

Before 1900 almost all the recruited free labourers were those brought by *kanganis*, recruitment of free labour through the promissory-note system being virtually non-existent. This was largely because prior to the passing of the Straits Settlements *Ordinance VII of 1897*, which came into effect from the beginning of 1899, there were no legal means of getting such immigrants to observe the agreements. They would sign the agreements in India, come to Malaya and then conveniently disappear. With the passing of this Ordinance, however, they were bound to honour the loan. They could be detained in the depot on their arrival in Penang and prosecuted if they refused to work for the stipulated year or pay the amount entered in the promissory-note.[4] But partly because of its indenture-like overtones and partly because of the development and systematization of the *kangani* system, the system of recruiting free labourers through the promissory-note method never

[1] *SSAR*, 1899, pp. 77–82; *SSAR*, 1900, pp. 188–90.
[2] *SSAR*, 1897, p. 170; *SSAR*, 1901, p. 177; *SSAR*, 1902, pp. 192–3; *SSAR*, 1903, pp. 270–3; *IO:EP*, 6364 (1902), pp. 857 ff.; Sanderson, 1910, part II, pp. 431–4; *PPSE*, 24 (1897–8), 4.8.1897, 14.9.1897; 25 (1899), 14.6.1899.
[3] *IO:EP*, 6564 (1902), pp. 855–6.
[4] *SSAR*, 1899, pp. 77–82; *SSAR*, 1900, pp. 188–90.

really got going. To begin with, the recovery from labourers, in any form, of any advances or expenses purported to have been incurred on their behalf was outlawed in 1909. Then, as noted in the foregoing pages, all forms of indenture were abolished in 1910.[1] Henceforth all contracts were limited to one month. In any case, employers of promissory-note labour, like those of indentureds, were already, before the end of the 1900s, beginning to switch to either the comparatively more popular and less expensive *kangani* recruits, who were traditionally— and from 1882 legally—engaged on one-month engagements, or to waive the promissory-note clauses and engage the labour so recruited on one-month engagements too. This change of heart on the part of these employers gave the professionally recruited labour stream a new lease of life. Even though the government ceased being a recruiting agency in 1915,[2] it appears to have continued to function side by side with the *kangani* system until the Great Depression of the early 1930s but, unlike the *kangani* system, it appears to have failed to survive this economic catastrophe for it ceased to feature thereafter in official documents.

No statistical data whatsoever appear to have been maintained for this movement, but from internal evidence in the *Minutes of meetings* of the Indian Immigration Committee and the *Annual reports* and files of the Labour Department, Malaya, it appears to have functioned primarily as an adjunct and corollary to the more important and senior partner—the *kangani* system. With the exception of the years 1926–7, which mark the high tide mark of Indian assisted labour immigration in response to a buoyant economy, the flow of professionally recruited labour into Malaya seldom, if ever, exceeded a few thousand entries per year until its apparent cessation in the early 1930s (Appendix 2).[3]

Kangani recruited immigration

The date of birth of the *kangani* system of labour recruitment, too, is hazy, but it appears to have begun at least as early as the late 1860s if not earlier.[4] However, it did not become significant until the establishment of large-scale commercial coffee cultivation in the 1880s and 1890s.[5] With the spread of coffee estates a difference of opinion developed between European sugar and coffee planters as to the type of labour desired in Malaya. The sugar planters, as we know, employed largely

[1] *IICMM*, 15.11.1908; *SSAR*, 1901, p. 116; *SSAR*, 1908, p. 69; *SSAR*, 1910, p. 500.
[2] *SSAR*, 1913, p. 35; *SSAR*, 1916, p. 155.
[3] The 1934 to 1938 figures in this Appendix for dependants and other types of assisted labourers refer only to dependants.
[4] *GMPPD*, 1870, 40–4 of 13.9.1870; *NAI:EP*, Sept. 1870, proc. 1–15.
[5] *SSG*, 1880, p. 507; *SSG*, 1883, p. 1183; *SAR*, 1896, p. 3; Parmer, 1960, pp. 7–8.

professionally recruited indentured Indians, but the coffee planters preferred to employ free labour recruited by *kanganis*, a procedure in vogue in Ceylon, from where most of the coffee planters had come. The rubber planters, too, favoured *kangani* labour, considering it far superior to the one recruited professionally. The *kangani*, as employee of the estate, was expected to do his best for his employer. He knew what was wanted. He had the confidence of his master. He recruited in his own village or taluk where he was known and where his apparent wealth and well-being would be all the more effectively employed in attracting emigrants, as it could be paraded as proof of the wealth awaiting them in Malaya. Moreover, *kangani* labour was cheaper since commissions paid to *kanganis* probably varied less directly with the demand for labour. Also of major importance was the fact that *kangani*-recruited labourers were considered free labourers and thus initially less subject to Government control and inspection.[1] The *kangani* system of the coffee and post-coffee era involved a short-term contract, generally verbal rather than written, which could be dissolved at a month's notice on the part of either party. It received its name because of the important role of the *kanganis*, or headmen, who in theory were foremen on estates or senior members of families, but in actuality were often only 'coolies of standing'. The *kangani*, like his garden *sirdar* and *maistry* counterparts of the Assamese tea plantations and the Burmese rice fields and mills respectively, was both recruiter and field foreman, at least in the case of those he recruited.[2] He was sent by an employer or association of employers to bring back his friends, neighbours and relatives in his home village and taluk. The *kangani*, on behalf of his employers, undertook to provide food, clothing and transit for the recruits in connection with the overseas trip. Frequently he was empowered to discharge their local debts or to leave money with their relatives. Considerable responsibility rested on him to choose the right sort of recruits and as compared with indenture there was a somewhat better chance that whole families or neighbourhood groups would come together.

On the Ceylon coffee, and subsequently tea, plantations, where the system appears to have been inaugurated, *kanganis* controlled gangs of labourers who were often composed of family units. Where several *kangani* gangs resided on the same estate there was often a head *kangani*. The *kanganis* in charge of the sub-groups were called *silara kanganis* (in Malaya, *cinna kanganis*) or deputy or minor *kanganis* who were responsible to the head *kangani*. The *kangani* was the all-important link

[1] *RLC 1890*, pp. 41, 47; *RLC 1896*, pp. C 224, 254; *SSAR*, 1934, pp. 851–5; Kondapi, 1951, pp. 29–45; Parmer, 1960, pp. 21–2; *ARSILFB*, 1959, pp. 31–2.
[2] Andrew, 1933, pp. 43–89; Kondapi, 1951, pp. 29–52; United Kingdom, 1931, pp. 349–442.

between the planter and his labour force. He recruited labourers in India, supervised their work on the estates and paid them their fares from a lump sum paid by the employer. In return for his services the head *kangani* received payments for recruits introduced on to the estate and also 'head-money', 3–6 rupee cents per day, for each resident labourer who showed up for work. In addition, he was occasionally paid a fixed salary for special services, and often also made a little more money by sharp practices. More important, he was able to exploit his position to his own advantage, particularly to gain control over the labourers so that they were constrained not to leave the gang. The *silara kangani* usually worked in the field, either as a labourer or sub-overseer. For this he received a 'name' which entitled him to a day's pay for each labourer in his group in addition to 'pence money', a sum of 9–12 rupee cents daily.

The labourer was obligated to pay within two years the sum advanced to bring him to the place of work. He could not be compelled to pay, since the law clearly allowed him to leave his job with thirty days' notice and did not hold him liable for any debt to the *kangani*, but in fact he would find it difficult to get work at another plantation if he failed to pay, and he took the debt as a point of honour.[1]

In Malaya, the *kangani* system differed from that practised in Ceylon. The coffee planters and following them the rubber and other planters and the government exerted more personal control over the labour force, chiefly by the payment of wages directly to each labourer. The hold of the *kangani* was thereby considerably weakened, though by no means entirely broken. Under this system of recruitment, Malayan employers paid the *kangani* the passage and expenses to and from India, plus a commission for each labourer recruited. These labourers were not required to enter contracts but were nevertheless expected to repay the cost of their importation to the employer, usually from wages. The employer's only remedy in cases of desertion without making full payment was a civil suit, but this was seldom done. Instead he relied on a combination of 'reasonable terms' and his *kangani's* influence to keep the labourer on the estate and recover expenditure. In any case, this worry also ceased with the inauguration of the Indian Immigration Committee in 1907 and its subsequent assumption of virtually all expenses connected with *kangani* recruitment, and the outlawing, in 1909, of recovering from the wages of the labourer any advances or debts incurred in the course of his emigration.[2]

[1] Ceylon, 1908, pp. vii–ix.
[2] *IICMM*, 15.11.1908; *SSAR*, 1922, pp. 511–12; *SSAR*, 1934, pp. 851–5; Parmer, 1960, p. 58; personal interview with the Commissioner for Labour, Federation of Malaya.

Immigration: origins and trends

Although from time to time important changes were made, the *kangani* system remained unaltered in its fundamental aspects until 1938 when it was abolished, following the ban by the Indian government on all assisted emigration of unskilled workers. The procedures of the *kangani* system under the aegis of the Indian Immigration Committee were not entirely new but mostly adaptations of earlier practices. In a pamphlet prepared in 1914 for distribution to prospective employers, the Deputy Controller of Labour, Malaya, described these procedures as follows:[1]

An employer in need of labour would obtain from a Labour Department office a blank *kangani* licence form. He would enter in this the *kangani's* name, the maximum number of labourers the *kangani* was to recruit, the wage rates the labourer would receive and the amount of the *kangani's* commission in respect of each labourer recruited. The *kangani* would proceed to Penang with the form where, if found satisfactory by the Deputy Controller of Labour, the licence was registered. The Deputy Controller especially wished to see that the *kangani* appeared old enough (twenty-one years or older), was a South Indian of labouring class, had been employed on the place for which he was to recruit for at least three months; also that the number of labourers he was recruiting did not exceed twenty,[2] the authorized limit in the first instance, that the validity of his licence did not exceed one year, and finally, that the commission paid to him in respect of each labourer recruited in no case exceeded Rs. 10 per head, the maximum permitted by the Indian Immigration Committee.[3] The *kangani* then embarked for India.[4] On arrival in India the *kangani* would have his licence endorsed by the Malayan Emigration Agent (later Commissioner) or his assistant at either of the two main Malayan emigration depots at Avadi (Madras) and Negapatam. The *kangani* then presented himself to the financial agents of his employers—generally two European firms, Messrs Binny and Company or Messrs Madura Company, which had formerly obtained indentured labour from professional recruiters for the Malayan employers and were now also agents for the British India Steam Navigation Company, the carriers of all assisted migrants between India

---

[1] *NAM:COHC*, 1919, 307, 12.8.1919.

[2] For subsequent recruitment this maximum was extended up to fifty men.

[3] The legally permitted commission paid to *kanganis* was as high as Rs. 26 per head before 1909. In that year it was reduced to Rs. 22 and finally to the lowly sum of Rs. 10, in order to prevent them from 'buying' labourers from professional recruiters. In practice, however, many employers paid them higher than the statutory Rs. 10, to ensure their *kanganis'* continued competitiveness in the recruiting districts of Southern India.

[4] After 1923, when the government of India appointed an Agent in Malaya, the *kangani* had to have his licence endorsed by this Agent prior to his departure for India.

and Malaya since the 1890s. These firms advanced money to the *kangani* for his travel and recruiting expenses.

Having obtained his advance, the *kangani* would proceed to recruit, ideally among his friends and relatives in his home village and certainly not outside his home taluk. Part of the money advanced by the financial agents was used to settle emigrants' debts or for gifts to those left behind and also for a farewell party (all considered part and parcel of the stratagem of getting the required number of emigrants). These were the only expenses of the *kangani* which were not recoverable from the Indian Immigration Fund. Having obtained the emigrants, the *kangani* then took them before the *munsif* of the village in which he had recruited the individuals, whose duty it was to see that there were no valid objections to the persons emigrating. If he was satisfied he initialled the entry of each intending emigrant's name on the back of the *kangani's* licence (fig. 1).[1] Having acquired the desired number of emigrants, the *kangani* took the recruits to the nearest railway station and from there to Avadi or Negapatam where they were kept in the camps until boarding the British India Steam Navigation Company's vessels. At some of the more popular interior railway stations, recruiting inspectors were employed (and sub-depots for the convenience of recruits were also maintained). These inspectors endorsed the *kangani's* licence with the number of recruits entraining and paid the cost of tickets. At other stations the *kangani* paid for the tickets from his advance and was reimbursed by the officials at the Malayan camps. Usually the *kangani* would go with his recruits to Malaya and receive his commission, less the advances received, on arrival. But sometimes he would send the recruits on and return to the villages for more emigrants. In this event, prior to leaving for the villages, he called in again at the financial agents where he not only collected the necessary advances for the new operations but also the commission due to him on the previous successful ventures. The agents also cabled the employer on the occasion of each shipment and periodically billed each employer for the expenses incurred on his behalf, adding a charge for their services.

The procedure at the emigration camps was equally, if not more, interesting. In an address given to the Planters' Association of Malaya in 1912 on his return from a visit to India, J. R. O. Aldworth, Controller of Labour, Malaya, described 'the scene on a busy day', the day prior to the departure of the weekly steamer, in the Negapatam camp as follows:

...Dr Foston (Malayan Emigration Agent) is early on the scene and while the coolies in camp are having their breakfast the arrivals by the first train are

---

[1] This was required only after the passing of the *Indian Emigration Act, 1922* in India.

admitted. First they come in the big gate into the admission yard where each kangani lines up coolies, holding in his hand his licence...Two clerks at tables in the office verandah are ready to write down details. There are two receptacles for the licences when they have been handed in by the kanganis. The Super-intendent of the Depot, the Resident Medical Assistant, and several peons are present. The first kangani advances with his men and hands his licence to the Medical Assistant who reads out the name of the estate, the number of coolies arriving and other details which are written down by the clerk. The licence is placed in one or other of the receptacles according to whether the railway tickets have been prepaid by the recruiting inspector or have been paid by the kanganis. Meanwhile the Doctor has been running his eye over the coolies and if any of them are obviously unfit, the whole batch, on leaving the yard, wait in one appointed spot. If nothing is wrong with them they wait in another place. The next batch advances...After the coolies arriving by the morning train have been either provisionally admitted, or rejected, they are again scrutinized by the Superintendent and probably some more are rejected for medical or other reasons. When the selection process has been completed all the coolies in camp are lined up and the camp regulations are read out to them. This procedure is gone through every morning and is a useful introduction to the estate discipline which is to follow. At muster every coolie is provided with a cheroot and some betel with the usual condiments for chewing. The muster having been dismissed, the new coolies are free to amuse themselves or make a few simple purchases in the shop, to be shaved or to rest for a few hours. Some estates desire all their coolies to undergo a vigorous medical examination before they are shipped; for which examination a fee of one dollar is charged. Every week a few coolies undergo this ordeal before shipping day. By two o'clock in the afternoon (on the day of shipping)...every man in the camp will have been shaved, and have had his hair cut in the few instances in which this is desired. Then they are all lined up for their gingelly oil bath. They squat on the ground with their hands extended in front of them, while two attendants, one with a large tin of oil and one with a dipper, pass down the row, and give each coolie a handful of oil and as often as not pour a quantity on their heads. Ten minutes are allowed for the rubbing of the oil, then at a given signal they move down in batches to the canal where five minutes is allowed for a good wash. At another signal they march up to the drying ground while their places in the canal are taken by another batch...[1]

While all this was going on the clothes and often the belongings of the emigrants were disinfected and those with insufficient clothing were issued with some new items.[2]

Rejection of *kangani* recruits was mainly on medical or political grounds. Rejected labourers were returned to their homes, the cost being paid by *kanganis* or debited to the *kanganis'* employers by the financial agent.[3]

[1] *PAMMM*, 27.4.1913.　　　[2] *Ibid.*
[3] *RLC 1890*, app. I; *PAMAR*, 1923–4, app. D.

Types of migrants

The task of shipping the emigrants to Malaya was undertaken by the financial agents usually directly from the camp premises to the ship, in the case of Avadi at the Madras wharves and at Negapatam in the outer roads. In the case of the latter, *toonis* (*dhoonies*) or large boats were used to convey the emigrants from the camp to the waiting ships, some two or three miles away. Prior to their embarkation on to these boats each labourer was given a 'tin ticket' bearing a number which represented the estate to which he was being dispatched. On arrival in Malaya, after a voyage of about five days, it was the usual practice for all assisted immigrant labourers to enter quarantine stations for one week or longer.[1] Here the immigrants were disinfected, fed, observed and allowed to recover from the rigours of the sea voyage, which to most of them was a new, strange and trying experience. From these camps they were sent to the nearby depots where, usually within one or two days, the employer or his agent came to remove his new labourers, by car, truck, boat, train or bullock-cart, as the case may be, to their place of employment.[2]

Penang was the sole port of entry for all assisted labour immigrants into Malaya from India until 1903. Thenceforth, however, Port Swettenham and subsequently Singapore were also added as points of entry. In fact, Port Swettenham in the ensuing years supplanted Penang as the major labour port of the country, handling 48 per cent of such traffic in the 1930s, compared with the 38 per cent by Penang and 14 per cent by Singapore.[3] On the Indian side, Negapatam remained the main port of *kangani* labour emigration until the Great Depression of the early 1930s, accounting for on the average about 60 per cent of the emigrants compared with Madras's 40 per cent. However, after the Depression, and the decline of *kangani* recruiting and the ascendancy of other forms of labour emigration, the roles were reversed, Madras now handling 70 per cent of the *kangani* traffic compared with only 30 per cent by Negapatam.[4]

As in the case of the indentured and professional recruits, it is impossible to know exactly how many *kangani* labourers entered Malaya from the inception of the system to its abolition in 1938. Continuous statistical data are available only from 1898. Between 1898 and 1938,

[1] This was only three days in the case of Singapore and five days at Port Swettenham. Detention for a week or longer only applied to Penang, the first port of call of *all* assisted labour immigrants.
[2] Personal interview with the Superintendent, Pulau Jerejak (Penang) Quarantine Camp.
[3] *SSAR*, 1904, p. 92; *SSAR*, 1934, p. 715.
[4] *GRAPM*, 1929–30, pp. 193–4; *GRAPM*, 1935–6, pp. 176–7; *MAREI*, 1908, p. 6; *MAREI*, 1929, p. 14; *MAREI*, 1937, p. 3.

1,153,717 *kangani* recruits were landed in Malaya, an average of more than 28,000 per annum. On the basis of the entries during 1898 and 1899, numbering 455 and 2,217 respectively, and the number of Indian labourers employed on the European coffee estates during the 1880s and 1890s,[1] it would appear not totally unreasonable to assume that there could have been at least some 1,000 *kangani* entries per year into Malaya during the nineteenth century. Furthermore, if we were to accept the middle 1860s as the beginning of the *kangani* system of labour recruitment, and apply the above average uniformly for the years 1865–97, it emerges that some 33,000 *kangani* recruits might have entered Malaya during that period. This number added to the 1,153,717 entries during 1898–1938 gives us a total of 1,186,717 *kangani* immigrants into Malaya during the period 1865–1938, the life of the *kangani* system of labour recruitment. This total represents more than 62 per cent of the total assisted labour migration, nearly 44 per cent of all labour and almost 28 per cent of the total Indian immigration into Malaya up to the end of 1957. Perhaps even more remarkable is the rapidity with which the *kangani* system, once accepted by the government in 1897 and systematized under the Indian Immigration Committee, supplanted the other forms of assisted labour migration. By 1902 the proportion of *kangani* recruits among the assisted immigrants had risen to one-third of the total. By 1907 this had reached almost three-quarters and five years later more than 95 per cent. This predominance, although not as marked as in 1912, continued through the subsequent years until just before the onset of the first rumblings of the Great Depression.

Then again, the average number of arrivals given above hardly tells the whole story of the *kangani* labour movement, for the arrivals in any one year varied from 435 in 1898 to 102,155 in 1926, nil in 1931 and 5,337 in 1937. However, within this fluctuating flow certain major trends can be distinguished. The period up to 1909 is the time of transition and the systematizing of the system and, with the exception of 1907, the number of arrivals in any one year did not exceed 20,000. The next decade or so, with the exception of the years marking the beginning and end of World War I, is a period of constantly large immigration of 50,000–80,000 persons per year. This is followed by the abrupt repercussions of the general trade recession of that period, and the fantastic rise in 1926, when no less than 102,155 *kangani* recruits are listed among the immigrants. This marked the apogee of *kangani* migration for, from thenceforth, this class of migration, with the exception of a few spasmodic recoveries, generally declined to nothing

---

[1] *SSSF*, 1891, 908/91; 1894, 3886/94; *SAR*, 1896, p. 3.

Types of migrants

Table 2a: Composition of Indian assisted labour immigration
into Malaya, 1844–1938

total number of arrivals	percentage						
	indentured						
	written contract	verbal contract	total	kangani	voluntary	others
1910820	9·5	3·5	13·0	62·2	15·3	9·5

Source: As for Appendix 3.

Table 2b: Composition of total Indian labour immigration
into Malaya, 1844–1941

total number of arrivals	percentage					
	Assisted					non-assisted
	indentured	kangani	voluntary	others	total	
2725917	9·1	43·7	10·7	6·6	70·1	29·9

Source: As for Appendix 3.

during the Great Depression and to only a few thousand entries in the years immediately preceding its demise in 1938. In contrast to the flow of indentured labourers, the number of arrivals in any one year under the *kangani* system appears to have been influenced more by such factors as demand in Malaya and the number of *kangani* licences issued, rather than conditions in India (table 2; Appendices 2, 3; figs. 6, 7).

Another significant feature of this *kangani* labour movement was that unlike its counterpart in Ceylon,[1] where it was largely a movement of families or equal numbers of males and females, the migration to Malaya consisted of predominantly adult males, at least until the late 1920s. Thereafter males still formed about 70 per cent of all the *kangani* immigrants.[2] Various attempts were made by the Malayan and Indian governments to improve the disproportion among the sexes. The Malayan government, for example, reduced the assessments paid on female workers in connection with the Indian Immigration Fund. It also increased the commissions paid to *kanganis* for female recruits and also

[1] Jackson, 1938, pp. 7 et seq.
[2] SSAR, 1921, p. 663; SSAR, 1929, p. 183; SSAR, 1937, p. 498.

for married men accompanied by their families. The Indian government on its part passed the *Indian Emigration Act, 1922* and the *Indian Emigration Rules, 1923*, which stipulated that there should be at least one female emigrant for every 1·5 males assisted to emigrate as labourers.[1]

These attempts, however, were only partially successful, and at times not even that. In the first place, the Indian government's stipulation was never implemented, partly because the Indian government had hitherto found the sex-ratio rule a 'useful means of bargaining' with Malaya. In any case it was not convinced that the sex ratio in Malaya was 'so bad as to give rise to grave abuses'.[2] Then, equally, if not more, important was the pressure from the planters, through the Malayan government, who feared that their supply of labour would suffer, ostensibly because it would be impossible to recruit sufficient suitable women to make up the stipulated sex ratio.[3] These fears were not unfounded. Female recruits were extremely difficult to come by. There were few unattached women available, partly because of the widespread practice of child betrothals and marriages before or at puberty. Then there was also the problem that women or minors were not allowed to emigrate on their own but had to be accompanied by their husbands, parents or relatives. In the case of families, the joint-family system made it difficult for them to leave. Moreover, it assured the female members protection while the males were away. Opposition of relatives to emigration was particularly strong in the case of the female members of the family. In addition to fears for their well-being, restraining wives and families from emigrating was considered probably the best way to ensure the return home of the male emigrants. Even if relatives permitted the wife and children to emigrate, it would still be considered imprudent of the man to expose her to the hazards and risks of a sea-voyage and living in a strange land among strange people. The males themselves were no whit less aware of this. In any case almost all of them appear to have been leaving India not in any permanent sense, at least then, but with the idea and aim of returning to it as soon as possible. In the meantime the family could best remain in India where maintenance was simpler and less costly.

Then, although no corroborative evidence has come to light, there was the feeling, amongst Indian labour leaders and others, that the Malayan employers while going through all the appropriate gestures of

[1] See pp. 145–6 below.
[2] *NAI:EP*, 1938, confidential file no. 44/38—L & O, serial nos. 1–133.
[3] *IICMM*, 21.5.1924; 24.11.1926; 24.11.1927; 19.2.1930; 8.5.1936; *MAREI*, 1934, p. 10; *MAREI*, 1936, p. 9; *NAI:EP*, March 1925, B proc. 27–44.

encouraging female emigration were in reality not very anxious to promote such migration. They considered the female labourers less efficient and productive and more costly to maintain in terms of supervision, accommodation, and maternity and nursery provisions.[1] In any case, unlike the tea planters of Ceylon, the Malayan rubber planters, the principal employers of *kangani* labour during the present century, could only employ a limited number of females on the estates. The International Labour Organisation's Committee on Work on Plantations has estimated that the proportion of male to female requirements of a rubber plantation are roughly in the order of five males to every three females, compared with the one to one ratio for tea plantations.[2] The sum total of the above factors was that the representative *kangani* emigrant was an adult male leaving the country for a short while and generally always with the idea of returning home. This is not to claim that there was no family emigration, but that it concerned a tiny minority of immigrants in the total stream, at least till the late 1920s. Neither is it to deny that a few left with the idea of permanent settlement, but that such elements were even more uncommon than the family emigrants.

Kangani labour immigration into Malaya was entirely a South Indian phenomenon, predominantly Tamil with a leavening of Telegus from Andhra Pradesh and Malayalis from the Malabar coast areas. The principal districts of origin were those adjoining or close to the ports of Madras and Negapatam—North Arcot, Trichinopoly, Tanjore, Salem, Chingleput and South Arcot (figs. 9, 10 *a*). These between them accounted for 70 per cent of the total emigrants, with North Arcot providing more than a fifth of the total. These migrants were drawn from a variety of castes and backgrounds, but predominantly from among the lower strata of South Indian society, especially its Untouchable or Adi-dravida sector of Pariahs, Pallas, Chamars and such like.[3] As stated above, the vast majority of these recruits were intended for the rubber plantations, and Selangor and Perak, two of the principal rubber areas of the country, between them absorbed nearly two-thirds of such entrants.[4]

The *kangani* system vastly improved Malaya's labour supply, but its method of recruitment left a lot to be desired. Bribery was frequently used to buy favours and it invariably entered into the several phases of immigration, especially where a lowly paid authority, as for example

[1] *NAI:EP*, 1932, confidential file no. 206–2/32—L & O; personal interviews with officials of the National Union of Plantation Workers, Petaling Jaya, Malaya, and the Department of Labour, Federation of Malaya, Kuala Lumpur.
[2] International Labour Organisation, 1950, pp. 29–30.
[3] *MAREI*, 1929, p. 10; *MAREI*, 1938, p. 22; India, 1932–7, vol. XIV, part II, pp. 87–91; *SSAR*, 1929, p. 197.
[4] *SSAR*, 1913, p. 35; *SSAR*, 1918, p. 472; *SSAR*, 1930, pp. 682–3.

the village *munsif*, was in a position to dispense privilege. Sharp recruiting practices on the part of the *kanganis* included purchasing recruits from professional recruiters or hotel keepers; forging signatures of village *munsifs*; exploiting family quarrels to get some member of the family to emigrate; promising young men that they would find wives in Malaya if they went there; catching recruits at weekly 'shandies', not unlike the practice of shanghaiing on the China coast; matching strangers in order to circumvent the rule that minors and women must be accompanied by a parent or relatives; misrepresentation of work and wages; substituting unfit persons for ones already passed as healthy; recruiting for estates other than their own; and, finally, not being *kanganis* at all but professional recruiters posing as *kanganis*.[1]

Furthermore, the *kangani* system was also criticized and disliked because it was more than a means of recruitment. It was a method of employment, too, in which liaison on estates between the labourers and the employer was chiefly through the *kangani*. This allowed the *kangani* to exploit the labourers' ignorance of rules and recruiting practices. In disputes between the *kangani* and labourers, the *kangani* usually had the support of the managers.

Kangani recruitment was under the control of the Indian Immigration Committee and the chief weapon that was available to the Committee to combat *kangani* abuses was the threat of cancellation or refusal of a recruiting licence. But this power only began effectively to be utilized in the late 1920s, primarily it appears through the efforts of the Government of India Agent, who assumed duties in Malaya in 1923.[2] Even then, too, this power was exercised in the face of stiff opposition from the Planters' Association of Malaya. This body violently opposed abolition of the system since it still implied low operating costs and effective control of cheap labour. But individual planters considered the system as already sacrosanct as early as the 1920s and favoured the creation of a permanent residential Indian population in Malaya. These sentiments also began to be echoed by the *Planter*, the official organ of the planting community.[3] More important, however, was the development of nationalism amongst educated and informed Indians within India and Malaya and growing criticism of labour emigration in general and the *kangani* system in particular.

Kangani emigration to Malaya began to be singled out as a topic of

[1] *MAREI*, 1926, pp. 5–6; *MAREI*, 1930, p. 6, *ARAGIBM*, 1926, pp. 5–11, 23; *ST*, 3.3.1912.

[2] For example, in 1927, when 7,882 *kangani* licences were outstanding some 8 per cent were refused reregistration or cancelled (*ARAGIBM*, 1927, p. 4).

[3] *PAMC*, 1928, 17, pp. 12–20; 1931, 5, p. 112; 1937, 7, pp. 3–4; *P*, 1922, I, xii, pp. 18–19; 1935, xvi, vii, pp. 289–312.

Types of migrants

comment at least as early as the beginning of the second decade of the present century. In 1913, for example, we find the *Amrita Bazar Patrika*, a Calcutta nationalist daily, publishing an article, by 'a correspondent' from Klang (Selangor), which stated:

...The recruiting Kanganies who generally belong to the lowest class and who do not care for the welfare of the coolies as long as they get a good commission from their employers give a glowing description of the new country...The Kanganies are easily believed by the simpletons because he...shines like a tin-god clothed in gorgeous velvet coat and lace turban and bedecked with costly jewels in his ears and his fingers...

The advertisement of the Federated Malay States Government which is displayed in all the Railway Stations and some public offices is an enchanting item. It gives all that are best here; the race courses which may not be seen by the coolie at all, the Mariamman temple within the radius of 50 miles, (*sic*) the coolie may not even tread, the Government Office in Kuala Lumpur with which the coolies have no connection whatsoever...the evry (*sic*) flowing river in Perak which contains water salter (*sic*) than that of the Sea and breeds myriads of crocodiles which make the river unbathable...

And the announcement at the bottom of each such alluring advertisement that coolies (males) get 7 annas a day is true enough. But...it is not coupled with a statement of the average cost of living for an average workman which is two and half times as much as it is in India...

...(The) conditions under which the coolies to be recruited are not properly explained to them and in majority of cases, the emigration agent does not even see the coolies until they are ready to be packed away.

According to the enactment in the States there are no statutory (indentured) emmigrants (*sic*). Everyone is a free coolie. He can leave the estate by giving an (*sic*) month's notice to the employer. It is all in theory. A coolie's notice is not generally accepted by the manager. In 99 out of 100 (*sic*), no coolie is allowed to see and speak to the manager. The coolie should give notice to the manager through the Kangany who, if he discharged a coolie from the estate, would lose two cents a day as he is given a head money (in addition to his wages) of two cents per coolie per working day. And naturally the Kangany informs the coolies that there (*sic*) indenture is not terminated...[1]

This was followed by petitions to the Colonial Office and further attacks in other publications too.[2] For instance the *Indian Emigrant*, a Madras monthly purporting to be a 'report of the status and doings' of Indian emigrants and 'an advocate of equal rights of British citizenship within the Empire', carried the following 'trumpet call' in its December, 1915, issue:

...In no other sphere of activity, the attention of the Indian public should be immediately directed than towards the methods adopted by the Kangany in India...

[1] *ABP*, 15.1.1913; *MM*, 30.1.1913.
[2] *C.O.273*, 404 (1913), 25.2.1913; 405 (1913), 25.3.1913.

...(The) Kangany on his arrival in India has only one object in view and that is to amass gold in plenty. First of all he looks to his personal appearance and very soon he is passed by all as a real and sympathetic gentleman. He, of course, hides his real intention and the object with which he is sent. He shows he does not care for money and gives any amount to his newly acquired friends ...He takes an interest in all matters concerning the welfare of the village or town he resides in...Soon he becomes popular with all...and is generally invited to all social and public functions. His gold attracts like magnet everybody, and his position is envied by many and our friend, the Kangany, is ready to help others to become like himself...He instils in the minds of these ignorant seekers of fortune that Malaya...(is an) El Dorado...where they could become very rich in the course of an year or two...Thus the ignorant people of the village are enticed away from their homes. Husbands and wives are separated, young girls kidnapped...(and) boys are spirited away from their...parents... A false impression prevails in our country about a Rubber Estate and the life led by the labourers. An Estate to translate into Tamil is a 'Thottam' and when this Thottam is again converted into English it becomes...a 'Garden'... Thus the labourer before leaving India imagines the work in an Estate is like the work he has to do in an Indian flower garden...[1]

Despite efforts by the Malayan government and some planters to show concern and to carry out inspection and so on, criticism from the Indians in India and Malaya not only continued but mounted in intensity. In 1936, the Indian government sent the Rt. Hon. V. S. Srinivasa Sastri, a leader of the Liberals in India, to Malaya to investigate the conditions of Indian labour. He received deputations from all sides.

Commenting on the *kangani* system he said,

...It is irrelevant to discuss here the merits or demerits of the administration of the system since the argument itself admits of the abuses to which it is liable...However careful the administration may be, the labourer may be under some concealed obligation to the kangany which will act to his disadvantage in Malaya...[2]

He recommended that the system be abolished.[3] By this time opposition from the Planters' Association of Malaya to the abolition of the system had also largely disappeared partly because of criticism of the system from the more sensitive of its own ranks and partly because of the availability of equally cheap alternative labour supplies, after the Great Depression, through the increasing movement of non-recruited assisted and independent Indian labourers to Malaya.[4]

Already declining in the late 1920s in the face of mounting criticism,

[1] *IE*, 1915, II, v, p. 135.
[2] Srinivasa Sastri, 1937, pp. 22–3; *PFC*, 1937, p. C 97.
[3] *Ibid.*   [4] *IICMM*, 27.3.1935.

legal restrictions and the growing knowledge and sophistication of the Indian labourers themselves the *kangani* system was suspended during the Great Depression of the early 1930s, when there was a surplus of Indian and other labour in Malaya. After this catastrophe, however, the system was resumed once again, but only on a very minor scale. Few licences were issued and these, too, mostly for the newly opened tea and oil palm estates and for employers whose labour connections were with remote parts of India, or were not well established to secure a sufficient supply of non-recruited labour.[1] For all practical purposes, therefore, it may be assumed that *kangani* recruitment ceased to be significant with the onset of the Great Depression. Formal abolition of the system, however, came in 1938 when the Indian government placed a ban on all assisted labour emigration.[2]

Assisted independent labour immigration

Kangani recruits, numerous though they were, were not sufficient to meet the large and increasing Indian labour needs of fast-developing Malaya. Consequently, to supplement the *kangani* and other streams of labour immigration, the Malayan government tried to stimulate a flow of so called 'independent', that is non-recruited, labour as well, by assisting such labourers to emigrate who voluntarily presented themselves at the Malayan depots in India.

In fact many of these independent labourers were recruited either formally, by *kanganis* who passed them off as voluntary emigrants, or informally, through letters from employers promising work.[3] Furthermore, independent migrants consisted really of three related but quite distinct categories—voluntary immigrants, *thitti-surat* and *puthal-surat* holders.

The first mention of a move to promote voluntary immigration appears to be that occurring on page 104 of the Straits Settlements' *Annual report of the Indian Immigration Department for the year 1896*. In that year $5,000 were voted by the government in its 1897 estimates 'to provide assistance to passages for bona fide agricultural labourers'. This was put into effect in 1900. But the response was disappointing as six and nineteen such emigrants only presented themselves at the Malayan depot in Negapatam in 1901 and 1902 respectively.[4] This was thought to be the result of having to pay for part of the fare. To rectify this the superintendent of the depot was authorized in 1903 to issue up to fifty

[1] *IICMM*, 8.5.1936; *ARAGIBM*, 1934, p. 2; *ARAGIBM*, 1936, p. 4.
[2] See p. 114 below.
[3] *NAI:EP*, 1935, confidential file no. 186/35—L & O.
[4] *SSAR*, 1900, pp. 188–9; *SSAR*, 1901, pp. 112–13; *SSAR*, 1902, p. 188.

free tickets to voluntary emigrants per steamer on the basis of first come first served.[1] As this move, too, did not have the desired effect, some employers suggested that returning labourers to South India should be provided with notices printed in Tamil and Telugu languages explaining how to obtain free passage to Malaya. This was attempted in 1913 and 1916 but nothing positive happened, principally because (*a*) many of these potential emigrants did not have the money to make the trip from their homes to the depot, (*b*) such emigration was contrary to the interests of the *kangani* and (*c*) the Indian Immigration Committee was not anxious to introduce any means of emigration that might undermine the *kangani* system.[2] From the middle 1920s, however, voluntary immigration rose substantially. The Committee's attitude, after years of vacillation and ambivalence towards such immigration, had undergone a radical change about this time. It now joined forces with the individual planters in stimulating voluntary emigration. These efforts took on added vigour with the decline of the *kangani* recruitment. As early as 1924, the Committee decided to pay a sum of $2.00 and $1.00 to each voluntary adult and minor emigrant, respectively, presenting himself at the Malayan depots in India. This was calculated to not only cover their travelling expenses to the depots but also to leave them a cash balance. This was in addition to the free passage to Malaya and maintenance while in the government depots.[3] The numbers henceforth were also swelled by many *kanganis* and their recruits and returning 'old hands' posing as new emigrants to get the voluntary 'bonuses'.[4]

The Agent of the Government of India in Malaya described the procedure of voluntary emigration to Malaya in 1925 as follows:

...Labourers who wish to go to Malaya independently of the Kangany appear at the nearest emigration depot at Avadi (Madras) or Negapatam. On being satisfied that they are *bonâ fide* labourers, the (Malayan) Emigration Commissioner or the Assistant Emigration Commissioner sends them on to Malaya at the cost of the Indian Immigration Fund. As soon as they are discharged from the immigration depots at the ports of destination in Malaya, they are at liberty to go to any place of employment they like...and are provided with free railway tickets...[5]

[1] *SSAR*, 1903, pp. 268–9.
[2] *IICMM*, 4.8.1912; 5.5.1913; *PAMMM*, 29.1.1919.
[3] *IICMM*, 19.11.1924; *PAMMM*, 8.8.1923.
[4] *ARAGIBM*, 1925, pp. 6–7; *PAMC*, 1926, 4, pp. 12–13. As a result of these developments voluntary emigrants made up 26 per cent of the total number of Indian labourers assisted to emigrate to Malaya in 1925 compared with only 9 per cent in 1913. In the 1930s the proportion was as high as 60 per cent (see Appendix 2 below).
[5] *ARAGIBM*, 1925, p. 6.

Types of migrants

Statistical data for voluntary emigrants in terms of the number of entries are comparatively more substantial. Between 1901 and 1938, when all forms of assisted immigration ceased, this stream had contributed 292,560 entrants; that is an average annual flow of 7,698 persons. Such an average flow is rather misleading in that voluntary immigration became really significant only from the middle 1920s in response to stimuli discussed above.

In fact, from 1925 to the time of the Great Depression, the average annual flow was more than 23,500. It was during this period, too, that the peak number of entries in any one year was registered—1927 with 32,302 voluntary immigrants. As in the case of the *kangani* system there was virtually no voluntary immigration during the Depression years.[1] But unlike its *kangani* counterpart, voluntary immigration was able to re-establish itself after the Depression. The flow in the post-Depression years would have been even higher than it was had it not been for the quota of only 20,000 such emigrants imposed by the Indian government for the years 1934 and 1935. This stemmed from the fears that there would be insufficient employment while Malaya recovered from the Depression.[2] Voluntary immigrants in these and the subsequent years of the 1930s nevertheless accounted for some 60 per cent of the assisted labour immigrants, 40 per cent of the total labour movement and nearly a quarter of the entire Indian immigration into the country. This compared with only about 15, 11 and 7 per cent respectively for the period as a whole (table 2; Appendices 2, 3). However, the dominance of voluntary immigrants in the assisted labour stream was short-lived, for their movement also met the same fate as the *kangani* counterpart. There was no escape from the Indian government's ban on all assisted labour migration in 1938.[3]

Voluntary emigrants appear to have come predominantly from the districts adjoining the ports of Negapatam and Madras, particularly the former. This was probably so because of the comparatively small expenses incurred in getting to the Malayan depots at these ports. Also, many of the voluntary emigrants appear to have been *pannaiyals* or serfs from the *mirasdar* estates of such districts as Tanjore, Chingleput, Madura and Trichinopoly (figs. 9, 10 *a*). Apart from such details, the voluntary emigrants were not substantially different from their *kangani*-recruited countrymen, that is they were mainly adult male emigrants drawn from the lower strata of the Tamil society.[4]

[1] The few who were assisted to emigrate during these years were *all* dependants of labourers already in Malaya.
[2] *IICMM*, 16.5.1934; 10.8.1935; *SSAR*, 1935, II, 769–70.
[3] See pp. 113–14 below.
[4] *MAREI*, 1934, pp. 3–5; *MAREI*, 1936, pp. 9–27.

Immigration: origins and trends

Thitti-surat immigration dates from the end of the Depression. During the Depression thousands of Indian labourers among others lost their jobs as the Malayan government retrenched many of its employees, and the plantations either closed down or functioned only on a care-and-maintenance basis. This resulted in a heavy exodus of Indian labour from Malaya, the government (including the Indian Immigration Committee) alone paying for the repatriation of nearly 250,000 such persons during the four years 1930–3 (Appendix 4).[1] Consequently when the Malayan economy partially recovered in 1934, there was a dearth of Indian labour, especially as the Indian government allowed assistance to Malaya of 20,000 new labour emigrants only in that year and also the year following. To meet some of the excess demand on the reopening estates, 'Malayan' Indian labourers, that is those who had previously worked in Malaya for five years and were now in India, were encouraged by their former employers to return to their jobs in Malaya. Such labourers did not count in the Indian government's quota of 20,000 and could receive free passage on furnishing proof at the Malayan depots in India that they had been in Malaya before. At the beginning a note from the estate manager was counted sufficient proof of previous residence. But from 1935, the Labour Department, Malaya, provided identification certificates for employers to give to their labourers returning to India. These were known as *thitti-surats*, literally, leave letters, and promised the labourers work on their return by a certain date. These labourers could bring their families along too.

In addition, as soon as the Indian government announced its intention of lifting its quota on independent assisted labour emigration with effect from the end of 1935, employers began to send to India, to friends and relatives of labourers already on the estates, letters promising work to them should they come to Malaya. In many cases small amounts of money too were remitted to such people to enable them to travel to the Malayan depots. There was a large response in 1936 and 1937 to such stimulation. In fact the Malayan government, though not the individual planters concerned, thought that this response was too large in relation to the labour needs of Malaya at that time. Accordingly, as in the case of the *thitti-surats* it took steps to regularize this movement also, so as to keep an effective check on its flow. Employers seeking labour through this method were now required to submit the names and other particulars of the labourers whom the employer expected to 'invite' for official approval. Furthermore, from 1937, these invitations were to be on official bearer letters, called *puthal-surats* or new immigrant

[1] *IICMM*, 24.10.1930; 11.2.1931; 24.6.1931; *SSAR*, 1930, pp. 678–702; *ARAGIBM*, 1931, pp. 2–9; *ARAGIBM*, 1933, pp. 8, 30.

letters, without which no such migrants were to be given free passage to Malaya.[1]

No statistical records were maintained in either India or Malaya of the bearer-letter migrants, but on the basis of the figures for the total assisted immigration and its voluntary and *kangani* components, it would appear that the bearer-letter arrivals comprised more than 30 per cent of the assisted migrants during the latter half of the 1930s. Neither are details available regarding the composition of this stream; but it is unlikely that it would have been in any way drastically different from that of its voluntary counterpart in terms of social class or sex and age structure. However, in terms of provenance, it is possible that since these bearer-letter migrants were either Malayan veterans or friends and relatives of such and others resident in Malaya,[2] they could have come from a wider area, possibly the same area as the *kangani* recruits.

Judging from the response to the *puthal-surats*, it is possible that bearer-letter emigration could have become even more significant than it did in its short life, especially as the Indian labourer by this time appeared to be becoming more mobile, better informed about Malaya and generally more sophisticated. But this has to remain in the realm of conjecture, for on 15 June 1938, the Indian government clamped a ban on all assisted labour emigration to Malaya. Although precipitated by a dispute over the amount of wages to be paid to Indian labour in Malaya, the ban had been pending for some time.

There was considerable abuse associated with assisted immigration in general. In addition to the abuses inherent in the *kangani* and other systems of formal recruitment, there were such other shortcomings as poor supervision, unsatisfactory shipping conditions and inadequate accommodation at emigration and quarantine depots. For example, in July 1900, the Penang depot was equipped to accommodate 800 persons, but held more than 2,000, and the 'appearance of cholera resulted in a great loss of life'.[3] As late as 1917 the anti-malarial works at Port Swettenham quarantine station, which opened in 1903, were yet to be completed,[4] while even as late as 1919 the principal medical and the senior health officers of the Federated Malay States were describing the immigrant ship conditions as 'incubators for cholera and all kinds of

---

[1] *MAREI*, 1934, pp. 3–6; *MAREI*, 1936, pp. 5–6; *ARAGIBM*, 1935, pp. 4–5; *SSAR*, 1934, pp. 855–8; *SSAR*, 1936, p. 499; *SSAR*, 1937, pp. 515–17; *IICMM*, 15.8.1936; *PFC*, 1937, p. C 376.

[2] *ARAGIBM*, 1935, p. 5; *IICMM*, 15.8.1936; personal interview with the Commissioner for Labour, Federation of Malaya.

[3] *PLCSS*, 1900, pp. B 147–55.

[4] *PAMMM*, 28.2.1917.

disease' and 'overcrowded and unsanitary tropical prisons'.[1] Through
representation and the work of the Agent of the Government of India,
efforts were made to improve conditions by introducing better vessels,
but overcrowding, and the occasional high mortality rate continued
throughout the 1920s, partly because the Malayan authorities and the
shipping companies tended to evade responsibility.[2] This attitude of
the Malayan government and its failure to ensure continuously satisfactory ship and camp conditions added more fuel to the already rising
flames of criticism in India against Indian labour emigration in general
and the assisted stream in particular.

We have seen how, in addition to the criticism of the indentured
system, *kangani* recruitment had been singled out for comment by the
Indian press as early as 1913, and that despite efforts by the Malayan
government to show concern the criticism had mounted. Hand in hand
with criticism of this particular mode of emigration was the overall
dislike of assisted labour emigration to the country. In addition to the
abuses inherent in the recruitment, transportation and employment of
Indian labourers in Malaya, the cause of the Indians in Malaya became
increasingly bound up with the political issue in India which concerned
the rights of Indians in not only their homeland but also overseas.[3] As
members of the one and same Raj, equal rights with the British were
demanded. The question of treatment of Indians overseas was debated
at almost every annual session of the Indian National Congress, from the
first decade of the present century.[4]

Messrs Gandhi, Polak and Andrews, the three leaders and authors
whom India looked up to on this subject, themselves time and again
condemned assisted emigration of labour and the treatment of Indians
abroad without reservation. In 1918, for example, we find them stating
that:

...the India Office and the Government of India...have not stood up for the
rights of the labourers or the honour of Indians to the same extent as they
are bound to do. Even the Government of (a) tiny (British Colony) seems to

[1] *IICMM*, 1.10.1919; Planters' Association for Malaya, 1919, sec. 2, p. 23.
[2] *IICMM*, 10.11.1919; *PAMAR*, 1919–20, p. 17; *ARAGIBM*, 1927, p. 5; *SSAR*,
1938, p. 13; Parmer, 1960, pp. 60–1.
[3] United Kingdom, 1918, p. 248; 1921, p. 8; 1923, pp. 73–91; Dev, 1940, pp. 5–6.
[4] See, for example, G. A. Nateson (compiler), *The Indian National Congress* (Madras,
1909), pp. 304 *et seq.*; B. P. Sitaramayya, *The History of the Indian National
Congress*, 2 vols. (Madras and Bombay, 1935–47), I, 76–82; II, 76–7, app. III;
All-India Congress Committee, *The Indian National Congress, 1930–1934* (Allahabad, 1934), p. 192; *PINC*, Minutes of the Working Committee, 9–11.9.1934;
Minutes of the All-India Congress Committee Meeting, 9–11.9.1934; Resolutions
of the Indian National Congress, 50th Session, 27–28.12.1936; 51st Session,
19–21.2.1938; Newsletter of the Foreign Department, 9.7.1946.

prevail in a dispute with the Indian Government. . . In being asked to give her labour under any terms to outside agency, India suffers a humiliation almost unexampled in the world . . . In fine, India neither needs nor countenances the idea of assisted emigration. . . [1]

As a result of the Montagu-Chelmsford constitutional reforms of 1918–19 in India, regulation of Indian emigration was placed in the hands of India's new bicameral central legislature. This body set up a joint Standing Emigration Committee in May 1922 to advise it on emigration questions. It also passed, the Malayan Government's objections notwithstanding, the *Indian Emigration Act, 1922*. These developments interposed the legislature of India in Malayan Indian affairs in a large way and this body became another centre of the storm raging round the question of Indian labour emigration. Moreover, this Act also provided for the appointment of an agent of the government of India in Malaya, to look after the welfare of the immigrants. The first such agent took up his appointment in 1923.[2] His on-the-spot accounts of the abuses inherent in assisted immigration further fanned the flames of criticism in India, where this form of emigration was becoming increasingly unpopular as it was regarded as an insult to the status of the Indian nation.

In addition to the *Amrita Bazar Patrika* of Calcutta, Indian emigration to Malaya began to feature prominently in both the moderate and radical Indian nationalist press and periodical literature, such as the *Swarajya, Servant of India, Indian Review, Modern Review, Young India* and *Hindu*, particularly the last. This paper, an influential and sober Madras daily, was the Malayan and Indian governments' chief critic, especially in the late 1930s, with regard to Indian migration between the two countries. For example, in 1937, it stated:

. . . The Indian in Malaya to-day is discriminated against on every side. His status is. . . far below that of other communities in the country. The public services are closed to him; under cover of protecting native interests arable land is denied to him; in the professions his existence is barely tolerated. . . Even the Malaya-born Indian, who does not know India, is treated as an alien in the land of his birth! To permit emigration of Indians to a country where they are treated with such little consideration seems consistent neither with the self-respect of India, nor with the best interests of prospective emigrants. . . [3]

The Rt. Hon. Srinivasa Sastri, although he avoided comment on the political and social issues of the Indians in Malaya, was nevertheless far from satisfied with assisted emigration. Besides recommending the

---

[1] *SI*, 1918, I, viii, pp. 88–9.
[2] *DLAI*, 1922, II, part ii, pp. 1755–89, 2049–50; III, i, p. 3; III, iii, pp. 1777–2146; *SEMMPI*, 1923–4, pp. 44–5; *NAI:EP*, Aug. 1923, B proc. 64.
[3] *H*, 6.3.1937.

abolition of the *kangani* system, he also deprecated, among other undesirable features, the 'prison-camp appearance' of the quarantine camps.[1] But neither these criticisms nor the visit of Pandit Nehru to Malaya in the following year, satisfied the ever mounting and increasingly militant anti-labour-emigration feeling in an awakening New India, keen on reform both at home and abroad.

Coupled with the rising unpopularity of assisted emigration in India was the growing criticism of this movement among the Indian intelligentsia in Malaya too. Usually it was expressed covertly in view of the severe discriminatory penalties against 'seditious stuff of any nature or form'. Occasionally, however, it did take an overt form. For example, we find the *Tamilaham*, a Kuala Lumpur Tamil weekly, in 1922, urging the Indians not to come to Malaya to work on rubber plantations. Then following the appointment of an Indian representative in the Federal Council and the Indian Immigration Committee in the latter half of the 1920s, questions on behalf of Indian labour began to be asked there.[2] Outside, the cudgels were taken up by such other Indian publications as the *Tamil Nesan, Indian Pioneer, Indian, Indo-Malayan Review* and *Indian Association (Penang) Bulletin* and by the Indian organizations, particularly by the Central Indian Association of Malaya. This association was formed in 1936 by business and professional class Indians. It was a pale reflection of the Indian National Congress, and certainly of a political bent. It set itself up as a watch-dog of Indian interests in Malaya. Until its voluntary liquidation after World War II, it waged an incessant war of memoranda, petitions, resolutions, meetings and speeches championing the cause of the Indian labourer in Malaya. Whilst constantly urging the Indian National Congress and legislature to ban emigration of labour, it kept these organizations and the Indian press minutely informed of the latest developments in the treatment of Indians in Malaya.[3]

The issue that finally precipitated the ban was the dispute between the two governments over the minimum standard wages to be paid to Indian labour in Malaya. Despite the fact that all the cost of importing a South Indian labourer under the Committee, on the average, amounted to only $29.39, from 1908 to 1938, compared with $47.50 in the late nineteenth century, wages remained ridiculously low and showed no drastic improvements over those prevailing in the last century. The

---

[1] Srinivasa Sastri, 1937, pp. 17–19; *PFC*, 1937, p. C 91.
[2] Parmer, 1960, p. 64; personal interviews with Mufti Nisar Ahmad Khan Sahib, retired Indian supernumerary officer, Malayan police force, and Mr N. Raghavan and Mr A. K. Sen, former President and General Secretary of the Central Indian Association of Malaya, respectively.
[3] *CIAMMM*, 27.3.1937; 18.7.1937; 27.3.1938; 27.11.1938.

wages tended to follow the prices of rubber, more downward than upward (Part 3). Finally, Indian government representation led to the imposition, from 1 June 1924, of a daily minimum standard wage rate of 35 cents for men and 27 cents for women. This was based on the prevailing cost of living.[1]

We have noted above that following the Great Depression there was a great exodus of Indian labour from Malaya and that upon the resumption of Indian assisted immigration in 1934 the Indian government limited such movement to 20,000 annually for that and the following year. In addition, it hoped that the prevailing wages would not be further depressed; in 1935 and 1937, following Sastri's report, it went a step further, and insisted, initially, on a partial and, finally, on a full restoration of the pre-Depression wages. Furthermore, it now recommended a basic level of earnings for each labourer per month, below which income would not drop, to ensure a living wage. Finally, it also suggested that the rise above this level should follow the state of the rubber market, in view of the rising cost of living which was estimated to be increasing by more than 10 per cent annually.[2]

By 1935 the Malayan government and the planting industry felt that the writing was already on the wall and sooner or later India would try to prohibit labour emigration. Moreover, in the estimation of many in the Labour Department and the planting industry, the country already had a large resident labour population.[3] Consequently, most of India's suggestions were rejected, with the exception of the restoration of wages to pre-Depression levels which the planters reluctantly agreed to in 1937. But in January 1938, without any consultation with the Indian government, some of the planters, apparently acting independently of their Association which was then against such a move, cut their wages by 5 cents per day in view of the reduced quantity of rubber that Malaya could export under the International Rubber Regulation Agreement of 1938. Two months later the planters' parent Association also followed the lead of its erstwhile errant mavericks, and from 1 May (1938) recommended similar wage reductions to all its members. Subsequently it went even further and suggested a further cut of 5 cents per day with effect from 1 July 1938.[4] In the meantime, however, the Central Indian Association of Malaya had been busy.

---

[1] *IICMM*, 9.2.1924; 12.5.1939.
[2] *IICMM*, 8.11.1935; *ARAGIBM*, 1936, pp. 8–9; *ARAGIBM*, 1937, pp. 5–6; *ARAGIBM*, 1939, p. 9; Parmer, 1960, pp. 74–7; *SSAR*, 1930, p. 678; *SSAR*, 1931, pp. 601–2 *et seq.*; *SSAR*, 1935, p. 678.
[3] Parmer, 1960, p. 75; *PAMC*, 1936, 6, app. A; *IICMM*, 18.6.1938.
[4] *PAMC*, 1938, 4, pp. 8 ff., addenda; 1938, 8, p. 12; *CIAMMM*, 2.4.1938; Parmer, 1960, pp. 75–6, 212–13.

Immigration: origins and trends

On learning of the decision of some of the planters to cut wages and strongly suspecting that the (United) Planters' Association of Malaya, despite its earlier opposition to the wage cut, was now itself on the point of officially recommending similar cuts to all its members, the Central Indian Association sent the following telegram to the central government of India, with copies to the Indian National Congress and the Minister of Labour, Madras, among others:

Reduction of Indian labour wages imminent. Main labour of Sastri delegation infructuous. Labour situation detrimental economic interests Indian labour. Suggest suspension assisted emigration. Respectfully urge firm determined stand safeguarding Indian rights.[1]

It followed this up with a letter to the Indian government:

The present evils are due to uncontrolled emigration from India. Unless India regains control of emigration in her hands it is impossible to maintain any high standard of living for our people or to maintain their wage level.[2]

Although the Indian government records are silent on this point, it is possible that the subsequent action of the government of India to halt assisted emigration to Malaya could have been based partly on the foregoing telegram (and letter). The European planters and press in Malaya and some of the Central Indian Association of Malaya leaders themselves, at least, certainly thought so.[3] Apparently basing himself on the above views, J. N. Parmer, in his recent study of colonial labour policy and administration in Malaya in the inter-war years, also comes to the same conclusion.[4] In fact, however, it was primarily the strong representations of the Agent of the government of India in Malaya, coupled with political expediency in the context of mounting nationalist Indian criticism—which would certainly have gained more ammunition through the Central Indian Association of Malaya's communications— and the dangers inherent in such agitation to the stability of the Raj in India that finally galvanized the government of India into action.

The Agent in Malaya worked in close co-operation with the local Indian leaders in matters affecting the well-being of the Indian community, particularly its labouring sector. Indeed, some of the memoranda and petitions of the Central Indian Association of Malaya on the need to improve the wages of labourers and the general position of the Indians in Malaya were reputedly inspired by the Agent. He felt convinced that a 'basic wage regulated on the cost of living budget' which

---

[1] *CIAMMM*, 2.4.1938; 30.4.1939; *PAMC*, 1938, 4, p. 2; *NAI:EP*, 1938, confidential file no. 44/38—L & O, serial nos. 1–133.   [2] *Ibid.*

[3] *PAMC*, 1938, 4, p. 2; *CIAMMM*, 30.4.1939; *MM*, 16.6.1938; personal interviews with Mr N. Raghavan and Mr A. K. Sen, former President and General Secretary of the Central Indian Association of Malaya, respectively.

[4] Parmer, 1960, p. 76.

would guarantee the Indian labourer 'a decent and reasonable standard of living' was an absolute necessity in Malaya.[1] To ensure this, he maintained, a change in the Indian government's emigration policy towards Malaya was imperative:

> ...It is not possible to maintain a proper wage level and increase the standard of living of the emigrants unless emigration is controlled and the policy of *laissez faire* abandoned. The present state of affairs practically makes us powerless unless the Government of India regain in their hands the initiative which they in a spirit of generosity have passed on to the Malayan authorities. For without it, we cannot say that our policy of emigration is purposeful...[2]

His fears appeared to be fully confirmed when, despite the 'assurance' of the Malayan government to him in February 1938 that there would be no reduction in the wages of Indian labourers, and in open defiance of his advice and the wishes of the government of India, the Planters' Association of Malaya decided to reduce the daily wages. In his opinion, this reduction was 'arbitrary, unjust' and 'definitely' imposed 'hardships' on the labourers. Furthermore, the planters were adamant and unlikely to change their attitude and so the intended reduction was 'not temporary or conditional'. He urged the government of India that a 'firm attitude' on its part was 'essential' in the matter, especially as there was already an estimated 60,000 surplus of Indian labour in Malaya and a further influx would only jeopardize the position of those already in the country.[3]

When the government of India learnt from its Agent of the impending wage cuts in Malaya it immediately got in touch with the Malayan authorities and asked them to confirm if the reports were true that the wages of Indian labourers were to be reduced. On being told that they were it seemed clear to the Indian government that it could not 'acquiesce in the reduction of wages', particularly as the reduction had been made 'without an investigation into the necessity for it, and without communication' to the Indian government of 'a detailed reason' for the measure.[4]

In the meantime, the Madras Provincial government, as the largest donor of emigrants and the most closely concerned of all the Indian states with the question of the Indian labourers in Malaya, had also been pressing for 'immediate action'. Irrespective of the outcome of the present correspondence between the Indian and Malayan governments and whatever reasons the Malayan authorities may eventually give for their proposed reduction of wages it wanted *all* unskilled labour emigration 'stopped or effectively controlled' forthwith.[5]

---

[1] *NAI:EP*, 1938, confidential file no. 44/38—L & O, serial nos. 1–133.
[2] *Ibid.*   [3] *Ibid.*   [4] *Ibid.*   [5] *Ibid.*

Finally, more important than any of the foregoing there was the political aspect. Public opinion in India had for long been clamouring for a display of authority by the government of India on the treatment of Indian labourers and others in Malaya and elsewhere. In the present circumstances this popular demand could not be safely ignored and it was feared that any weakness on the part of the government in its stand against the reduction of wages would arouse public opinion, thereby possibly further weakening the British government's position in India.[1] In this setting of mistrust and lack of co-operation on the part of the Malayan government, the government in India was forced to take 'drastic' action. Abroad and more especially at home it had been faced with unavoidable and increasingly embarrassing pressures. Accordingly, it placed a formal and complete ban on all assisted labour emigration to Malaya with effect from 15 June 1938, under its *Notification No. F–44/38—L & O, dated Simla, the 8th June 1938*, which reads as follows:

Whereas it appears that the number of Indian labourers now in Malaya States (*sic*) is in excess of the present requirements of industry and continuance of emigration to those States is therefore undesirable, the Central Government in exercise of the powers conferred by sub-section (i) of Section 13 of the Indian Immigration Act 1922 (VII of 1922) is pleased to prohibit with effect from the 15th June 1938, all persons from emigrating...to the Straits Settlements, the Federated Malay States of Perak, Selangor, Negri Sembilan, and Pahang to the Unfederated Malay States of Johore, Kedah, Kelantan (and) Trengganu ...for the purpose of unskilled work.[2]

The effect of the ban was that no labourer was allowed to receive assistance to come to Malaya from India to work for hire or to engage in agriculture. Wives and children could join husbands and parents but not to work. Furthermore, no labourer could leave for Malaya even at his own expense if it was known that he was going to work for someone else. Even Indian labourers who had worked in Malaya and had subsequently gone to India for a holiday and had remained there for more than two years were not allowed to return. *Mandurs* (overseers) and *kaṇakkapiḷḷais* (foremen) and railway porters were classified as skilled workers and allowed to return to Malaya. Similarly no restrictions were imposed on labourers emigrating on their own, provided they gave proof that they had independent means and had not been promised work by some private or government labour-hiring agency on arrival in

---

[1] *IICMM*, 24.6.1931; *NAI:EP*, 1935, confidential file no. 186/35—L & O; 1937, file no. 36–11/37—L & O B: 1938, confidential file no. 44/38—L & O, serial nos. 1–133; *PAMC*, 1938, 4, p. 6.

[2] *DLAI*, 1938, IV, 120; *NAI:EP*, 1938, confidential file no. 44/38—L & O, serial nos. 1–133.

Malaya. The Malayan government approached the government of India in 1939, 1940, 1941 and also after the Japanese occupation to allow resumption of assisted labour emigration to Malaya.[1] But this produced no tangible results and the ban still remains and is likely to remain.

NON-ASSISTED LABOUR IMMIGRATION[2]

The movement of non-assisted independent labourers into Malaya goes back to the beginnings of British rule in the Straits, but no separate statistical data are available for such arrivals until 1916.[3] However, this movement appears to have become significant only in the present century, particularly after the Great Depression.

We have noted above the heavy exodus of Indian labour to India during the Depression, the imposition thereafter by the Indian government of a quota of 20,000 emigrants per annum only, and finally, the limitation by the Malayan government of free passage only to those who were voluntary emigrants, *kangani* recruits or in possession of officially approved identification letters. Such letters became increasingly difficult to acquire as the Malayan government, at this time, often felt that there was already a sufficient, if not surplus, supply of Indian labour in the country. This view, however, was not shared by many of the planters. Unable to acquire the desired numbers through the official channels, such planters remitted the passage and other expenses of the potential immigrants, usually, as before, through their friends and relatives in Malaya. Then some of those who had been repatriated in the early 1920s and were unable to acquire free passage either through official channels or through employers, paid their own passage or got friends or relatives already in Malaya to send them the money. Finally,

---

[1] *PAMC*, 1946, 6, p. 5; *DLAI*, 1939, ii, 1010–11; Parmer, 1960, p. 77; Ton That Thien, 1963, pp. 229–38; personal interview with Mr N. Raghavan, former President of the Central Indian Association of Malaya; *IDM*, 30.4.1947, 1.12.1947; *PINC*, Proceedings of the Working Committee, held at Wardha, 3–13 August 1946; *H*, 12.8.1946.

[2] Labourers arriving in Malaya as 'passengers', that is fare-paying deck travellers, were officially designated as 'non-recruited' and 'non-assisted' independent labourers. For the present purposes this classification has been retained for convenience, but it is a misnomer. Less than 20 per cent of these labourers are estimated to have been genuinely non-recruited independent arrivals, the remainder being either formally or informally recruited or assisted by kith and kin and future employers or brought in by speculators who, like the Chinese brokers with their human cargoes, hoped to 'sell' them to the highest bidders among the prospective employers (see p. 55 above).

[3] The figures in Appendix 1 for the period prior to 1916 are merely a guess based on nineteenth and early twentieth century official estimates of between 'two-thirds' and '70 per cent' of the deck passengers arriving in Malaya from India being 'coolies' or belonging to the labouring classes.

8-2

some newcomers too were similarly aided.[1] As a result of such developments the annual average number of arrivals between 1934 and 1937 rose to 32,000, double that of the 1920s (Appendix 1).

This enhanced flow was short-lived, however, for the Indian government, having banned assisted-labour emigration, soon turned its attention to the so-called 'non-assisted' and 'independent' labour movement which it had so far exempted from the ban. It appears to have known that much of this latter kind of migration was in actuality an assisted movement. In any case it felt that such a flow of labour was 'bound to have repercussions on the conditions of labour prevailing in Malaya'. Consequently an amendment to the 1922 Emigration Act (*Indian Emigration (Amendment) Act, 1922 (XXI of 1938)*) was passed by the Legislative Assembly and became law on 22 September 1938. It gave the government of India power to control unassisted labour emigration as well, and almost immediately after the government began to take steps to prevent 'unskilled workers' from proceeding to Malaya 'even at their own expenses'. To put this into practice it began to examine every passenger leaving South India. Moreover it decided that '...all passengers proceeding overseas should be in possession of a certificate under the Indian Emigration Act from a local magistrate, or the Protector of Emigrants, to the effect that the passenger is not an "Emigrant" (that is a labourer) for the purpose of the Act'.[2] Shipping companies were informed of this and instructed not to issue tickets unless the passengers were in possession of these certificates.[3] There was a sharp fall in the movement of independent labour as well, caused first of all by the restrictive measures of the Indian government and finally by the lack of deck-space resulting from military requisition.[4] For example, compared with 50,128 independent labourers arriving in Malaya in 1937, there were only 2,166 and 500 such entries in 1939 and 1941 respectively (Appendix 1). Even with the restoration of normal travel conditions after the war there was no change in the position of this labour migration. Therefore, for all practical purposes, labour migration ceased with the Japanese invasion of Malaya. The cessation of the independent labour movement also marked the end of all types of Indian labour immigration into Malaya, as the other types had already ceased immigration prior to this. Henceforth, with the exception of those who managed to 'get round the regulations', the labourers

[1] *IICMM*, 15.8.1936; *NAM:COHC*, 1937, 149, 15.7.1937; *ARAGIBM*, 1936, p. 4; *ARAGINM*, 1938, p. 3; *MAREI*, 1936, pp. 5–6; *SSAR*, 1935, II, 771–2.
[2] *MAREI*, 1939, pp. 4–5; *NAI:EP*, 1938, file no. 149/38—L & O, serial nos. 1–24; 1939, file no. 48/–7/39—Os.
[3] *Ibid.*
[4] *MAREI*, 1940, p. 4; *MAREI*, 1941, p. 6.

entering Malaya were either those returning from India after a visit or dependants of labourers already in Malaya.

It is impossible to know exactly how many non-assisted independent labourers arrived in Malaya during the lifetime of the movement, because, as stated earlier, separate records of such immigration were only begun after 1916. However, on the basis of the statistical data for the period 1916–41 and of the nineteenth and early twentieth century official estimates which place about two-thirds of the deck-passengers in the independent labour category, it would appear that more than 815,000 such people had entered British Malaya up to the Japanese occupation. This figure represents about 30 per cent of all the labour and 20 per cent of the total Indian immigration into Malaya (table 2; Appendices 1, 3).

The independent labour immigrants appear to have been mainly boatmen, building and factory workers, cooks and other domestic servants, toddy tappers and washermen. Like the rest of the labour movement, adult South Indian males predominated in the non-assisted sector also; females, minors and North Indians forming less than 10 per cent of the total movement. However, within this structure there were two noteworthy differences *vis-à-vis* the rest of the labour migration. In the first place, although the exact figures are not available, it appears that the Malayali element from the Malabar coast was equal, if not greater than, its Tamil counterpart. In certain sectors, such as waterfront and construction labour, it was in fact the dominant element. Secondly, Muslims formed a significant portion of the labour; in some years they comprised more than 30 per cent of the total independent labour migration, although virtually absent in the rest of the labour stream.[1]

NON-LABOUR IMMIGRATION

Although non-labour immigrants were fewer in number—amounting to less than 35 per cent of the total migration stream (table 5a; Appendix 3)—they, particularly the commercial and professional class élite amongst them, exercised a monopoly of political, economic and social influence in the Indian community. The factors that stimulated the movement of the non-labour classes into Malaya have been discussed above.[2] The rest of the details can be given here. We could well begin with the commercial immigrants, who appear to have formed the vast majority of the non-labour migrants.

[1] *IICMM*, 23.3.1924; *MAREI*, 1938, p. 22; *MAREI*, 1939, p. 14; *SSAR*, 1891, p. 160; *SSAR*, 1916, p. 153; *CARWIEA*, 1935, p. 9.
[2] See pp. 67–74 above.

Immigration: origins and trends

Commercial immigrants

We have observed that although they had declined considerably in influence and numbers following their heyday in the pre-European era, some Indian traders were nevertheless still to be seen, at times in highly influential positions, at the Malay ports and courts at the time of Francis Light's landing at Penang. With the foundation of Penang some of this Indian mercantile class, presumably those less favourably placed in the existing locations in the Malay States, shifted their businesses to this port shortly after its occupation by Light. The first arrivals were almost entirely from Kedah and Perlis, but they were soon joined by others from such places as Prai, Selangor, Acheh, Borneo and, more significant for our purposes, India. We have it on the unimpeachable authority of Light himself that before the end of the 1780s 'Chooliar (Chulia, South Indian) vessels from Nagora (*sic*), Negapatam, Porto Novo and Pondicherry' had already become a common sight in the Penang waters. Links with the Bengal ports, too, appear to have been firmly established by this time; and, if not earlier, certainly by the early 1790s, Indian ships from the north-western ports of the Sub-continent were also beginning to call at Penang.[1]

These vessels from India brought not only goods but always appeared to be 'full of people, a great many of whom (were) merchants having each a small adventure'.[2] By the beginning of 1794 this movement of merchants and others to Penang from India had reached '1,300 to 2,000 men' per year.[3] In the meantime, the construction and occupation of the first shop-house to be built in Penang by an Indian trader, arriving at this port directly from India, had already taken place as early as 1788; the trader was a Bengali from Calcutta.[4] He was soon joined by others as the number of the commercial groups venturing to Malaya increased substantially in the subsequent years.

Although Northern Indians were among the first commercial immigrants into British Malaya from the Subcontinent and were then and subsequently far more significant amongst this class of immigrants than any of the foregoing, they were nevertheless still a minority. South Indians also made up the majority of the commercial immigrants. The South Indians were mainly Malabar and Coromandel coast Muslims and Chettiar Hindus of the Puddukkottai and Ramnad districts—the *Cettinaatu*—and the city of Madras (fig. 9). Some of the Chettiars in Malaya were agents of ancient trading and financial houses and corpora-

[1] *SSFR*, 1 (1769–95), 1.7.1787; 14.9.1787; 2 (1786–7), 13.12.1786; 22.1.1787; 3 (1788–9), 25.8.1788; 10.4.1789; 4 (1790–1), 5.1.1791; 5 (1792–3), 5.4.1793.
[2] *SSFR*, 5 (1792–3), 5.4.1793.   [3] *SSFR*, 6 (1794), 1.8.1794.
[4] *SSFR*, 3 (1788–9), 10.4.1789.

tions with headquarters in the Madras province. These corporations maintained Nakarattaar (Chettiar) 'lodges' at almost all main sea-ports of the country for the use of their representatives in particular and the Chettiar community in general. Here they not only sheltered in between journeys to and from their homeland and overseas but also gathered the up-to-date intelligence on the situation in Southeast Asia, the traditional and principal area of their overseas enterprise.[1]

The South Indian Muslims, too, maintained their own houses, although not on the same scale as the Chettiars. Such facilities existed at all the main Coromandel coast ports handling passenger traffic between South India and the Straits, namely Nagore, Negapatam, Madras, Karikal, Pondicherry, Cuddalore and Porto Novo.[2]

Until the early years of the present century the Northern Indian[3] commercial immigrants consisted almost wholly of Bengalis, Parsis and Gujaratis. But with increasing Sindhi and Sikh immigration in the ensuing years the Gujaratis, Parsis and Bengalis were superseded by these newcomers, together with a few Marwaris, both numerically and gradually commercially. The Sikh commercial immigrants were mainly from and around the Rawalpindi, Lahore, Ludhiana, Jullundur and Amritsar urban centres of the Punjab. While the majority of them arrived in Malaya directly from India, substantial numbers also came from such places as Rangoon and Bangkok, where they had first settled prior to moving to Malaya. Like the Sikhs, the Sindhis and Gujaratis were also principally from areas in and around urban centres of their respective provinces, such as Karachi and Hyderabad in the case of the Sindhis and Ahmedabad and Surat in the case of the Gujaratis. The vast majority of the Sindhi and Gujarati immigrants appear to have arrived in Malaya either directly from their home provinces or from the city of Bombay, where they had first settled prior to venturing to the Straits.

The Parsis and Marwaris were almost wholly from the city of Bombay and the princely state of Bikaner, respectively, while the Bengalis were principally from the Calcutta, Dacca, Chittagong and Midnapore areas of their home province. There were also a few 'U.P. wallas' (natives of

[1] Madras, 1930, I, 29–30; III, 1101–92, 1216; V. Krishnan, *Indigenous banking in South India* (Bombay, 1959), pp. 29–192; Moothedan, 1932, pp. 40–5; Krishnan, 1936, p. 24; personal interview with officials of the Chettiar Chamber of Commerce, Singapore.

[2] Personal interview with officials of the Indian Chamber of Commerce, Singapore.

[3] The following description of the North Indian commercial immigrants in Malaya is based on the oral testimonies of a number of Bengalis, Parsis, Sindhis, Punjabis, Gujaratis, Marwaris and 'U.P. wallas' (Hindu and other inhabitants of the United Province (Uttar Pradesh)) interviewed by the writer in Malaya and India in 1962 and 1966.

the United Provinces or Uttar Pradesh) amongst the North Indian commercial immigrants. In contrast to the foregoing groups they appeared to have been drawn from a somewhat wider area within their native state, with Gorakpur district and the rural areas round Benares, such as Azamgarh and Ramnagar, and those round Lucknow, Allahabad, Sultanpur, Rae Banchi and Fyzabad being the main contributors.

Nowadays the Northern Indian travelling by sea between Malaya and the Indian subcontinent may use Bombay, Karachi, Calcutta or Madras as his port of embarkation or disembarkation as the case may be. Until the outbreak of World War II, however, Calcutta, and to a much lesser extent Madras, was almost the sole point of entry and departure of such migrants. The bulk of the passenger shipping plying between India and Southeast Asia was concentrated at these ports and Negapatam. It was far cheaper and more convenient, even for those from the coast of northwestern India to make the journey overland by train and take a ship at the Bay of Bengal end than attempt a passage by a Straits-bound steamer from Europe, virtually the only other alternative to the Bay of Bengal shipping.

The Northern Indians also maintained organizations and facilities at Calcutta for the benefit of the migrants, along similar lines and with the same functions as those run by their South Indian counterparts. These *sewa* or sort of 'migrants' aid' or mutual benefit associations usually formed part and parcel of general *gurdwaras*, dharmasalas and *musafirkhanas*, catering for Sikh, Hindu and Muslim needs respectively. In turn, these institutions were considerably aided and improved by donations from the more successful among the migrants. The number of such *sewa* institutions maintained by each community depended very largely on the volume of migration traffic involved. For example, while the Sikhs and Sindhis maintained two *gurdwaras* and two dharamsalas, respectively, the Bikanerwallas (Marwaris) were content with one such institution. Although nowadays, with migration limited only to very highly qualified or wealthy individuals, these facilities are comparatively little used and then almost completely by the poorer sections of the migrant communities visiting or returning permanently to India, in the past they were made use of by almost all of the North Indian migrants setting out on their first trip to Malaya.

Although North Indians were among the first commercial immigrants into British Malaya,[1] their movement in substantial numbers only really began with the advent of Sindhis and Sikhs in significant numbers from about the late 1920s, and especially in the years before and after World War II. But then, just when this movement appeared to be gaining

[1] See p. 118 above.

momentum, and even looked like overtaking its South Indian counter-part in numerical terms, it was cut short by the immigration restrictions introduced by the Malayan government in 1953 and 1959 and thereby lost whatever chance it had of equalling the numbers of its Southern cognate.

The vast majority of the commercial immigrants were salesmen, pedlars, petty entrepreneurs, traders and shopkeepers, street-side vendors, medicine-men, stall-holders and such like. Merchants, financiers and contractors of substantial means—principally Chettiars and Marakkayar Muslims of the Madras coast and Parsis, Sindhis and Sikhs—were a tiny minority, estimated at less than a fifth of the total commercial movement entering Malaya. But despite the great disparity in capital assets amongst the different categories of commercial immi-grants the groups, as a whole, had at least two notable features in common. In the first place, like their labour-migrant countrymen they were predominantly adult males, there being little family movement until the 1930s. Secondly, free immigrants in every sense of the word, generally of higher caste than those who had come as labourers, these commercial immigrants usually came on their own or family resources, invariably with some capital, however small, and experience in the kind of trade they sought to practise. More accustomed to travel, and more resourceful, aggressive and ambitious, the more successful amongst them, in conjunction with others like them from such classes as the professional groups, gradually assumed the role of a *petite bourgeoisie* among the Indian community of Malaya.

No separate worthwhile records relating to commercial immigrants have been kept. The various figures cited above are estimates only, derived through calculations based on interviews and the data available for the other types of migrants. In the same way, it is estimated that these commercial immigrants formed some three-quarters of the non-labour passenger arrivals in Malaya. With the exception of occasional fluctuations and the total cessation of the movement during the Japanese occupation the annual movement of commercial immigrants into Malaya increased substantially from the early years of the present century. This was particularly so in the late 1930s and the early post-war years. Far more economically minded than their labouring country-men, the annual movement of the commercial immigrants was influenced to a considerable extent not only by conditions in Malaya but also by those in India. For instance, there was a big influx of these immigrants, many of them refugees, in 1947–8, 1951 and 1953. They followed, respectively, the political unrest in the Indian subcontinent just before and after its partition into India and Pakistan, the trade boom generated by the war in Korea and the Malayan government's notification to restrict immigration in general with effect from 1 August 1953. The *Straits Times*, a Singapore daily, in discussing the increased movement of commercial immigrants in 1948, described the arrival of Northern Indians alone as 'an invasion':

...Hundreds of Sindhis have arrived in Singapore in the last few months... Singapore Sindhi merchants who are concentrated in High Street set up an organisation early this year to receive and disperse the new arrivals.

Many have been helped to set up their own businesses while others have been absorbed...in existing Sindhi shops...New Sindhi textile shops have sprung up in Changi, Nee Soon, R.A.F. Seletar, Naval Base, Middle Road, Arab Street, and in the centre of the town...

Besides Sindhis, Sikhs have also been arriving in large numbers, some of these Sikhs, well established businessmen in Bangkok, have opened up branches in Singapore...Other Sikhs are from West Punjab.[1]

Although it was not as spectacular and in any case did not get the same publicity as the Northern Indians, the movement of South Indians at this time was about equally significant in terms of numbers. However, both these movements were drastically reduced with the 1953 immigration restrictions and even more so with the 1959 amendment of the above.[2] Fresh immigration of the commercial classes became limited almost entirely to a few highly paid executives and wealthy capitalists and the wives and children (if the latter were below twelve years of age) of such people or of those already in Malaya (Appendix 3; figs. 6, 7).

Professional and clerical immigrants and those of other backgrounds

Unlike their commercial counterparts, some of those Indians who came to Malaya to join government departments or private commercial and other undertakings in such roles as skilled workmen, priests, clerks, administrators, technicians, teachers and doctors, were recruited in India and assisted to migrate by their employers. This was generally the case for clerks working in Indian firms.[3] From time to time the government also obtained some of its staff through secondment or recruitment in India.[4] The former practice, however, virtually ceased with the transfer of control of the Straits Settlements from the India to the Colonial Office in 1867. The latter method of staff recruitment continued. Even a few years ago the government, faced with an acute shortage of such people following the rapid expansion of services and the departure of

---

[1] *ST*, 6.12.1948.　　　　　　　　[2] See pp. 149–51 below.
[3] *MAREI*, 1934, p. 11; *FMAR*, 1955, p. 18; personal interview with officials of the Indian Chamber of Commerce, Singapore.
[4] *NAI:RAD(S)P*, March 1884, proc. 8–27; *SSSF*, 1892, 950/92; personal interview with Mr R. Thambipillay, retired schoolmaster, Victoria Institution, Kuala Lumpur.

many of its British officers under the Malayanization of the services policy, recruited about a hundred Indian doctors and highly qualified teachers on three to five year contracts. But generally, most of these immigrants (almost all English-speaking) either came on their own or, more usually, were sent for by relatives or friends already in Malaya, who possessed the necessary money.

The majority of these immigrants also came from South India. Most prominent among them were Malayalis, especially those from the Vallam sector of Kerala, and, to a lesser extent, Tamils. Perhaps it should be pointed out that the Tamils had a much larger role in this movement until the 1920s. Thenceforth, however, with the great influx of Malayali labour, particularly waterfront, building and factory workers, the number of English-speaking Malayali immigrants also increased proportionately. They were found to be useful in dealing not only with their own countrymen but also with the Tamils, as nearly all of them spoke Tamil as well. Once they had established a bridgehead in Malaya, they rapidly extended their field of endeavour; in addition to monopolizing almost the whole of the civilian clerical and junior officer grades of the British War Department's installations in Malaya by the 1930s, they had very largely succeeded in supplanting the Ceylon and Madras Tamil conductors, clerks and assistants on the European-owned rubber, oil palm and other plantations.[1] They consolidated their position even further after the war following a further expansion of military installations and the arrival of more Malayalis. It is possible that in the ensuing years they would have become a significant force in the other services too if it had not been for the 1953 and 1959 immigration restrictions of the Malayan government. These limited fresh entry of such immigrants to those with very high professional qualifications.

The few Northern Indians amongst the English-speaking immigrants were principally Bengalis, mainly from the Calcutta and Dacca areas, and Punjabis from approximately the same districts of the Punjab as their fellow-countrymen who came to join the ranks of the armed services, the police, the prison service and other similar organizations.[2]

In contrast to the foregoing migration types, the Indians entering Malaya to join the security forces were almost all Northern Indians. Amongst them the Sikhs were the most prominent group, although such other notable elements as Pathans, Punjabi Hindus and Muslims, Rajputs and Mahrattas—all members of the much publicized 'martial races of India'—were also present.

[1] Personal interviews with officials of the National Union of Plantation Workers and the All-Malayan Estates Staff Union, Petaling Jaya, Malaya.
[2] See p. 124 below.

Immigration: origins and trends

The Sikhs were almost all from the Mahja, Malwa and Dhoaba areas of the Punjab (fig. 12b). The proportion of immigrants from each of these areas in the total Sikh movement of this type is uncertain, but on the basis of inferential evidence in Malayan government records, sample surveys and interviews with the older members of the Sikh community, it is estimated that the Mahja and Malwa areas were approximately equally represented with about 35 per cent of the total immigrants each; about 20 per cent came from the Dhoaba region.

These Sikh migrants found their way to Malaya mainly through three channels. We have seen above[1] that the first Sikh migrants to enter Malaya were those recruited by Captain Speedy of Perak. We also know that some of these pioneer recruits were subsequently drafted into the government service to form the nucleus of the police and para-military forces of that state, following its passing under British control. Furthermore, the government, to meet its growing needs for Sikh recruits for the security forces, now began to recruit Sikhs in India on its own. This was done for some time through the Indian government but later on through its own officers, usually Sikh non-commissioned officers on furlough in India.[2] The common practice of recruitment of Sikhs, however, was to enlist them in Malaya, because, as the word spread of the opportunity in Malaya, more and more Sikhs were coming into the country on their own[3] or, more correctly, were being brought along by their relations and friends, returning from a visit to India, or were in other ways assisted by such people to reach Malaya.[4] Not all such immigrants were absorbed by the government and quasi-government departments. At times, for every candidate accepted another was rejected, partly because only a limited number were needed in any one year and partly because of strict and high physical requirements. Those who failed in their bid for the cherished government *pukka nawkris* either drifted, occasionally out of the country to such places as Sumatra and Thailand or, more usually, into the private sector of the Malayan economy to work as caretakers, watchmen, bullock-cart drivers, dairy-keepers and mining labourers.[5]

Although some of them did send for their families subsequently, few

[1] See p. 73 above.
[2] *NAI:EP*, Dec. 1904, secret memorandum by Swettenham dated 12 Aug. 1904; *MSGAR*, 1913, p. 1.
[3] *MSGAR*, 1899, p. 1; *MSGAR*, 1900, p. 5; *SSG*, 1882, p. 365; *JAR*, 1926, p. 27.
[4] Personal interview with the late Jemadar Bishen Singh of the Federated Malay States Police Force; *C.O.273*, 291 (1903), 12.8.1902.
[5] *MSGAR*, 1908, p. 2; *MSGAR*, 1909, p. 1; *FMSPAR*, 1909, p. 1; *JAR*, 1927, p. 27; *JAR*, 1931, p. 31; *NAI:EP*, Dec. 1904, secret memorandum by Swettenham dated 12 Aug. 1904; Oct. 1915, secret file no. 154, serial no. 1; *MCECLFMS*, pp. 19 *et seq.*

Types of migrants

Sikh immigrants arrived in Malaya with families until after World War II. But whether accompanied by families or not, with the exception of a tiny minority that used Madras, almost all the Sikhs arriving in Malaya used the port of Calcutta, and the *gurdwara sewa* facilities there.

The total number of these Sikh immigrants into Malaya is unknown. Judging from the number of candidates offering themselves for recruitment into the country's military and police forces in certain years, it would appear that the movement was not large and at the most hardly more than a couple of thousand arrivals in any one year; generally it was less than this.[1] This is not entirely surprising.

The vast majority of these Sikh migrants were illiterate and had little to offer beyond their martial bearing, physical strength and willingness to be trained.

Employment in the government's security forces, the goal of almost all the early Sikh immigrants, was limited. Moreover, even within this, an important avenue of employment was lost in 1919 with the disbanding of the Malay States Guides, a predominantly Sikh regiment of about 700 men, formed in 1896.[2]

More important, a potential Sikh migrant making his own way, say to Southeast Asia or southern Africa, in the pre-World War II period, needed to have about Rs. 40–60 in cash—the approximate cost of travel expenses between the Punjab and these areas. Few Sikh potential migrants had ready cash of this 'magnitude'. In most cases their only hope of getting this was to wait for some more fortunate and sympathetic relative or friend to make the trip, earn sufficient money and send them the necessary fare for the passage. Needless to say this was a slow process. Another possible means of raising the fare was to mortgage the family plot of land—that is if they still had it—to the local *baniya* or *shahukar*. This most Sikhs were reluctant to do; the *raison d'être* for emigration and the enduring of all the imaginary and real *dhuks* of *pardesi* travel, was to make sufficient *paisa* to either buy a few *bighas* of *zamin* or redeem the already mortgaged family plot. In any case, those still in possession of their plots of land were not the ones most likely to migrate.[3]

Moreover, Malaya had to compete with other equally, if not more, desirable areas of Sikh immigration. For example, if they were able to

---

[1] *JAR*, 1927, p. 27; *JAR*, 1930, p. 33; *FMSAR*, 1900, p. 5; *FMSAR*, 1902, p. 15; *MSGAR*, 1909, p. 1.

[2] *MPM*, I (1928), 17–23; II (1929), 382; *MSGAR*, 1902, p. 15; *OGMSG*, pp. 1 ff.; *C.O.273*, 283 (1902), 1.5.1902; 291 (1903), 12.8.1902.

[3] Personal interviews with Sardar Balwant Singh, Secretary of the Barra Singh Sanghat Gurdwara, Calcutta, and the late Jemadar Bishen Singh of the Federated Malay States Police Force; Punjab, 1930, I, 129–45, 163–5, 377; United Kingdom, 1927–8, VIII, 622–78.

raise the money, it was not Malaya but 'Miriken' (America) or 'Kaneida' (Canada)—the lands of fabulous wealth in their estimation—that were the first choice of many Sikh emigrants. This fascination of America and Canada persisted even after the discriminatory restrictions imposed on their entry and employment there by the American and Canadian governments from the beginning of the second decade of the present century. This was illustrated by the 'Komagata Maru' incident when some 380 Sikh migrants, denied entry into the country by Canadian law, tried to land—albeit unsuccessfully—at Vancouver in 1914.[1]

Also, with the vast expansion of the armed forces in India and the increasing emphasis by its government on recruiting from the so-called martial races of the country, there was considerable scope for Sikhs for employment in India itself.[2]

Finally, there was a change for the worse in the British Indian government's attitude towards Sikh emigration in general. Up to the turn of the century it had not discouraged Sikh emigration. Indeed, it had itself recruited Sikhs for security duties on behalf of the Malayan and other governments. But about this time its attitude began to change. In the first place, it stopped recruiting for other governments. Henceforth it also began to frown upon recruitment by other means as well.[3] At times it virtually prohibited fresh emigration altogether.[4] The reasons for this change in policy are unclear, but four possibilities could be suggested.

First, that the government needed Sikhs for its own armed forces and that the comparatively better terms offered by colonial and other governments were leading to a Sikh 'brawn drain'. Secondly, there was the danger of Sikh emigrants, once abroad, enlisting in foreign armies, which could one day conceivably be opposing their British counterparts.[5] Thirdly, many Sikh emigrants were a constant source of administrative trouble and political embarrassment to their home government. For example, a number of Sikh emigrants were entering or trying to enter 'white' countries such as South Africa, Canada, the United States and

---

[1] *NAI:EP*, Nov. 1914, confidential A proc. 97–177; March 1915, confidential A proc. 1–13; personal interview with Sardar Balwant Singh, Secretary of the Barra Singh Sanghat Gurdwara, Calcutta; United Kingdom, 1927–8, viii, 629–30; 'Emigrant', 1924, pp. 75–8; Kondapi, 1951, pp. 207–11.

[2] *FMSAR*, 1915, p. 1; *FMSAR*, 1918, pp. 8–11; *SSAR*, 1897, p. 61; *HCIOL*, Curzon to Hamilton, 4 Sept. 1902.

[3] *HCIOL*, Curzon to Hamilton, 24 Sept. 1902; *NAI:EP*, May 1922, file no. 40/22, B proc. 12–14; *SSAR*, 1897, p. 61.

[4] *NAI:EP*, Nov. 1915, confidential A proc. 1–2; Jan. 1918, confidential A proc. 18.

[5] *C.O.273*, 291 (1903), 12.8.1902; Colonial Office, minute no. 33335; *NAI:EP*, May 1922, file no. 40/22, B proc. 12–14.

Australia, which were far from anxious to have them. As British subjects they expected and demanded the British government to support their case on the same basis as it would have done, say, for fellow citizens of the United Kingdom.[1]

This position also applied to the extra-territorial agreements that Britain had with some countries, as for instance Thailand and China. One of the reasons for these agreements was the protection of the interests of the British people there. The entry of substantial numbers of Indians, predominantly Sikhs and other Punjabis and Pathans, into such countries as Thailand and their insistence on equal treatment threatened to queer the pitch of extra-territorial privileges that in theory applied to all British citizens, but in practice were apparently extended to whites only.[2]

These developments created a serious problem for the British Indian government. Political expediency, in the context of the Indian Nationalist movement and the security of British interests in India, demanded that the myth of equal rights, as between Indians and the people of the United Kingdom, be maintained; but at the same time, especially in view of the ambivalent position of the Indian government within the British Empire, the wishes and sentiments of white settlers and the foreign governments could not be lightly or safely ignored. Maintenance of an ambivalent posture in this matter was becoming increasingly difficult. Finally, Sikh emigrants, particularly those in the United States, Canada and Southeast Asia, were becoming an increasingly dangerous source of supply for arms, men and money to the Indian revolutionary movement, which was dedicated to the overthrowing of the Raj by force of arms.[3]

Needless to say, this dampening of enthusiasm for Sikh emigration in general on the part of the British Indian government would to some extent also have inhibited their movement to Malaya. But, though no more than one or two thousand in any one year, these Sikh immigrants nevertheless represented the major stream, numerically, of all Sikh immigrants until the 1930s. Thereafter, with the increasing numbers of other Sikh immigrants and changes in employment opportunities in the country, the proportion of these Sikhs in the total Sikh migration to Malaya appears to have declined gradually.

There was no such movement between Malaya and India during the

[1] *NAI:EP*, May 1913, confidential file no. 3, serial nos. 17–18; United Kingdom, 1927–8, VIII, 630–1; One of them, *The Sikh at home and abroad* (Vancouver, 1917), pp 3 ff.; 'Emigrant', 1924, pp. 76–7.
[2] *F.O.* 69/145, 21.1.1891, 4.3.1891; 69/168, 17.8.1895; *F.O.* 17/1268, 20.6.1895.
[3] *NAI:EP*, Nov. 1914, confidential A proc. 97–177; *C.O.273*, 408 (1914), 24.12.1914; 429 (1915), 10.8.1915; Colonial Office, minute no. 38661.

Japanese occupation. After the war this immigration was resumed, but it did not last long. First, the policy of the British Malayan government *vis-à-vis* the employment of Sikh immigrants in the government forces had undergone a drastic change since the war, in so far as it now no longer appeared keen to have such recruits. The reasons for this virtual *volte face* are not wholly clear, but the consensus of opinion of those interviewed on this topic and the little literary evidence that is available appears to be that it was the result of the following developments:

Up to the war, Sikhs arriving in Malaya from India were moving from one British area to another. The emergence of an independent India ended this and it meant that henceforth Malaya, still a British colony, would have to deal with a foreign Indian government, which in any case did not appear at all sympathetic to its citizens emigrating for the purpose of taking up such low-income jobs as labourers, policemen, watchmen and so on.[1] Then there was the fact that many Sikhs, including members of the British Malayan police force, had espoused the cause of the wartime anti-British Indian National Army, and with such affiliations were considered politically tainted and a security risk.

Moreover some of them were either known or suspected of collaborating with the Japanese and of ill-treating British prisoners-of-war. More important, there was the intensification after the war of the government's policy, which appears to have begun in the 1920s,[2] of limiting government employment to locally domiciled people, as far as possible. Greater implementation of this was now possible as with the rapid growth and increasing stabilization of the country's population, large numbers of locally domiciled people were available for government jobs. In any case, if some special para-military recruits were required and could not be acquired locally, they could be more conveniently drawn from the ranks of the Gurkhas, whose loyalty was above reproach and with whose government Britain still had a treaty allowing it to recruit its citizens for British military needs. Some Gurkhas were in fact recruited for services in Singapore, as a 'Special Force' or 'Reserve Unit', that is, as an anti-riot squad.

Secondly, employment in the private sector also became increasingly difficult for new Sikh immigrants after the war. Perhaps partly because of the government's lead and partly owing to the increasing availability of local Malay-speaking candidates, commercial organizations also began to limit their recruitment largely to locally domiciled elements. This became increasingly true after 1948, when, at the outbreak of an armed

[1] Ton That Thien, 1963, pp. 233–5; *ST*, 26.4.1949, 27.4.1949.
[2] *FMSAR*, 1924, p. 35.

128

Communist revolt, a number of Sikh policemen with sufficient years of service to exercise their pension rights began leaving the government service for the comparatively safe commercial sector.

Finally, there was the general immigration restriction by the Malayan government in 1953. This was the *coup-de-grâce*, for it completely stopped the entry of potential policemen and other immigrants who could be employed in comparable jobs.

The pattern and characteristics of the immigration of Pathans, principally from the Hazara and Mardhana areas of the North West Frontier Province, and the Punjabi Muslims and Hindus, from about the same areas as their Sikh cognates, were more or less identical with those of the Sikhs. In terms of employment in the Malayan forces they were, however, not as fortunate, for it was not long after their first arrival in Malaya with Captain Speedy that they began to acquire the reputation of being inferior to the Sikhs in terms of general work and discipline. Consequently from as early as the 1890s they began actively to be replaced by Sikhs.[1] The final blow to this movement too was the change in the Malayan immigration policy in the 1950s.

The comparatively small numbers of Rajputs—almost wholly from those areas of Rajputana adjoining the Punjab—and Mahrattas—mainly from the Belgaum, Bombay State Agency and the villages in the neighbourhood of the city of Bombay—were almost all associated with such employment as watchmen, caretakers and guards in commercial organizations. The pattern and characteristics of their movement were very similar to that of their other Northern neighbours; their movement too ceased with the change in the Malayan immigration policy in the post-war years.

Garrison and camp-follower immigrants

Almost certainly the first person from Light's party to go ashore at Penang on 17 July 1786 was an Indian lascar, of the garrison-elect. Throughout the period of Indian government control of Malaya (1786–1867) and occasionally thereafter, the military garrison of the country was wholly or partly drawn from units of the regular British Indian army. Occasionally, as in the 1820s, volunteer corps or militia were also raised in India to supplement the regular army units in Malaya. The provenance of the military forces varied, but until the change from Indian to Colonial Office control, the Indian units of the Malayan garrison were drawn first from Bengal (until 1827) and thereafter from Madras. Subsequent to the transfer, the Indian elements in the garrison

---

[1] *C.O.273*, 198 (1894), 4.12.1894; personal interview with Mufti Nisar Ahmad Khan Sahib, former Indian supernumerary officer, Malayan police force.

appear to have come more from the ranks of such Northerners as Punjabis and Pathans.[1]

Until about the middle of the nineteenth century, in addition to their normal duties, it was the accepted form and practice for the employees of the Company, including the garrison, to engage in business activities, farming and other commercial enterprise in order to supplement the Company's wages. Consequently, Indian sepoys, and probably some lascars too, were among the first to take up plots of land for commercial farming. They appear also to have engaged in moneylending, with funds saved from their wages, and also in the financing of enterprise in the bazaar:

...Every female slave brought to market is purchased by them at price hitherto unknown to the natives who cannot enter into a competition and are either kept for their use or exposed to prostitution for their emolument. They are the money-lenders of the settlement and by an influence from mutual support they are enable (*sic*) to recover when due the most nefarious engagements. They live in a style equal to the more opulent inhabitants expending large sums on their weddings and feasts and annually remitting to their friends at Bengal...[2]

Apparently these undertakings were so profitable that by the beginning of 1791 we find Light writing to his superiors in Calcutta, asking them to send him a replacement for the two companies of sepoys in Penang, as these were anxious to become 'riotts' (*sic*) in Penang 'rather than return to Bengal'.[3] This was complied with, and on the arrival of the replacements two months later the existing two companies were demobilized.[4] Similarly the militia that was raised in Bengal in 1820 and brought over to Penang was also subsequently disbanded in Penang. There is no record of their having returned home after their demobilization.[5] Presumably they also assumed the role of civilian immigrants. There were also cases of some soldiers, who had previously been members of the garrison forces, returning to Malaya once they had obtained their discharge in India.[6]

In addition to the foregoing accretions to the general migration stream, there were the *chaiwallas*, grooms, dhobis and other similar camp-followers of the garrison. This 'bazaar contingent', as the camp-

---

[1] *SSFR*, 1 (1769–95), 1.9.1787; 2 (1786–7), 2.3.1786; 20.3.1786; 154 (1827), 8.6.1827; 165 (1826–7), 10.6.1827; 185 (1805–30), 12.11.1805; 17.1.1807; personal interview with Mufti Nisar Ahmad Khan Sahib, former Indian supernumerary officer, Malayan police force; *JIA*, IV (1850), 117, 629.
[2] *SSFR*, 6 (1794), 1.8.1794.   [3] *SSFR*, 4 (1790–1), 5.1.1791.
[4] *SSFR*, 4 (1790–1), 20.4.1791.   [5] *JIA*, IV (1850), 117.
[6] Personal interview with Mufti Nisar Ahmad Khan Sahib, former Indian supernumerary officer, Malayan police force.

follower population was at times called, appears on occasions to have matched the regular soldiers in numbers, at least in the early days. Generally, however, they were proportionately far less significant.[1] Judging from post-World War II experience, some of these camp-follower immigrants would presumably have detached themselves from the garrison entourage and entered the world of their non-military immigrant counterparts.

Farmer immigration

This type of Indian immigration appears to date from 9 February 1790, when Francis Light, returning to Penang from Calcutta, brought with him some 'Bengal farmers', as part of his campaign to develop the agricultural resources of the island. Each one of these farmers was given four acres of land and a loan to tide him over his first year of pioneering.[2] The subsequent progress of these farmers is unknown, as they cease to feature in the records of the ensuing years, but a similar attempt a century later by Dennis, the Superintendent of Lower Perak, to settle twenty-four Tamil families was not very successful. It appears this was due largely to lack of support from the central Malayan authorities and the attraction of cash wages on adjoining plantations and in government projects.[3]

These are the only two known instances of government-sponsored, Indian farmer immigration.[4] There may well have been others too, but by the early 1900s the government appears to have definitely decided against any government sponsorship of Indian farmer immigration.[5] Henceforth the few immigrants of this type who did enter Malaya apparently came of their own initiative or were assisted by their relatives and friends already in the country. Although no conclusive evidence is available, some such types may also have arrived in the country prior to the early 1900s.

Apart from the Tamils and Bengalis, the farmer immigrants also included Hindu *doodwallas* or dairy-keepers from the Bihar and Uttar Pradesh areas of the Ganges valley. In fact, together with some Sikhs, they appear to have been almost the sole farmer immigrants from Northern India during the present century. No statistics are available

[1] *SSFR*, 1 (1769–95), 1.9.1787; 2 (1786–7), 2.3.1786; 20.3.1786; 154 (1827), 8.6.1827; 165 (1826–7), 10.6.1827.
[2] *SSFR*, 4 (1790–1), 24.3.1790.
[3] *SSSF*, 1886, 970/86; *SSAR*, 1890, p. 287; *PLCSS*, 1893, paper no. 6, Superintendent, Lower Perak, to Secretary to Government, Perak, 10 October, 1892.
[4] There was an Indian farm settlement at Kajang, Selangor, in 1885, but it is unknown if these settlers originally came into Malaya as labourers, who subsequently took up farming, or as farmers (*SAR*, 1886, pp. 209–10).
[5] *MMECSS*, 6.7.1896; 7.7.1896; *C.O.273*, 217 (1896), 1.9.1896; 324 (1906), 3.1.1906.

but it is possible that their numbers may also have increased in proportion to the Northern commercial immigrants during the late 1930s and
after the Japanese occupation until the stream was dammed by the
Malayan immigration restrictions of the 1950s.

Indian convicts[1]

When Lord Cornwallis arrived in India in 1786 to take up his post as
Governor-General, he found that inefficiency, corruption and cruelty,
including the forfeiture of limbs, were common features of indigenous
criminal law courts. Quite apart from various other considerations, he
saw that an effective deterrent was urgently needed to halt the depredations of such desperadoes as the dacoits. At the same time this deterrent
had to be compatible with his sense of justice based on English law.

Transportation to the Company's possessions in the East, an idea
which had been gaining ground at about this time amongst the resident
Europeans, appeared to be just the solution needed. Accordingly, in
1788 the Governor-General in Council recommended that persons sentenced to life, seven years' imprisonment or the forfeiture of their limbs
should henceforth be transported to Penang or some similar place.[2]

By this time the first effort to get Indian convicts to Penang had
already been made. In June 1787 an enterprising Calcutta resident
named Crucifix suggested that Penang might be 'a convenient dumping
ground' for convicts who, he considered, should be given to him for a
term of some years and made to work for his private profit on the land.
But this was not accepted by the government.[3] The reasons for the
refusal are unstated but were in all probability connected more with the
timing and the terms of the offer than concern over the principle of
transportation, as this mode of punishment was already in vogue in
England. This assumption appears to be borne out by the fact that in
January 1789—by which time transportation to Penang as a form of
punishment had been finally decided upon—the Governor-General gave
permission to one Mr Julius Griffith to transport twenty dacoits from
Bengal to Penang. He could employ them there for a period of three
years for his own profit with certain conditions relating to the treatment.[4]

---

[1] Besides the Indians, some Ceylonese, Chinese and European convicts were also
transported to the Straits Settlements during the nineteenth century. However,
compared with the Indians, their numbers were small; Indians generally formed
more than 85 per cent of the total transmarine convict population of the Colony
during its tenure as a penal station. Following agitation by the resident European
population, transportation of European, Chinese and Ceylonese convicts ceased in
1854, 1856 and 1873 respectively (*SSR*, S23, 1856, items, 39, 189; *IO:JP*, proc.
13–15 of 20.10.1854; *SSAR*, 1859–60, pp. 197–206; *C.O.273*, 66, 1873, 22.4.1873).
[2] (N.) Majumdar, 1960, pp. 235–333.   [3] Aspinall, 1931, p. 203.
[4] *SSFR*, 4 (1789–91), 30.1.1789; (N.) Majumdar, 1960, p. 272; Aspinall, 1931, p. 203.

However, whether Julius Griffith did in fact bring these convicts to Penang is unknown, the first verifiable convict entry into Penang was that of two men, named Eyeno Deen Sheikdar and Mohamed Heiant, sent by the Governor-General in March 1790. Both these convicts were under sentence of 'perpetual confinement' and were to be maintained in Penang at the expense of the island's government. To offset some of this expenditure the Penang authorities were free to employ the convicts in any manner they thought proper.[1]

Before many convicts had been sent to Penang, however, the place of transportation for Indian convicts was changed to the Andamans in 1793; but in 1796, when the British settlement on those islands was abandoned, the convicts transported there were removed to Penang. From that time, with the exception of the years 1811 to 1813 when the punishment of transportation was suspended in India, a number of Indian convicts arrived in Penang every year till 1860, after which they ceased to be sent to the Straits Settlements.[2]

When the British gave up their settlement at Bencoolen, Sumatra, in 1825 (following the Anglo-Dutch treaty of 1824) Singapore was also pressed into service as a penal station to accommodate some 600 Indian convicts then in Bencoolen; this settlement had been another of the Company's 'Botany Bays of India'. The first batch of these convicts arrived in the Lion City in April 1825. The others followed soon after. Subsequently Singapore also began to receive convicts direct from India itself. This practice continued till the final cessation of the movement in 1860.[3]

Malacca got its first group of Indian convicts in 1805, when 'two complete companies', consisting of some 100 men and 4 overseers, were sent from Penang to help in the destruction of the Dutch fort and other fortifications. But this proved to be only a temporary stay, ceasing with the return of Malacca to the Dutch in 1808. However, Malacca did finally become an official penal colony seventeen years later when it received its first 'official' consignment of convicts from Penang. Thenceforth it, too, joined Singapore and Penang as an annual recipient of those deported from India.[4]

Exactly how many Indian convicts entered the Straits Settlements during their term as penal stations is unknown, no continuous records being maintained of the number of arrivals in any one year. However, on the basis of the available figures for the annual numbers of arrivals in the early 1820s and the late 1850s, it would appear that, besides the

[1] *SSFR*, 94 (1824), 15.4.1824.
[2] *SSFR*, 94 (1824), 15.4.1824; *PP*, XL (1862), paper no. 12, p. 56.
[3] *SSFR*, 100 (1825), 13.3.1825; Buckley, 1902, I, 108; McNair, 1899, pp. 38–41.
[4] *PLCSS*, 1870, pp. 114–21.

600 transferred from Bencoolen, some 15,000 Indian convicts may have reached the Straits Settlements from India between 1790 and 1860, at an average of about 200 arrivals per year.[1] But despite the almost continuous movement of such numbers of new convicts into the country each year, there were seldom more than 4,000 Indian convicts in the Straits Settlements in any one year. More than half of these were in Singapore from the 1830s, the remainder being principally in Penang (table 3).

The comparatively small number of convicts in the Straits Settlements in any one year, despite the virtually uninterrupted additions of new-comers every year, was mainly the result of a very high death rate. Between the years 1820 and 1824, for example, for every 192 new convicts entering the Colony, there were 103 deaths in each year. In some years the number of deaths in fact exceeded the arrivals, as for instance in 1859–60 when there were 236 deaths amongst the convicts compared with 171 new arrivals.[2]

About the beginning of the nineteenth century approximately 10 per cent of the Indian convicts in the Straits Settlements were set free at the end of their term, each year. While some of these remained in the Straits Settlements others returned to India. Till the early 1830s return passages were paid by the Indian government for freed prisoners. In those days some 90 per cent of the convicts left Malaya after their terms expired. But afterwards payment of return passages was stopped by the Indian government and more and more of the Indian convicts found it difficult to go back to India. By 1838, only about 60 per cent were returning to India and by the 1860s very few at all returned home at the end of their sentence. Not all those who returned to India re-mained there; some of them, finding it difficult to fit into their old community, came back to the Straits Settlements. In some years, as for example in the 1860s, as many as 200 to 300 discharged prisoners were settling down in the Straits Settlements annually. Some of them married, either their fellow ex-prisoners, other Indians or Malays, and thereby contributed to the increase in both the Indian and Jawi Pekan population. The latter is to this day still largely concentrated in the Straits Settlements, particularly Penang.[3]

[1] *SSFR*, 94 (1824), 15.4.1824; *SSAR*, 1859–60, pp. 197–8; *PP*, xl (1862), paper no. 12, pp. 11–16.

[2] Most of the deaths, we are told by official records, were due not to any excessive punishment or other forms of ill-treatment but to such causes as 'nostalgia', 'mental depression' caused by the forcible removal from their native country, and change of climate, diet and work (*SSFR*, 94, 1824, 15.4.1824; *SSAR*, 1859–60, pp. 197–8; McNair, 1899, pp. 147–55).

[3] *SSFR*, 94 (1824), 15.4.1824; *C.O.273*, 40 (1870), 22.10.1870; McNair, 1899, p. 145; Nathan, 1922, p. 86.

Table 3: *Number of Indian convicts in the Straits Settlements, 1810–1873*

year	Penang			Malacca			Singapore			total		
	M	F	T	M	F	T	M	F	T	M	F	T
1810	N	N	1300	—	—	—	—	—	—	N	N	1300
1824	N	N	1462	—	—	—	—	—	1839	N	N	1462
1855	N	N	1358	N	N	648	N	N	2275	N	N	3 845
1860	1163	93	1255	532	—	532	2151	124	1798	3846	217	4 063
1865	728	73	801	743	2	745	1681	112	N	3152	187	3339
1873	N	N	N	N	N	N	N	N	N	N	N	1815

M = male.   F = female.   T = total.

N = No information available.

Source: Compiled from *SSFR*, 94 (1824), 15.4.1824; *SSAR*, 1859/60–1864/5; *C.O. 273*, 19 (1868), 4.6.1868; 66 (1873), 9.5.1873; *PP*, XL (1862), paper no. 12, pp. 5–54.

The number of discharged prisoners settled in the Straits was augmented by the decision of the Indian government to grant pardons to 1,815 of the prisoners scheduled to be transferred to the Andamans in 1873.[1] When the final shipment took place they were allowed to remain in the Straits Settlements. With the exception of 125 of them, who were sick and incapable of earning a living and were to be supported by Indian government funds, the rest of these convicts were left to merge into the local population.[2]

Then, from the early years of the nineteenth century there was anything up to 650 convicts on ticket-of-leave in the Straits Settlements. They, too, were allowed to marry whomsoever they could, and some of them did.[3]

Finally, some ten to twenty convicts escaped, or to use the official phrase 'deserted', every year, principally into the adjoining Malay States. While some of them were apprehended and others perished in the Malayan jungles, some made good their escape and ended up as far off as Pahang and Kelantan. While some of these were finally returned to the Straits Settlements, others remained at large and eventually, it is presumed, also merged into the Malayan population.[4]

As in the case of several other aspects of their immigration, the regional provenance of the convicts is also poorly documented. However, an examination of the evidence at hand suggests that, although most parts of the Indian subcontinent contributed their share of felons, the majority came from the Bengal Presidency, that is the lower Ganges–Brahmaputra basin. This was certainly the case till the early 1820s, when 'Bengalis' formed nearly two-thirds of the total convict population of the Straits.[5]

Some female Indian convicts were also sent to the Straits Settlements. However, they were comparatively few in number, seldom exceeding 200 in any one year.[6]

Almost every stratum of Indian society was represented amongst the convicts, including Benares *brāhmaṇas*, Sikh and Dogra *kṣatriyas*, Chettiar, Bengali and Parsi financiers and ryots and untouchables from the various parts of the Subcontinent.[7]

---

[1] See p. 140 below.

[2] *C.O.273*, 66 (1873), 9.5.1873; McNair, 1899, p. 183.

[3] *SSFR*, 94 (1824), 15.4.1824; *C.O.273*, 40 (1870), 22.10.1870; McNair, 1899, pp. 143 ff.; *SSAR*, 1865–6, p. 62.

[4] *SSAR*, 1861–2, pp. 45–6; *SSAR*, 1862–3, pp. 42–4; *SSAR*, 1863–4, pp. 42–4; *SSAR*, 1864–5, pp. 68–72; *SSAR*, 1865–6, pp. 61–5.

[5] *SSFR*, 94 (1824), 15.4.1824; *SSAR*, 1859–60, pp. 197–8; *PP*, XL (1862), paper no. 12, pp. 11–16.   [6] *Ibid.*

[7] *SSFR*, 94 (1824), 15.4.1824; McNair, 1899, p. 89; Singh and Ahluwalia, 1963, pp. 42–54; *NAI:FPP*, Jan. 1850, secret consultations, 46–57 of 25.1.1850, 27–8 of 26.1.1850;

Types of migrants

Most of the convicts appeared to have been sentenced for such crimes as thugee, dacoity, robbery, 'professional poisoning' and murder. There were also some political prisoners and, after 1857, some mutineers. More than three-quarters of the convicts were those sentenced to transportation for life, the remainder serving terms ranging from seven to twenty-five years.[1]

The management of the convicts in the Straits was both liberal and effective. The whole tenor of their treatment was more in the spirit of such measures as those introduced in Norfolk Island by Captain Alexander Maconochie than of anything in contemporary India.[2] While serving their sentences the convicts were taught useful trades. Beginning from the 1820s they were divided into six classes. The first class consisted of trustworthy convicts allowed out of jail on ticket-of-leave. They had to attend muster on the first of every month, had to keep the Superintendent of Convicts informed of their place of residence, and were bound to sleep in it every night, but there were few restrictions on their place of residence or work within each territory.

The second class comprised the convict petty officials, both male and female, and those employed in hospitals and public offices. They were allowed to go out of jail during and after working hours, but had to report at an 8.00 p.m. roll-call daily and, except for those working in hospitals or other similar special duties, were required to sleep in prison at night.

The third class was composed of convicts employed on roads and public works. Some of them worked in the country, in which case they were housed in temporary jail accommodation at their place of employment. Those in the town, provided they were of approved conduct, were allowed to be out of jail after working hours until 6.00 p.m.

The fourth class was made up of convicts newly arrived, and those degraded from other classes or promoted from the fifth class. They were not allowed to leave the prison except for work.

The fifth class was a punishment class consisting of convicts degraded from the higher classes, and those requiring more than ordinary vigilance to prevent escape, or regarding whom special instructions had been

March 1850, 89–94 of 22.3.1850; July 1850, 27–8 of 26.7.1850; Aug. 1856, political consultations, 225–7 of 29.8.1856; Oct. 1857, 17–20 of 2.10.1857; Feb. 1860, 296–8 of 17.2.1860.

[1] *SSFR*, 94 (1824), 15.4.1824; McNair, 1899, p. 146; *PP*, XL (1862), paper no. 12, p. 7; Singh and Ahluwalia, 1963, pp. 42–54; *NAI:FPP*, Jan. 1850, secret consultations, 46–57 of 25.1.1850, 27–8 of 26.1.1850; March 1850, 89–94 of 22.3.1850; July 1850, 27–8 of 26.7.1850; Aug. 1856, political consultations, 225–7 of 29.8.1856; Oct. 1857, 17–20 of 2.10.1857; Feb. 1860, 296–8 of 17.2.1860.

[2] J. V. Barry, *Alexander Maconochie of Norfolk Island* (Melbourne, 1958), pp. 69 ff.; *SSFR*, 94 (1824), 15.4.1824; McNair, 1899, pp. 84 ff.

received from India. They too were not allowed to leave prison except for work.

The sixth class was comprised of invalids and superannuated convicts. The superannuated men were exempt from all work while some of the others were employed for such light work as the sweeping and caretaking of government bungalows. Until granted ticket-of-leave, all female convicts belonged to this class.[1]

In terms of employment, many ticket-of-leave men and women worked for wages for private employers, such as planters. Some became gardeners, syces and domestic servants. Others either took up such pursuits as shikar, tailoring or well-digging or, once they had saved sufficient, set up their own farms, dairies, forges, cart and furniture making and other such enterprises. Besides such direct contributions to the development of the country, these free and ticket-of-leave exiles also appear to have been innovators. Besides setting up their own forges and kilns, making carts and furniture and spreading these and similar skills amongst their neighbours, they seem to have been the first to discover the *pelas tikus* palm (*Licuala acutifida*, Mart.) in Penang. From this palm were constructed walking-sticks called Penang lawyers and the process of preparing them—scraping off the outer skin with glass prior to straightening over a fire—was not dissimilar to the present-day Malay method of making Malacca canes. Some of these 'Penang lawyers' were sold by the convicts on the spot, and many more were exported to Europe and America.[2]

The rest of the convicts were almost wholly employed in government undertakings. These included jobs as snake and tiger killers, firemen, *pankhawallas*, canal, well and grave diggers, drain and road makers, bridge-builders, brick and tile-kiln operators, lime and charcoal burners, bricklayers and plasterers, masons, carpenters, tailors, weavers, blacksmiths, basket and furniture makers, coopers, painters, gardeners and syces, shoe and sandal makers, wheelwrights, boatmen, signalmen, nurses, orderlies, master-builders, draughtsmen, printers and scavengers.[3]

---

[1] There was another group of Indian exiles which did not strictly come under the category of convicts. This was a number of families of Polygar feudal chiefs of South India. They were deported to Penang in 1800 for their part in the Polygar wars of the eighteenth century. These exiles were paid stipends while in Penang and were allowed to move about freely on the island. Their numbers were seriously decimated by disease and by 1817 there were only fifteen of them surviving in Penang. Within the next three years they lost another five of their number before being finally repatriated to Madras (*SSFR*, 181, 1814–18, 21.9.1814; 6.5.1815; 22.11.1817).

[2] *SSFR*, 65 (1818), 22.1.1818; 94 (1824), 15.4.1824; *SSAR*, 1862–3, p. 43; McNair, 1899, pp. 19–24, 145.

[3] *SSFR*, 65 (1818), 22.1.1818; 94 (1824), 15.4.1824; *SSAR*, 1862–3, p. 43; Makepeace, 1921, I, 283; McNair, 1899, pp. 47 ff.

This list can be continued, but it is sufficient to say that 'for years the history of (these) convicts is the history of the Public Works Department'. They have left an indelible print behind them. Buildings like the Mariamman Hindu temple, St Andrew's Cathedral and the Government House in Singapore are standing monuments to their skill and labour.[1] Their effect on Singapore, which, together with Penang, was the main beneficiary of the 'Convict Era' of Malaya, is perhaps best summed up in the words of the Governor of the Straits Settlements, Colonel Blundell, a man in close touch with the doings of these convicts:

> ...The whole of the existing roads throughout the Island...every bridge in both town and country, all the existing canals, sea wall, jetties, piers, etc., have been constructed by convict labour. But not only is the community indebted for these essential works to the mere manual labour of convicts, but by the introduction among them of a system of skilled labour, Singapore is indebted for works which could not otherwise have been sanctioned from the State funds. A church has been erected, every brick and every measure of lime in which has been made and laid by convicts, and which in architectural beauty, is second to no church in India. Powerful batteries have been erected at various points...which would have been too expensive for sanction if executed by free labour while by means of convict labour, the whole of the public buildings in the place...(were) kept in a state of efficiency and repair without exhibiting in the annual accounts any large items of expenditure for such necessary work...[2]

Despite the obvious usefulness of convict labour there was a steady undercurrent of resentment amongst the local British residents against the use of the Straits Settlements as dumping grounds for, what they termed, the 'concentrated scourings of the Indian jails'.[3] These mutterings became louder in the 1850s, especially following the Muslim Muharram celebrations of 1855. At Muharram the convicts were usually given permission to carry tabuts in procession through the towns. But in 1855 there was such hooliganism that the government forbade such processions next year. This order was enforced in Malacca, in Penang it was withdrawn for fear of the reaction of the convicts. In Singapore the defiant convicts overpowered the sepoy guards, marched through the town and planted their tabuts in front of the Resident Councillor's house.

With previous Chinese and Indian bloody riots in mind the European community panicked and objections were publicly raised not only against the sending of Indian convicts to the Straits Settlements but

---

[1] *JIA*, v (1851), 1–9; vi (1852), 18, 83, 143, 218, 521, 618; McNair, 1899, pp. 19 ff.; Makepeace, 1921, I, 283.
[2] *PP*, xl (1862), paper no. 12, pp. 32–3.
[3] *PP*, xl (1862), paper no. 12, p. 5; *SFP*, 10.9.1857.

also, for the first time, against the practice of allowing ex-convicts to settle in the Straits and permitting life convicts ticket-of-leave after sixteen years. Hasty measures passed by the Indian government, in August 1857, to transfer 'dangerous' prisoners of 'unusual audacity and boldness' from the Calcutta jail to the Straits Settlements in order to make room for mutineer prisoners aroused further agitation and protests. To add to their worst fears, transportation of a number of mutineer prisoners to the Straits began in November 1857. One such party, which arrived in Singapore in March 1858, had in fact attempted to seize the ship en route. Some of these were heavily guarded and manacled while on ship but let loose in the ordinary jail in Singapore.

This was virtually the last straw. Public meetings were called and the decision taken to petition the Indian and British governments to cease sending mutineer and other convicts to the Straits Settlements. To give more weight to their agitation they even deputized their members on leave in England to take up the cudgels in person, and in London itself, against the sending of convicts.[1]

As the pressure from the European residents against the presence of the convicts increased in intensity, the Indian government gave in. Beginning with an order in mid-1858 to remove all mutineer prisoners from the Straits Settlements to the Andaman Islands, it agreed, in September 1860, to prohibit any further sending of Indian convicts to the Straits. Finally, following the British government's decision in 1866 to transfer the Straits Settlements from Indian to Colonial Office control, the Indian authorities also agreed to remove all Indian convicts still under sentence to the Andamans. This was done on 8 May 1873.[2]

[1] *SFP*, 6.8.1857; 10.9.1857; 1.10.1857; 15.10.1857; 19.11.1857; 10.12.1857; 31.12. 1857; 13.5.1858; 20.5.1858; 3.6.1858; *ST*, 22.9.1857; 13.10.1857; 5.6.1858; C. M. Turnbull, 'The movement to remove the Straits Settlements from the control of India, culminating in the transfer to the Colonial Office in 1867', unpublished Ph.D. thesis, University of London, 1962, pp. 103–7; C. T. Saw, 'Transported Indian convicts in Singapore, 1825–1873', unpublished Academic Exercise, University of Malaya, Singapore, 1955, pp. 36–44; *PP*, xl (1862), paper no. 12, p. 5.
[2] *C.O.273*, 27 (1869), 1.3.1869; 66 (1873), 9.5.1873; *PP*, xl (1862), paper no. 12, p. 51.

4

EMIGRATION–IMMIGRATION LAW
AND PRACTICE

Indian immigration into Malaya was accompanied by a great deal of legislative interference, succinctly summarized in the following remarks of a Straits Settlements Legislative Councillor in 1898:

If we make a pilgrimage back through the desert of debate and discussion, we find the route mapped out for us by bleaching skeletons of its predecessors. Amended Ordinances, suspended Ordinances, repealed Ordinances—Ordinances which strangled themselves by the complexities and incongruities of construction...[In short] Ordinances...of every sort and description...

In all this the speaker was impressed by two features—the ambivalence and procrastination of the Malayan government in the promotion of Indian immigration and the best means of achieving this, and the generous consideration (often, it could be added, to the detriment of the immigrants themselves) shown by the Indian government to this aspect of the Indo-Malayan relations.[1]

Indian emigration policy and practice

Indian emigration policy towards Malaya, though quite distinct in its administrative and clausal details, nevertheless formed part and parcel of the Indian government's overall attitude towards emigration in general.

Emigration of Indians to foreign countries, as far as significant numbers are concerned, began in the 1830s when colonial planters and governments turned to India to meet their growing needs for labour, and office and technical assistants. The subsequent decades saw thousands of Indians leaving the Subcontinent not only for such nearby places as Ceylon and Burma but also for far off colonies like the West Indies and Fiji.[2]

Migration from India, especially to tropical lands, was not altogether a natural process and was not caused by the spontaneous action of the

[1] *PLCSS*, 1898, p. B 28.
[2] Geoghegan, 1873, pp. 1 ff.; Davis, 1951, pp. 89–105; Kondapi, 1951, pp. 8 ff.

141

people, but rather brought about to a considerable extent by the persuasions of agents and recruiters. It therefore required supervision on the part of the Indian authorities.[1] Moreover it was felt that

> a European proprietor of an estate in the tropics is, as a rule, unlike the proprietor of an estate in England, in the respect, that he does not look upon his estate as a life investment for his money; but he, as well as his European employé, looks to making large profits with as little outlay and delay as possible, with the view of 'going home' to live on the capital he shall have made out of the estate...

Under these circumstances, he limited his expenditure to the barest minimum.[2] Consequently, the immigrant labourer was in danger of being neglected and periodically in the nineteenth and early twentieth centuries the Indian government passed such laws which it thought would protect the prospective emigrant from force and fraud and secure satisfactory conditions such as sanitation. This was about as far as it was prepared to go with regard to assisted labour emigration. As for the movement of free or non-assisted emigrants, it generally did not interfere at all, individuals of independent means being free to leave or not as they saw fit.[3] Apart from the two notifications issued in 1857 and 1859 to prevent overcrowding on 'native' passenger ships, the Indian government's first efforts to supervise labour, or for that matter any emigration to Malaya, began in 1870, when it prohibited labour emigration to the Straits Settlements, following the denunciation in that year of the traffic as a system for 'kidnapping of minors and abduction of women'.[4] But the prohibition was not strictly enforced and was formally removed two years later, following the assurance given by the Straits government that it would provide adequate protection for Indian immigrants.[5] Subsequently, although certain checks were enforced provisionally from time to time to protect the emigrants, the Indian government was generally disinclined to interfere in the movement. Consequently, it is not at all surprising that, once it had assured itself that the Indian labourer would be adequately looked after by the Malayan authorities, it relinquished all direct control of labour emigration to Malaya in 1897.[6]

This fitted in with the ideals prevailing among the British rulers in India at that time. As K. Gillion has stressed in another context, they

[1] *BM:BP*, Ad. MSS 36473, ff. 91–8, 7.10.1836; ff. 159–75, 14.7.1837; *SEMMPI*, 1871–2, p. 786.   [2] *PLCSS*, 1878, paper no. 35, p. 16.

[3] *IO:EP*, 1502 (1890), pp. 80–167; 8241 (1909), pp. 455–71; *DLAI*, 1921, I, 1461–4, 'Emigrant', 1924, pp. 15 ff.; *MRM*, III (1928), 78–83.

[4] Geoghegan, 1873, pp. 63–4; *IO:EP*, 14 (1871), pp. 986–93; *GMPPD*, 1870, 40–4 of 13.9.1870; *NAI:EP*, Sept. 1870, proc. 1–15.

[5] *IO:EP*, 692 (1873), proc. 12–15 of March 1873.

[6] See p. 62 above.

lived in an age of individualism and *laissez faire*, and, it might be added, imperial strategy and needs. While they frequently saw the interests of India as being distinct from those of Britain, they nevertheless seldom appear to have totally ignored the urgings of the Empire builders or the call of the 'larger and common good of the British Empire'. Their policies appear to have been based not so much on respect for the views and needs of the Indians but more on the desire for internal security and the stability of the Raj. In any case, they were strongly paternalistic and felt they knew what was best for their subjects. They had witnessed the launching of some of the world's greatest inter- and intra-continental population movements and wanted the fewest possible checks on the flow of merchandise, men and money, especially within the Empire.

Just as the demands of the political economy of England sanctioned the conversion of India from an exporter of manufactured goods to that of a supplier of raw materials to the British industrial complex and a market for the products of those machines, so-called free trade ideas and imperial requirements, coupled with the belief in individual rights of movement and employment, sanctioned the recruitment of Indians for indentured and other forms of labour overseas. The government of India, right up to the time it began reforming its emigration policy in the second decade of the present century, continued to describe its stand on this issue as being neutral, that is one of non-interference, apart from seeing fair play towards the parties in a commercial trans-action.[1] Accordingly, its regulations were designed to achieve this end. However, although this stand of the Indian government was largely consonant with contemporary European ideas, it was not only unrealistic but probably hypocritical as well. First, as we have already seen, the government of India often assisted or discouraged emigration in practice despite its professed neutralistic position in the matter; the appropriate action depended on the circumstances and class of emigrant involved.[2] In the case of labour emigrants, for example, every now and then instructions were issued to officials to render all assistance possible to recruiters while special government facilities were provided to facilitate the departure of such emigrants from their homes to the ports of embarkation.[3] On the other hand the movement of non-labouring

[1] *IO:EP*, 1502 (1880), pp. 80–167; 8241 (1909), pp. 455–71; *DLAI*, 1921, I, 1461–4; 'Emigrant', 1924, pp. 15 ff.; *MRM*, III (1928), 78–83; Gillion, 1962, pp. 23–9; *GMPPD*, 1900, 558–9 of 13.6.1900; 726–7 of 27.7.1900; 1914, 1476–7 of 16.11.1914; *PLCSS*, 1900, p. C 117; *NAI:EP*, July 1917, confidential A proc. 3–4; Oct. 1920, A proc. 5–6; March 1922, A proc. 154–6.

[2] See pp. 62, 126 above. Cf. pp. 146–7 below.

[3] *GMPPD*, 1871, 1313 of 25.8.1871; 1900, 558–9 of 13.6.1900, 726–7 of 27.7.1900; Vermont, 1888, pp. 1–60.

Immigration: origins and trends

elements, especially Sikhs, was frequently interfered with, at times even to the extent of virtual stoppage,[1] partly as some of them were needed for service in India itself and partly because many of these emigrants were a constant source of administrative trouble and political embarrassment to their home government.[2]

Secondly, it neither made adequate allowance for the actual economic, social and administrative conditions in India nor the place of emigration. Such aspects of the Indian peasant life as poverty, ignorance, illiteracy and fear of authority were general knowledge. Apart from comprehending the laws governing emigration and service abroad, many of them had little more than a hazy idea of where they were going, and were often unable to distinguish between the various emigrant-receiving colonies.[3] Then it will be remembered that it was well known and considered hardly an exaggeration that the Indian labourer was highly gullible, even for his kind; that political economy had virtually no meaning to him; and perhaps most important of all, that an agent or recruiter could, if it was made worth his while, 'persuade' him 'to go anywhere'. That the methods of persuasion employed by the recruiters included bribery, kidnapping, coercion and fraud were not outside the knowledge of the Indian government.[4] It was also known that a number of officials administering the migration regulations were not only inadequately trained but often corrupt as well. Regardless of the foregoing features of the community and the defects in the recruiting system, the government insisted on treating the peasants of India as free or independent individuals—at least until they had thumb-printed their freedom away —who were able to protect their interests and rights themselves, both at home and abroad.[5]

Finally, it failed to take cognizance of the social and political consequences of emigration and ran foul of Indian public opinion.

We have already noted that emigration, especially for the purpose of unskilled labour overseas, does not seem to have been popular with the people of India. Indeed, it was often opposed; but until the turn of the century, this opposition was more in the form of silent disapproval than active resistance. With the political awakening of India at about this time, however, this disapproval, particularly from the beginning of the second decade of the present century, became not only increasingly vocal and vehement but also more and more politically motivated.

The cause of the Indians overseas became inextricably linked with the general freedom struggle of the Indian nationalists.

[1] *NAI:EP*, June 1917, B proc. 8; confidential file no. 44/38—L & O, serial nos. 1–133.
[2] See pp. 126–7 above.   [3] Rai, 1914a, p. 18.
[4] See pp. 79–80 above.   [5] See pp. 142–3 above. Cf. Gillion, 1962, pp. 19–58.

Emigration–immigration law

The exploitation, degradation, indenture and criminal prosecution by employers of Indian labour for labouring offences and the development of discrimination and prejudice against Indians in general, in terms of employment and political status in Malaya, was considered not only harmful to Indians and Indian interests in Malaya but also discreditable to India as a nation, and inconsistent with sentiments of national self-respect. The nationalists felt morally bound to obtain justice for their overseas comrades.[1] Moreover, the treatment of the Indians abroad was, in all probability, valuable additional ammunition to feed the batteries against the Raj. Henceforth, every little bit of real or imagined grievance or slight of the Indian emigrants in Malaya, as elsewhere, was seized upon with alacrity both by the nationalist press and leaders, and exploited for all it was worth.

As the nationalist movement increased in strength and militancy the government realized that the opposition to emigration of labour could not be safely ignored; some shift, however small, from the traditional *laissez faire* attitude, was imperative to sop or draw off some of the heat at least from the nationalist agitation which was now becoming politically increasingly dangerous. At the same time, as stressed earlier on, the Agent in Malaya and the Madras authorities were also keen on reform. Their pressure on the central Indian government and support, albeit covertly expressed,[2] for the efforts of the Indian leaders further strengthened the hands of the nationalists. As the latter consolidated their position so that of the government weakened, leading finally to a complete *volte face* in the 1930s.[3]

The first positive step away from the traditional policy came in 1916[4] when the indenture system was abolished and all indenture contracts in operation at that time were to cease in 1920.[5] There still, however, remained labour emigration under other forms of assistance and in 1922 the *Indian Emigration Act 1922, of 5 March 1922 (No. VII of 1922)* was passed by the Indian Legislative Assembly and Council of State. This

---

[1] *CIAMMM*, 27.1.1936 to 7.10.1941; *PCGGI*, 1911–12, L, 363–93; *PCGGI*, 1914–15, LIII, 5–15; *DCSI*, 1922, II, 871; Dev, 1940, pp. 5–6, 70–98; *PINC*, Resolutions of the Indian National Congress, 29th Session, VI; 39th Session, XVII; Annual report(s) of the Indian National Congress for the year(s) 1910 (pp. 37–44), 1913 (pp. 85–90), 1923 (p. 184) and 1924 (para. 14); Summary of the proceedings of the Working Committee, 5 March 1926.

[2] Personal interviews with Mr N. Raghavan and Mr A. K. Sen, former President and General Secretary of the Central Indian Association of Malaya, respectively.

[3] See pp. 109–14 above.

[4] It may be recalled that Malaya abolished Indian indenture in 1910. But, though Indian agitation did play a part in this abolition, the main act took place in London. Moreover, the legal abolition was at the Malayan and not the Indian end. (See p. 86 above.)

[5] Andrews, 1930, p. 434.

Act sought not only to consolidate and renovate previous regulations but also to create a machinery for future control of emigration in order to help and protect Indian emigrants abroad. It will be remembered that prior to this, a standing emigration committee, consisting of Indian members drawn from both chambers of the Indian legislature, had also been created to advise the government on all matters relating to emigration. The creation of this committee and the passing of the Act marked the transition from *laissez faire* to a much stricter form of legal and administrative control of labour emigration.[1]

In the case of Malaya, individuals below the age of eighteen years were not allowed to emigrate unless accompanied by a guardian or relatives over eighteen years of age, while Rule 23 of the Rules under the Act, designed to promote a healthier community life by reducing the preponderance of males amongst the emigrants,[2] stipulated that 'the number of male emigrants unmarried or unaccompanied by their wives being assisted to emigrate must not exceed one in every five persons over eighteen' in any one year. Every case of recruiting was placed in the hands of a Malayan Emigration Commissioner, who was to be solely responsible for all recruiting transactions carried out in the name of his country. However every recruiting agent was required to obtain permission to recruit from the local government of the port from which the emigrant was to depart. He was also required to obtain the sanction of the headman of the village for each and every one of the emigrants recruited. In addition to the above safeguards, there was to be an Agent of the government of India in Malaya to look after the welfare of the Indian immigrants there. He was also required to 'vet' every recruiting licence.[3]

However, partly as a result of it seeing no pressing urgency in the matter and partly because it was not prepared to jeopardize the interests of another British government, the government of India once again failed to use its powers effectively to bring about any significant improvement in either the system of labour recruitment or the general position of the Indians in Malaya. In the first place, not all the foregoing stipulations of the Act were enforced. For instance, it will be recalled that Rule 23 was never put into effect. Also, even where the clauses were implemented, the enforcement was seldom strict.[4] In these circumstances some of the abuses inherent in the system of assisted emigration still continued, and consequently so did Indian criticism, culminating

[1] *DCSI*, 1922, II, 890–1110; *DLAI*, 1922, II, 1755–2196; III, 3.
[2] India, 1935, pp. 3–13; India, 1941, pp. 2–17.
[3] *GMPPWLD*, 1927, 2424—L of 22.10.1927.
[4] *NAI:EP*, 1935, confidential file no. 222/35—L & O; *GMPPWLD*, 1927, 2424—L of 22.10.1927.

finally in the imposition of the total ban on assisted labour emigration in 1938.

With the ban on assisted labour emigration, the movement of other types of labour also began to come under stricter control. We have seen above how every passenger leaving India was required to have a clearance from the government authorities before he could obtain passage, to the effect that he was not an assisted labourer or some similar kind of emigrant.[1] These regulations began rigorously to be enforced from 1939 and especially by independent India. In the meantime activity, pointing to a change in migration policy there as well, became discernible in Malaya.[2]

Malayan immigration policy and practice

Although not a declared policy, the Malayan government's immigration legislation pertaining to Indians during the pre-World War II period was almost wholly concerned with the movement of labour. The other Indians, in terms of immigration control, were either ignored or, if noted at all, then primarily in so far as they affected the existing order and, ultimately, British rule in general and labour relations in particular. In practice, this meant that Indians capable of leadership or political agitation and who might conceivably rock the labour boat or 'the larger and common good of the Empire' were not welcome and, from the 1920s at least, often actually barred from entering Malaya.[3]

Common features of the Malayan immigration legislative measures were the lack of consistency; vacillation and instability were the keynotes. However, throughout the long melancholy tale of '...Amended Ordinances, suspended Ordinances, repealed Ordinances...'[4] a connecting theme can be pieced together. The fundamental aspects of this theme appear to be the Malayan government's desire to acquire and maintain a constant and large supply of cheap Indian labour on one hand, while on the other to accept only the minimum moral responsibility for these labourers on the grounds that they were temporary sojourners in Malaya. To this end it offered the Indian immigrants little more than what was necessary for the efficient functioning of the capitalist enterprise of the country, while it strove hard to systematize and assure a sufficient flow of Indian labour into Malaya.[5]

---

[1] See p. 116 above. [2] *ST*, 9.12.1935; *H*, 7.7.1946.
[3] See pp. 45–6 above. [4] See p. 141 above.
[5] *C.O.273*, 40 (1870), 22.10.1870; 300 (1904), 17.9.1904; Colonial Office, minute no. 29635; 317 (1906), 28.2.1906; *NAI:EP*, March 1922, proc. 178–80; 1935, confidential file no. 186/35—L & O; file no. 330/35—L & O; *ST*, 14.5.1933; 19.5.1933; 12.6.1933; 2.9.1933; 23.10.1933; *MM*, 18.8.1910; *IMR*, I (1935), 16–19; Jenks, 1920, pp. 73 *et seq.*; Parmer, 1960, pp. 65–6.

Immigration: origins and trends

The creation of the Indian Immigration Committee was the major breakthrough in this direction. The subsequent expansion of its operations and scope and the systematization of labour immigration under its control was considered 'an unqualified success' by the government.[1] A measure of its confidence in the system was the decision to extend the machinery to the importation of Javanese labour, following the Indian government's ban on assisted labour emigration and its refusal to lift the ban despite the Malayan representations of 1939, 1940 and 1941.[2] This was the only alternative supply suitable, as China was at war and the Chinese labour already in Malaya was becoming increasingly restive under the influence of Communist and Kuomintang nationalist agitators. However, before the scheme to import Javanese labour in place of Indians could be fully launched the Japanese invasion intervened. It was resurrected after the war but once again it could not be satisfactorily implemented, this time due to the unsettled conditions in Indonesia as a result of the Indonesian–Dutch conflict. Baulked here, the Malayan government once again appears to have appealed to the Indian government in 1946, but, as noted already, in vain.[3]

In the meantime estates and government departments had been carrying out their rehabilitation and day-to-day work almost wholly with the labour already in Malaya. Needless to say, given the prevailing unsettled situation in Java and China and the inflexible attitude of the Indian government, it was abundantly clear that from now on Malaya would have to try and meet its labour needs locally. Nor did this prospect seem as alarming as it appeared on the surface, for not only had the country by this time acquired a large and rapidly increasing settled population, but the Malays, for the first time, were now beginning to enter the labour market in substantial and ever increasing numbers.[4]

Moreover, latent Malay opposition to Chinese and Indian immigration was becoming more overt. As early as 1944 a group of Malay students in London, including some future leaders of the country, had petitioned the Colonial Office not just to restrict[5] but, if possible, to bring a total halt to all Chinese and Indian immigration.[6] The essence of their argument was this: as living standards in Malaya were much higher than those prevailing in China and India, or for that matter any of the

[1] *ARLDM*, 1938, p. 10; Parmer, 1960, pp. 61, 250.
[2] *PAMC*, 1946, 7, pp. 5–6; *H*, 22.11.1941; Parmer, 1960, pp. 112, 252.
[3] See p. 115 above.
[4] *MUARLD*, 1947, pp. 23, 41.
[5] Chinese immigration had already been limited from as early as 1933 when the entry of males was restricted to an annual quota of between 500 to 6,000 persons. Female immigration, too, was similarly restricted from 1938 (Sandhu, 1961*a*, pp. 16–17).
[6] *BM*, Dec. 1944, pp. 89–91; Jan. 1945, pp. 100–2.

neighbouring countries, there was a constant influx of Chinese, Indians and others coming in almost solely for economic gain. They showed little interest in the life of the country other than as a 'milch cow'. Neither did they care who held this cow as long as they could milk it. If all these persons were allowed unrestricted entry into Malaya their large numbers would result in a lowering of wages and conditions of employment. Finally, Malays, the indigenous people, were in danger of being swamped in their own land.

These sentiments gathered momentum with the emergence of organized Malay nationalism in the post-war years. Additional support for these aspirations was also forthcoming from a number of retired British Malayan civil servants. Even though some of them in their active careers had actually helped to formulate the existing immigration policy, they were now solidly behind the Malays. They constantly pressured the Colonial Office to respect the wishes of the Malays who, they insisted, were after all Britain's wards.[1]

Up to now the paramount consideration influencing immigration policy in Malaya had not been so much the wishes of the Malays, but more the development of the country's resources and the maintenance of law and order and ultimately British rule. This was possible because there was little cohesion in the incipient Malay nationalism until after the war. This situation changed with the formation of the pan-Malayan United Malays' National Organisation in 1946. Then too, the primary aim of the Malayan immigration policy had been the promotion and control of labour migration. Now this labour was no longer available; there was, instead, a rising influx of traders, pedlars, petty shopkeepers, hawkers, shop-assistants, clerks and watchmen—types of little value to British business or government.[2] There was therefore little in this immigration to recommend itself from the point of view either of the government or the British commercial organization. Consequently, a bill was drafted in 1949 to restrict the entry of all types of new immigrants in order, according to the official statement, 'to prevent a deterioration in the present standard of living and to safeguard, for those who have made their homes in Malaya and are going to form the Malayan Nation, the medical, education, social and other benefits which are at present available for them'.[3] The bill, *Immigration Ordinance*

[1] *MP*, Jones to Maxwell, 20.1.1943; *BM*, April 1946, pp. 291–4; Asian Relations Organisation, 1948, p. 81; Ton That Thien, 1963, pp. 230, 237.
[2] Although there appears to be no direct connection between it and the change in migration policy, the Emergency in Malaya (Part 2) may also have contributed to the need for a strict control on all migration, especially since almost all the rebels and their supporters were from the immigrant communities.
[3] Public Relations Department, Singapore, 1953, p. 3.

(*No. 68 of 1952*), was passed by the Malayan government on 24 April 1952, and came into operation on 1 August 1953.

With this Ordinance and its corollary, *Immigration (Prohibition of Entry) Ordinance, 1953*, entry to *all* Indians in Malaya was controlled for the first time. Right of entry was limited to British subjects born or naturalized in Malaya, subjects of the ruler of a Malay state, federal citizens, British subjects ordinarily resident in Malaya, aliens who were holders of Residents' Certificates, and the wives and children under eighteen years of all these persons. Fresh immigration was restricted to any person who:

(*a*) had professional or specialist qualifications which would enable him to follow his profession or occupation without prejudicing the interests of persons already resident in Malaya and possessing corresponding or similar qualifications; or

(*b*) was an employee of the owner of a substantial or well-established business and held a contract of service with such owner providing for his employment in Malaya on such terms and conditions as to the minimum period of engagement and minimum remuneration as the Member for Home Affairs (or, as in Singapore, the Colonial Secretary) may from time to time approve; or

(*c*) was a member of the family of any person permitted to enter Malaya under paragraph (*a*), (*b*); or

(*d*) was a member of the family of a person lawfully resident in Malaya otherwise than on a Pass or on a pass issued to him under the provision of any law relating to immigration for the time being in force in Malaya.[1]

In practice even this selective immigration was restricted, and amendments introduced by an independent Malaya in 1959 further limited the right of free entry of dependent children of citizens, initially, to those under fifteen years and, finally, to those under six years of age. Moreover, every new immigrant entering Malaya for the purpose of employment was now required to furnish proof that he was 'entitled to a salary of not less than one thousand and two hundred dollars (Malayan) a month'. Furthermore, the government had to be satisfied that such an entry would not be prejudicial to any local interest. Even if an applicant fulfilled all the above conditions the government still reserved the right to refuse admission.[2] It could therefore be said that fresh immigration of Indians into Malaya virtually ended with the passing of these regu-

[1] Singapore, 1955–6, vol. II, chapt. 102, part 2; *MCPFLC*, 1953–4, paper no. 29; Federation of Malaya, 1952, pp. 3 ff.; *FMAR*, 1950, p. 2; *FMAR*, 1952, p. 27; *FMAR*, 1953, p. 9.
[2] Federation of Malaya, 1959, paras, 5 ff.; Singapore, 1959, paras. 3 ff.; *CSAR*, 1959, pp. 53–5.

lations. The present movement consists almost wholly of returning residents of the country, their wives and children, and a small trickle of new immigrants—nearly all highly qualified professional or commercial persons. In 1962, for example, out of 680 Indians granted entry permits into Singapore more than 90 per cent were wives and children of citizens of the Island City State.[1]

[1] *SSARID*, 1962, p. 13.

5

FLOW AND CHARACTERISTICS
OF MIGRATION

The significant features of the total Indian movement to Malaya between 1786 and 1957 seem to be, first, that the total volume of immigration has been remarkably small in relation to India's total numbers. This has been so despite (*a*) the size, destitution and disabilities of India's population, (*b*) the virtual lack until the 1930s and 1950s of any substantially prohibitive measures against Indian migration in India and Malaya respectively, and (*c*) Malaya being comparatively empty, wealthy and socially free. Secondly, the movement has been largely of a transitory character. Thirdly, much of the migrational surplus or excess of immigration over emigration appears to have been eliminated by disease, exhaustion and other such agents of destruction. Fourthly, as stated earlier on,[1] it was predominantly a movement of labourers from South India. Finally, it was essentially a movement of male adults.

The exact total of Indians arriving in Malaya between 1786 and 1957 is unknown, but we know that it was never as large as the estimated 15,000,000 Chinese, and certainly nothing even remotely approaching the flood of Europeans into North America during the pre-war period.[2] An estimate, based on available data, would place the total number of Indian immigrants at about 4,250,000 (table 5*a*; Appendix 3), or less than 2 per cent of the total population in India in 1900.[3] However in this sense Malaya's case was not unique because the number of Indian emigrants in the other countries was also small in terms of India's total population. For instance, Davis has estimated that the total number of Indians leaving India between 1834 and 1937 did not exceed 31,000,000, or less than 11 per cent of the total population in 1900. It is, however, possible that, in view of the data on migration from India being incomplete and the system of registration in the country appearing to record the number of immigrants more fully than emigrants, the actual

---

[1] See pp. 81–117 above.
[2] League of Nations, 1937, p. 2.
[3] The year 1900 has no particular significance here apart from being a convenient date for which comparable data are available for several nations.

movement out of the Subcontinent was substantially higher during the 1834–1937 period, say in the region of 40,000,000 to 45,000,000 or approximately 15–16 per cent of the total population of India in 1900.[1] Even if we were to accept the latter statistics, they compare unfavourably with similar figures for, say, the British Isles and Italy, where the overseas departures during roughly the same period are estimated to represent more than 43 and 31 per cent of their total population in 1900 respectively.[2] Comparative figures for China are not available, but needless to say the number of Chinese leaving their homeland would almost certainly have been proportionally higher than the Indians.

The most common explanation given in official publications for this comparative inertia amongst the Indians was that it resulted from the Indians' innate love of their homeland, which precluded their leaving on the same scale as, say, the Europeans or the Chinese.[3] In actual fact, worthwhile information on this vexing question is either obscure or scrappy, but the most reliable indicates that this official explanation is at the best only a half-truth and at the worst a gross fallacy.

Part of what follows has been stated earlier on,[4] but it can stand some repetition and elaboration here. To begin with, there was a strong repugnance to emigration in general in India. In the first place, there was the deep-rooted aversion to strange and foreign places. To a large extent Indian life is, and has been, a community life. This was, and continues to be, particularly so in the case of the rural folk.

Then there was the traditional conservatism of the essentially agrarian society of India. The general mode of life, tied as it was to a farm, and centuries of isolated living in the customary and familiar environment of virtually one and the same village appears to have endowed the Indian peasant with more than the usual reluctance to move than is normally associated with his kind. Moreover, inheritance laws in India called for an equal division of property and so no group of sons was forced to leave by an inferior right of inheritance.

Social customs and institutions militating strongly against emigration further reinforced this stay-at-home attitude. For instance, travel overseas for the orthodox Hindus involved the risk of compromise or loss of caste through contamination of food, contact with *mlecchas* and the crossing of seas. Then the joint-family system which, while granting security to its members, also imposed certain obligations that required

---

[1] Davis, 1951, pp. 27, 99; India, 1901–5, I, 26; Kumar, 1965, p. 136.
[2] Carr-Saunders, 1936, p. 49; Davis, 1951, p. 98.
[3] See, for example, Nagam Aiya, 1894, I, 550; India, 1911–15, vol. I, part 1, p. 91; India, 1921–4, vol. I, part 1, pp. 62–83; India, 1932–7, XXI, 33–4.
[4] See pp. 59–60 above.

their presence at home. There was also the tendency to accept one's lot as that preordained by karma. Furthermore, with the exception of some Northern Indians, particularly Punjabis, the Indian peasant was generally not the abstract economic man in the sense of, say, his Chinese counterpart. Consequently he needed far stronger forces of propulsion and attraction than was customary in many other societies. Even under the most desperate conditions he seldom left immediately, preferring to hang on to the bare thread of life in his familiar milieu on the chance that his karma might change for the better. Then, if he conquered his fears of the unknown, he seldom knew where to go, for apart from his horizon being limited through inadequacies in education, the virtual absence or shockingly bad state of roads and other forms of transport and communication in the countryside restricted his movements to journeys little further than his home village or taluk (tahsil). Perhaps far more important than any, if not all, of the foregoing was the fact that even if there were adequate transport facilities and he knew the way to the nearest port, he seldom had the ready cash for his trip from the village to the port, let alone the voyage beyond. Finally, there was the prevalence of the truck system of employment in parts of India and the almost universal indebtedness amongst the peasantry to the landlord or moneylender. These people, as well as other local employers of labour, such as the planters,[1] were keenly alive to the value of their existing or potential labourers, debtors or serfs and adopted every stratagem fair or foul to retain their services. In this setting we have seen the direct or indirect services of recruiters or *agent provocateurs* become imperative if the dam of prejudices and obstacles was to be breached to any appreciable degree.[2]

As required by the Indian emigration machinery, each recruiter had to fulfil a number of official mandates before he could successfully see his catch safely aboard a steamer. To this end he had to present himself before administrative officials. But to gain access to these inner sanctums he had first of all to run the gauntlet of the *darwans* and babus, who often required to be bribed, otherwise they could keep the recruiter waiting and in the meantime dissuade the prospective emigrants. In any case, recruiters were an unpopular class and were considered fair game not only by office and railway caretakers and clerks but also by the policemen along the recruiters' routes.

Registration officers, most of whom were Indians, were also often unsympathetic to emigration. Some of the more zealous amongst them

---

[1] *PMBR*, 23.11.1843; *GMPPD*, 1912, 24 (Misc.) of 8.1.1912; Kumar, 1965, p. 139; *IE*, 1914, I, i, pp. 2–3; Rai, 1914*a*, pp. 13–14.

[2] See pp. 64–7 above.

at times even went to the extent, quite contrary to the government's policy and instructions, of actively endeavouring to dissuade emigrants. The general public, too, regarded emigration with disfavour well before nationalist feelings on the subject were aroused, and there were occasions when crowds actually tried to stop recruiters from departing with their recruits.[1] With the development of nationalism, these sentiments took on a much sharper edge, recruiters and their calling were denounced in no uncertain terms and a vigorous campaign mounted to end assisted emigration of labour altogether.[2]

These factors contributing to the general immobility of the Indian population do not exhaust the topic. They nevertheless serve to illustrate some of the main features and to show that the lack of large-scale emigration amongst the Indians was not the result, in any appreciable degree, of something mystic in their character or their 'innate love of home' as some officials would have us believe. Moreover, they also imply that we should be on guard against the widespread tendency to give too much importance to the stabilizing effects of the Indian social milieu or family structure in accounting for the lack of a mass overseas movement amongst the people of the Subcontinent.[3]

In the case of Malaya, there were other obstacles besides the factors operating against emigration from India in general. These included the Malayan government's immigration policy and the competition from the other Indian immigrant-receiving countries. Each one of these factors in its own way also appears to have tended to reduce the number of Indians arriving in Malaya.

We have noted above that the Malayan government's Indian immigration policy was geared almost totally to the promotion and regulation of a constant and adequate supply of labour and that except in a few isolated instances it made no attempt to sponsor the immigration of other types of Indians. Indeed, articulate Indians, who might conceivably rock the labour boat, were not welcome and from the 1920s at least were often actually barred from entering the country.

The movement of assisted labour, as well, was by no means on an unlimited scale, the volume being controlled to fit in with the prevailing demands. This was being done certainly by the 1920s by which time a

---

[1] Personal interviews with Kanganis Kundan and Subbiah of Negapatam, India, and Ipoh, Malaya, respectively; *IO:EP*, 1862 (1882), pp. 177–750; 2058 (1883), pp. 810–1364; British Guiana, 1916, pp. 6–68; Sanderson, 1910, part II, p. 29; Gillion, 1962, pp. 31–42; *SSAR*, 1937, p. 492.

[2] See pp. 108–14 above.

[3] With regard to *internal* migration within the Subcontinent itself, the role of the Indian social structure and family relationships as barriers to population mobility may have been even less, if not almost negligible (see, for example, Morris, 1960, pp. 124–33; 1965, pp. 42–83; Srinivas and Shah, 1960, pp. 1375–8).

considerable pool of Indian labour had already built up in Malaya. The method used to achieve this was the lowering or raising of the number of *kangani* recruiting licences issued and the number of voluntary emigrants to be assisted in any one year.[1] Then there was also the rejection of emigrants at the Malayan depots in India on such grounds as unsuitability and irregularities in recruiting. Stringency in applying the rules for rejection appears to have varied with the demand in Malaya. For example in 1928, owing to a temporary lull in demand for labour on rubber plantations in anticipation of the international scheme to control rubber production, more than 42 per cent of the labourers entering the Malayan depots in Madras and Negapatam were rejected, compared to the 21 per cent in 1924 and less than an estimated 10 per cent in 1912.[2] The number of *kangani* licences issued in 1928 also dropped from 7,882 in 1927 to 2,913, while the number of voluntary migrants assisted similarly decreased from 32,302 to 10,980 during the same period. In the next year, when conditions stabilized a little following the implementation of the Stevenson Rubber Restriction Scheme, the number of *kangani* licences issued was increased to 5,312 and the voluntary immigrants to 28,917. In the same manner during the Great Depression years, when there was a surplus of labour in Malaya, no *kangani* licences were issued while assistance to voluntary migrants was also virtually halted. Instead nearly 250,000 Indian labourers were repatriated to their homeland to reduce the number of unemployed and under-employed in Malaya. After the Depression, once sufficient labour had again entered Malaya, checks were once more introduced to reduce the chance of excessive surplus (Appendices 2, 4; figs. 6, 7).

The 1920s and 1930s were also the period when, with growing sophistication and knowledge, the Indian people showed less reluctance to emigrate; and signs were not wanting that if it had not been for the restrictive steps taken by the Malayan authorities the number of Indian labour immigrants would have been greater than those allowed to enter the country in the late 1920s and late 1930s.[3]

We have seen how Malaya, to compete with the more favourably situated Ceylon and Burma, had improved its conditions of service to make them competitive with those prevailing in the other two areas. But, despite these changes and indeed the superiority of service terms in Malaya, these two nearby areas never quite lost their attraction for the Indian emigrants. In fact, up to about the outbreak of World War II,

---

[1] Personal interview with Mr T. P. Sundaram, former Assistant Controller of Labour, Federation of Malaya; Parmer, 1960, p. 44; *SSAR*, 1935, pp. 769–70.

[2] *SSAR*, 1912, pp. 279–94; *SSAR*, 1924, p. 352; *SSAR*, 1928, pp. 359–70.

[3] India, 1932–7, xxi, 33–4; *SSAR*, 1935, p. 772; *SSAR*, 1937, pp. 491–2; *PFC*, 1934, pp. C 311–12; *PFC*, 1937, p. C 376.

Flow and characteristics

Table 4: Comparative flow of Indian immigrants
into Burma, Ceylon and Malaya, 1910–1935

Burma		Ceylon		Malaya	
year	number of immigrants	year	number of immigrants	year	number of immigrants
1910	331 100	1910	118 613	1910	91 723
1915	338 800	1915	94 809	1915	76 323
1920	341 100	1920	45 946	1920	99 474
1925	372 700	1925	223 798	1925	97 159
1930	368 500	1930	202 282	1930	86 152
1935	296 600	1935	144 427	1935	81 350
TOTALS	2 048 800		829 875		532 181

Source: Compiled from *SSAR*, 1910–35; Baxter, 1941, p. 121; Jackson, 1938, p. 42.

the annual movement of Indians to Ceylon and Burma generally
exceeded that to Malaya (table 4). Then places like the United States,
Canada and Kenya, despite their blatant anti-Indian immigration
policies, still retained their attraction for some Indians, especially Sikhs.
Needless to say the existence of all these rival competitors for the
relatively small number of Indian emigrants would have siphoned off
some emigrants who in other circumstances would probably have ended
up in Malaya.

But so much for the probabilities, now for the actual movement to
Malaya. The great bulk of this movement was of a transitory character,
with some 4,250,000 entering and about 3,000,000 leaving the country
between 1786 and 1957 (table 5a; Appendices 3, 4).

The trend of immigration shows several major fluctuations, with six
prominent periods (Appendix 3; fig. 8). The first, running approximately
from the 1840s to 1900, is the period of relatively unrestricted indentured
immigration, representing by and large a steady rise in immigration
until about the beginning of the present century. The second period,
from 1901 to 1922, saw the increasing regulation and final abolition of
the indenture system but on the other hand a rise in the *kangani* and
other individual contract methods. With the exception of a few small
drops in total immigration, as for example during World War I when
restrictions were imposed on Indian emigration and immigration by
the Indian and Malayan governments respectively (Part 2), there was
also an increasing volume of Indian immigration. The third period,
from 1923 to 1929, represents the spurt of immigration under the *Indian
Emigration Act, 1922* and under conditions of general prosperity in

157

Malaya. The fourth, from 1930 to 1933, marks the highest reversal of flow, as a result of the Great Depression and economic hardships in Malaya. More than 370,000 Indians left Malaya, during 1930–3, compared with less than 188,000 coming in (Appendices 3, 4). The fifth, from 1934 to 1938, witnessed the revival of the migratory flow towards Malaya, though not on the same scale as the late 1920s. This was largely because of the dampening aftermath of the Depression, a symptom not only confined to Malaya but a general feature distinguishing world population movements during this period. The final period, 1939 to 1957, shows not only the disruption of the Japanese invasion, but also the restricting influence of the Indian government's ban on assisted labour emigration and the increasingly stringent selective immigration policy of post-war Malaya. Fresh immigration in large numbers, with the exception of a few instances, as for example in 1952 and 1953 when many tried to beat the new entry regulations, virtually came to an end (Appendix 3). The movement of Indians after this was confined chiefly to those going to India to visit relatives and homes and returning to their place of work in Malaya.

The above changes in the current of Indian immigration into Malaya were the result mainly of fluctuations in the economic conditions in Malaya, particularly in the rubber industry, and to legislative enactments, initially in India and subsequently in Malaya (figs. 7, 8).

The largest average annual flow of the Indians into Malaya was during the period 1911–30, when more than 90,000 persons were landing in the country every year. This movement was about double the arrivals from 1901 to 1910. From 1921 to 1930 there were some 98,000 arrivals annually, after which there was a marked decline. In the future, there is little likelihood that Indian immigration into Malaya will regain even the volume it had prior to 1900.

With the increased Indian movement into Malaya from the beginning of the present century, the already exceptionally high percentage of those who returned also increased. For example, compared to the more than 30 per cent of Europeans who returned home after emigrating to the United States between 1821 and 1924,[1] more than 60 per cent of the Indians moving into Malaya during the same period went home. For the period 1925–57, those returning exceeded 80 per cent of the total immigration. This large percentage of returnees among the Indians was chiefly due to the fact that most of the Indians migrating to Malaya came primarily as short-term labourers and were more seasonal migrants than immigrants in any permanent sense. Many of the non-labour immigrants also came as short-term entrants, to earn money quickly

[1] Carr-Saunders, 1936, p. 49; Davis, 1951, pp. 99–100.

Flow and characteristics

Table 5a: Composition of total Indian immigration
into Malaya, 1786–1957

period	total number of arrivals	percentage		total	
		labourers	non-labourers	South Indians	North Indians
up to 1941	3823812	72·5	27·5	92·3	7·7
up to 1957	4245990	65·3	34·7	91·3	8·7

Source: As for Appendix 3.

Table 5b: Ethno-linguistic composition of Indian labour
immigration into Malaya, 1844–1941

total number of arrivals	percentage					
	Tamil	Telugu	Malayali	other South Indian	total South Indian	North Indian
2725917	85·2	6·8	6·4	0·8	99·2	0·8

Source: As for Appendix 3.

and then return home to the family hearth. The return flow thus largely reflected the economic health of Malaya, being highest when Malaya's economy was at its lowest and vice versa (Appendix 4; figs. 7, 8).

The total current of Indian migration to Malaya was a summation of the many lesser currents generated by and distinguishing the different categories of the migrants moving in and out of Malaya. The outstanding feature of these lesser currents which influenced the main flow was the fact that the Indian migration to Malaya consisted predominantly of adult labourers, generally between the ages of fifteen and forty-five years. These labourers comprised about 70 per cent of all the Indians entering Malaya before the Japanese occupation. Some 70 per cent of these labourers were assisted immigrants, principally *kangani* recruits (tables 2, 5a). Fluctuation in the flow was marked in the labour movement, since it was this section of the Indian immigration which was most sensitive to economic changes in Malaya and legislative sanctions in India (Appendix 3; figs. 6, 7).

More than 98 per cent of the labour immigrants were from South

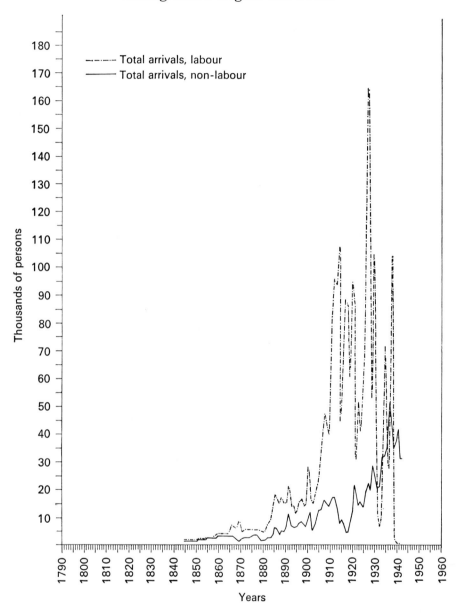

Fig. 6. The flow of Indian labour and non-labour migrants into Malaya, 1844–1941.

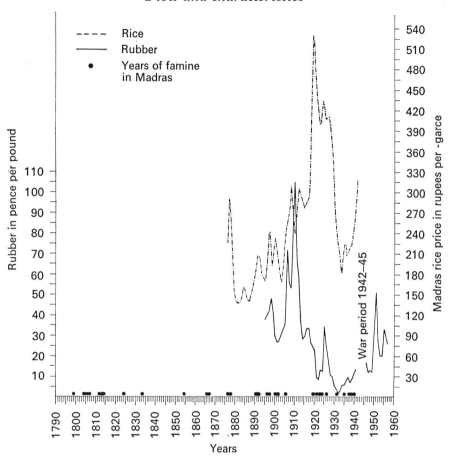

Fig. 7. Famines in India and the average annual London and Madras prices for rubber and rice respectively, 1867–1957.

India, largely Adi-dravida and other low-caste Tamils from such main localities as the North Arcot, Trichinopoly and Tanjore districts of the Madras Presidency (table 5b; figs. 9, 10a). Most of the non-labour immigrants were also from approximately the same areas (figs. 10b, 12a), further emphasizing the dominance of the South Indian elements in the total Indian movement. For example, between 1929 and 1938, more than 80 per cent of the total Indian arrivals in Malaya were from South India. Before 1929, the proportion of South Indians among the Indian migrants was even higher, as North Indian migration to Malaya in substantial numbers was a comparatively recent phenomenon (Appendix 3).

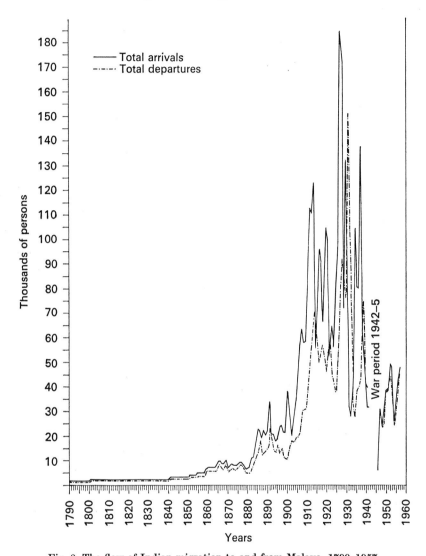

Fig. 8. The flow of Indian migration to and from Malaya, 1790–1957.

The majority of the South Indians were from the Madras Presidency (Province), the remainder being from the areas now included in Kerala and Andhra Pradesh States. The relatively small number of North Indian migrants into Malaya were chiefly from the Punjab, mostly Sikhs from the Malwa, Mahja and Dhoaba areas of the Land of Five Rivers (figs. 11, 12).

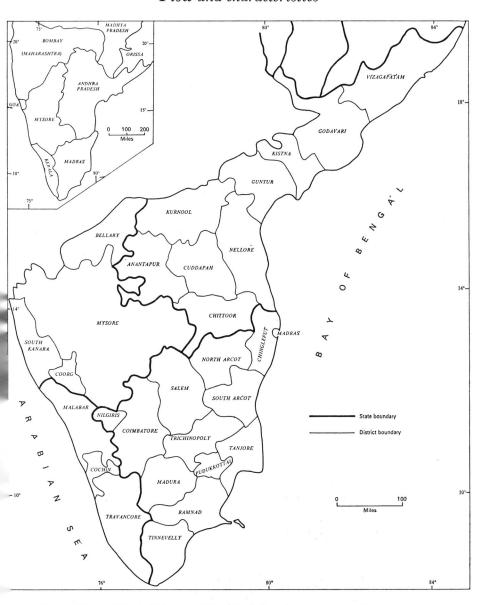

Fig. 9. The political divisions of South India: districts, 1941. For comparative purposes the state boundaries included here are those for 1957. Inset: states, 1957.

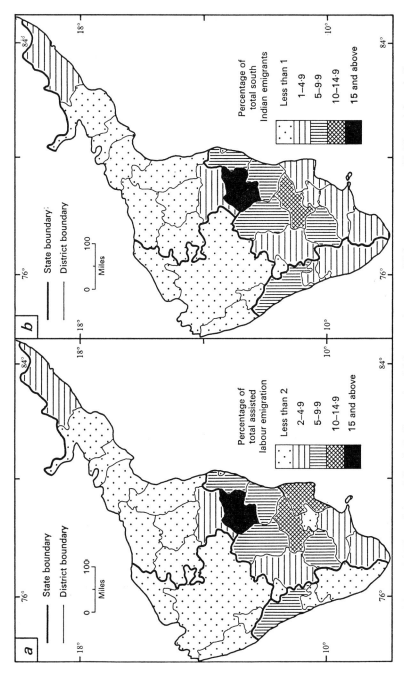

Fig. 10. (a) The origins of South Indian assisted labour emigrants to Malaya, 1844–1938. (b) The origins of all South Indian emigrants to Malaya, 1891–1941.

Map a legend:

Percentage of total assisted labour emigration

Less than 2
2–4.9
5–9.9
10–14.9
15 and above

State boundary
District boundary

0   100
Miles

Map b legend:

Percentage of total south Indian emigrants

Less than 1
1–4.9
5–9.9
10–14.9
15 and above

State boundary
District boundary

0   100
Miles

164

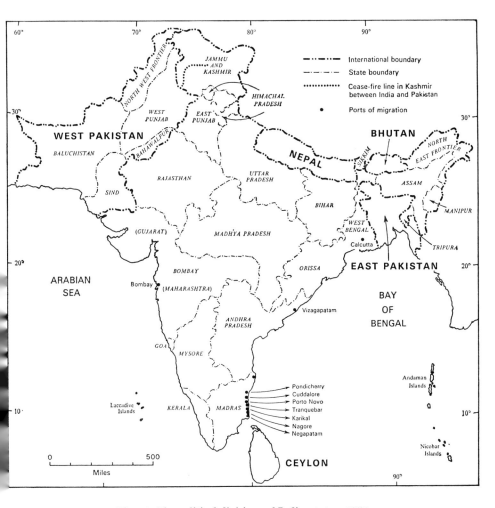

Fig. 11. The political divisions of India: states, 1957.

Information on the ultimate destinations of the Indian immigrants disembarking at Malayan ports is incomplete but it is estimated that more than half of them were heading for the Federated Malay States, especially Perak and Selangor.

We have noted above that one of the features common to all categories of migrants was the preponderance of males amongst them. The cumulative total of the main stream, quite naturally, reflects this pattern. For instance, between 1907 and 1938, the effective life period of the Indian Immigration Committee, females averaged only 24 per cent of

165

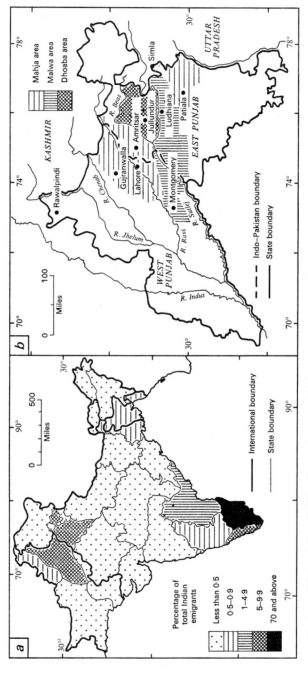

Fig. 12. (a) The origins of all Indian emigrants to Malaya, 1891–1957. (b) The origins of Sikh emigrants to Malaya, 1874–1957.

166

the total assisted labour immigration (Appendix 2). The proportion of females amongst the other types of immigrants was even smaller.[1] This predominantly male character of the Indian movement was due to the fact that the majority of the Indian immigrants were simply birds of passage, sojourners only in Malaya, and preferred to leave their families in India.

Another significant feature of the Indian movement to Malaya was that it consisted very largely of Hindu immigrants, who formed some 80 per cent of the total movement, the remainder being principally Muslims, Christians and Sikhs, in that order of numerical strength.

Finally, the difference between the recorded number of Indian arrivals and departures, the net immigration, is 1,234,000 for the 171 years between the British landing at Penang and *Merdeka*. Perhaps more significant, more than three-quarters of this net immigration took place after 1900 (Appendix 4). Under normal conditions, given this substantial migrational surplus and the fact that the majority of the net immigrants were comparatively recent arrivals, there should have been a large Indian, especially immigrant, population in Malaya at the end of British rule. However, the Indian population of Malaya in 1957 numbered only 820,270. More important, less than 311,000 of these Indians were recorded as being immigrants or born in India, the remainder being Malayan-born.[2] There is thus a considerable discrepancy between the total Indian net immigration into Malaya and the number of survivors. Similar analysis of other population censuses containing comparable data seems to reveal the same story:[3] the migration records generally appear to register a migrational surplus out of all proportion to the number of Indian survivors returned at census counts, leaving a very large number of *net immigrants* unaccounted for.

Four possible explanations suggest themselves. First, these people could have been absorbed into other population groups of the country, as for instance the Malays, and therefore were counted as members of these communities at census counts rather than as Indians. The process of *masok Melayu*, assimilation into the Malay community through conversion and marriage, appears to have taken place from the very early times and continues to this day. However, since the establishment of Islam and the abolition of slavery in Malaya in the fifteenth and early nineteenth centuries, respectively, intermarriage between Indians and Malays has been confined almost entirely to Indian Muslim males and Malay females, as Islamic and other social taboos formed serious barriers

[1] *SSAR*, 1906, p. 20; *SSAR*, 1924, pp. 352–3; *SSAR*, 1934, p. 859.
[2] Fell, 1960, table 7C; Chua, 1964, table 27.
[3] See, for example, Nathan, 1922, table 30; Vlieland, 1932, table 103 and del Tufo, 1949, table 45.

for other Indians, especially Hindus and Sikhs. With regard to the intermarriage between Indian Muslims and Malays, it is true that this gave rise to a mixed Indo-Malay community, Jawi Pekan, which since the end of the nineteenth century was enumerated as Malay for all practical purposes. However, the number of Indian immigrants involved in this process has been very small in terms of the total Indian population of Malaya.[1] The number of Indians assimilated into other population groups such as the Chinese and Eurasians is even smaller. In short, assimilation leading to enumeration in a community other than Indian can account for only a very tiny percentage of the net missing numbers.

There is the chance that they could have gone to other countries from Malaya. There was some movement to parts of Southeast Asia and the China coast and beyond, but it was confined almost wholly to non-labourers, mainly Northern Indians, as labour immigrants were specifically barred by law from leaving Malaya except to return to India. In the case of the non-labourers, the movement in and out of Malaya *vis-à-vis* these other countries appears to have been of about equal strength—a few thousand arrivals and departures annually.[2] Therefore, neither is this avenue of much help in explaining the unaccounted for net migrants.

The third possible explanation is that the migration statistics are unreliable as a whole or that while the immigration data are accurate, the number of departures recorded is hopelessly inaccurate and too low. It is true that the Malayan Indian migration statistics are far from complete or totally reliable (Aide-mémoire), but in terms of presenting a picture of the pattern of arrivals and departures they do not appear to be grossly off the mark.[3] In short, we must look elsewhere for the key to the enigma of the missing migrants.

---

[1] The exact number of Jawi Pekans in Malaya is unknown as no record was maintained of their numbers after 1911. Prior to this, too, the information is far from complete. On the basis of such data, it is estimated that the Jawi Pekan population of Malaya did not exceed 20,000 in 1957.

[2] *SSAR*, 1933, p. 472; *SSAR*, 1936, pp. 1042–4.

[3] We have noted that the Indian migration was predominantly a South Indian phenomenon. Until the 1930's almost all of these migrants travelled as deck-passengers, principally on boats of the British India Steam Navigation Company. The first Malayan port of call of these boats was Penang, where all the deck-passenger arrivals from India were recorded from 1879. The procedure for departures was very similar, the last port of departure also being Penang, where the number departing were also recorded. South Indians arriving and departing as deck-passengers by boats other than those of British India were comparatively few, the highest known number of arrivals and departures recorded in any one year being 1,578 and 720 respectively. Furthermore, these deck arrivals were also recorded, as a separate category amongst the total Indian migrants, prior to 1927 occasionally but continuously since then. No account of cabin-class passengers travelling by these other lines or by British India was taken till the beginning of

Flow and characteristics

This brings us to the last, and perhaps the most likely, explanation, that the mass of these *net immigrants* were killed by exhaustion, malnutrition, disease, snake bite and so on.

Till the systematization and control of the indenture and *kangani* systems of recruitment, recruiting often consisted of 'sweeping up of the dregs of humanity from the highways and byways and bringing them forward as emigrants', if they could 'only pass muster physically, no attention being paid to their fitness in other respects'.[1] After this as well, except in the case of the indentureds, neither the medical examination nor inquiry into the authenticity of the potential emigrants' agricultural heritage, was rigorous, unless specifically demanded by a particular employer.[2] As a result a number of the Indian immigrants arriving in Malaya were not fit or at any rate were hardly pioneer-type immigrants. Then, in addition to subsequent ill-usage, many of them suffered the disillusionment of things being not quite what they had been led to believe.

We have seen how many of the indentured got caught up in the vicious circle; a low daily income, insufficient food, deterioration in health and a reduction in their ability to work regularly; in turn a diminution in the already insufficient earnings resulted and they were obliged to eat still less, which caused a further deterioration in their health until death supervened. The position of many of the other labourers was not much different in that they were also paid only for the days for which they actually worked, medical leave and sick-pay being recent innovations only.

Then the average Indian labourer was a shockingly inefficient house-

the 1930s, when migration statistics began to be collected on a pan-Malayan basis of all Indians arriving and departing by *all* means of transport. In any case, the number of Indian cabin passengers, prior to the 1930s, was almost infinitesimal. Similarly no account was taken of the North Indian arrivals and departures by deck, cabin or by any other mode of travel till the beginning of 1929, but we know that the movement of Northern Indians in significant numbers did not begin much before this. Then there are also the statistics of South Indian arrivals and departures from and to Malaya collected by the Madras authorities. Although these differ from their Malayan counterparts from time to time, the overall pattern of arrivals and departures that they convey is not greatly dissimilar to that of the Malayan version. Therefore, while by no means complete, it does not appear that any significant numbers of Indians escaped being recorded since the 1870s. Then too, if there were gross errors in the migration statistics one sees no valid reason why these should be any more inaccurate in the case of the departures than arrivals or vice versa. Although no proper statistics are available for the period prior to the 1870s, we know that the pattern of movement then was essentially similar to that of the later period (*SSFR*, 6, 1794, 1.8.1794; *SSG*, 1880, p. 1068; *SSAR*, 1927, pp. 303–5; *SSAR*, 1937, pp. 1036–8; *GMPPD*, 1870, 40–4 of 13.9.1870).

[1] *RLC 1890*, p. 42; app. A, p. 37; app. L.
[2] *PAMMM*, 27.4.1913.

169

keeper. Even when he could afford to have better food, he tended to stint in this direction, not so much because of any superior endowment of thrift but to spend the savings thereof on drink, tobacco and the like.[1] Moreover, the Indian labourer was notoriously careless in his eating habits and hygiene—often eating food that was frequently stale or which only remotely resembled anything fit for human consumption. In addition, quite apart from the usual prejudices against going to a hospital when sick, he seldom took any proper precautions against infection of any kind.[2] In this setting of indiscriminate eating habits and poor hygiene, bowel complaints and infections were almost universal among the Indian labourers.[3] The debilitating effects of this and other infections, such as yaws, further sapped the resistance powers of the Indians, and this in an area in which malaria was hyperendemic and a major killer before the advent of modern anti-malarial controls and biotics.[4]

On top of this medical facilities were far from adequate. On some estates these were totally absent till recently. Then, in the case of those that possessed them, these medical facilities often consisted of only a shack and a compounder who had picked up the rudiments of medicine along the way. Even as late as 1918 there were only eight doctors to 1,006 estates in the Federated Malay States. Estates could use the government hospitals in the urban centres but, more often than not, these were fully extended in meeting urban needs. Then, for many of the isolated estates access was not easy at any time. Finally, there was the fear amongst many estate managers, especially in the early years of the present century, that their labourers would run away or be crimped if they were allowed to leave the estate. In these circumstances they often delayed sending sick labourers to government hospitals, preferring to treat them in their own medical facilities in the hope they would get better. When this did not work out, only then did they take steps to

[1] For example, according to a 1957–8 government sample survey of household budgets amongst a group of Malay, Chinese and Indian labourers and others, the Indian labourers spent less than 59 per cent of total earnings on food compared with 69 and 67 per cent, respectively, by the Malays and Chinese. On the other hand the Indians expended more than 13 per cent of their earnings on drink and tobacco compared with 5 and less than 8 per cent by their Chinese and Malay counterparts respectively (Department of Statistics, 1958 *a*, tables 1–18).

[2] For instance, despite the fact that in many rural areas there was a complete lack of proper disposal of excreta and that the milieu of most of them was the largely and constantly damp soils and atmosphere, most of them went about barefoot.

[3] An illustration of this is that government sample surveys, before and after World War II, of bowel infections amongst rural dwellers have revealed that more than 70 per cent of the Indians in these parts were infected by ankylostomiasis (Ooi, 1959, p. 67).

[4] Ooi, 1959, pp. 46–60, 68–9; *RCHE 1924*, pp. A 4–77.

take their sick to the hospitals. Often this was too late. In some cases where such estate managers themselves realized it was too late, rather than take their dying labourers into the hospitals and have to explain their actions, they resorted to the safer device of leaving the moribund labourers—who invariably had no idea of the actual name of the estate on which they worked, knowing it only by its colloquial Tamil soubriquet —on the side of main roads, away from their own properties, in the hope of their being picked up by some passing Samaritan. Even as late as the 1930s labourers in a moribund state were being picked up from the roadsides by government vans that chanced to be passing or were summoned by some passer-by who had stumbled on the near corpses.[1]

Then, if not succumbing to exhaustion, malnutrition and disease, the Indian labourers, living as many of them did on the fringe of the Malayan jungle, had also to survive encounters with snakes, particularly cobras, crocodiles, tigers and other dangerous reptiles and beasts.[2]

In the face of these overwhelming odds it is not at all surprising that, up to the abolition of indenture, on some estates as many as 60 rising to 90 per cent of the labourers died within a year of their arrival.[3] Conditions improved after this, but even then the deaths remained high till the 1920s.[4]

Quite separate from the foregoing mortality there was the havoc of the Japanese occupation when more than 50,000 Indian immigrant labourers are estimated to have lost their lives (Part 2).

The fate of the comparatively better off and organized non-labour Indian immigrants was, quite naturally, somewhat better in terms of survival. But deaths amongst them too, although nothing like that amongst their labour compatriots, were high till the 1920s. Then, they also suffered many casualties during the Japanese occupation (Part 2).

In this setting of high death rates till the 1920s and again during the Japanese occupation, it seems probable, and by no means unduly surprising, that more than 750,000 Indian immigrants may have died in Malaya during the period of this study. Many of the Indian labour leaders certainly appear to have no doubts about this as becomes apparent from the following remark of one of them: 'Every railway sleeper and rubber tree in Malaya marks the remains of an Indian.'

To sum up, following the establishment of British rule in India and

[1] *ARLDM*, 1918, p. 11, apps. D, E, F, G; *CSSMRCA*, p. 26; *RCHE 1924*, pp. A 4–77; *PMOJMCCEL*, pp. 3–7.
[2] *FMSAR*, 1905, p. 10.
[3] Sanderson, 1910, part II, p. 432; *IO:EP*, 8522 (1910), p. 228; *FMSAR*, 1908, pp. 2–17.
[4] In 1918 the number of deaths amongst the Indian labourers in the Federated Malay States alone amounted to 20,000 compared with 5,571 births (*ARLDM*, 1918, p. 11, apps. D. E. F. G).

the consolidation of their power in Malaya, Indian interests were largely subordinated to the needs of the paramount power. Consequently the character of Indian contacts with Malaya also changed. In the first place, whereas the earlier immigrants were mainly merchants, traders, adventurers and purveyors of a superior civilization, the modern migrants were chiefly unlettered labourers coming in to work for a pittance on some plantation or government project. Secondly, in contrast to the earlier phase, the modern migration was not to any extent spontaneous but rather politically arranged by the British and brought about to a considerable degree by the persuasions of agents and recruiters. Finally whereas the earlier movement was small in volume, the later migration was on a large scale.

Much of the modern Indian migration to Malaya, during the period 1786–1957, however, was a short-term migration with an extremely high proportion of returnees. The flow of migration was affected primarily by legislation enacted both in Malaya and in India and the economic conditions prevailing in Malaya from time to time. Within this framework probably the peak of Indian immigration was reached in the late 1920s. After that increasing legal restrictions in India and Malaya, coupled with the growth of a local labour supply and strident nationalism, have seen the decline and, finally, the virtual cessation of Indian immigration into Malaya. The present movement of Indians to and from Malaya is limited almost wholly to Indians of Malayan domicile. The above factors which contributed to the decline of Indian immigration are likely to persist in the future. Thus, leaving aside the question of Indian immigration ever regaining the volume it had prior to the Great Depression, there appears to be little likelihood of fresh immigration, even in small numbers.

PART 2

THE INDIAN POPULATION OF MALAYA GROWTH AND ASSOCIATED CHARACTERISTICS

6

GROWTH AND STRUCTURE

Malaya's population has grown rapidly, especially over the last sixty years; by 1957 it numbered 7,725,000 persons and eight years later more than 10,000,000. The growth of the Indian section of the country's population has been equally spectacular, though with considerable fluctuations over the inter-census periods (fig. 13; table 6a).

Table 6a: Growth and racial composition of the population of Malaya, 1891–1965

year	total population (in thousands)	percentage of total			
		Malays	Chinese	Indians	others
1891(a)	1 500	65·0	25·0	5·0	5·0
1901(a)	1 800	60·0	30·0	6·6	3·4
1911	2 645	53·3	34·6	10·1	2·0
1921	3 327	48·8	35·2	14·2	1·8
1931	4 348	44·4	39·2	14·3	2·1
1947	5 849	43·5	44·7	10·3	1·5
1957	7 725	42·9	44·2	10·6	2·3
1965	10 047	43·4	44·0	10·5	2·1

(a) The figures for 1891 and 1901 are estimates as no worthwhile information is available on the population of the Unfederated Malay States for these years.
Source: Compiled from del Tufo, 1949, table 2, app. c; Fell, 1960, table 1; Chua, 1964, table 2; *MSB*, Dec. 1966, p. 3; *MDS*, Jan. 1967, p. 11.

Table 6b: The Indian population of Penang, Malacca and Singapore, 1794–1871

Penang		Malacca		Singapore	
year	population	year	population	year	population
1794	1 000	1817	2 986	1821	132
1812	7 113	1834	2 403	1833	2 324
1833	10 346	1860	1 026	1850	6 284
1871	18 611	1871	3 277	1871	11 501

Source: Compiled from *SSFR*, 6 (1794), 1.8.1794; del Tufo, 1949, app. c.

The Indian population of Malaya

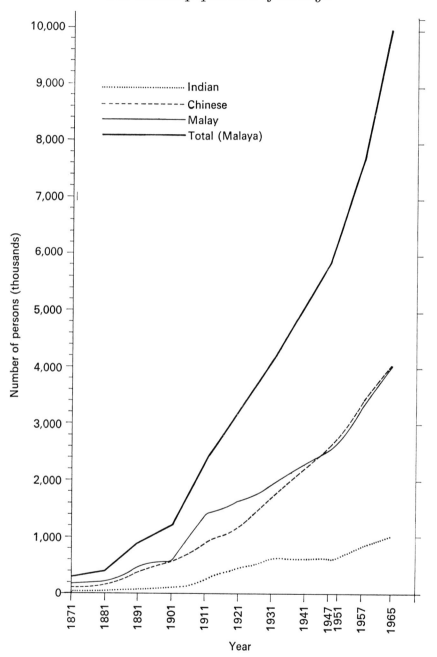

Fig. 13. Growth of the population of Malaya, 1871–1965.

176

Growth and structure

The period 1786–1873

It will be remembered that prior to the establishment of Penang, Indian contacts with Malaya passed through two distinct phases. The first ended with the coming of the Portuguese in 1511, and was associated with the dominance of Indian concepts and institutions in the political, social and economic life of the country. The second ended with the arrival of the British, and was characterized by the waning of Indian influence. With the purchase by Francis Light of the island of Penang from the Sultan of Kedah, new and quite different Indian connections were forged with Malaya. Now, while Indian sepoys and lascars helped to maintain law and order, Indian labourers and convicts toiled to develop the new settlements (Part 1). Indian traders were also present but not in the same exalted roles as some of their brethren in Malay courts. They were nevertheless, it seems, forging profitable commercial links because increasingly large numbers of them began to move into these settlements. A similar tendency could also be detected among other classes of immigrants, especially with the expansion of government works and commercial agriculture in the nineteenth century. Some of these migrants, like their predecessors, took local brides from amongst the Malay and slave populations. Fed by two streams, immigration and natural increase, particularly the former, the numbers of Indians in the Straits Settlements increased from an estimated total of less than 2,000 in 1786 to 33,389 by the time of the first population census in 1871 (table 6 b).

No statistical data are available for the rest of Malaya, but the number of Indians there is unlikely to have been more than a few hundred up to the time of the British occupation of Perak, Selangor and the Sungei Ujong area of Negri Sembilan in 1874.

Growth of state populations, 1786–1873

We know that Indian sepoys, lascars and domestic servants were present at Penang from the very first day of its occupation by the British (Part 1). On the second day, if not from the start, they were joined by other Indians, from Kedah.[1] Others from the same source and other Malay states and from India followed. By 1794 the resident Indian population of the Island, according to Francis Light, was second only to that of the Chinese, who although later arrivals than the Indians had nevertheless moved in in larger numbers:

...The Chinese...are men, women, and children, above 3,000...The second class of our inhabitants consists of the Chooliars (Chulias) or people from the several ports on the Coast of Coromandel. The greater part of these have long

[1] *JIA*, IV (1850) 629–62; *SSFR*, 1 (1769–95), 1.9.1787.

been inhabitants of Queda (Kedah) and some of them born there. They are all shopkeepers and coolies. About one thousand are settled here some with families. The vessels from the Coast bring over annually 1,300 or 2,000 men who by traffic and various kinds of labour obtain a few dollars with which they return to their homes and are succeeded by others...[1]

In addition to the above there were also the garrison, convicts and the camp-followers and Bengali, and possibly Parsi and Gujarati, traders and others (Part 1).

The next available population count for Penang giving details comparable to the above is that of 1812. By this year there were 7,113 Indians in a total population of 26,107 in Penang and Province Wellesley. The first twenty-one years saw this number rise to 10,346 and this in turn to 18,611 by the beginning of the 1870s (table 6*b*). By this time Indians had already replaced the Chinese as the principal labourers in the expanding European sugar industry of Province Wellesley (Part 3).

The fortunes of Malacca were more varied as it struggled to develop its new livelihood of agriculture to replace its former lifeblood, commerce. This transition stage appears to have affected the number of Indians among others (table 6*b*).

In Singapore, other than one Naraina Pillay, a Hindu trader from Penang, and the 120 sepoys and lascars, and possibly camp-followers, assistants and domestic servants, in Raffles' entourage, there is no record of Indians at its foundation in 1819.[2] Two years later 132 Indians, apart from the garrison and camp-followers above, were enumerated in a total population of 4,727. With the influx of increasing numbers of traders, labourers and the like, in response to Raffles' liberal policies and rapidly expanding opportunities for employment and gain, the Indian population rapidly increased and by 1871 had reached a total of 11,501. This number of Indians was exclusive of the garrison and its camp-followers and convicts (table 6*b*).

No information is available for the number of Indians in the other Malayan states during this period. It is certain, however, that some Indian immigrants arriving in the Straits ports subsequently moved into the Malay States to augment the numbers already there. But this movement is unlikely to have involved many persons in view of the generally unsettled conditions in the mainland interior. Indeed in one case—Kedah—the movement *out* of the area towards the British settlements appears to have been more marked. At the time of the British acquisition of Penang the affairs of Kedah were under 'the

[1] *SSFR*, 6 (1794), 1.8.1794.
[2] *SSFR*, 185 (1805–30), 8.3.1819; Ministry of Culture, Singapore, 1966, p. 213.

guidance of a Chuliah (Chulia) or Coromandel Coastman bearing the title of 'Dattoo (Dato) Sri Raja' or 'Most Illustrious One'—a Kedah title normally conferred by the Sultan on the state *shahbandar*, or a sort of municipal-cum-port officer responsible for the commercial affairs of the state in general and the reception and treatment of foreign merchants in particular. Besides the Dato and his underlings, other Indians were present as traders and farmers. In the 1790s more Indians were engaged, probably from Penang, to erect and man the state's defences. Contemporary accounts give the impression that despite the probability of a greater out- than in-migration there were still, at least, a couple of hundred Indians in Kedah at this time, principally in and around the capital at Alor Star. Indeed, the inhabitants of two of Alor Star's satellite *kampongs*, Limbong and Anak Bukit, were 'chiefly Chuliah (Chulia)'.[1] But continuingly unsettled conditions, and finally the invasion and depredations of the Siamese army in 1821, appear to have resulted in an exodus of Indians to Penang, for little is heard of Indians actually resident in Kedah till much later.[2]

There is no reference to any Indians being present in Selangor at this time, but there may well have been some. In Pahang and Kelantan only some runaway convicts were mentioned as being present.[3] As several convicts usually escaped from the Straits Settlements every year (Part 1), it is possible that other areas of Malaya, including Selangor, may also have received such 'immigrants'. A few Indians are recorded as being present at Rembau in Negri Sembilan and, according to the observations of Francis Light and his correspondence with the Sultan of Trengganu, Kuala Trengganu, the capital, then consisted of 200 houses some of which were occupied by Indian traders.[4]

In the case of Perak, no definite information is available concerning the fate of the Indians recorded to have been there before the founding of Penang.[5] But it is known that subsequent to the establishment of Penang, runaway Indians—possibly convicts, other criminals or labourers—were sold as slaves in Perak if captured by the local people. At other times, other Indians, ostensibly brought for work in Penang, were actually being taken to Perak to be sold into perpetual indenture

---

[1] *SSFR*, 1 (1769–95), 'Some account of Quedah and of adjacent countries', unsigned and undated; 2 (1786–7), 13.12.1786; *C.O.273*, 1 (1838–58), 24.4.1842; Bassett, 1964, pp. 121–2.

[2] As many of the 'Indians' in Kedah were probably really Jawi Pekans, it is possible that those who did not flee passed into the Malay community. This is not to say that Indian contacts with Kedah entirely ceased then, but rather than reside in Kedah they operated from the comparatively safer sanctuary of Penang. The reappearance of Indians in substantial numbers in Kedah had to await the return of more normal conditions in the ensuing years.   [3] *C.O.273*, 5 (1861–2), 3.9.1860.

[4] *SSFR*, 3 (1788–9), 13.2.1788.   [5] Nathan, 1922, p. 85.

by Indian speculators.[1] Then, from an unknown date, possibly after the discovery of the Larut tinfield in 1848, a number of Indian bullock-cart owners and drivers and the like, presumably from Penang Island and Province Wellesley, began to move into the Larut–Matang area of the State. Here, according to both the diary of the first British Resident of Perak, J. W. W. Birch, and the first report of Capt. Speedy, the Assistant Resident, these Indians for some time enjoyed a monopoly of the bullock-cart carrying trade.[2]

Indians were making their presence felt in Johore too, although in a somewhat different role from that in Perak. R. O. Winstedt and the Governor of the Straits Settlements record the presence of Tamil advisers and moneylenders in the royal court of Johore.[3]

Although there is no mention in contemporary literature, it is possible that other classes of Indians such as traders and labourers may also have been present in this state at this time. Indian merchants, particularly those from the Malabar coast, for example, were certainly still prominent in the international trade of early eighteenth-century Johore,[4] and it is not impossible that some such contacts—albeit it would seem in ever decreasing volume, frequency and status—may have continued thereafter as well.

The period 1874–1957

The British occupation of the Federated Malay States in the 1870s and 1880s started a fresh wave of expansion in plantation agriculture.[5] On a smaller scale there was further expansion in the commercial agricultural enterprises of Kedah, Johore and the Straits Settlements as well.[6]

[1] C.O.273, 2 (1858–9), 8.12.1858.

[2] BP, 1st Diary of J.W.W. Birch in Perak, 15.4.1874; SSG, 1875, pp, 291–3.

[3] Sultan Hussein, whom Raffles installed as Sultan of Johore in order to acquire Singapore, was indolent and extravagant. This led his wife to get a Tamil friend, Abdul Kadir, to manage the royal house. Infuriated by the Tamil's economies, the Sultan's dependants started a scandal about the Tamil and his royal mistress, which forced Hussein to move both his own household and the Tamil to Malacca. There the Tamil was given a title and married to a daughter of Sultan Hussein. Then Sultan Ali, Sultan Hussein's heir and successor, was heavily indebted to a Tamil moneylender and gave him in 1868 'the right to sell Muar to the British or anyone else'. In the same year, Sultan Ali also gave power of attorney to an Indian schoolmaster, Babu Ramasamy, 'to collect the non-existent revenue' from his small territory (Winstedt, 1932, pp. 89 et seq.; C.O.273, 110 (1881), 31.12.1881).

[4] Bassett, 1964, pp. 121–2.

[5] For example, there were already forty sugar estates in Perak by 1899, covering 50,000 acres and employing 8,000–9,000 labourers. Coffee was another major crop, which spread rapidly, especially in the Federated Malay States. By 1896, Selangor alone had seventy-two estates comprising 47,000 acres (PAR, 1899, pp. 14–15; SAR, 1896, p. 3; Parmer, 1960, pp. 7–8).

[6] The sugar acreage in Penang, for instance, increased from 13,500 acres in 1871 to 15,000 by 1901, and tapioca to 9,300 acres from 7,650 in 1891 (SSBB, 1871, pp. W4–5, X8–10; SSBB, 1901, pp. W4–5, X8–10).

Growth and structure

The labourers and subordinate staff on these new plantations, as well as in the rapidly expanding government services, were chiefly Indian, following an increasing volume of fresh immigration in the 1880s and 1890s. By 1891 the Indian population had jumped to about 76,000 and ten years later to some 119,000 (table 7).

The story of the growth of the Indian population after 1901 is tied very closely to the expansion of the government services and projects and of the oil palm and rubber estates, particularly the latter, which now replaced the sugar and coffee enterprises. Rubber grew rapidly from some 50,000 acres in 1900 to 543,000 in 1911 and 3,272,000 in 1938 (Part 3). The growth of the Indian population was equally spectacular as increasing numbers of Indians flowed into the country to man the new projects. The number of Indians in Malaya spiralled to 268,269 by 1911 and 470,180 ten years later (table 7).

The increase in the Indian population would have been considerably higher during the 1911–21 period had it not been for a number of adverse factors. First, in August 1914 the European War broke out and for a month or two there was a dislocation of trade, many mines closed down and great difficulty was experienced in obtaining remittances from England to continue development projects on newly opened rubber estates. The number of labourers thrown out of employment was so large that immigration from India was totally prohibited. The embargo was only lifted in 1915. Secondly, there was an outbreak of influenza in 1918 which killed more than 40,000 people, many of them Indian, who had little resistance and contracted pneumonia easily. During the epidemic the death rate per thousand for the Indians was 372·0 compared with 129·6 for the Malays and 158·4 for the Chinese. Finally, in 1916, there was a general rush for land for rubber and the area alienated was so large that there was an almost unprecedented demand for Indian labour and the probability of the then record figure of immigrants, that for 1913, being exceeded in 1917. But in April 1917, the Indian government stopped all emigration of labour from India except under licence, and limited the number of labour recruits to 82,000 adults. In 1918 this number was reduced to 73,000 and, owing to the urgent need of recruits for labour battalions both in India and Europe, the emigration of males between the ages of eighteen and twenty-five years was prohibited. With the exception of those returning to their place of residence or work, the emigration of some non-labouring classes, especially Sikhs, was also discouraged. At times it was almost stopped, partly, as noted above, because they were needed at home for the armed forces and partly on grounds of security. In 1919 all restrictions on emigration were removed but an outbreak of cholera in the Malayan depots in India halted operations. Furthermore, the unfavourable rate of exchange between the Indian rupee and the Straits dollar limited the numbers immigrating while, towards the beginning of the 1920s, the world trade depression also began to affect Malaya, reducing immigration further.[1]

Nevertheless, the increase of more than 75 per cent in the Indian population between 1911 and 1921 was proportionately far higher than that for any other community; for the Chinese increased by 28 per cent and the Malays by less than 15 per cent during the same period.[2] But such a high rate of increase was not maintained in the ensuing decades. With the growth of a large pool of labour in the country, and the introduction of the Stevenson Rubber Restriction Scheme in 1928 (to combat over-production) and the first rumblings of the Great Depression, immigration—the main factor in the rate of increase up to now—began to taper off from its 1926 peak value (Part 1). These changes are reflected in the inter-census population change between 1921 and 1931, when the Indian population increased by only 32·2 per cent. In the ensuing years even this rate of increase was interrupted by the Great Depression, the Indian Government's ban on labour emigration, the outbreak of World War II and finally the occupation of Malaya by the Japanese in 1942.

We know that during the Great Depression, while 187,000 Indians arrived in Malaya, 373,000 fled the country during the four years from 1930 to 1933, a net loss of 186,000 persons (Part 1). Hardly had this loss been made good when the Indian government clamped its ban on labour emigration. This dried up an important source of Indian population increase. Then there was the total stoppage of Indian migration following the Japanese occupation of Malaya and the consequent disruption of normal passenger services between India and Malaya. Perhaps more important, the Malayan economy came to a virtual standstill.

At the time of the Japanese attack on Malaya, both the rubber and tin industries were working at maximum capacity. But by 1943 the Japanese had insufficient ships to take away the rubber, and their efforts to distil it into motor fuel failed. Rubber became almost unsaleable. Tin dredges were either sunk or out of action for want of spares. Many workers lost their means of livelihood. At the same time the price of food soared. Former sources of food—countries like China, Australia, India, Indonesia, Thailand and Burma—were now totally closed or difficult to reach. The food stockpile left behind by the British administrators had disappeared within a few months. The people of Malaya

[1] Nathan, 1922, pp. 19–21; *IICMM*, 1913–20.
[2] Nathan, 1922, pp. 30–4.

Table 7: Growth of the Indian population of Malaya, 1881–1957

numbers at each census

state/year	Singapore	Penang	Malacca	Perak	Selangor	Negri Sembilan	Pahang	Johore	Kedah	Perlis	Kelantan	Trengganu	un-located	MALAYA
1881	12138	27202	1891	N	N	N	N	N	N	N	N	N	N	44000 (E.T.)
1891	16035	35987	1647	15143	3592	1117	583	700	800	N	100	N	N	76000 (E.T.)
1901	17845	37774	1276	35037	16847	5526	1227	N	N	N	N	N	N	119000 (E.T.)
1911	28454	45901	7527	74771	74079	18248	6611	5669	6074	114	731	90	—	268269
1921	32687	49656	18857	132215	132561	33658	8694	24184	33071	811	3575	211	—	470180
1931	50860	53119	23237	162846	155823	50096	14544	51025	50808	966	6745	1371	407	621847
1947	68978	57157	19718	140176	145184	38082	14744	55044	51347	1684	4940	1761	801	599616
1957	124084	69035	23266	178623	201048	54399	21838	70948	67094	1539	5665	2731	—	820270

inter-census percentage increase/decrease

state/year	Singapore	Penang	Malacca	Perak	Selangor	Negri Sembilan	Pahang	Johore	Kedah	Perlis	Kelantan	Trengganu	MALAYA
1881–1891	32·1	32·3	−12·9	N	N	N	N	N	N	N	N	N	56·5
1891–1901	11·2	4·9	−22·5	131·3	369·0	394·7	110·4	N	N	N	N	N	56·5
1901–1911	59·4	21·5	498·8	113·4	339·7	230·2	438·7	N	N	N	N	N	125·4
1911–1921	14·8	8·2	150·5	76·8	78·9	84·4	31·5	326·6	444·4	611·4	389·0	134·4	75·2
1921–1931	55·5	6·9	23·2	23·1	17·5	48·8	67·2	110·9	53·6	19·1	88·6	549·7	32·2
1931–1947	35·6	7·6	−15·1	−13·9	−6·8	−24·0	1·4	7·9	1·1	74·3	−26·8	28·4	−3·6
1947–1957	79·8	20·8	18·0	27·4	38·5	42·8	48·1	28·9	30·7	−8·6	14·7	55·1	36·7

N = No information available.

E.T. = Estimated total.

Some of the sources contain numerous errors of addition. In such cases the errors have been corrected and the totals adjusted accordingly.
Source: Compiled from Scott, 1912, table 4; State of Kelantan, 1911, table 1; Nathan, 1922, table 2; Vlieland, 1932, table 18; del Tufo, 1949, table 4, app. c; Fell, 1960, table 1; Chua, 1964, table 2.

realized that the only hope of survival lay in the cultivation of their own foodstuffs. Their efforts in this direction, however, were only partly successful and the loss of life through malnutrition was considerable.

There were other adverse factors which aggravated the food shortage and caused abnormally high death rates, particularly amongst the very young and old. The Japanese rationing system failed to operate effectively outside the larger towns and villages, resulting in an inflation of the prices of basic commodities, whilst black-marketing became an established mode of business. Worse still, many families lost their bread-winners through the forced recruitment of able men into labour gangs for various Japanese constructional projects, notably though not solely the notorious Siamese Death Railway. More than 85,000 Indians, chiefly those living on estates, are reputed to have been amongst those mobilized for this project. Only about half of these Indians survived to rejoin their families. The birth rate of the Indian population fell as a result of the long absence of husbands, while the mortality rate increased due to the lowered levels of nutrition. The deterioration of medical facilities through lack of adequate funds, personnel and medicines aggravated this increase.[1]

The combined effect of all the foregoing factors was that the Indian population, which stood at 621,847 in 1931 and, in normal circumstances, might have been expected to reach at least 800,000 in 1947, actually declined: only 599,616 Indians being enumerated in 1947. This represented a drop of more than 3·5 per cent on the 1931 figure (table 7). With the full recovery of the Malayan economy, health services, shipping and other immigration facilities, reunion of war-separated families and completion of delayed marriages by the beginning of the 1950s, the rate of population growth picked up once again and by the last census, in 1957, there were 820,270 Indians in the country, a rise of nearly 37 per cent over 1947 (table 7). Official estimates place the number of Indians living in Malaya at the end of 1965 at 1,063,000, representing an increase of almost 30 per cent over the 1957 total.[2] If such rates of increase are maintained the Indian population is expected to pass the 2,000,000 mark by 1987, if not earlier.[3]

[1] del Tufo, 1949, pp. 33–6; Smith, 1952, p. 84; personal interview with the Commissioner for Labour, Federation of Malaya; *BM*, May 1946, pp. 13–14; *H*, 5.3.1946.
[2] *MSB*, Dec. 1966, p. 3; *MDS*, Jan. 1967, p. 11.
[3] Cf. Fell, 1960, pp. 46–50.

Growth and structure

The changing balance between immigration and natural increase

Up to World War II the dominant factor in the increase of the Indian population in Malaya was the excess of immigrants over emigrants.[1] Few Indians had any intention of settling permanently in Malaya until comparatively recently. If married, they almost invariably left their wives and families in India and returned to them as soon as they had saved enough money or finished their contracts in Malaya. If unmarried they had generally little opportunity of finding wives in Malaya owing to the shortage of women of their own kind. The difficulties imposed by religion formed an almost unsurmountable barrier restraining most of them from intermarriage with other communities, even if they overcame their own prejudices. Therefore, although poverty may have kept them a longer time in Malaya, a stretch of three to five years was about the longest they endured before the urge to return to India, at least for a visit, became too great. Nevertheless, transitory though the Indian migration to Malaya was, there was a net migration of more than 1,200,000 Indians into the country between 1786 and 1957 (Part 1). It is interesting to speculate what the demographic structures of the Indian and the total population of Malaya would have been if all these immigrants had survived. Sufficient numbers, however, did survive and it was primarily they who were responsible for the increases in the Indian population until the late 1930s.

In the earlier stages Indian migration to Malaya was nearly all male; in 1901 there were only 171 women to every 1,000 men in Malaya. Following the systematization of the labour immigration machinery, migration of female labour became comparatively greater. As they settled in Malaya and as their means improved, other Indians, too, like their labour compatriots, began to bring in their womenfolk. This, coupled with the natural increase in Malaya, gradually augmented the number of women in the Indian population (table 8 a). This change in the male: female ratio is reflected in the increasing normalization of the age-structure of the Indian population (fig. 14).

The improvement in the sex-structure, together with the expansion

---

[1] This point is stressed by the superintendent of the 1921 population census of Malaya, '. . . in British Malaya the main factor which governs the increase in the (Indian) population is not, as in European countries, the excess of births over deaths but immigration . . . Deaths during the past decade have been largely in excess of births and were it not for the stream of immigrants from . . . India . . . there would have been a decrease in the population instead of an increase . . .', and reiterated by his successor in 1931: '. . . the dominant factor in the growth of the . . . (Indian) population is not, as in European countries, the excess of births over deaths but the excess of immigrants over emigrants . . .' (Nathan, 1922, p. 18; Vlieland, 1932, p. 32).

The Indian population of Malaya

Table 8a: Number of females per 1,000 males in the
total Indian population of Malaya, 1891–1965

1891	1901	1911	1921	1931	1947	1957	1965
18(a)	171(a)	308	406	482	637	692	750

(a) = Excluding the Unfederated Malay States for which no information is available.
Source: As for Table 6a.

Table 8b: Percentage of Indian, Chinese, Malay and
total population born in Malaya, 1911–1967

year	Indian	Chinese	Malay	total
1911	12·0 (a)	16·0 (a)	85·0 (a)	50·0 (a)
1921	12·4	22·0	87·4	53·2
1931	21·1	31·2	91·3	56·3
1947	49·8	62·5	95·4	75·4
1957	62·1	74·7	96·9	77·9
1967	70·0 (a)	85·0 (a)	98·0 (a)	85·0 (a)

(a) These figures are estimates as the birthplace information available is incomplete.
Source: Compiled from Nathan, 1922, pp. 93–101; del Tufo, 1949, pp. 83–6; Fell, 1960, pp. 45–50, 77–84; Chua, 1964, tables 24–25; MSB, Dec. 1966, pp. 3–6; MDS, Jan. 1967, pp. 11–14.

of health services and consequent reduction in mortality rates, especially in the rural areas, resulted in natural increase becoming a significant factor in the growth of the Indian population from the beginning of the 1930s.[1] By 1937 the annual rate of natural increase among the Indians was 2 per cent. Twenty years later it had reached 3·5 per cent, the highest of any community in Malaya, with the exception of the Malays.[2]

Since the Japanese occupation the increase in the total Indian population has been predominantly the result of a birth rate outstripping a death rate, the migrational increase having become a relatively minor feature. The replacement of net immigration by natural increase as the dominant factor contributing to the growth of the Indian population is reflected in the increasing proportion of the local or Malayan-born group amongst the Indians in Malaya (table 8b). Today about 70 per cent of the Indians are estimated to be local-born and a

[1] It was not until 1929 that there was an excess of births over deaths amongst the Indians in Malaya in any one year (ARAGIBM, 1929, p. 14).
[2] ARAGIBM, 1937, p. 30; FMAR, 1957, p. 9; CSAR, 1957, pp. 24–7.

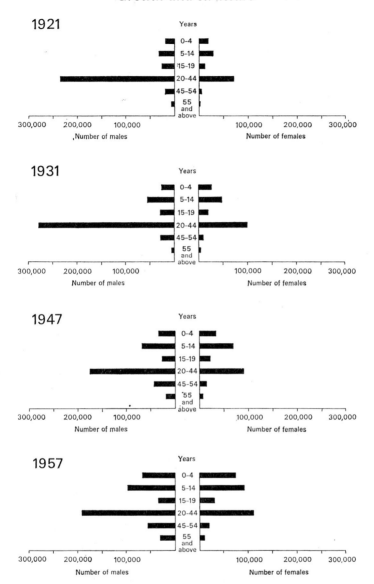

Fig. 14. Age-structure of the Indian population of Malaya, 1921–1957.

further 25 per cent have been resident in Malaya for more than ten years. Fresh immigration has virtually ended and, barring a major catastrophe, the future growth of Indian population in Malaya will be determined by the rate of natural increase.

187

The Indian population of Malaya

Patterns of growth in state and 'mukim' populations, 1874–1957

Within three decades of their occupation by the British, the rate of increase of the Indian population in the Federated Malay States had equalled and then surpassed the rate of increase in Penang; numerically, too, the rate of increase was greater here (table 7). These large increases were chiefly because the Federated Malay States were in a transitional stage and large numbers of labourers and other workers moved into them from India to work the new development projects. In the Straits Settlements by 1901 much of the more accessible and suitable land had either been already alienated for such crops as coconuts, sugar, tapioca and *padi* or was occupied by Chinese squatters.[1] In these circumstances the increases in the Indian population were chiefly in the urban centres of Georgetown and Singapore, mainly it appears through the movement of traders, shop-assistants, clerks and other such people. Malacca, having no attraction comparable to that of the entrepôts of Singapore and Penang, actually registered declines of 12 and 22 per cent for the respective periods 1881–91 and 1891–1901 (table 7).

Most of the non-British territories were in a state of political flux and the numbers of Indians there were small (table 7).

The story of the 1901–11 inter-census period was very similar to the previous decade, with spectacular increases in population in the Federated Malay States resulting from the spread of rubber cultivation and the continuing rapid extension of communications coupled with other developments (Part 3). The extension of rubber planting was felt in most parts of the Straits Settlements and the Malay States, but particularly in the relatively sparsely occupied and more accessible Perak, Selangor and Negri Sembilan, where it was undoubtedly the main cause of the very large increases in population over the ten years (table 7).

The highest percentage increases, however, were in Pahang and Malacca, but the total number of Indians in these two states in 1901 was little more than a thousand each. In Malacca the recruitment of Indian labour for the rubber estates was mainly responsible for the 6,000 new arrivals, while in Pahang the Indian population was inflated by the entry of Tamil labourers employed on railway works.

In the ensuing decade rubber continued to spread further into Malaya following the acquisition by Britain of Kelantan, Trengganu, Kedah and Perlis in 1909 and of Johore in 1914. At the same time as this expansion in economic activity there was an increase in the number of Indian immigrants.

[1] *SSAR*, 1893, p. 115; *SSAR*, 1895, p. 309; Sandhu, 1961a, pp. 10–14.

Growth and structure

The demand for land to grow rubber and other plantation crops in the newest territorial additions to British Malaya—the Unfederated Malay States—over the period 1911–21, was as brisk as it had been in the Straits Settlements and Federated Malay States before them. The most remarkable percentage increases were therefore in these Unfederated Malay States (table 7).

The Federated Malay States, with the exception of Pahang, showed increases of more than 75 per cent for the decade 1911–21. The lower rate of increase in Pahang was due to the departure of large numbers of the Tamil labourers employed in railway construction in the state following completion of the project, and the comparative unattractiveness and inaccessibility of much of the state.

In the Straits Settlements, with the exception of Malacca, the rate of increase of the Indian population was low compared with the Malay States. This was natural in the case of Singapore and Penang because there was little land left for expansion of agriculture and the increase was largely in the urban population of the cities. In Malacca the large increase was due not so much to expansion in cultivation, but largely to the gradual substitution of Indian for Chinese labour on the estates. Province Wellesley estates had had for a long time settled Indian labour forces, but on the Malacca estates Chinese labour predominated till 1911 and it was only in the few years preceding the 1921 census that systematic recruiting in India had led to the introduction of Indians in large numbers.[1]

In the decade 1921–31 Perak and Selangor still showed big increases in absolute numbers and contained about half the total Indian population of Malaya in 1931 (table 7). All the other states also showed increases but, with the exception of Trengganu, not on the same scale as in the previous decade. The case of Trengganu is quite different as its development began comparatively late. However, the Indian population of the state in 1921 was so small (211) that the increase of 549·7 per cent for the decade 1921–31, considered alone, can be misleading. As for the other Unfederated Malay States, the rate of increase slackened as the movement in the direction of large-scale rubber cultivation lost its impetus after the depression in the rubber industry of the 1920s.

The exodus of Indians from Malaya during the Great Depression, the Indian government's ban on the emigration of labour and the depredations of the Japanese occupation were felt most strongly in the states with the largest Indian estate populations. The Federated Malay States, particularly Perak, Selangor and Negri Sembilan were the hardest hit.

[1] SSAR, 1911, pp. 472–3; SSAR, 1916, pp. 163–71.

All three of them showed decreases in their population in 1947 compared with 1931. With the exception of Perlis, there was also a sharp drop in the rate of increase in the Unfederated Malay States, the other area of large Indian estate population. Perlis was mainly a rice-growing area and as such was not as hard hit as some of the other states. Indeed, following the stoppage of tapping on estates a number of Indian labourers and others from the nearby states appear to have moved into Perlis to take up rice planting.

There was a normal increase in the Indian population of Singapore during the 1931–47 period. But this is of little significance for increases of the same order were observable in most of the other main urban centres of the country.[1]

The post-war years have seen stabilization of the Indian population. With the return to normal conditions and the rehabilitation of the rubber industry, Perlis lost some of its wartime attractions for the Indians. Then, despite considerable improvement in communications and general development in the post-war years, this state, together with Kelantan and Trengganu, was still regarded as an unattractive and out-of-the-way place *vis-à-vis* Kuala Lumpur and Singapore. It is, therefore, not surprising that these states, with the exception of Trengganu, should show the lowest rate of increase during the 1947–57 inter-census period; Perlis in fact registered an actual decrease, as more people left than entered it between 1947 and 1957 (table 7).[2] Apart from the growth in the number of government employees consequent upon the state being absorbed into the Federation of Malaya in 1948, the comparatively inflated increase in Trengganu was probably the result, largely, of a number of Indian labourers and others brought in by the British Colonial Development Corporation Ltd. (to work its experimental cocoa and abaca plantation projects at Jerangau in southwest Trengganu) and the Eastern Mining and Metal Company (for its iron mines at Dungun). The rate of increase in the other states also rose appreciably during the 1947–57 decade (table 7). Singapore, for example, registered a record increase of nearly 80 per cent, the highest since 1860, following the influx of job seekers from the Federation and refugees from the Indian subcontinent after partition.

Statistical information on the inter-census changes in the number of Indians in each *mukim* of Malaya is available only for the periods 1891–1901, 1931–47 and 1947–57. Even here there are gaps in the data for 1931–47 while the 1891–1901 information covers the Straits Settlements only. But despite the shortcomings of the *mukim* data for com-

[1] del Tufo, 1949, table 7; Vlieland, 1932, tables 14, 18.
[2] *1957 PCFM*, 2–12, table 9C; Chua, 1964, tables 24–7.

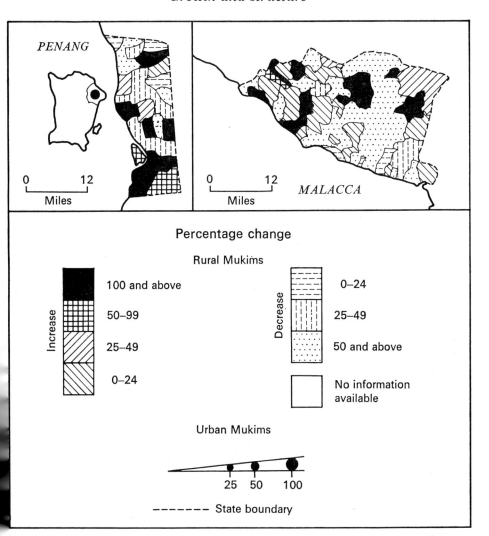

Fig. 15. Inter-census change in the Indian population of Penang and Malacca between 1891 and 1901, by *mukims*.

parative purposes, they do give some indication of the pattern of population change at the grass-root administrative levels.

So far we have seen how, with the exception of Malacca, the Indian population of each of the other parts of British Malaya increased from the 1890s to the 1930s. During 1931–47, on the other hand, five states registered decreases, but only it appears temporarily for population

191

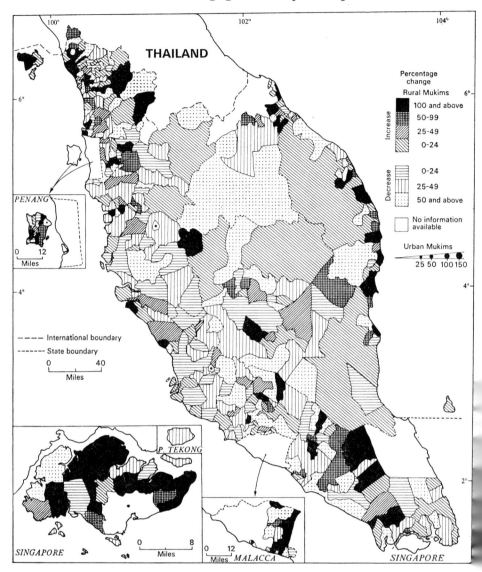

Fig. 16. Inter-census change in the Indian population of Malaya between 1931 and 1947, by *mukims*.

growth had once again revived in all these states, including Malacca, in the 1950s. But these overall figures, however, do not tell the whole story of inter-census population change in each state. In some *mukims* there were phenomenal increases and in others big decreases. For

192

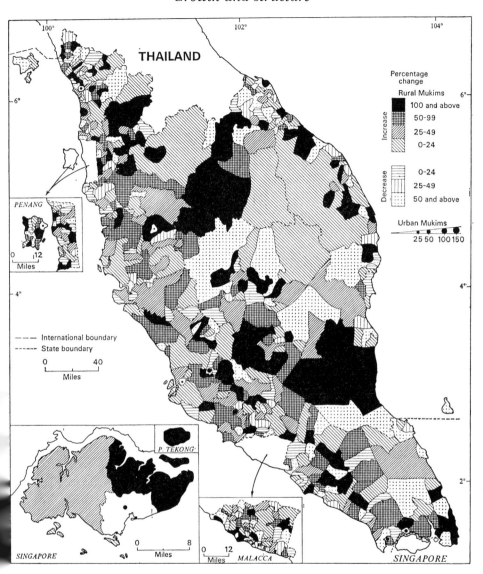

Fig. 17. Inter-census change in the Indian population of Malaya between
1947 and 1957, by *mukims*.

example, Mukims VI (Penang), Bakai (Kedah) and Karangan (Kedah)
showed increases of 2,738, 6,655 and 3,776 per cent over the 1891–1901,
1931–47 and 1947–57 inter-census periods respectively, whereas in
Mukims Ayer Molek (Malacca), Galas (Kelantan) and Sidim (Kedah)

there were decreases of 100, 100 and 99 per cent respectively over the same periods.[1] Then the inter-census decreases were confined to rural *mukims*, all urban *mukims*[2] experiencing continuous increases during these times (figs. 5, 15, 16, 17). The causes of such changes in the Indian population are not clear but were in all probability linked with (*a*) immigration and emigration, especially before the Japanese invasion, between India and the place of occupation in the individual *mukims*; (*b*) internal migration, associated with changes in employment, from *mukim* to *mukim* and shifts in government labour and staff forces to new projects; and (*c*) the period after the war, when such factors as the resettlement of rural populations during the Emergency had their effect. The increase and decrease in the Indian population numbers of Karangan and Sidim *mukims*, respectively, during the 1947–57 inter-census period appear to have been largely the result of the third phenomenon.[3]

Internal migration of the Indian population of
the states and 'mukims'

No record has ever been maintained of intra- or inter-state migration in Malaya, the only information available being that inferred from Malayan birthplace data. Unfortunately these statistics cannot in any way represent a precise picture of internal migration because they totally exclude the Indians born outside Malaya, who till recently formed the major portion of the Indian population in Malaya. Even then, the published birthplace statistics are only on a state basis, related data for districts and *mukims* being excluded.

Meagre though they are, these statistics are nevertheless useful: the Malayan-born Indian is comparatively better informed, more sophisticated and less bound by the proverbial inertia-generating religious and social institutions of Indian society as a whole. Therefore, it is not unreasonable to assume that, if anything, the Malayan-born Indians

[1] Innes, 1901, tables 13, 33–7; Vlieland, 1932, table 19; del Tufo, 1949, table 5; *1957 PCFM*, 1, table 2.

[2] Unless otherwise stated an 'urban *mukim*' is taken to be a *mukim* containing an urban centre of 50,000 or more inhabitants.

[3] Perhaps it should be mentioned that not infrequently the apparently large turnover in *mukim* populations, in terms of inter-census percentage increase or decrease, actually involved only small numbers of people. Two examples must suffice. Mukim Bera in Pahang had a solitary Indian in 1931 and three in 1957. In terms of inter-census change, however, this represents an increase of 200 per cent during the 1931–57 period. Similarly, although the number of Indians in the *mukim* of Bukit Senggeh in Malacca in 1931, 1947 and 1957 was 140, 33, and 48 respectively, the percentage change during the 1931–47 and 1947–57 inter-census periods was −76 and 45 per cent respectively (figs. 5, 16, 17).

were likely to be more mobile than their Indian-born compatriots. In these circumstances therefore, these statistics not only give a picture of the inter-state movement of the Malayan-born Indians, but they can also be taken as useful indicators of the movement of the Indian population as a whole, since the movement of the total Indian population would in all likelihood have been proportionately less than that of the Malayan-born sector alone.

Until recently, the Malayan-born Indians were highly immobile. For example, even as late as 1947 eighty-five per cent of the Malayan-born Indians were enumerated in their state of birth.[1]

This, however, is hardly to be wondered at. For one thing, there was the traditional aversion to change (Part 1), an aversion which had by no means totally disappeared from the ranks of the Malayan-born, despite birth in a foreign land. Then, perhaps more important, was the fact that the vast majority of these Indians, like the rest of their compatriots in Malaya, were engaged in permanent or semi-permanent wage occupations, which tended to tie them and their children to particular places. This was especially so in the case of government servants since, with the exception of a few services, each state engaged its own personnel for services within its borders.

This situation changed noticeably only after World War II, primarily it appears as a result of three developments. First, there was the political unification of the states, Singapore excepted, into a single political unit—the Malayan Union and subsequently in 1948 the Federation of Malaya (Aide-mémoire). Among its many centralizing features was the creation of federal departments which absorbed their state counterparts making the personnel of these liable for service in any part of the new federation. Secondly, there was the Emergency and the enforced and voluntary movement of people for security reasons.[2] Thirdly, there was the rapid expansion in communications during the Emergency, especially in the hitherto largely neglected *hulus* of the country—the milieu of the Communist guerrillas.

The result of these developments was increased internal migration. Coupled with increasing education and sophistication, further movements appear to have been generated in turn, but the full extent and effect of these will not be known till the next census in 1970. In the meantime, however, nearly 25 per cent of the Malayan-born Indians were enumerated outside their state of birth in 1957, compared with 15 per cent in 1921 and 1947. This represents a significant numerical

[1] Nathan, 1922, table 30; Vlieland, 1932, tables 103–6; del Tufo, 1949, table 45; Chua, 1964, tables 24–7; *1957 PCFM*, 2–12, table 9C.
[2] See pp. 214–16 below.

increase and possibly points to a trend of increasing inter- and intra-state migration in the future.[1]

Perhaps even more than the migration of state populations, such internal migrations would undoubtedly have also affected—albeit in a way that cannot be measured statistically—the growth of *mukim* and district Indian populations. However, it is possible that much of this movement may have cancelled itself out in the sense that the difference in the numbers moving in and out of one *mukim* or district to another may not have been very great. This certainly appears to have been the case with regard to inter-state migration: with the exception of post-war Singapore, the difference between the in- and out-migration from one state to another was seldom more than 3,000 persons up to 1957.[2]

The case of post-war Singapore is an anomaly. A recent survey seems to suggest that some 40,000 Indians may have entered Singapore from the Federation between 1947 and 1957.[3] This represents more than two-thirds of the absolute increase of 55,106 persons in the Indian population of the Island during the 1947–57 period. This estimated flow across the causeway is in all probability on the high side, but there is little doubt that this movement was on a substantial scale during the period under discussion. The Federation (or States of Malaya as it is now called) was at this time in the throes of a costly and dangerous campaign against armed Communist-led rebels. Contemporary Singapore, on the other hand, was a comparative haven of peace. Also quite apart from the attractions of a fast developing city, Singapore's economy was booming and salaries were generally higher and services better than those prevailing in the Federation. There was, therefore, a constant influx of people into the Island from across the causeway.

To sum up, although it is possible that inter-state migration will play a more important role in the growth of state populations in the future

[1] This is corroborated by oral evidence and field checks in selected areas. For example, according to the managers of ten estates visited by the writer in 1961 in Johore, Perak and Kelantan, in contrast to the 1930s when about 80–85 per cent of the Indian population of their estates stayed on the estates on a permanent basis and left them, almost always, only to visit or return to India, in 1961 less than 60 per cent of the Indians were 'old hands' or descendants of such, the remainder being post-war employees, some only since the previous year. This fits in with the National Union of Plantation Workers' estimate that, compared with the pre-war days when more than 80 per cent of the children of estate workers stayed on the estates of their parents, only about 50–60 per cent were doing so in 1961–2, mainly because of better communications, education and contacts with the other estates and the non-estate world. The majority of those leaving tended to gravitate towards the nearby urban centres or some other better paying or located estate.

[2] Nathan, 1922, table 30; Vlieland, 1932, tables 103–6; del Tufo, 1949, table 45; Chua, 1964, tables 24–7; *1957 PCFM*, 2–12, table 9C.

[3] United Nations, 1962, pp. 23–9.

than hitherto, it was, on the whole, with the exception of post-war Singapore, of minor significance up to 1957. On the other hand, inter-*mukim* movement of population appears to have been more significant and there is no reason why it should not continue to be so in the future.

Proportion of Indians to the total population of Malaya

The proportion of Indians in the Malayan population increased steadily till the outbreak of World War I and thence generally maintained its level until adversely affected by the Great Depression, the Indian government's ban on labour emigration and the depredations of the Japanese occupation (table 6 a). This is also reflected in the state populations (table 9). For instance, in 1891 only in one state, Penang, did the Indians make up more than 10 per cent of the total population. In 1901 and 1911 Perak, Negri Sembilan and Selangor also joined the ranks of such states, with Indians making up more than a quarter of the total population of Selangor in 1911. In 1921, almost a third of Selangor's population was Indian while by 1931 in Johore and Kedah as well Indians comprised 10 per cent or more of each state's total population. The decrease in the total Indian population during the 1931–47 period occurred mostly in Selangor, Perak and Negri Sembilan, three of the main rubber areas of the country. In Selangor, for example, less than 21 per cent of the total population was Indian in 1947 compared with 33 per cent in 1921. During the 1947–57 decade, increases of any note in the Indian proportion in the total population were limited to rapidly developing states like Singapore and Pahang (table 9).

Analysis of the proportion of Indians in the total population on a state basis is a useful guide, but by itself does not reveal their full significance, as it is far too coarse a mesh. To obtain a truer picture of this aspect of the community, it is imperative that analysis on a state basis should be supplemented by a similar exercise on a *mukim* basis, as the latter serves to weed out certain conclusions which tend to escape the coarser mesh of the former. For instance, from state figures it would appear that, with the exception of Trengganu, Indians formed at least 1 per cent of the total population of all parts of the country by the 1920s; or that in no part of Malaya did the Indians ever form more than a third of the total population (table 9). The *mukim* figures on the other hand reveal that while large tracts of the country were virtually empty of Indians, there were others, especially those with undertakings in which Indians specialized, which were literally little Indias; they formed more than half and at times more than 90 per cent of the total population. A few examples must suffice.

For the *mukims* for which the relevant information is available,

197

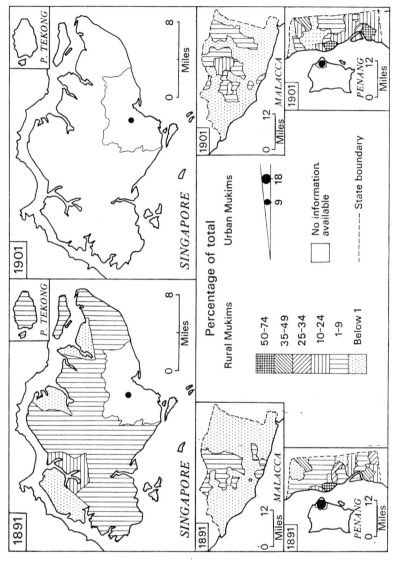

Fig. 18. Indians as a percentage of the total population of the Straits Settlements in 1891 and 1901, by *mukims*.

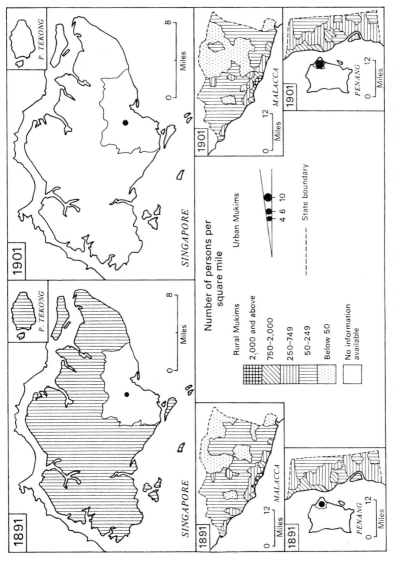

Fig. 19. Density of total population in the Straits Settlements in 1891 and 1901, by *mukims*.

199

Table 9: *Indians as a percentage of the total population of the individual states and of Malaya, 1891–1957*

territory	percentage of total population						
	1891	1901	1911	1921	1931	1947	1957
Singapore	8·7	7·8	9·2	7·7	9·1	7·4	8·9
Penang	15·5	15·5	16·9	16·9	15·7	12·8	12·0
Malacca	1·7	1·3	6·0	12·2	12·4	8·2	8·0
Perak	7·0	10·5	14·9	21·9	20·8	14·7	14·6
Selangor	4·4	9·9	25·2	33·0	29·2	20·4	19·7
Negri Sembilan	1·7	5·7	14·0	18·8	21·4	14·2	14·9
Pahang	0·9	0·2	0·7	1·1	2·4	5·9	7·0
Johore	N	N	3·1	8·6	10·1	7·5	7·7
Kedah	N	N	2·5	9·8	11·8	9·2	9·5
Kelantan	N	N	0·3	1·2	1·8	1·1	1·1
Trengganu	N	N	0·03	0·1	0·7	0·7	0·9
Perlis	N	N	0·3	2·0	1·9	2·4	1·7
MALAYA	5·0 (a)	6·6 (a)	10·1	14·2	14·3	10·3	10·6

N = No information available.

(a) = These figures are estimates.

Source: Compiled from del Tufo, 1949, table 2, app. c; Chua, 1964, table 2; *1957 PCFM*, 1, table 1.

Indians formed 10 or more per cent of the total population in 12 per cent of the *mukims* in 1891 and 1901. In two of these *mukims*, both in Penang, the state with the largest concentration of Indians at that time, they formed more than half of the total population in 1901. In Mukim I, in fact, they formed 70 per cent of the total population in 1901; ten years earlier their proportion in the total population of this *mukim* was 64·7 per cent[1] (figs. 5, 18, 19). By 1931, the next date of similar information, Indians formed 10 per cent of the total population in 31 per cent of the *mukims*, compared with only 12 per cent of them in the nineteenth and early part of the twentieth centuries. Moreover, they now comprised half or more of the total population of a total of 14 *mukims* in Selangor, Kedah, Negri Sembilan, Johore and Malacca; Penang by this time had lost much of its earlier momentum in rapid agricultural expansion as land space was limited. In two of these *mukims*, Sg. Tinggi and Damansara of Selangor, Indians formed more than 90 and 81 per cent of the total population respectively[2] (figs. 5, 20, 21).

The decrease in the total Indian population during the 1931–47 inter-census period is also reflected in the changes at *mukim* level. The

[1] Innes, 1901, tables 33–7; Merewether, 1892, tables 22–6.
[2] Vlieland, 1932, table 19.

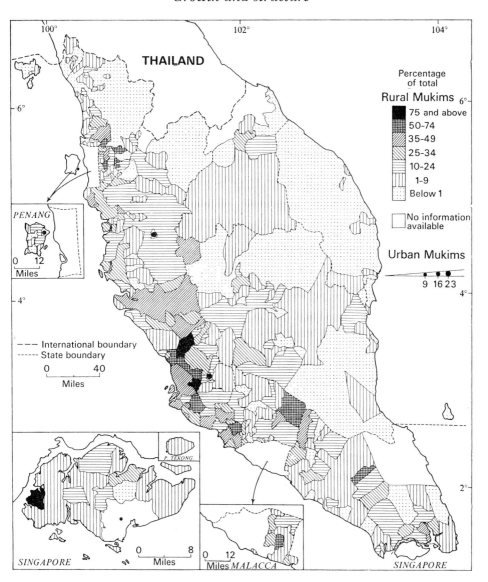

Fig. 20. Indians as a percentage of the total population of Malaya in 1931, by *mukims*.

proportion of *mukims* in which Indians formed 10 per cent or more of
the total population decreased from 31 to 26 per cent between 1931 and
1947. The number of *mukims* in which they formed half or more of the
total population also decreased from 14 to 7—a 50 per cent drop. Mukims

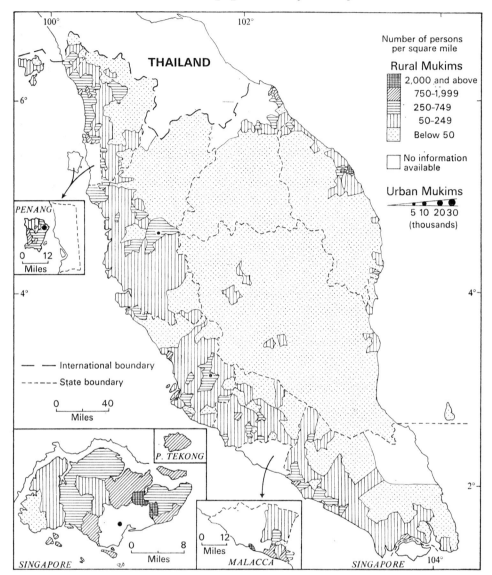

Fig. 21. Density of total population in Malaya in 1931, by *mukims*.

Damansara and Sg. Tinggi reflect this change in that the proportion of Indians in their population declined from more than 81 and 90 to less than 66 and 63 per cent respectively, over the same period.[1] The turning

[1] del Tufo, 1949, table 5.

202

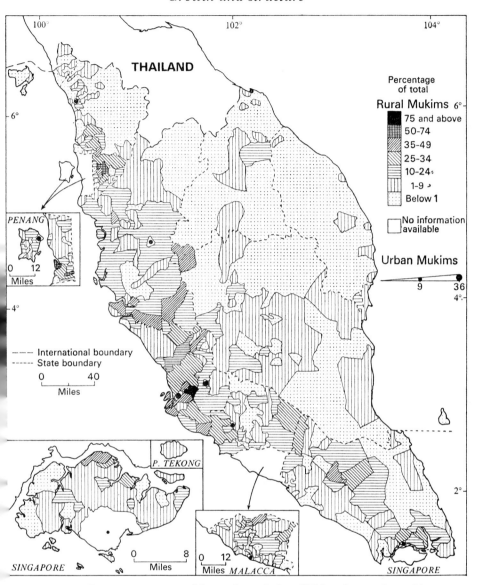

Fig. 22. Indians as a percentage of the total population of Malaya in 1957, by *mukims*.

of the tide in terms of population numbers during the 1947–57 decade is similarly indicated in the number of Indians in these *mukims* where they now formed 75 and 69 per cent of the total population respectively[1] (figs. 5, 22, 23).

[1] *1957 PCFM*, 1, table 2.

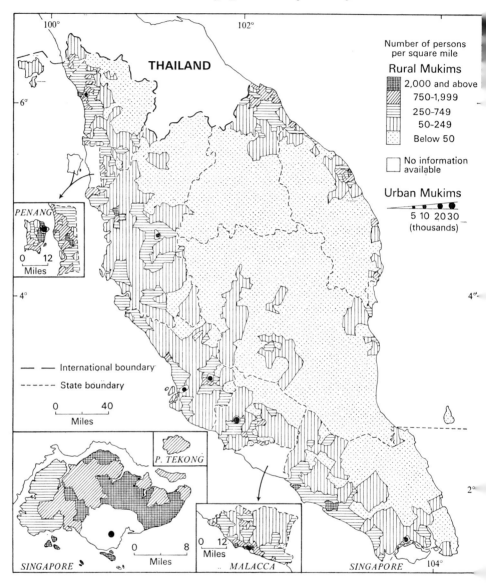

Fig. 23. Density of total population in Malaya in 1957, by *mukims*.

7

PATTERN OF DISTRIBUTION

The spread of Indian settlement in Malaya has been closely linked with the pattern of economic development in the country. Prior to the arrival of the main streams of immigrant peoples, the distribution of the comparatively small numbers of the indigenous Malays was largely confined to the coastal riverine sectors of the country. This basic pattern was undoubtedly set in the first instance by physical environmental conditions. The principal impediments were first the prevalence of sizeable swamps landward of the coastal belt; second, the prevalence of all but impenetrable swamp forests further inland and third, the hilly nature of the terrain culminating in a high mountain backbone, that was covered with near-equatorial forests and extended almost the length of the peninsula (fig. 2). This fundamental structure was adversely affected still further by the high rainfall and its unseasonable nature so that the interior of the country was denied to all but perhaps a few wandering aboriginal groups. In these early days therefore the more sedentary settlements were along the periphery of the Peninsula. These were the settlements of the indigenous Malays who appear to have subsisted on an economy based on *padi*-cultivation and fishing.

The later forms of economic growth introduced from the East and South Asia or from the West were in their initial phases more confined to areas west of the central cordillera and more particularly to the western littoral. The motivating factors were again environmental: the relative proximity and accessibility of the western littoral to the new socio-political influences, the greater suitability of the protected west coast for the establishment of anchorages and ports, the high proportion of alluvial flats in the western half of the country, and the bigger deposits of minerals (i.e. alluvial tin) in the same western belt.

Consequently the movement of immigrant peoples in the first phase up to the beginnings of British rule witnessed a rise in population in the more favoured sectors of the western littoral and at the expense of settlement growth in the eastern littoral (Part 1). The second phase, under British influence, saw the immigration of large numbers of Chinese and Indians into these same regions of the west or areas closely adjacent to them; and these favoured areas continued to absorb the

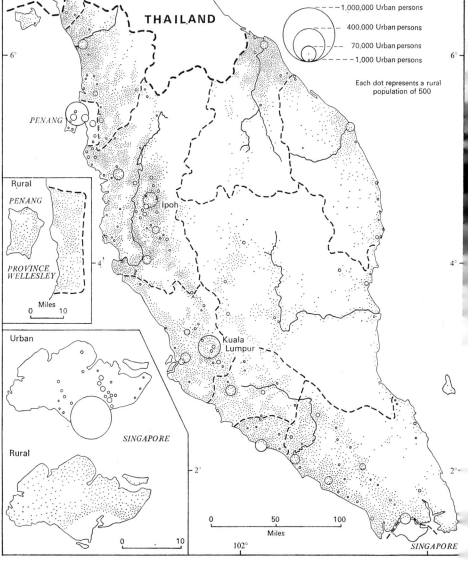

Fig. 24. Distribution of the total population of Malaya, 1947.

bulk of even the later immigrant Indian population as indeed they did
the Chinese (figs. 24, 25). The present-day pattern of population distribution is consequently an example on the one hand of the persistent
influence of natural environmental conditions coupled with historical

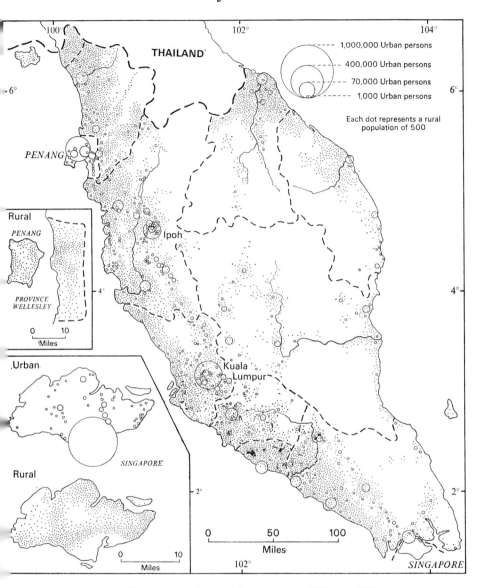

Fig. 25. Distribution of the total population of Malaya, 1957.

factors, and on the other a product of the selective areal concentration or intensification of the more rewarding aspects of economic activity which have demanded a higher input of adaptable labour. Even at the time of writing, the disparities between the western sector, the highland

207

The Indian population of Malaya

Table 10: Percentage distribution of the Indian population
of Malaya by states, 1891–1957

territory	percentage of total Indian population						
	1891	1901	1911	1921	1931	1947	1957
Singapore	21·0	14·9	10·6	6·9	8·2	11·5	15·2
Penang	47·3	31·7	17·1	10·6	8·5	9·5	8·4
Malacca	21·1	1·0	2·8	4·0	3·7	3·3	2·8
Perak	19·9	29·4	27·9	28·1	26·2	23·4	21·8
Selangor	4·7	14·1	27·6	28·2	25·1	24·2	24·5
Negri Sembilan	1·4	4·6	6·8	7·2	8·1	6·4	6·6
Johore	0·9	1·0	2·1	5·1	8·2	9·2	8·6
Kedah	1·0	N	2·2	7·0	8·2	8·6	8·2
Perlis	N	N	0·1	0·2	0·2	0·3	0·2
Western Malaya	N	N	97·2	97·3	96·4	96·4	96·3
Pahang	N	N	2·4	1·8	2·3	2·5	2·7
Kelantan	0·1	N	0·3	0·8	1·1	0·8	0·7
Trengganu	N	N	0·1	0·1	0·2	0·3	0·3
Eastern Malaya	N	N	2·8	2·7	3·6	3·6	3·7

N = No information available.
Source: Compiled from del Tufo, 1949, table 2, app. c; *1957 PCFM*, 1, table 1; Chua, 1964, table 2.

core and the eastern marchlands are significant, despite the efforts of the present government to further agricultural settlements in the high-land areas and to rehabilitate if not to develop the economy of the eastern lands.

Up to and during the nineteenth century, Indian contacts with Malaya were for the most part limited to the Straits Settlements and these places quite naturally had the highest concentrations of Indian population. Only after the 1870s did the Indians begin to move in substantial numbers into the rest of the country. But their spread was rapid and by the turn of the century the pattern of the present distribution of the Indian population was already formed.

Besides Penang and Singapore their main concentrations were, first, in the sugar and coffee, and following them the rubber, areas of western Malaya; secondly, along lines of communications; and finally, in and/or close to established urban centres such as Kuala Lumpur, Seremban, Ipoh and Taiping. In subsequent years, though there was a gradual spreading out of the population throughout western Malaya and also, on a very much smaller scale, into eastern Malaya, the overall pattern of population distribution did not change. Rather it was confirmed, for in

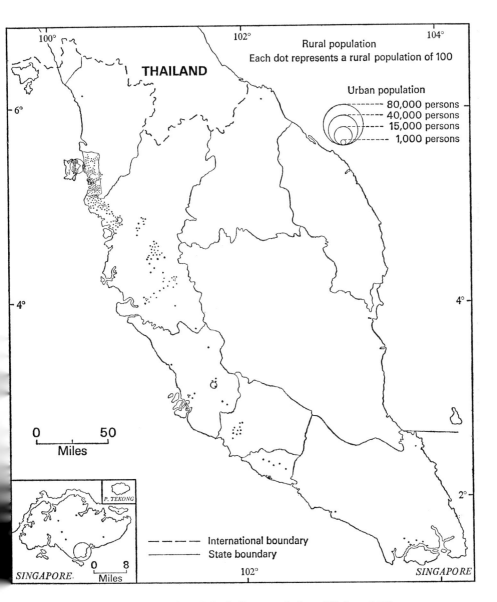

Fig. 26. Distribution of the Indian population of Malaya, 1891.

1957 almost 97 per cent of the Indian population was still in western Malaya (table 10; figs. 26, 27, 28, 29, 30).

With the exception of the large Indian agglomeration of Singapore, the densest concentrations of Indians in 1957 were in west-central

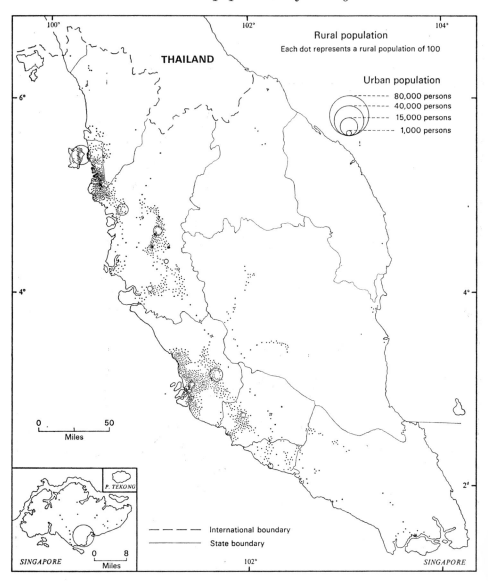

Fig. 27. Distribution of the Indian population of Malaya, 1911.

Malaya—the region of greatest economic development—from central Malacca in the south to southern Kedah in the north. Kedah, Penang, Perak, Selangor and Negri Sembilan between them contained more than 69 per cent of the total Indian population in 1957, compared with

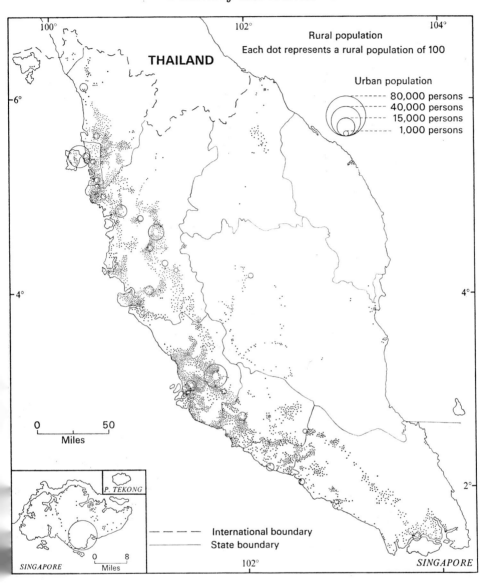

Fig. 28. Distribution of the Indian population of Malaya, 1931.

81 per cent in 1911 and 1921, 76 per cent in 1931 and 72 per cent in 1947, respectively (table 10). Within this area there were further pockets of concentration, mainly in (i) the port-city and island of Penang; (ii) the intensely developed agricultural region of Province

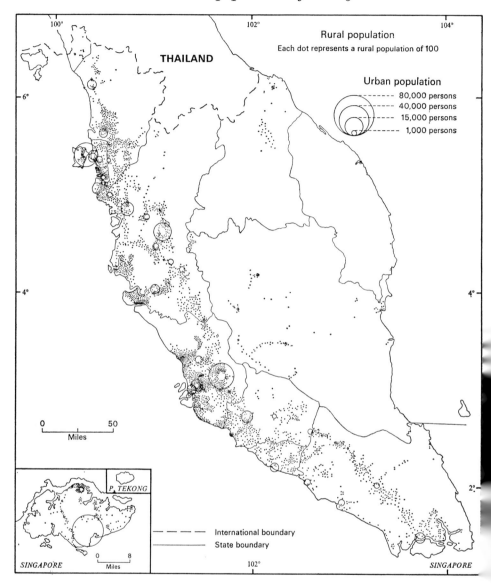

Fig. 29. Distribution of the Indian population of Malaya, 1947.

Wellesley, southern Kedah and north-western Perak; (iii) the rubber, coconut and oil palm complex of Ipoh–Telok Anson, Kuala Selangor–Kuala Lumpur–Klang and Seremban–Port Dickson, including the urban concentrations of Ipoh, Kuala Lumpur and Klang (figs. 3, 4, 38, 43).

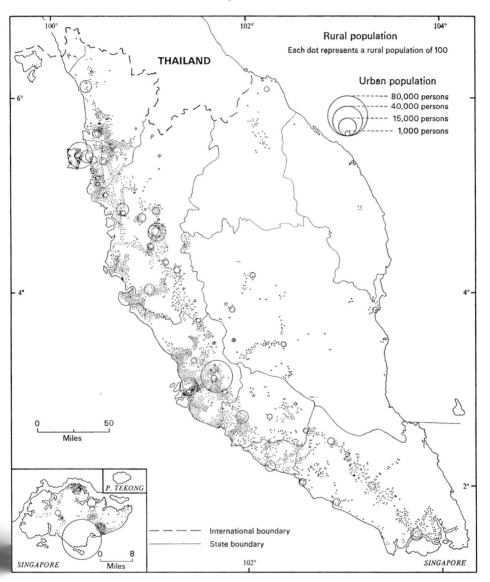

Fig. 30. Distribution of the Indian population of Malaya, 1957.

These places, in addition to being regions of intense economic development, had the advantage gained from the momentum of an early start,
all of them being centres of settlement from the time the country began
to be opened up.

213

The Indian population of Malaya

Urban–rural structure and distribution[1]

For a producer of primary raw materials, Malaya has been a highly urbanized country for the last fifty years. Twenty-three per cent of the country's population in 1911 was urban, and by 1947 this figure had increased to 35 per cent (table 11 a). In comparison, about 15 per cent of the total population of Southeast Asia was estimated to be urban in 1947, while only 10 per cent of Indonesia's population was classified as urban.[2]

The high proportion of urban dwellers in the population of Malaya was further increased following the declaration of the Emergency in 1948. The campaign against the guerrillas necessitated the shifting of about 573,000 rural dwellers into nucleated settlements called New Villages. These were located along main roads for convenience of administration, access and supervision. They thus accentuated the existing pattern of urban concentration in the rubber and tin belt of western Malaya, which in 1947 already had most of the towns and more than 90 per cent of the urban population of Malaya.[3] In terms of numbers the resettlement programme, together with the drift of rural dwellers to urban centres, and the normal growth of the existing populations of these centres, increased the number of urban centres from 187 to 445 and the proportion of urban dwellers in the total population from 35 to 48 per cent between 1947 and 1957. This made Malaya, after Japan, the most highly urbanized country in Asia (figs. 24, 25; tables 11 a, 11 b).[4] Even if we were to accept the suggestions of some writers[5] and take 2,000 or 5,000 people as the numerical minimum qualifying a place as urban, Malaya would even then be a fairly highly urbanized area, in the sense that by 1957 some 44 and 38 per cent of the country's population were already living in urban centres of 2,000 and 5,000 or more, respectively.[6]

The urban Indian population has been increasing steadily. In 1891 there were four towns in Malaya with an Indian population of more than 1,000 persons. But by 1947 there were thirty-two centres among

[1] There is as yet no satisfactory definition of the terms 'urban' and 'rural' which can be applied uniformly to any part of the world. In Malaya, for census purposes urban areas are categorized as settlements having 1,000 or more inhabitants. Many people feel that this is too low a minimum and tends to over-emphasize the degree of urbanization in the country. This is probably so, but for the sake of convenience this classification is retained for the purposes of this study.
[2] Ginsburg and Roberts, 1958, pp. 53–4.
[3] del Tufo, 1949, table 7.
[4] Sandhu, 1964, pp. 157–80.
[5] See, for example, Ooi, 1963, pp. 135–7; Sendut, 1962, pp. 117–18; Jones, 1965 a, p. 44.
[6] Fell, 1960, table 2; Chua, 1964, tables 3–4.

Pattern of distribution

Table 11a: Proportion of urban dwellers in the total Indian, Chinese and Malay populations of Malaya, 1911–1957

		percentage urban		
year	total	Indian	Chinese	Malay
1911	22·7	24·0	50·0	8·0
1921	27·7	27·4	52·8	9·0
1931	29·5	30·5	49·3	10·6
1947	35·1	39·0	53·7	14·1
1957	48·0	47·2	72·7	21·6

Table 11b: Racial composition of the urban population of Malaya, 1911–1957

	total urban population (in thousands)	percentage			
year		Chinese	Indians	Malays	others
1911	608	65·0	12·9	17·8	4·3
1921	921	66·6	13·8	16·0	3·6
1931	1284	65·4	14·8	15·9	3·9
1947	2054	68·3	11·4	17·4	2·9
1957	3709	67·1	10·4	19·3	3·2

Table 11c: Comparative growth of the total urban and rural Indian population of Malaya, 1921–1957

	absolute increase/decrease (in thousands)			percentage increase/decrease		
type	1921–31	1931–47	1947–57	1921–31	1931–47	1947–57
total	150	−22	220	32·2	−3·5	36·7
urban	39	65	153	30·2	38·9	65·5
rural	112	−87	67	33·0	−19·3	18·3

Source: State of Kelantan, 1911, table 1; Pountney, 1911, tables 2–6; Marriot, 1911a, table 4; 1911b, tables 1–4; Cavendish, 1911, tables 2–3; Scott, 1912, table 2; Nathan, 1922, tables 2, 11; Vlieland, 1932, tables 1, 14, 18; del Tufo, 1949, tables 4, 7, app. c; Fell, 1960, tables 1–2; 1957 PCFM, 1, table 3; Chua, 1964, tables 3–4.

Malaya's 187 towns while a decade later this figure had risen to forty-five out of a total of 445 urban centres.

The resettlement programme did not affect the Indian population in the same manner as the Chinese, or the number of towns with 1,000 or

more Indians would have been greater. Only about 21,000 Indian rural
dwellers were removed to New Villages compared with some 500,000
Chinese. This was largely because most of the rural Indians were on
estates. With the exception of a few, the vast majority of the estates
did not move their labour populations to the New Villages. Instead
each estate merely regrouped its labourers and other inhabitants at one
or more defended points within it. As the numbers involved in each
such shift were comparatively small, regroupment did not give rise to
large Indian villages on the same scale as relocation, which involved the
wholesale shifting of rural dwellers to New Villages, did for the Chinese.[1]
The Emergency, however, led to an increasing drift of Indians from the
rural areas to comparatively safer urban centres. Then, from the early
1950s there were also growing numbers of Indian labourers and others
being thrown out of employment as a result of the sale and subsequent
subdivision into small plots of some European-owned rubber estates.
While some of these unemployed, with their families, returned to India,
others drifted to nearby urban centres in search of work (Part 3).

Such rural–urban drifts, coupled with the normal growth of the
existing urban populations and the absorption by such populations of
the adjoining New Villages, substantially altered the urban–rural ratio
of the Indian population. For more than a hundred years, since the
beginning of the Indian indentured immigration into Malaya, little
more than a third of the Indians had lived in urban centres. But by
1957 more than 47 per cent of the Indians were in centres of 1,000 or
more persons, while today this figure is estimated to be higher than 50
per cent (tables 11 a, 11 c). If we were to employ a minimum of 2,000 or
5,000 persons as a requisite for urban status, even then a substantial
portion of the Indians in Malaya would be urban dwellers: by 1957, for
example, more than 43 and 38 per cent of the total Indian population
of the country was already living in urban centres of 2,000 and 5,000
or more inhabitants, respectively, while the relevant figures for today
would be higher than 45 and 40 per cent.

Indian urban dwellers have habitually tended to congregate in the
larger urban centres of the country, that is places containing 50,000 or
more inhabitants. From 1921 to 1957, for example, between 52 and 57
per cent of the urban Indian population was in such centres. Amongst
these Penang, Kuala Lumpur and Singapore have been the chief centres
of Indian concentrations ever since the nineteenth century. In 1931,
for instance, 54 per cent of the total Indian urban population was in
these three places. Lately, their share of the total urban Indian population has been decreasing following the expansion of other towns like

[1] Sandhu, 1964, pp. 174–7.

Pattern of distribution

Table 12: The Indian estate population of Malaya, 1921–1957

year	total Indian estate population (in thousands)	estate as percentage of the total Indian population	estate as percentage of the rural Indian population
1921	258	54·9	75·7
1931	304	48·8	67·0
1947	241	40·2	66·0
1957	226	27·5	52·2

Source: Compiled from Nathan, 1922, table 58; Vlieland, 1932, table 20; del Tufo 1949, table 111; personal communiation from the Ministry of Labour, Federation of Malaya.

Ipoh and Klang. In 1957, Singapore, Penang and Kuala Lumpur, nevertheless, still had more than 42 per cent of the total urban Indian population of Malaya.

The rural Indian population in Malaya has been chiefly associated with the estate economy. In 1947, two-thirds of the rural Indian population were on estates, while in 1921 the proportion of the estate dwellers in the total rural Indian population was as high as 75·7 per cent (table 12). The significant point to note here is the fact that although most of the rural Indian population was still on estates in 1957, the proportion of this segment in the total rural population had been gradually decreasing over the last few decades. This decline was the result partly of the lack of any fresh immigration from India, partly of the drift of some rural Indians to urban centres or their return to India, and partly of the increasing flow of Malay and Chinese labour into the estate economy (Part 3).

The densest concentrations of Indian estate and other rural dwellers have traditionally been in the highly developed agricultural coastal districts of central Selangor, southern and northern Perak and Province Wellesley. Other concentrations of such Indians have been in the rubber and oil palm areas of southern Kedah, Negri Sembilan, Malacca and Johore, though not on the same scale as those of either Perak or Selangor (figs. 26, 27, 28, 29, 30, 38, 40).

8

SETTLEMENT CHARACTERISTICS

The settlements of the Indians in Malaya have been, and are, markedly nucleated, in contrast to the comparatively largely dispersed and sprawling settlements of the indigenous people. This characteristic of the Indian settlements has been chiefly the result of the fact that, as discussed above, the majority of the Indians came to Malaya as gangs of labourers, mainly to work the estates. For convenience of management and security these undertakings, many of them employing hundreds of labourers, usually grouped the labourers together in dwellings located close to the office, factory and managerial staff quarters.[1] This pattern did not change very much after its inception in the pioneering stages. In fact, it was further accentuated by the Emergency resettlement programme of the Malayan government.

Those Indians who did not enter the estate economy settled mainly in towns. The majority were absorbed by the government services and the commercial trades. The government, though maintaining field camps, housed its employees in or adjoining existing urban centres, while the commercial Indian community was quite naturally chiefly in the urban areas, though many of them did travel to the rural areas to conduct their business. This picture of the Indian population outside the estates did not change to any marked degree over the years. In fact, the trend over recent years has been for the rural farm population to drift towards the urban centres, thereby further emphasizing the nucleated pattern of Indian settlement.

The tendency of the Indian settlement to be nucleated is nothing new, in the sense that almost all the Indian immigrants into Malaya came from traditionally nucleated villages in India. But, other than the ubiquitous temples, the form of the Malayan nucleation bears no relation to the generally compact, wall-to-wall and back-to-back village forms of India. This is chiefly because the Indians came to Malaya largely as wage-earners and not as colonizers, and their settlements and dwellings were designed and provided by their employers, usually Europeans. Furthermore, the constantly wet Malayan climate and other

[1] Field work; *IO:EP*, 2278 (1884), pp. 707–29; *SJ*, IV (1896), 442; Edgar, 1937, pp. 10 ff.; *JIA*, V (1851), 108–9.

environmental factors are not conducive to the Indian village life (mud houses, for example) in Malaya. In any case, until recently the Indian regarded his stay in Malaya as a temporary exile from the village in India, and he was not concerned with establishing familiar settlement types: Indian permanent settlement is thus comparatively recent. Those who settled have been in Malaya for a long time and their outlook towards settlement has been conditioned to an appreciable extent by the Malayan environmental conditions and local municipal requirements.

The urban centres of modern Malaya are principally the creation of Europeans, Chinese and Indians. Here, too, they bear little or no resemblance to the traditional town patterns of India or China, but have been laid out more on the lines of English towns. Furthermore the Malayan towns were subject to European municipal regulations, which prevented, or at least hindered, the earlier tendencies of the Indians, Chinese and other Asian immigrants to continue to huddle together.[1]

There have been few settlements in Malaya designed exclusively for, or peopled wholly by, Indians. Even these, apart from being inhabited by Indians, have not always been markedly different in their layout from the analogous types of the other immigrant groups. In these circumstances the settlements of the Indians, or more usually settlements containing Indians, are most conveniently discussed as part of the overall Malayan settlement pattern.

Sectionalism in urban settlement

The Malayan urban centres consist chiefly of a nucleus of streets laid out on a grid pattern and lined with wooden, brick or concrete shops, godowns and entertainment buildings, and surrounded by areas of irregularly spaced streets, winding between government buildings and through residential districts and sprawling timber and thatch dwellings, which gradually merge with the surrounding rural landscape. These rectangularly organized patterns are usually aligned either along a railroad, road or waterfront. More often than not, their primary function is, and has been, that of centres for administration and for the gathering and processing of Malayan produce, the distribution of consumer goods and the provision of financial, social and other services, for the surrounding rural populations besides their own. Except for some of the larger ones, the Malayan urban centres have had virtually no manufacturing functions.

In the absence of any established canon of classification, we have to be content with grouping the Malayan urban centres purely on the basis

[1] *SSFR*, 4 (1789–91), 21.8.1789; 10 (1808–23), 27.9.1814; *JIA*, v (1851), 108–9; vii (1853), 333–9; viii (1854), 100–11; ix (1855), 452.

of population size. Using this criterion we could divide the Malayan urban centres into cities with 100,000 or more inhabitants and towns of up to 100,000 persons.

The cities of Malaya (i.e. in 1957, Singapore, Kuala Lumpur, George-town (Penang) and Ipoh), though differing in detail, have been remark-ably similar in their development. Moreover, apart from such continual modifications as outward expansion and new building materials and design, they have generally retained much of their initial layouts. They consist largely of a central core area of wholesale stores and shops, usually double-storeyed, and tall many-floored financial and com-mercial institutions and offices. Government buildings are prominent just outside the core. Immediately adjoining these is a central area of entertainment houses, food markets, factories, stores, and closely packed double-storeyed retail shops and multi-storeyed flats, occupied chiefly by people doing low-grade work.

Surrounding this central area is usually a suburban belt of houses with gardens. Such houses have usually been occupied by higher grade workers. Further out there are often outer suburbs and/or a market-gardening belt. Most of these outer areas contain ornate bungalows, set amidst broad tree-lined avenues, large gardens, and usually occupied by wealthy people. The market gardens have been, and continue to be, stocked with vegetables, fruit and poultry intended for the city markets. In some of these cities, as in Singapore, there are now separate industrial centres and largely self-contained satellite housing estates.

Traditionally the Chinese have been the predominant population in the cities of Malaya. For example, in 1957 Indians formed less than 12 per cent of the cities' total population compared with 73 per cent of the Chinese element. Although found in almost all parts of the cities, the Indians have tended to congregate in certain sections. In Singapore, for example, five such concentrations can be distinguished. The earliest of these, which existed before the 1830s, lies along the western fringe of the central business core, in the Chulia and Market Street areas. Most of these Indians were, and to a large extent still are, South Indian Chettiar and Muslim Tamil traders, financiers, money-changers, petty shopkeepers and boatmen and other kinds of quayside workers. A second grouping, this time largely of Sindhi, Gujarati and Sikh cloth merchants, exists in the High Street area, while a third grouping of Gujarati and other Muslim textile and jewellery merchants can be distinguished in the Arab Street region, further to the east of Singapore River. The fourth grouping of Indians is the Tamil shopkeeping element on Serangoon Road, one of the main roads along which settlement fanned out from the centre of the city during the nineteenth century.

Settlement characteristics

Lack of space to organize a homogeneous community within the central core led the Indians to establish a ribbon development along Serangoon Road. This was later intensified and confirmed as a dominantly Indian area through the government's siting there of labour lines for a pre-dominantly Tamil labour force and the overflow of shopkeepers and traders from the central core. The last prominent concentration of Indians is that around the docks and railway, where many of the workers were Tamils, Telugus and Malayalis (fig. 31).

Similar concentrations occur in Georgetown, Kuala Lumpur and Ipoh, though Indians are to be found in all sections of these cities (fig. 32). As in Singapore, these concentrations have largely been the result of such factors as a kind of historical momentum, the siting of the government's labour lines close to the labourers' place of work, the traditional Indian tendency to congregate in homogeneous communities coupled with their generally marked occupational specialization, and last, but by no means least, the efforts of British administrators to plan urban development and fit the indigenous and foreign populations into convenient moulds.

The impact of this last factor is particularly clearly exemplified in the case of Singapore, where as early as 1822 a town committee was appointed by Raffles 'for appropriating and marking out the quarters or departments of the several classes of the native population'.[1] The dispositions decided on at that time are still fairly characteristic of the city though, of course, there have been extensive changes in detail during the past 145 years.

The heart of this newly planned city, as well as that of each of its sister-cities on the mainland, was the European-dominated centre focused on a spacious administrative enclave, large *padang*, substantial club and an imposing Anglican church. The Asian areas of settlement were relegated to the peripheries of this central focus. Although there does not appear to have been any declared policy on these lines, in practice the distance from the colonial focus of the Eurasian, Chinese, Malay, Indian and other ethnic groupings seems to have varied in accordance with the respective community's social status *vis-à-vis* the *tuan besars*. In this scheme all the Indian communities—in the eyes of some of the colonial élites forever doomed, irrespective of their economic or social position, to be the coolies and 'blackmen' of Malayan society— seem to have been almost always relegated to the lower rungs of the social order.[2] Consequently, it is not surprising that the Indian concen-

---

[1] *JIA*, v (1851), 108–9; viii (1854), 100–11.
[2] Cameron, 1865, pp. 281–2; *C.O.273*, 376 (1911), Colonial Office, minute no. 24942; 378 (1911), 25.10.1911, Colonial Office, minute no. 33284; *BP*, E. W. Birch,

trations within the Malayan cities usually tended to be further away from the European-dominated orthodox centre than, for example, the Eurasians or Chinese, who were nearly always placed well above the Indians in the colonial social hierarchy.

There has been a considerable loosening, if not virtual disappearance, of the foregoing colonial social order in the post-war years. However, the full effect of this emancipation, in terms of settlement reorientation in the context of the existing racial concentrations within the Malayan cities, has yet to be seen. To this day the Indian enclaves continue to be predominated by South Asians. However, other racial groups and especially the Chinese have been moving into these areas in growing numbers thereby reducing their racial exclusiveness to some extent.

The land area—both legal and real—of the Malayan cities has tended to be small. Moreover, the legal limits of these cities were fixed early on and seldom extended to keep pace with population growth. For example, while Singapore's population increased by nearly three and a half times between 1891 and 1947 the city limits remained the same throughout this period.[1] In these circumstances, the average population densities rose correspondingly higher with the passage of years. For instance, Singapore's 912,343 persons in 1957 were crowded on to less than thirty-eight square miles, giving an average density of more than 24,000 persons per square mile. In the central zone of this city, the densities were even as high as 370,000 persons per square mile.[2] Kuala Lumpur and Penang both had 100,000 or more persons per square mile in their central zones in 1947 (figs. 31, 32).[3]

In these crowded cities, the Little Indias, Little Delhis or the Indian Quarters, as the Indian central concentrations are sometimes known, have formed distinctive, monotonous blocks of closely packed, low, narrow, double-storeyed shop-houses, in which the Indians have lived and worked cheek by jowl, often with ten to twenty-five or more inhabitants to each dwelling.[4] The monotony of the nondescript shop-house structures is broken only by temples, often elaborately ornamented and decorated, and other institutional buildings. The atmosphere and mode of life in these Indian sectors is, and has been, very reminiscent of India and, were it not for the presence of Malayan elements such as shop-styles and transport, the scene could well have had its setting in Calcutta, Bombay or Madras.

'Memorandum on the Malay race in the Federated Malay States, dated Taiping, 28th May, 1906'; *MP*, Jones to Maxell, 20.1.1943; Neelakandha Aiyer, 1938, pp. 92–4.

[1] Merewether, 1892, map 1, tables 8–24; del Tufo, 1949, p. 601, table 7.

[2] Chua, 1964, table 3.　　　　　　　　　[3] del Tufo, 1949, pp. 602–3.

[4] Singapore Department of Social Welfare, 1948, pp. 69–87.

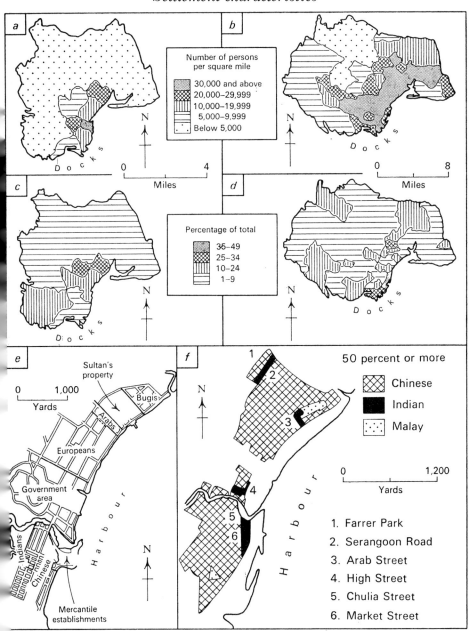

Fig. 31. (a) and (b): Density of total population in Singapore city in 1891 (a) and 1957 (b), by census divisions. (c) and (d): Indians as a percentage of the total population of Singapore city in 1891 (c) and 1957 (d), by census divisions. (e) and (f): Racial groupings in the centre of Singapore city about 1828 (e) and in 1952 (f).

223

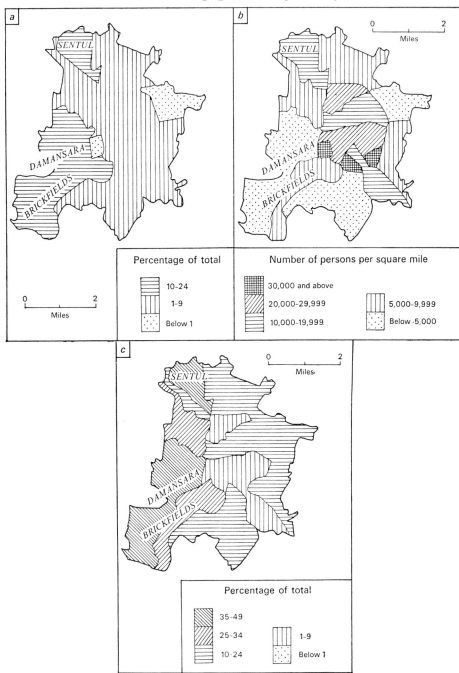

Fig. 32. (*a*) Percentage distribution of the Indian population of Kuala Lumpur in 1947, by census divisions. (*b*) Density of total population in Kuala Lumpur in 1947, by census divisions. (*c*) Indians as a percentage of the total population of Kuala Lumpur in 1947, by census divisions.

Settlement characteristics

The information on the way in which the Indian sectors of the colonial cities were governed is meagre and obscure and the resulting picture of patterns of urban authority rather hazy. For example, as early as 1796 we find Major Macdonald, who took up the post of Superintendent of Prince of Wales Island (Penang) on the death of Francis Light, appointing 'a Captain to each language' to assist in the administration of the Island.[1] But it is not clear as to whether, in view of their linguistic heterogeneity, this meant the appointment of one or several 'Captains' in the case of the Indian population. Again, in 1801 the Chulias or South Indian Muslims of Penang are recorded as having a captain of their own: the leadership position of the other contemporary Indian communities is unknown.[2] Finally, twenty years later we have the Chulias of Singapore petitioning the government to appoint 'a headman or captain' for 'the mercantile and labouring classes'. Here, too, it is unclear whether this person was to be in charge of all the mercantile and labouring classes or just the Chulias. Moreover, the outcome of this petition is unknown.[3]

What emerges from such scanty sources of information as the foregoing is that there is no record of any *one* Indian official, comparable to, say, the Capitan China or Headman of the Chinese community, being appointed in any of the modern Malayan cities to be in charge of *all* the Indians there. Neither is there any evidence of the Indian sectors as a whole ever having enjoyed any significant degree of self-government, as for example did the Chinese. Even if an Indian counterpart of the Capitan China had existed, it is unlikely that he would have wielded the same degree of influence or power among his countrymen as did his Chinese colleague, because of the extremely heterogeneous and fragmented ethnic, religious, economic and linguistic composition of the Indian urban communities and the apparent lack of any substantial cohesive centripetal force to counter the numerous inherent fissiparous tendencies amongst them.

The towns of Malaya have usually had the same morphological features as the cities, the variation being principally only in size. But while a few of the larger towns have almost all the trappings in terms of size, features and functions of the cities, most of the remainder are little more than overgrown rubber and tin-mining villages, that still have the air of recent and rapid developments.

Indians in the towns have been generally even more insignificant than in the cities.[4] In 1957, for example, Indians formed less than 10 per cent

[1] *JIA*, v (1851), 109.   [2] *JIA*, v (1851), 192.   [3] *JIA*, ix (1855), 452.
[4] Marriot, 1911a, table 4; Marriot, 1911b, tables 1–4; Pountney, 1911, tables 2–6; Cavendish, 1911, tables 2–3; State of Kelantan, 1911, p. 1; Scott, 1912, table 2; Nathan, 1922, table 11; Vlieland, 1932, table 18; del Tufo, 1949, table 7.

of the total population of the 441 towns of the country.[1] Moreover, even these small numbers were generally widely dispersed in a Chinese-dominated urban landscape. The main features of the Indian settlement here—shops, social clubs, temples, residential houses and labour lines—were usually found scattered among their Chinese and Malay counterparts. The picture today is no different.

Rural settlement units

Rural settlements containing significant numbers of Indians have been and are of the following main types: farm, New Village and estate settlements.

Estate settlement has been the dominant form of Indian rural settlement from the latter half of the nineteenth century.[2] Almost all Indian estate settlement has been connected with sugar, coffee, coconut, rubber, oil palm and tea cultivation (Part 3). These estates, generally along roads and railways, have been closely tied to transport routes, as has the settlement within them.

The settlement unit on an estate, whether it has been under sugar, rubber or oil palm, has been quite similar. It has usually consisted of a number of buildings, for the most part labourers' quarters, residences of the manager and other administrative and technical staff, a factory, office, estate shop, dispensary, toddy shop,[3] school and, on the larger estates, a hospital and recreation facilities, all concentrated at a focal point on the estate. In the case of the very large properties, besides the main (headquarters) concentration, there have also been one or more minor settlements. These have usually been dispersed in smaller nucleations about the estate, for convenience of work, normally along the estate roads (figs. 33, 34). Some of the smaller estates, too, have followed this pattern of decentralization. However, the dispersed settlements on the estates now no longer exist, for under the same conditions that created the New Villages, the dispersed estate population was gathered and regrouped in closely packed settlements. These measures also introduced such new features as barbed-wire fencing, guardhouses and communal kitchens where all labourers' food was kept, cooked and distributed, thereby preventing it from being passed on to guerrillas.

On some estates all labour lines were concentrated at the factory. In

[1] Chua, 1964, tables 3–4; Fell, 1960, table 2.
[2] Personal interview with Mr R. Thambipillay, retired schoolmaster, Victoria Institution, Kuala Lumpur; *IO:EP*, 2278 (1884), pp. 707–29; Wright, 1908, pp. 334 ff.
[3] This feature disappeared from a number of estates in the 1930s and after the Japanese occupation, following agitation by Indian nationalists against the sale of toddy to labourers.

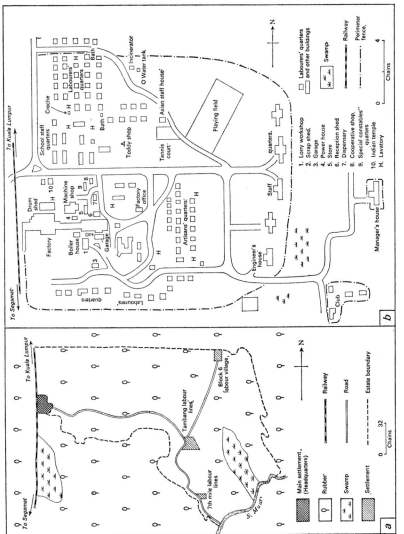

Fig. 33. Location (*a*) and layout (*b*) of the main (headquarters) settlement of a rubber estate in north Johore: an example of a large estate settlement, 1957.

227

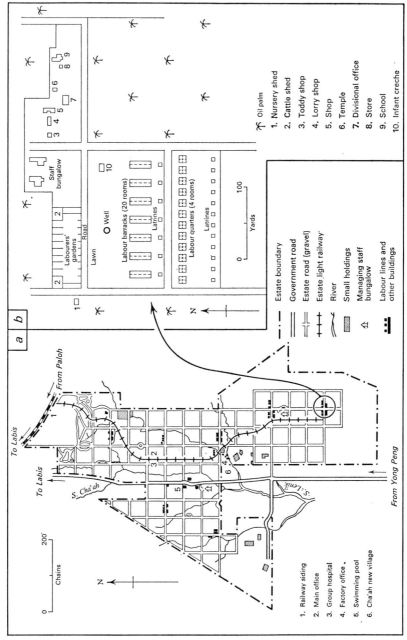

Fig. 34. (a) An oil palm estate in north Johore: An example of the distribution of settlement units on a large (multi-divisional) oil palm estate, 1957. (b) Layout of a single divisional settlement unit of the above estate, 1957.

a   b

From Paloh

To Labis

To Labis

S. Cha'ah

S. Lenik

From Yong Peng

1. Railway siding
2. Main office
3. Group hospital
4. Factory office
5. Swimming pool
6. Cha'ah new village

0   200
Chains

N

Staff bungalow

Labourers' gardens

Lawn   Road

Well

Labour barracks (20 rooms)

Latrines

Labour quarters (4 rooms)

Latrines

0   100
Yards

N

Estate boundary
Government road
Estate road (gravel)
Estate light railway
River
Small holdings
Managing staff bungalow
Labour lines and other buildings

Oil palm
1. Nursery shed
2. Cattle shed
3. Toddy shop
4. Lorry shop
5. Shop
6. Temple
7. Divisional office
8. Store
9. School
10. Infant creche

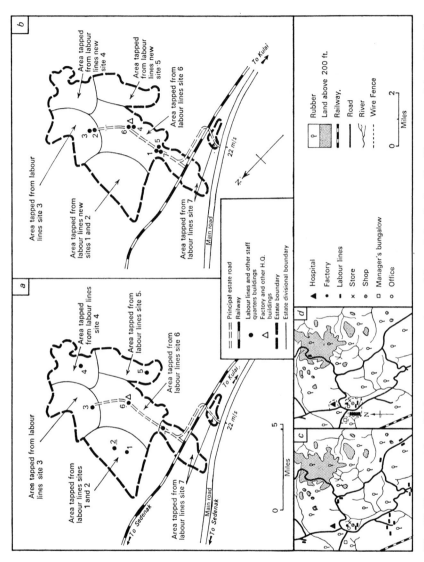

Fig. 35. Two examples of labour regroupment on rubber estates during the Emergency. (a) and (b): An estate in south Johore, before (a) and during (b) the Emergency. (c) and (d): An estate in central Johore, before (c) and during (d) the Emergency.

229

others, especially the large ones, two or more concentrations were not uncommon (fig. 35). The standard regroupment centre consisted of closely packed but neatly arranged labour lines and other buildings. The additional accommodation was obtained either by transferring the buildings from the old sites or by the construction of new buildings according to government specifications. The settlements were fenced and guarded by special constables, mostly Malays (fig. 35). In this sense the fenced life of the Indian labourer on the estates took on the same features as that of his countryman or the Chinese resettled squatter in the New Villages.[1]

Indian farm settlement can be thought of in two categories: the first the product of private individual enterprise and the second that based on forms of sponsorship.

Sponsored Indian farm settlement, in turn, has again been mainly of two types, non-government-sponsored settlement, meant specifically for labourers or former labourers, and government-sponsored settlement open to all Indians capable of farming (Part 3). The former has been wholly Indian and has consisted for the most part of individual houses set along a road, behind which stretched the gardens of the inhabitants.[2] The ubiquitous temple (or occasionally church), school, shop(s) and office, together with cattlesheds and other buildings for stock, has completed the picture. With the exception of the late nineteenth century coffee-planting colony in Kajang (Selangor) and the contemporaneous but abortive attempts at *padi* cultivation in Perak, there have been no government land-development schemes designed solely for Indians. They have, however, been admitted into some of the schemes designed to take settlers from all communities. The layouts of the settlement units in these schemes have been prepared by the government and, apart from standard-type dwellings, have included such facilities as roads, transport and police stations, religious buildings, parks and playgrounds, schools and an industrial area. Within such settlements, Malay, Chinese, Indian and other settlers have been generally allotted separate sectors to allow what was officially termed as 'homogeneity of community'.[3]

Non-sponsored independent Indian farm settlement has not been so prominent since it has consisted chiefly of individual farms set amidst the farms of other communities. Variations have occurred, depending on the economic activity. For the most part these farm settlements have comprised one or more dwellings, depending on the number of farmers, stock-sheds, a well and at times small shrines for religious purposes.

[1] See p. 231 below. [2] See pp. 263–70 below.
[3] Personal communication from the Federal Land Development Authority, Kuala Lumpur.

Settlement characteristics

A unique feature of the non-estate rural settlement has been the labour lines for the government's Indian work-gangs in the Public Works Department and Malayan railways. These have usually consisted of a single wooden or concrete structure, divided into rooms, a well, bathroom and lavatory. They have been, and still are, found more often than not in isolation, away from any other settlement, but alongside roads or railways. They have been situated for convenience of maintenance of the transport system and have been supplied from the near-by urban centres.

There have been no separate Indian fishing or mining settlements. The few Indian fishermen and miners have lived scattered amidst the other communities.

As noted above, the New Villages came into existence as a part of the Malayan government's plan to combat the Communist-led rebellion which broke out in 1948. The standard New Village possessed such amenities as a police post, dispensary, school and a communal kitchen, the last only in villages under severe food restriction. For the most part these New Villages were similar in appearance. Many of them were little more than closely packed shanty-towns, with small houses or large *kongsis* made of wood, *atap*, *lalang* or zinc, with bare laterite roads and unfinished drains, all fenced in with barbed wire.

It will be recalled that the New Villages, even more than the cities and towns, were predominantly Chinese. Moreover, the few thousand Indians in them were widely distributed amongst a number of New Villages with the result that there were seldom more than a small number of Indians in any one New Village. Here their dwellings were generally tucked away in almost wholly Chinese surroundings.

The exceptions were a few New Villages meant for Indians only. The largest of these was Changkat (also known as Boyd Road Indian Settlement) in Perak, with a population of about 900.[1] After some time this rigid rule was relaxed and a few Chinese and Malays were allowed into Changkat and the other Indian New Villages. However, despite their almost exclusively Indian populations, there was, and still is, little in the outward appearances of the Indian New Villages to distinguish them from their Chinese-dominated cognates, except for the introduction of such items as cattle sheds in place of pigsties and Hindu and Sikh temples in place of Buddhist shrines.

[1] Sandhu, 1964*b*, fig. 1; Corry, 1954, app. A; *SNVFM*.

Types of buildings

Indian buildings can for convenience be divided into two classes, dwellings and institutions, though these types may not always be discrete. There always has been little or nothing to distinguish the Indian dwellings in Malaya. Indeed the difference between them and the Chinese or Javanese equivalents, for example, has often been only in the fact that their occupants have been Indians.

Buildings which have housed Indians have ranged from large villas and bungalows to miserable tenements; but the most common house type of the urban Indians has been the ubiquitous shop-house, while that of their rural countrymen (has been) the estate dwelling designed to house labourers.

The shop-houses have varied, mainly in detail and building materials used, depending on the date of construction, but their pattern has been very similar.[1] They have usually been double-storeyed buildings, in which the lower part has been used for business and the upper for dwelling. These dwellings have frequently been divided into cubicles, which have almost invariably been overcrowded and insanitary; as many as twenty-five persons living huddled together in a small area 20 feet by 70 feet by 15 feet has not been at all uncommon in the post-war years. These modern Black Holes of Calcutta have been incubators for tuberculosis and other similar diseases.[2]

Until recently the estate dwellings designed to house labourers consisted largely of *atap, kajang* or wooden shacks either raised or on the ground and divided into a number of cubicles arranged back-to-back. Kitchens for these structures, reminiscent of Bornean longhouses, were usually either at the back or below the dwellings, depending on the style of the buildings, while lavatories were separate from the main structures (figs. 33, 34).

In these rural slums there was little privacy. The tiny rooms, generally 10 feet by 12 feet by 10 feet, at times housed whole families of five or even more persons.[3] Following the representations made before World War II by the Agent of the government of India, the emergence of strong labour trade unions in the post-war period and a developing concern for health and welfare on the part of the Malayan government, conditions improved considerably.[4] In the first place, a number of the

[1] Wright, 1908, pp. 647–8 *et seq.*; *SSAR*, 1935, II, 161; Dobby, 1940, pp. 98–104.
[2] Federation of Malaya, 1949, pp. 1–3; Singapore Department of Social Welfare, 1948, pp. 67–87.
[3] *IO:EP*, 2278 (1884), pp. 707–29; *RLC 1890*, p. 48; International Labour Organisation, 1950, pp. 119–21; Jackson, 1961, p. 104; *C.O.273*, 404 (1913), 25.2.1913; 405 (1913), 25.3.1913.
[4] Personal interview with the Commissioner for Labour, Federation of Malaya; *ARAGIBM*, 1926, p. 13; Gamba, 1962, pp. 10 ff.

barrack-like quarters were converted either into two or four family cottages through the removal of some rooms, or were given more privacy by the provision of additional screens. Later, the new labour quarters were almost wholly concrete-and-tile single, or semi-detached cottages.

There has been a plethora of Indian institutional buildings in Malaya, ranging from athletic associations and women's sewing clubs to *āśramas*,[1] and political *sabhas* or *caṅkams*; but the most common have been the religious buildings, and to a lesser extent, toddy shops.

Although by no means as prominent as in India, nevertheless Indian temples, churches and mosques have been a significant feature of the Malayan landscape.

The Indians in Malaya, like their fellow-countrymen in India, have professed a variety of faiths. No statistics of Indians by religious affiliation are available for either the present day or 1957 or 1947, but in 1931, out of the 621,847 Indians in the country 81·5 per cent were Hindus, 9·0 per cent Muslims, 5·9 per cent Christians, 2·9 per cent Sikhs, while the remainder followed a variety of other faiths such as Buddhism, Jainism and Zoroastranism.

The old Tamil saying

> *kovil illa uril kuti irrukka vendam*
> (do not live in a town where there is no temple)[2]

appears to have been particularly observed by the Hindus, for not only have their temples been the most numerous amongst the Indian religious buildings in Malaya but also the most widely known and distributed; almost every urban centre and large estate has had at least one. These temples have been maintained principally by Indian public subscription and donations. The temples on the estates have been on the whole simple structures but those in the towns have usually been highly decorated and ornamented buildings.

The estate temples and shrines have primarily served the needs of the estate dwellers but the urban temples have drawn a variety of worshippers from far and wide. The Kaliamman temple in Serangoon

---

[1] The Indian *āśramas*, in Malaya, such as those maintained by the world-wide humanitarian organization, the Ramakrishna Mission, have not only been sanctuaries for the poor and the weary but have also housed libraries and other facilities for study and meditation. With their banana plant-fringed and saffron-coloured walls and buildings with wide courtyards, reminiscent of the Indian homeland *āśramas* and *kuttees*, these *āśramas* have often stood out as uniquely Indian features of the Malayan landscape. The number of *āśramas* in Malaya has, however, been limited and the few that have existed have almost all been located in the larger urban centres of the country.

[2] This saying is of unknown origin but has traditionally been ascribed to the sage Auvaiyar (personal communication from Dr Rama Subbiah of the Department of Indian Studies, University of Malaya, Kuala Lumpur).

Road at Singapore, for instance, has drawn its congregation from as far afield as Bukit Panjang and Seletar, besides serving those Indians living in its immediate precincts in the city. Other Hindu places of worship such as the Batu Caves outside Kuala Lumpur, and the Sri Poyatha Vinayagar temple in Malacca (constructed in the early eighteenth century and the earliest extant Hindu temple of Malaya), have drawn worshippers and visitors from all over the country.

The Sikhs have their own *gurdwara* in almost every substantial urban centre in Malaya. Some of the larger towns and cities, like Singapore and Kuala Lumpur, have a number of Sikh temples. These have been built and supported by public subscription and donations from the Sikh community. The *gurdwaras* have been for the most part simple utilitarian structures along modern architectural lines and have served not only the needs of the Sikh community but also those of the Sindhis, who have had no proper temple of their own in Malaya.[1]

The *gurdwaras* have been, and are, much more than temples to the Sikh community, for they have also served as *Gurmukhi* schools, centres of social gathering and places where general matters affecting the Sikh community and the country as a whole have been discussed and debated. Each of the temples has been administered by a *gurdwara* committee, elected by the congregation. The priests in the Sikh temples have been appointed by the respective *gurdwara* committees.

The Indian Christians, who are virtually all South Indian Tamils, Mysoreans, Malayalis and Telugus, have been a small community and financially far poorer than either Hindus or Sikhs. Furthermore, the religious needs of many of them have been adequately met by the churches maintained by other Christian groups such as the Chinese, Eurasians and Europeans. In these circumstances there have been few Indian churches in the country, and when there have there has been little to distinguish them from those maintained by the other communities.

Indian Muslims, as well, have maintained few mosques of their own. As the Malays are Muslims and the Malay States constitutionally Islamic States, there has been little need for the Indian Muslims to have separate mosques. A mosque or *surau* has existed in every *kampong* and urban centre since well before the influx of Indian immigrants in modern times (Part 1). The few Indian mosques that were established have mostly had a distinctive Indian quality about them, in that their architectural style has exhibited a closer affinity with South India than

---

[1] The Sindhis (natives of the Province of Sind, now part of West Pakistan) in Malaya are almost all Hindus. However, their brand of Hinduism appears to be such that its needs are apparently more adequately met in Sikh rather than in orthodox temples.

with Malaya, while their congregations have generally consisted almost completely of Indians.

The few Indians professing other faiths (such as Buddhists, Jainists and Zoroastrans) either have had their own communal shrines or have had to make do with some other individual alternatives for their religious needs. Many of the Indian Buddhists, for example, appear to have gone to the temples maintained by the Chinese, Sinhalese, Thai and Burmese members of the sect. Some of the larger and more ornate Buddhist temples have formed striking features in the Malayan landscape.

Religion, as an aspect of the Indian social organization in Malaya, has not been so significant as in India, but (as will be apparent from the foregoing pages) it has exerted a considerable influence in the everyday life of the immigrants. The frequent comings and goings between home and temple, shrine, mosque or church have formed an integral part of the Indian social scene in Malaya. On festive occasions the scenes enacted at some of these religious places, especially the Hindu temples and shrines, could well have come straight from India.

The ordinary *kallukkaṭais* or toddy[1] shops of Malaya have not had any unique architectural style, but they have had a distinctive general appearance, which has tended to set them apart from their surroundings. Owing to their prohibition in Madras, it has not been possible for the writer to gain any impression of the design of toddy shops there for comparative purposes, but some of the people who have had experience of seeing both the Madras and Malayan types think they exhibit some prominent features in common. This may well be the case for the following description of a toddy shop in Southern India in the early centuries A.D. could well fit its Malayan counterpart of recent times, flags excepted:

> The gates of toddy shops have flags
> As sign of sale, where drinkers come
> In numbers, and the noisy yard
> Where fish and meat are fried, is heaped
> With sand, and with flower gifts is strewn...[2]

---

[1] The 'term toddy' or palm wine appears to be a corruption of the Hindustani *tari*, that is the fermented sap of the *tar* or Palmyra (*Borassus flabellifera*; Sanskrit *tāla*) and also of other palms such as date and coconut. In Malaya, toddy is derived solely from the coconut and is used almost wholly for drink, though it can be used to leaven bread and for the production of *gula melaka* or jaggery.

The amount of alcohol in freshly drawn toddy is practically nil, but rises rapidly and attains its maximum within forty-eight hours. It may then contain as much as 8 per cent absolute alcohol by volume. As fermentation proceeds the alcohol diminishes until in a toddy a few weeks old there is the merest trace. At its strongest —that is in a forty-eight-hour old toddy—it may be compared in alcoholic strength to pale ale or nearly double the strength of the ordinary Pilsner or Lager beers.

[2] *Pattu-Paṭṭu* (U.V. Saminath'-aiyar, Madras, 1889), canto II, vv. 200–10; J. V. Chelliah, *Pattupaṭṭu: Ten Tamil idylls* (Colombo, 1946), p. 33.

9

ETHNO-LINGUISTIC COMPOSITION

Local usage in Malaya tends to designate every South Indian a *Keling* while all North Indians are likewise dubbed *Bengalis*, irrespective of their territorial or ethnic origins. While this blanket division into North and South Indians is convenient, the ethno-linguistic composition of the Indian population is much more complex and can here be treated only in very general terms. Almost all the major ethno-linguistic groups of the Indian subcontinent are represented in Malaya but the most prominent are the South Indians. British Malaya's contacts with India have been chiefly with South India, and the South Indians formed more than 94 per cent of the total Indian population in Malaya in 1921.

Subsequently the relative proportion of South Indians in the total Indian population declined. This was the result of several factors. More North Indians immigrated and their death rate was lower. The Indian government's ban on labour emigration affected the South Indian almost exclusively and during the Japanese occupation a large number of South Indian labourers died. However, though their proportion has been generally decreasing, the South Indian element was numerically still the dominant element in the Indian population of Malaya in 1957 (table 13), and continues to be so to this day; and there is no reason whatsoever why it should not maintain its dominance in the future too.

Among South Indians, the Tamil group has been the largest in Malaya since the early days of Penang, and in 1921 formed nearly 87 per cent of the South Indian and more than 82 per cent of the total Indian population of Malaya. Over the next three decades the proportion of the Tamil population in the total and South Indian population on the whole declined for the same reasons as cited for the whole of the South Indian element. Indeed, the decline in the total South Indian population was largely the result of the decrease in the Tamil proportion since it was the latter that was the dominant South Indian group. Thus any change in the Tamil population has affected the whole of the South Indian population.[1]

---

[1] For example, as the proportion of Tamils in the Indian population declined to less than 77 per cent between 1931 and 1947, there was a concomitant, albeit smaller, decrease in the proportion of South Indians as a whole in the total Indian population (table 13).

Ethno-linguistic composition

Table 13: Ethno-linguistic composition of the Indian population of Malaya, 1921–1957

ethno-linguistic group	1921	1931	1947	1957
A. South Indian groups:				
Tamils	387509	514778	460985	634681
Telugus	39986	32536	24093	27670
Malayalis	17190	34898	44339	72971
Other South Indians	2000 (a)	4000 (a)	15968	20000 (a)
TOTALS	446685	586212	545385	755322
B. North Indian groups:				
Sikhs	9307	18149	10132	N
other Punjabis	6144	N	20460	N
Pathans	804	N	3166	N
Bengalis	5072 (?)	1827	3834	N
Gujaratis	403	N	1301	N
Mahrattas	29	N	556	N
Sindhis	N	N	728 (?)	N
Rajputs and Marwaris	N	N	1834	N
Parsis	N	N	98	N
TOTALS	21759	34156	42109	N
C. Other and indeterminate people of India	1736	1479	12122	N
Total Indian population in Malaya	470180	621847	599616	820270

(a) = Estimates.
N = No information available.
The figures in this table have limited reliability because of changes in classification and the uncertain quality of enumeration in past censuses.
Source: Compiled from del Tufo, 1949, p. 78; Fell, 1960, table 3; Chua, 1964, table 36; personal communication from the Superintendent of Census, Singapore.

More than a third of the Tamils have been on estates, where they have formed the bulk of the labour force. Since the beginning of the present century they have been found mainly in the Federated Malay States. These States contained nearly 80 per cent of the Tamils in Malaya in 1957. Within the Federated Malay States the largest concentrations have always been in the states of Perak and Selangor, particularly in the Kinta, Krian, Larut, Lower Perak, Klang, Kuala Langat and Kuala Lumpur areas. For example in 1957 these areas contained nearly half the Tamils of Malaya (figs. 4, 36a).

The Tamils are all from Madras State, the chief labour supply centre of pre-war Malaya. Until the 1930s the Tamil population was predomi-

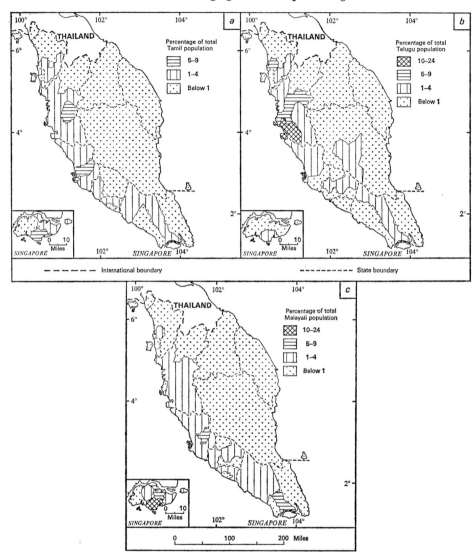

Fig. 36. Percentage distribution of (*a*) Tamil, (*b*) Telugu and (*c*) Malayali populations of Malaya in 1957, by districts.

nantly migrant and natural increase or decrease was of little significance in its growth. Further, this population was, except for a very small clerical, professional and mercantile element, largely a labouring population, mainly employed on the estates and, to a smaller extent, in government services and general labour. It followed that the increases

238

in the Tamil population were closely dependent on the state of develop-ment of the country, and more particularly on the health of the rubber industry. Following the Indian government's ban on labour emigration (which affected chiefly the Tamils) and the improvement of sex-ratio among them, the Tamil population became a little more settled. Further-more, though many of them were still on estates, the more enterprising non-labour elements had spread to almost every walk of Malayan life by 1957 (Part 3).

The Telugus, natives of the Andhra Pradesh region of South India (fig. 11), have also been chiefly connected with the estate economy of Malaya. They too, like their Tamil countrymen, declined in number from 39,986 in 1921 to 27,670 in 1957, making up little more than 3 per cent of the total Indian population and less than 4 per cent of the South Indians. This compares with 8·5 and nearly 9 per cent, respec-tively, in 1921 (table 13). The Telugus, unlike the other Indians, brought their womenfolk with them in considerable numbers and their sex-ratio has always been the highest among the Indian population. In 1957, for example, the sexes were almost equally divided and the community led a normal settled life.[1] The Telugus have traditionally been most strongly represented in Perak, Johore and Kedah, chiefly on the rubber and coconut estates (figs. 4, 36b, 38, 39).

The Malayalis, whose ethnic home is the Malabar coast area com-prising present-day Kerala State (figs. 9, 11), are the only major South Indian group in Malaya which did not decrease in numbers during the present century. In 1957 they numbered 72,971, compared with 17,190 in 1921. Their proportion in the Indian population had increased to more than 8 per cent in contrast to less than 4 per cent in 1921 (table 13).

The Malayalis suffered less from the ravages of diseases and the Japanese occupation than the Tamils and Telugus, partly because of their superior health and partly because the majority of them lived in towns where they enjoyed comparatively higher incomes in such jobs as stevedoring, clerical services and building trades. The Malayalis in the rural areas have lived mainly on the estates where besides being labourers they have also provided most of the subordinate administrative and technical staff. The numbers of the Malayalis in Malaya were further swelled following the influx of large numbers of their countrymen into the country in the first few years of the post-war period. These new arrivals found employment in the fast-expanding British military bases, where they formed the largest Indian group in 1957 (Parts 1, 3).

The Malayalis have been most numerous in southern Malaya, es-pecially in Singapore, south-central Johore and central Selangor (figs. 4,

[1] Fell, 1960, table 3; Chua, 1964, table 36.

The Indian population of Malaya

36c). Of the Indians in Malaya, the Malayalis appear to have been the least anxious to bring their womenfolk with them. Their sex-ratio was lowest in 1957, with about 480 females only to every 1,000 males compared with the more than 900:1,000 female-male ratio of the Telugus.[1] They are the least settled Indian group in Malaya and many of them, even to this day, generally seem to regard Malaya as a place to earn an income to support families in India.

Other South Indians include Kanaras (Kanaris, Canarese), Oriyas, Hyderabadis and Mysoreans, but the statistical information on them is wholly unreliable. In any case they always have been a numerically insignificant element in the South Indian population. Their occupations and distribution have more or less followed the pattern of the Malayalis. As for the North Indians, by far the most numerous among them have been the Punjabis. In 1947 they numbered 30,592, or more than 72 per cent of the total North Indian population of Malaya (table 13). The most conspicuous of the Punjabis are the tall, and generally bearded and turbaned, Sikhs. The Sikhs, according to the 1947 census, numbered 10,132 compared with the 18,149 enumerated by its 1931 counterpart. This decrease, however, is unlikely to have been entirely real, because many Sikhs were in all probability wrongly classified under some other heading, presumably as other Punjabis in view of the large unexplained increase attributed to this latter group (table 13). If anything, the Sikh population appears to have been steadily increasing, at least since the Japanese occupation, and is at present estimated to number about 30,000.

Initially concentrated in such services as the police and military forces, Sikh and other Punjabi immigrants and their descendants are today found in almost every sphere of the country's economy, being particularly prominent in the professional, mercantile and moneylending groups (Parts 1, 3).

By the end of the Japanese occupation the Sikhs and other Punjabis were found in most parts of Malaya but mainly in and near the large towns. The largest numbers of these people were in Singapore, Selangor and Perak, particularly the last which was one of the first areas of Punjabi immigration into Malaya (figs. 4, 37a). The pattern today is unlikely to be very different.

The rest of the North Indians have been present only in small numbers in Malaya, generally in and around the main urban centres and following such occupations as lawyers, textile merchants, *jagas*, milkmen and *chaiwallas* (table 13; figs. 4, 37b–h).

Summarizing, it could be said that the number of Indians in Malaya

[1] *Ibid.*

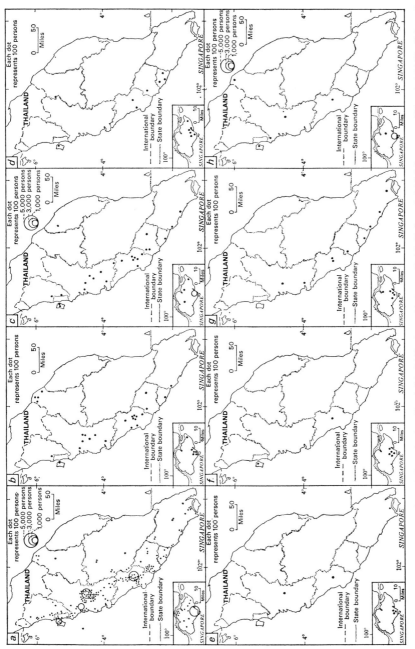

Fig. 37. (*a–g*) Distribution of (*a*) Sikh and other Punjabi, (*b*) Pathan, (*c*) Bengali, (*d*) Gujarati, (*e*) Mahratta and Parsi, (*f*) Sindhi, and (*g*) Rajput and Marwari populations of Malaya, 1947. (*h*) Distribution of the Hindustani (Uttar Pradesh) population of Malaya, 1931.

16

241

S II

increased rapidly, principally through immigration in the earlier phases, and later, with the improvement of the sex-ratio and general health, through natural increase. Almost half of the Indian population in Malaya in 1957 was below fifteen years of age and its annual rate of increase (3·5 per cent) was one of the highest in Malaya. Furthermore, its earlier transient character gradually changed, and by the beginning of the 1960s the major portion of the Indian population was stabilized and Malayan-born and domiciled.

Until the middle of the nineteenth century the Indian population was located along the coast, almost completely in the Straits Settlements. But with the establishment of law and order in the Malay States and the consequent development of modern transport and of sugar, coconut, tapioca, coffee, rubber, oil palm and tea plantations, the concentration of population moved inland from the coast, principally to rubber areas in the foothills of western Malaya. Except for slight modifications it has remained there ever since.

Finally, over the last two decades, the rate of urbanization among the Indians has been remarkable. For example, the proportion of the urban dwellers in the total population is estimated to have been less than 35 per cent up to the end of the Japanese occupation, but within the next twelve years it had increased to more than 47 per cent. Today it is estimated that well over 50 per cent of the Indians in Malaya are living in urban centres of 1,000 or more persons.

PART 3

INDIANS IN THE MODERN MALAYAN ECONOMY

10

AGRICULTURE AND INDUSTRY[1]

The economic development of Malaya has focused to a large extent on the production of rubber and tin for export, and on the output of a variety of foodstuffs and secondary manufactures mainly for domestic consumption (fig. 38). Financial and commercial services for domestic markets and for the large entrepôt trade with most of Southeast Asia are also important undertakings. The role of Indian labour, and to a lesser extent capital and enterprise, has been of special significance in the economic development of the country.

Agriculture has occupied a dominant position in the economy of Malaya, contributing some 40 per cent of the gross national income and about two-thirds by value of total exports in the 1950s and early 1960s.[2] The majority of the Indians have been directly or indirectly connected with this undertaking, especially from the latter half of the nineteenth century, although in smaller numbers they have also been found in almost every other sector of Malayan economic life. For example, in 1931 some 60 per cent of the total gainfully occupied Indian population was engaged in agricultural pursuits while by 1947 and 1965 the proportion were still respectively 53 and 45 per cent (tables 14, 15). In the case of the Indian female workers alone, this concentration in the agricultural sector has been even more marked. Females have generally formed between 25 and 45 per cent of the total Indian labour force of the country and more than 80 per cent of them have been in agricultural pursuits since the early years of the present century. While still on the subject of Indian woman employment, it may be worthwhile to note that their rate of participation in economic activity has been propor-

[1] The collection and publication of comprehensive statistical material relating to the structure and characteristics of the economic activities of the people of Malaya is closely linked with the periodic censuses of population. As stated earlier on (Part 2), the last census of population in Malaya was taken in 1957 and the next will not be taken until 1970. In these circumstances, while every attempt has been made to incorporate as many of the post-1957 statistical data as were necessary and available, this in practice often meant being satisfied with material pertaining to the 1950s only, little comparable information being available for the later years.

[2] International Bank for Reconstruction and Development, 1955, pp. 9–16 *et seq.*; *FMOYB*, 1964, pp. 670–90; *SYB*, 1964, pp. 69–105; Silcock and Fisk, 1966, pp. 93 ff.

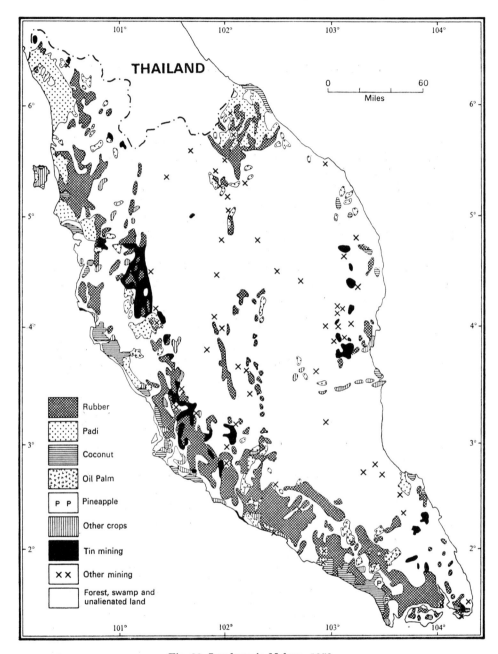

Fig. 38. Land use in Malaya, 1953.

246

Agriculture and industry

Table 14: Percentage occupational grouping of the gainfully occupied Indian population of Malaya, 1931–1965

occupational group	percentage			
	1931	1947	1957	1965*
agricultural pursuits	60·5	53·4	47·4	45·0
mining and quarrying	1·8	1·7	1·8	1·0
manufacturing	2·0	4·9	10·3	10·0
transport and communications	8·0	5·9	6·2	6·0
commerce and finance	5·6	10·1	13·4	16·5
services	21·0	23·1	19·9	19·5
other and indeterminate occupations	1·1	0·9	1·0	2·0

* The employment data for Malaya for 1965 are incomplete. The figures included here are estimates based on Department of Statistics, 1963, tables 2.8, 4.7; 1965, pp. 4 ff.; Department of Labour and Industrial Relations, 1966, apps. 12–14; *ARLDS*, tables II, III; *MDS*, Jan. 1967, pp. 17–25; *MSB*, Dec. 1966, pp. 131–6.

Source: The figures for 1931 to 1957 are compiled from Vlieland, 1932, tables 118–44; del Tufo, 1949, tables 78–110; Chua, 1964, tables 84–7; Fell, 1960, tables 11–17.

tionately higher than their numerically superior Malay and Chinese counterparts. In the Federation of Malaya in 1947, for example, about 41 per cent of the Indian females aged ten years and over were economically active compared with less than a quarter of the Malays and Chinese. The corresponding figures for 1957 were almost 52 and less than 25 per cent respectively.[1] This high activity rate among the Indian females has been not so much a question of attitudes or inherent ethnic propensities but rather of features associated with the place and type of Indian female economic activity. About three-quarters of the Indian female workers have been on plantations where wages have been generally low and it has been normal for almost all working-age members, including females, of families to work, the main obstacles to this being removed by the provision of creches, ayahs and other child-minding facilities. Outside the plantation sector of the Malayan economy the activity rate of Indian females has been low—on the whole less than 20 per cent compared with more than 30 per cent for the Chinese. In the larger urban centres the rate has been even lower. In Singapore, for example, only about 7 per cent of Indian females aged ten years and over were economically active in 1957. This situation is not totally surprising:

[1] It should, however, be noted that these comparatively low activity rates amongst the Chinese and Malay females may not be a true index of their overall participation in economic activities: though it is known that substantial numbers of Chinese and Malay females are economically active such activities are often in circumstances which do not easily lend themselves to definitive recording.

247

Indians in the modern Malayan economy

Table 15: Racial composition of the gainfully occupied
population of Malaya (by industry), 1931–1965

industry	year	percentage				
		Indians	Chinese	Malays	others	total
agricultural pursuits	1931	17·0	27·0	55·0	1·0	100·0
	1947	14·5	29·9	54·6	1·0	100·0
	1957	13·6	26·9	58·5	1·0	100·0
	1965 (a)	12·5	25·5	61·0	1·0	100·0
mining and quarrying	1931	13·5	76·5	8·5	1·5	100·0
	1947	12·4	74·5	11·6	1·5	100·0
	1957	11·5	68·8	17·2	2·5	100·0
	1965 (a)	11·0	62·0	25·0	2·0	100·0
manufacturing	1931	6·5	72·0	20·0	1·5	100·0
	1947	7·6	69·4	21·3	1·7	100·0
	1957	12·2	67·2	18·9	1·7	100·0
	1965 (a)	9·0	70·0	20·0	1·0	100·0
transport and	1931	22·5	55·0	20·5	2·0	100·0
communications	1947	18·0	56·4	22·9	2·7	100·0
	1957	18·5	50·1	27·5	3·9	100·8
	1965 (a)	17·8	49·2	29·5	3·5	100·0
commerce and finance	1931	11·5	78·3	8·5	1·7	100·0
	1947	13·5	72·3	12·5	1·7	100·0
	1957	15·6	70·1	12·1	2·2	100·0
	1965 (a)	16·0	68·5	13·0	2·5	100·0
services	1931	25·0	46·0	24·5	4·5	100·0
	1947	23·3	43·3	29·0	4·4	100·0
	1957	15·3	42·7	33·0	9·0	100·0
	1965 (a)	15·0	40·0	37·0	8·0	100·0
other and indeterminate	1931	10·5	70·0	12·0	7·5	100·0
occupations	1947	10·8	69·1	12·7	7·4	100·0
	1957	18·0	60·0	20·0	2·0	100·0
	1965 (a)	18·5	60·0	19·5	2·0	100·0
all occupations	1931	18·5	44·2	35·8	1·5	100·0
	1947	15·1	43·2	39·8	1·9	100·0
	1957	14·2	42·4	40·9	2·5	100·0
	1965 (a)	14·0	42·0	42·0	2·0	100·0

(a) See footnote to table 14.
Source: As for table 14.

with the exception of some such groups as those engaged in low-income
manual labour, a high rate of participation in urban economic activity
has seldom been a characteristic of the urban Indian female population,
principally because of, first, the various social barriers and prejudices
within the Indian community itself against females leaving homes in
search of employment and, secondly, the strong competition from the

better placed, socially freer, more mobile and generally better educated Chinese womenfolk in, as will be seen later,[1] a traditionally Chinese-dominated sphere of activity.[2]

AGRICULTURE, FORESTRY AND FISHING

Malayan agriculture consists essentially of two types of cultivation—smallholdings and plantations or estates,[3] with the latter being commercially the more important. In 1957 and 1965, out of a total of 5,000,000 and 6,400,000 acres alienated for agriculture, more than 2,200,000 and 2,100,000 respectively were in estates (table 16a).

Estate or plantation agriculture

Plantation agriculture, based on the production of raw materials in substantial quantities by cheap labour from largish land-holdings, is essentially a modern phenomenon. Malaya's association with this type of cultivation began with the planting of pepper and spices on Penang Island in the 1790s.[4] Subsequently a variety of other crops, including gambier, tapioca, ramie, sugar, coffee, coconuts, rubber, oil palm, tea, pineapples and cocoa were also tried, especially in the western coastal regions of the country. Of these only the last six crops have survived—the remainder ceasing to be of any commercial significance as estate crops by the second decade of the present century.[5]

The cultivation of coconuts is an old-established undertaking. It has, however, largely remained a Malay smallholder enterprise, though important plantations were developed from as early as the nineteenth century, particularly in Province Wellesley and the Bagan Datoh and Krian areas of Perak. In 1957 there were 95 coconut estates covering 85,560 acres and producing 36,000 tons of copra.[6]

The history of the introduction of Para rubber, *Hevea brasiliensis*, Muell.-Arg., its period of trial in Malaya, and its subsequent phenomenal

[1] See pp. 281–9 below.
[2] del Tufo, 1949, pp. 101–16, 354–549; Fell, 1960, pp. 86–157; Chua, 1964, pp. 79–96, 162–254; Jones, 1965a, pp. 44–72; 1965b, pp. 61–82.
[3] There is as yet no clear definition or criteria in Malaya as to what constitutes a smallholding. It is, however, generally accepted that all agricultural holdings below 25 acres in size are smallholdings except in the case of rubber and oil palm cultivation when the ceiling is 100 acres. Bigger holdings are classified as estates or plantations.
[4] *SSFR*, 9 (1805–10), 30.9.1805.
[5] *NHGMP*, pp. 17–26; *JIA*, iv (1850), 378; *PP*, xxiii (1847–8), part i, paras. 333–609; *SFP*, 7.10.1841; 13.2.1962; *PAR*, 1899, pp. 14–15; *SSBB*, 1897, p. X4; *SSG*, 1880, p. 507; *SSG*, 1883, p. 1183; *SAR*, 1896, p. 3; Wheatley, 1954, pp. 63–6; Grist, 1936, pp. 10 ff.; Parmer, 1960, pp. 7–8; *FMAR*, 1957, p. 161.
[6] *FMAR*, 1957, p. 160.

success, has been described in a large number of publications.[1] For our purposes it is sufficient to say that rubber was first grown as a commercial crop in Malacca by a Malacca-born Chinese, Tan Chay Yan. After some experimental planting in 1895, and recognizing that rubber had a market, he organized a Chinese rubber-planting syndicate and in 1898 planted the first rubber estate (Bukit Asahan Estate) in the northeast corner of Malacca territory. His example was soon followed by sugar and coffee planters and others. Some of these planters, with their sugar, coffee and other plantations rapidly declining in the face of falling prices, rising costs of production and increasing competition from better organized production in other countries,[2] had already been experimenting with *Hevea* prior to this and who now either took up new land or began converting their existing properties into rubber estates.

The area for rubber production grew rapidly—from less than 5,000 acres in 1899 to 543,000 and more than 3,000,000 by 1911 and 1938, respectively—and from the first recorded export of some 100 tons in 1904–5, Malaya's production rose, in 1920, to 196,000 tons or 53 per cent of the world's production.[3] Although Malaya's production subsequently decreased to about 40 per cent, following development of the crop in Indonesia and elsewhere, production had reached 638,700 tons by 1957 and more than 859,000 from 4,269,000 acres eight years later (table 16 a), almost all of which was exported. Nearly 60 per cent of the exports came from estates.[4]

In 1957, rubber made up two-thirds of the cultivated area of 5,600,000 acres, contributed 59 per cent of the total exports of $4,171,000,000 and employed about a quarter of the economically active population of the country—a clear indication of its role and importance in the everyday lives of the people and the national well-being of the country (figs. 38, 39). In spite of the efforts of the government to diversify the economy by such means as the encouragement of manufacturing and the cultivation of commercial crops other than rubber, Raja Rubber continues to dominate the Malayan economic scene, and is likely to do so for many a year to come.[5]

The oil palm, *Elaeis guineensis*, Jacq., coming originally from West Africa in 1875, was not commercially cultivated in Malaya till 1917,

[1] See, for example, Mills, 1942, pp. 183–214; Grist, 1936, pp. 73–101; J. H. Burkill, *A dictionary of the economic products of the Malay Peninsula* (London, 1935), pp. 1150–60.
[2] *NHGMP*, pp. 22–6; Grist, 1936, pp. 10 ff.
[3] Department of Statistics, 1958 b, table 4; Ooi, 1959, pp. 17–18; *RSB*, 1959, xiii, iv, p. 39; A.W.S., 1910, pp. 12–13.
[4] *FMAR*, 1957, p. 148; *CSAR*, 1957, p. 110; *MSB*, Dec. 1966, pp. 18, 31–40.
[5] Malaysia, 1965, pp. 1 ff.

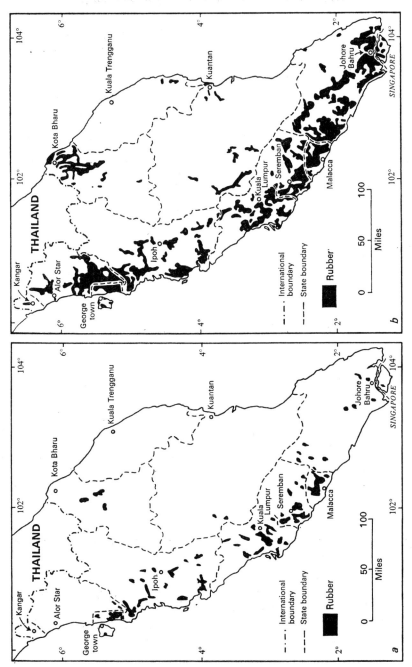

Fig. 39. Rubber cultivation in Malaya, 1910 (*a*) and 1953 (*b*).

251

Indians in the modern Malayan economy

Table 16a: Crops and cultivated areas in Malaya, 1957–65

	per thousand acres					
	estates		smallholdings		total	
crop	1957	1965	1957	1965	1957	1965
rubber	2011	1859	1725	2410	3736	4269
rice	—	—	748	865	748	865
oil palm	116	208	—	18	116	226
coconut	85	68	433	445	518	513
pineapples	20	27	25	20	45	47
cocoa	1	2	N	N	1	2
tea	3	3	7	5	10	8
others	N	N	N	N	447	503
TOTALS	2236	2167	2938	3763	5621	6433

N = No information available.

Source: *MSB*, Dec. 1966, p. 17; personal communications from the Department of Agriculture, Malaysia, and the Land Office, Singapore.

Table 16b: Ownership of rubber estates in Malaya, 1931–1957

year	total number of estates	total acreage	percentage distribution							
			number				acreage			
			European	Chinese	Indian	other	European	Chinese	Indian	other
1931	2301	2320300	42·4	42·4	10·5	4·7	75·9	16·9	2·9	4·3
1947	2316	1945600	39·2	41·1	16·9	2·8	74·5	17·1	4·9	3·5
1957	2473	2477900	24·1	52·9	17·9	5·1	65·7	24·5	7·5	2·3

Source: Compiled from Grist, 1933, p. 26; Department of Statistics, 1948, p. 11; 1958*b*, pp. 9–10; personal communications from the Ministry of Labour and Industrial Relations, Malaysia, and the Land Office, Singapore.

when H. Fauconier established the first plantation in the district of Kuala Selangor, in southwestern Malaya. Its cultivation was a monopoly of estates until a few years ago when an experiment was started to popularize it as a smallholder crop. In the early years, from 1917 to 1924, cultivation of oil palm was confined to Selangor, but it then spread to Negri Sembilan, Perak, and Johore.[1] By 1957 Johore, into which the crop was introduced in 1925, had 42,900 acres out of the total of 116,000 (table 16a; fig. 38).

[1] Jagoe, 1952, pp. 3–10.

252

Agriculture and industry

Pineapples were first grown for canning purposes in about 1888, the earliest factories being opened by Europeans in Singapore and Penang. While the factories in Penang ceased operations because of the difficulty of obtaining sufficient supplies of fruit, those in Singapore prospered, chiefly as a result of the expansion of the crop in south Johore since 1920. In the post-World War II rehabilitation of the industry, the emphasis has been on permanent plantations in contrast to the largely catch-crop system current before the war. Out of a total acreage of 45,000 in 1957, nearly half was in estates, chiefly in Johore, Selangor and Perak (fig. 38; table 16 a).

Although tea had been grown by Chinese smallholders in Malaya for many years previously, estate cultivation of the crop only came into prominence in the late 1920s with the development of the Cameron Highlands area of northwestern Malaya. The total tea estate acreage in 1957 was estimated at 3,000 while production was 5,247,000 lb., of which about three-quarters was exported.[1]

Cocoa is a comparatively recent estate crop in Malaya, and is still very largely in its experimental stage, though a pilot scheme had already been established by the Colonial Development Corporation in Trengganu in 1957. Up to 1965, however, the total area under cocoa here and elsewhere did not exceed 2,000 acres (table 16 a).

Indians and plantation agriculture have been almost synonymous terms in Malaya since about the second half of the nineteenth century. Indian associations with plantation agriculture began virtually from its inception, though they did not become prominent until after the middle of the nineteenth century, the principal plantation workers up to this time being Chinese. With increasing immigration thereafter, Indians rapidly replaced Chinese as the main plantation labour force. For example, as early as the 1860s Indians had already replaced the Chinese as the principal labourers on sugar estates, not only on European-owned properties but also on some of those belonging to the Chinese *towkays* of Penang.[2] Thereafter their numbers increased and by 1931 they formed more than 70 per cent of the total estate population of 424,000. Although their predominance declined subsequently from its peak, Indians nevertheless still formed 52 per cent of the estate population in 1957 (table 17 a; fig. 40).

The principal role of the Indians in the estate economy has been that of labourers and, to a smaller extent numerically, they have been subordinate administrators and technicians as well as estate owners and managers.

[1] *FMAR*, 1957, p. 160.
[2] Jackson, 1961, pp. 26–9; *RLC 1890*, app. A.

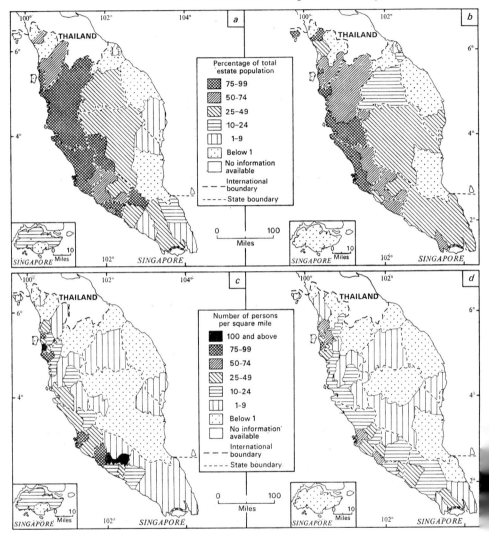

Fig. 40. (*a*) and (*b*): Indians as a percentage of the total estate population of Malaya in 1921 (*a*) and 1947 (*b*), by districts. (*c*) and (*d*): Density of total estate population in Malaya in 1921 (*c*) and 1947 (*d*), by districts.

Indian estate labour

As the discussion in Parts 1 and 2 showed, Indian immigration into British Malaya was essentially a movement of manual labour from about the middle of the last century, and they have continued to be the most numerous element in the Indian population since then. In 1931, for instance, about 75 per cent of the gainfully occupied Indians were labourers, while in 1947 and 1965 the percentages of labour in the gainfully occupied Indian population were approximately 70 and 60 per cent respectively. The most important labour group has been the estate workers, who comprised more than 85 per cent of all the Indians engaged in manual work in 1931.

Since the 1930s, and especially over the last decade, there has been an overall decline in the estate group as a proportion of the total Indian labour force following a decreasing proportion of Indians living on estates on account of such developments as the Emergency, increasing urbanization (Part 2) and the fragmentation of estates. The problem of the fragmentation of estates, resulting in Indian and other workers losing their jobs and having to leave the estates, has been assuming dangerous dimensions of late. It has been caused by the sale and subsequent subdivision into small plots of European-owned rubber estates employing Indian and other labourers.[1] These sales began about 1950, mainly, it seems, as a result of fears and problems of security generated by the Emergency and impending *Merdeka* and the extra-ordinarily high prices offered for rubber estates by speculators. The speculators in turn hoped to make handsome profits through the subdivision of such properties into small plots and the sale of these plots to land-hungry immigrant Malayan, more particularly Chinese, smallholders who were finding the acquisition of fresh rubber-lands extremely difficult.

The acreage of rubber estate land so subdivided became really significant in the post-*Merdeka* period and by 1965 more than 200,000 acres of European-owned estate land had already been sold and sub-divided into small units, generally of 50 acres or below. More significant from our present point of view, this had resulted in the unemployment, among others, of some 18,000 Indians. As noted earlier (Part 2), while some of these Indians, with their families, returned to India, others drifted to nearby urban centres in search of work.[2]

The exodus of Indians and other people from the estates would have been even higher had it not been for the intervention of the National Land Finance Co-operative Society. This society was formed in 1960 by a group of people headed by Dato (now Tan Sri) Sambanthan, President

---

[1] A few other European-owned properties, mostly oil palm and coconut estates, have also been sold and subdivided, but up to the present the acreage involved here has been insignificant compared with that of rubber estates.

[2] *RSE 1957*, table I; Aziz, 1962, I, 35, 174–90 *et seq.*; Federation of Malaya, 1961, pp. 3–10; *ES*, 18.2.1967; 19.2.1967; *ST*, 15.12.1966; 6.2.1967; personal interviews with the officials of the National Union of Plantation Workers and the All Malayan Estates Staff Union of Petaling Jaya, Malaya; Gamba, 1962, pp. 231–4.

of the Malayan Indian Congress, to 'raise funds from the estate workers and to buy rubber estates to combat fragmentation and its attendant evils'. By the end of 1966 this society owned six estates covering some 12,000 acres. It had a membership of 48,000 at that time and employed some 2,000 workers on its estates. Most, if not all, of these workers would have lost their jobs if the estates had been fragmented.[1] But, despite the efforts of the society and other well-wishers, the threat of fragmentation continues to become increasingly more menacing for the estate workers.[2] The full impact of this growing danger has yet to be felt but, together with the other developments mentioned above, there has already been a decline in the formerly predominant position of the estate workers in the total Indian labour force. However, although declining, the estate group is still the most numerous. In 1957, for example, it formed about two-thirds of the total Indian labour force of the country, and eight years later nearly 60 per cent.[3]

Since the 1860s Indians have been the most important group of all the communities engaged in estate labour. In 1931, for example, they formed nearly 75 per cent of the estate labourers. During the ensuing three decades, following the Great Depression, the Indian government's ban on labour emigration just before the outbreak of World War II and the increasing movement of Malays and Chinese into the estate economy, the predominance of the Indians in the estate labour force suffered a relative decline; nevertheless they still constituted the single largest element in 1965, comprising 48·5 per cent of estate labour compared with 22·6 per cent for the Malays and 28·7 per cent for the Chinese (table 17 b).

From the beginning of the present century the largest numbers of Indian labourers, both male and female, working on estates have been in the rubber industry. In 1957 and 1965 there were 134,000 and 120,000 on rubber estates, representing more than 88 and 87 per cent respectively of all Indian estate labour. The Indians were always the predominant racial group on rubber plantations until the early 1930s. Thereafter their predominance declined for virtually the same reasons as the contemporaneous decline in the proportion of Indians in the total estate labour force. Nevertheless they still constituted the major element in the rubber estates' labour force in 1957 and 1965, with nearly 52 and more

[1] National Land Finance Co-operative Society Limited, 1962, p. 5; *ES*, 27.9.1966; personal communication from the Secretary, National Land Finance Co-operative Society Limited, Kuala Lumpur.

[2] *ES*, 16.12.1966; 18.2.1967; *ST*, 15.12.1966; 6.2.1967; *MM*, 6.2.1967.

[3] Vlieland, 1932, tables 127, 135, 143; del Tufo, 1949, tables 87–8; Fell, 1960, tables 11–12; Chua, 1964, tables 65, 84; Department of Labour and Industrial Relations, 1958, tables 1–2; 1966, apps. 12–14; *ARLDCS*, 1957–8, table II; *ARLDS*, table II.

Table 17 a: Racial composition of the estate population
of Malaya, 1921–1957

year	total estate population (in thousands)	percentage			
		Indians	Malays	Chinese	others
1921	372	69·5	10·2	19·0	1·3
1931	424	71·7	6·7	20·2	1·4
1947	412	58·5	12·8	27·7	1·0
1957	435	52·0	19·0	28·0	1·0

Source: As for table 17 b.

Table 17 b: Racial composition of the estate labour force
of Malaya, 1921–1965

year	total estate labour force (in thousands)	percentage			
		Indians	Malays	Chinese	others
1921	279	77·8	4·9	16·4	0·9
1931	200	73·5	2·8	23·1	0·6
1947	326	50·1	20·9	28·7	0·3
1957	290	52·8	18·6	28·2	0·7
1965	283	48·5	22·6	28·7	0·2

Source: Compiled from *ARAGIBM*, 1925–40; *ARLDFM*, 1947–57; Department of Labour and Industrial Relations, 1966, apps. 12–14; *ARLDCS*, 1957–8, table II; *ARLDS*, table II.

than 47 per cent of the 260,000 and 254,000 labourers respectively in the industry.[1]

The next important estate crop employing Indians has been the coconut industry. Here, as in rubber cultivation, Indian labour has played a dominant role and in 1957 and 1965 it comprised 84 and 85 per cent, respectively, of the total labour force engaged on coconut estates. However the numbers involved were comparatively small, for there were only some 7,500 Indian labourers in the industry in 1957 and 4,300 eight years later.[2]

On oil-palm estates, too, Indians have been the main group from the very inception of the industry. In 1957 they formed 54, and in 1965

[1] Department of Labour and Industrial Relations, 1958, table 1; 1966, apps. 12–14; personal communication from the Labour Department, Singapore.
[2] Department of Labour and Industrial Relations, 1958, table 1; 1966, app. 12.

58, per cent of all the labour employed on oil-palm estates. As on the coconut estates, the numbers involved were small compared with rubber. In 1957 and 1965 there were under 10,000 Indian labourers on oil-palm estates, or less than 8 per cent of the total Indian estate labour force then.[1]

Tea plantations have provided the other principal employment of Indian agricultural labour, and between 1957 and 1965 there were some 2,500 to 2,900 Indian labourers engaged in tea cultivation. However they formed between 59 and 70 per cent of the total labour force on the tea estates at that time.[2]

The last plantation enterprise of note in which Indian labour has been engaged has been pineapple cultivation. Essentially this has been a Chinese-dominated undertaking. There were less than 400 Indian labourers on these estates in 1957, forming 19 per cent of the total labour force engaged in the industry. By 1965 there were only 20 Indians in a total work force of 2,740, of whom 2,290 were Chinese.[3]

The vast majority of Indian estate labourers have always been directly employed on a long-term basis, in contrast to the Chinese, for example, who have usually preferred working on a contract system. In 1957, for example, whereas more than 90 per cent of the Indian estate labourers were directly employed, some 62 per cent of their Chinese colleagues were on contract engagements.[4] This prevalence of the direct method of employment amongst the Indian labourers has been so largely because of the mode of their initial recruitment and engagement (Part 1) and their general preference for working for fixed wages and security of tenure.

Indian estate labourers have received their wages either fortnightly or monthly, the amount paid depending on the prevailing daily wage, the number of days actually worked and, of late, the sum total of work completed or commodity produced. Until a few years ago wages were seldom constant from year to year, but tended to fluctuate with the market price of the commodity produced. While wages were generally reduced in proportion when commodity prices toppled, they rarely rose proportionately when prices appreciated. In short, while the labourers nearly always felt the trade and commodity recessions, they cannot be said always to have shared in the booms.[5]

The wages paid to the Indians have varied with the commodity and

[1] Department of Labour and Industrial Relations 1958, table 1; 1966, app. 12.
[2] *Ibid.* [3] *Ibid.* [4] Department of Labour and Industrial Relations, 1958, table 3.
[5] Kumaran, 1964a, pp. 1 ff.; Gamba, 1962, pp. 25 ff.; National Union of Plantation Workers, 1965, pp. 45–50; Department of Labour and Industrial Relations, 1958, table 6; *IICMM*, 1907–41, *passim*; *RSB*, 1965, xix, ix, table 55; Parmer, 1960, table 8.

the nature of work, but generally they have been less than those paid to their Chinese co-workers.[1] This willingness of the Indian to accept lower wages was in fact his major attraction as a labourer in the first instance, at least where planting interests were concerned. This was fully appreciated by the general planting community which, with the exception of some individual planters who frequently spoke out and worked for better treatment of Indian labourers, took the necessary steps to ensure that *Ramasamy* never lost his virtue as a cheap and docile labourer. To this end, through such powerful media as their own Planters' Association of Malaya, the Rubber Growers' Association of London, their representatives in the Indian Immigration Committee and the Malayan legislature, a sympathetic Malayan government and a largely European-dominated press, they generally prevented wages from rising higher than they wished. Until the 1940s they also prevented the rise of effective trade unions or other movements claiming to represent estate labourers.[2]

Then, while paying lip-service to the government's exhortations to encourage Indian labourers to settle permanently in Malaya through liberal land grants, generally little was done in this direction, partly from fear that it would lead to a neglect of estate duties by such labour-farmers and, if they were successful, to the withdrawal of their labour altogether.[3]

A final example of the determination of planters to oppose any measure that might disturb the *status quo* was their attitude towards the establishment on estates of schools for the labourers' children. From almost the very beginning they were against such schools, ostensibly on grounds of cost, as they would have had to have been provided for almost wholly from estate funds. But when they failed to prevent the enactment of the *Labour Code* of 1923, which stipulated the provision of a school on every estate containing ten or more children of school-going age,[4] the planters made certain that the schools remained ineffective. Before

---

[1] It should be noted that all directly employed labour has received, in addition to wages, such other benefits as free accommodation and medical attention. As the vast majority of the Indians have been directly employed, in contrast to the largely contractor-engaged Chinese, they have enjoyed these additional benefits. However, it has been estimated that even taking this into account the total *real* wage of a Chinese tapper has been usually at least a third higher than that of his Indian counterpart (*PAMC*, 1941, 2, pp. 20–2; 1946, 2, p. 4; *NAI:EP*, 1939, file no. 48–7/39–0s; Parmer, 1960, table 8).

[2] *PAMC*, 1946, 2, p. 3; 3, pp. 6–8; 4, pp. 4–6; 5, pp. 13–15; Parmer, 1960, pp. 166–221; Kumaran, 1964*a*, pp. 1–4; Gamba, 1962, pp. 10–20.

[3] *PAMC*, 1936, 6, app. A; *NAI:EP*, confidential file no. 227/36—L & O 1936B.

[4] Some of the larger estates already operated schools for their labourers' children prior to this. Indeed, the establishment of estate schools in Malaya dates from the nineteenth century, but it was purely a voluntary affair until 1923.

World War II few of them had qualified teachers. Most were *kanganis*, clerks and other similar part-time teachers. The schools were usually simple sheds, often with no provision for separate classes, all the grades being taught in one class by the same teacher. Attendance was seldom compulsory. Indeed, most estates provided job opportunities for children from the age of ten to twelve years. This incentive, coupled with the general ignorance and illiteracy of the parents and the need for the children to work in order to supplement the family income, meant that most children left school after a few years. In any case these were only primary schools and no skills, other than the tautological rudiments of the three R's were taught. Moreover, the medium of instruction in these schools was not English, the passport to a better-paid job in contemporary Malaya, but Tamil, Malayalam or Telugu.[1]

The Malayan government, for its part, refused to support English education in estate schools, principally on grounds of cost. Furthermore, instruction in the mother tongue of the immigrants was acceptable to the Madras authorities.[2] There were English schools in the urban centres, but the labourers' earnings were generally so low as to leave them little margin for such luxuries. Thus the one language—English— in the country which might have enabled the children of labourers to find other occupations was on the whole denied to them. Furthermore, the parents, segregated by language, culture and conditions of service from the mainstream of Malayan life and themselves appallingly ignorant and almost always illiterate, were hardly in a position to inculcate in their children anything more than what they knew themselves, that is the wielding of the *manvetti* or the *katti*.

Finally, excessive supervision, patronage and paternalism, both on the part of the Indian and Malayan governments and the planters, were hardly the conditions to generate initiative or ambition in the Indian labourers.

In these circumstances, while a number of Chinese who began as labourers alongside Indians later emerged as millionaires or at least as successful *towkays*, the number of Indian labourers or their children who became anything else than rubber tappers, coconut pluckers, weeders and such like, was negligible. The few descendants of Indian estate labourers who managed to find other occupations almost all became

---

[1] *NAI:EP*, Oct. 1929, B proc. 58–67; *PAMC*, 1933, 2, pp. 10–11; 5, p. 9; 1946, 7, p. 7; *C.O.273*, 352 (1909), 27.12.1909; *ARAGIBM*, 1926, p. 14; *PFC*, 1923, pp. 107–11; Parmer, 1960, pp. 124–5; personal interviews with officials of the National Union of Plantation Workers, Malaya, and Mr T. P. Sundaram, a former Assistant Controller of Labour, Federation of Malaya; Cheeseman, 1955, p. 39.

[2] *IO:EP*, 1502 (1880), p. 166; Cheeseman, 1955, p. 39; Indian Education Committee, 1951, p. 2; *PAMC*, 1933, 5, p. 9.

clerks, teachers and office assistants, and there is no known case of any ex-estate labourer or his descendant becoming a millionaire or a successful *mutalaaḷi*.

Indeed, far from experiencing any spectacular improvement in their fortunes, the Indian labourers in pre-war Malaya generally continued to form a poor landless rural class, fixed in status by the terms of their employment, education and total earnings. The average monthly earnings of an adult Indian labourer on a rubber estate then seldom amounted to more than $10–15 compared with the $30–35 earnings of his Chinese colleagues. After the war, with the emergence of an organized labour movement and the establishment of trade unions amongst labourers, the lot of the Indian labourer began to improve. Daily rates of pay of rubber tappers, for example, had risen to $2·60–2·80 by 1957 and the total monthly earnings of a tapper averaged $65–80 compared with the $10–15 of the pre-war days. Two years later, and for the first time, rubber-estate workers were guaranteed a minimum basic wage while the ceiling of the maximum was removed. In practical terms this meant that before the end of 1959 the average monthly earnings of an Indian rubber tapper had reached $75–100.[1]

Even allowing for the rise in cost of living, this was an increase in real income. There was also an improvement in the provision of services such as better educational facilities, including easier access to English education. The full effects of these improvements have yet to be felt, but even now there are signs of bigger family incomes, better education and greater geographical and occupational mobility among Indian labourers. However, while he has certainly advanced, the Indian labourer has still some way to go before he can either match the generally 50–100 per cent higher earnings of his Chinese counterpart or accumulate sufficient capital to set himself up as a smallholder or small-scale entrepreneur.

Indian subordinate administrative and technical estate staff

With the exception of approximately fifty years between 1880 and 1930, when Ceylon Tamils also appear to have been prominent, Indians have held a virtual monopoly of the subordinate managerial, clerical

---

[1] Department of Labour and Industrial Relations, 1958, tables 6–20; Kumaran, 1964*a*, pp. 16–22, apps. A–B; personal interviews with officials of the National Union of Plantation Workers of Petaling Jaya and the Ministry of Labour, Malaysia, Kuala Lumpur. There are some discrepancies in both the government's and the National Union of Plantation Worker's figures for the total monthly earnings of estate workers, the latter's being generally about 10–15 per cent lower than those of the government. The earnings cited in the text above are adjusted totals based on all available data, both official and private.

and technical posts on estates from almost the beginning of large-scale European plantation enterprise in Malaya. In 1957 and 1965, for example, they formed more than 88 and 80 per cent, respectively, of the approximate 6,700 and 5,500 persons so engaged in the plantation economy.[1]

The Indian community that has been the most prominent in this sector of the plantation economy has been the Malayali group. Kerala has had one of the highest literacy rates in India from the nineteenth century and some of the earliest assistants employed on estates appear to have been Malayalis. Once established, this community entrenched itself in the estates and, as the industry grew, they brought in their relatives and friends to try, as far as possible, to maintain it as a 'closed' preserve for Malayalis. Following the post-World War II trend of allowing more Asians into senior executive posts on European properties, a number of these Malayalis have become managers of estates.

Indian estate ownership

Plantation agriculture in Malaya has been largely controlled by European, mostly British, capital and management. For example, in 1931 more than 75 per cent of the total estate rubber acreage of 2,320,300 was in European-owned estates. In the post-war years the dominant position of the Europeans gradually decreased, mainly through the sale of smaller properties to local Asian buyers, but they still controlled nearly two-thirds of the estate acreage in Malaya in 1957 (table 16b).

Next in importance have been the Chinese-owned estates, followed by Indian estates. Indian-owned estates have been concerned almost exclusively with rubber. These numbered 242 in 1931 and 400 in 1957, out of a total of 2,301 and 2,473 respectively. But the average size of Indian estates has generally been small compared with either European or Chinese. For instance, while the European and Chinese estates averaged 1,800 and 400 acres in size in 1931 and 1,600 and 350 in 1947, the estates of the Indians averaged only 280 and 240 acres respectively (table 16b).

The small acreage of the Indian-owned estates has been largely the result, first of the late entry and inexperience of Indian estate owners; secondly, the lack of large amounts of capital and of instruments for concentrating it, both vital in the pioneering big estates; thirdly, the British Malayan government's land policy which was strongly biased towards large-scale estates; fourthly, the strong competition for what-

[1] Personal interviews with officials of the All Malayan Estates Staff Union and the National Union of Plantation Workers, Petaling Jaya, and Mr R. Thambipillay, retired schoolmaster, Victoria Institution, Kuala Lumpur.

ever land was left and available to the small-scale operators from the more experienced and already established Chinese investors; and finally, until recently, the reluctance on the part of many Indians to undertake long-term permanent investment owing to the transitory nature of their stay in Malaya.

Almost all of the Indian estates have been privately owned, principally by the Chettiar Tamils of South India. As will be seen shortly,[1] they have been the chief Indian financiers of Malaya and have also owned most of the other Indian land-holdings in the country.

The majority of the Indian estate owners, both Chettiars and others, have been absentee landlords, who have invariably left the workings of their estates in the hands of Indian assistants or Chinese *kepalas* and have employed mostly a mixed labour force of Indians, Chinese and Malays.

Smallholding agriculture

Smallholding, the traditional form of *kampong* agriculture, has been based on the cultivation of foodstuffs for domestic consumption and the raising of livestock or poultry as cash products. The farms of the smallholders have generally ranged from less than an acre to ten acres in size.[2] Work on them has almost always been done wholly by family labour.

From about the turn of the present century smallholders increasingly began to concentrate on the production of cash crops, both for local and foreign markets, and soon constituted an important element in primary agricultural production. For example, in 1931, 1,215,000 acres of the 3,071,000 acres under rubber cultivation were in smallholdings which produced 195,000 tons of rubber, or more than 40 per cent of the total production for that year.[3] By 1965 the area under smallholding rubber had grown to 2,400,000 acres, representing more than 50 per cent of the total rubber acreage of the country then (table 16*a*).

Indians in smallholding agriculture

In addition to individual Indians settling down to small-scale farming on their own amidst the other communities of Malaya (Part 1), several attempts have also been made to sponsor agricultural settlement by groups or a number of Indian smallholders together.

Sponsored Indian farm settlement in Malaya dates from almost the beginning of British rule. However, it was not until comparatively recently that it assumed any notable dimensions.

[1] See pp. 290–2 below.
[2] Dobby, 1957, pp. 3–143; Wilson, 1961, tables 18–19.
[3] Grist, 1932, tables 2, 6.

For convenience, sponsored Indian farm settlement can be divided into two categories, namely non-government-sponsored settlement meant specifically for labourers or ex-labourers and government-sponsored settlement open to all Indians capable of farming.

Non-government sponsored settlement of labourers and ex-labourers on agricultural land has consisted of two main types: (a) that which has been estate sponsored and (b) that which has been sponsored by some other private or semi-official agency.

The *Labour Code* of Malaya at an early stage stipulated that an allotment of one-sixteenth of an acre of land be made to each Indian labourer on an estate for his own cultivation. This was designed, first to ensure a settled labour force in the country; secondly, to enable the labourer to supplement his wage income by growing vegetables, fruits and the like, and thereby generally to improve his economic position and health; and, thirdly, to give the Indian labourer a stake in the country, thereby promoting loyalty to Malaya and also giving him an alternate means of livelihood during periods when there was little demand for labour.

But despite this early provision of land for labourers in the *Labour Code*, it was not until after the 1929–33 slump that this stipulation came into general and effective use. Till then, only a few Indian labourers made use of this provision. There were a number of reasons for this. First, the proportion of families among the Indian labourers was small. Bachelors were not attracted by fruit and vegetable gardens as they usually planned to return home after a few years in Malaya. Secondly, farming conditions in Malaya were for the most part strange to these Indians and there was virtually no example to follow. In any case, food was cheap and most of them did not see the necessity of growing foodstuffs. Thirdly, the average planter or visiting agent had very little idea of the aims of settling Indian labourers on land. Furthermore, to many planters and nearly all visiting agents, a green shoot appearing above the soil which was not rubber or some other commercial seedling was likely to be *lalang* and therefore something to be destroyed rather than encouraged. Fourthly, a planter who had his own vegetables sent to him from distances of a hundred miles, along with his cold-storage requirements, was not likely to be enthusiastic over cultivation of vegetables among his labourers. Fifthly, there was also a reluctance on the part of planters to encourage agricultural plots for labourers on grounds of health, especially for fear of the spread of malaria. Furthermore, gardens close to homes were regarded as a great hindrance by planters and actually discouraged as far as possible.[1]

[1] Interview with Mr T. P. Sundaram, a former Assistant Controller of Labour, Federation of Malaya; *ARLDM*, 1938, p. 49.

Agriculture and industry

During and after the 1929–33 slump, conditions for settlement became more favourable and led to numbers of Indian labourers taking up agricultural plots. This was because, in the first place, the Indian labourers who were left in Malaya during the Great Depression (Part 1) consisted to a large extent of families and a large proportion of those who came back after the slump were labourers who had married while in India. Then, as no alternative means of livelihood were available, the Indian labourers had little choice but to produce their own food-stuffs in order to survive. Finally, the lesson taught by the Great Depression on over-dependence on one source of income led to a change in attitude among both planters and labourers themselves. They no longer regarded agricultural plots close to dwellings as unsafe and in fact this cultivation came to be regarded as a necessity against over-dependence.[1]

For the most part these labourers' allotments have consisted of a strip of land divided into plots of one-sixteenth of an acre in area, either adjoining labour lines or separate from dwellings but close by. Where the labourers have lived in separate cottages the agricultural allotments have usually adjoined and stretched behind each cottage.

Another type of settlement for labourers on estate land, but one which was rather rare in Malaya and in any case has now virtually disappeared, has been that where large areas of estate land have been set aside for the exclusive settlement of dependent labourers on plots averaging more than an acre in area on a permanent or semi-permanent basis. The best example of this type of land settlement in Malaya was the Permatang Estate Settlement, owned by Permatang Estate of Morib, Selangor.

The directors of this estate set aside an area of 63 acres of land for the benefit of their labourers in November 1936. The idea behind the scheme was

...to get a number of non-working dependent labourers to take up blocks of land and contribute something to the exchequer instead of loafing about the lines and being a drag on their relatives. It was hoped that some of the older workers would also take up land with a view to developing it in their spare time and returning to live on it when they were no longer fit for work...[2]

The whole area of 63 acres was, with the exception of 5 acres set aside as common grazing ground for livestock, divided into single-acre blocks, and each labourer was given one of these blocks, both for his quarters and for cultivation. At first there was some reluctance among the labourers to take up the land, but once the initial suspicion that

[1] *ARLDM*, 1938, p. 51.   [2] *MAJ*, xxvi (1938), 454.

there was no ulterior motive behind the offer had been overcome, it was readily taken up by the settlers. By 1938 there were already thirty settlers and by the time of the Japanese invasion almost all the blocks were occupied.

The subsequent history of this settlement is a little hazy but, according to the oral testimony of some of the descendants of the original settlers, it appears that deterioration set in during the Japanese occupation.[1] This resulted partly from the forced recruitment of several of the able-bodied settlers by the Japanese for their wartime labour battalions (Part 2) and partly on account of the generally disturbed conditions that characterized the period. Things improved a little after the war but not for long, for with the declaration of the Emergency (Part 2), the settlers, though allowed to attend to their plots during the day-time, were forced to abandon their dwellings in the settlement and return to the estate labour lines. With the intensification of the guerrilla campaign, even the daytime care of the fields became increasingly difficult and it was not long before almost all the plots were under *lalang* or *belukar*. In the meantime the ownership of the estate had changed hands and the new proprietors seem to have decided to do away with the settlement altogether, for they refused an application by some of the descendants of the original settlers a few years ago to be allowed to go back to their family plots. At the time of the interview, virtually the whole of the former settlement had been cleared by the estate and planted with oil palm.

It is apparent from the foregoing account of the Permatang Estate Settlement that on nearly all the estate-sponsored Indian 'colonies' the settlers have not owned their plots, and have been totally or partially dependent on the estates for their holdings. On the other hand, they have paid no land taxes for their gardens of foodstuffs, vegetables and fruit, except for a nominal quit rent paid to the estates.

Labour settlement sponsored by private or semi-official agencies has been on a much larger scale. In such schemes the labourers have been given title to the land on which they have settled. But they have had to finance themselves, largely through the sale of jewellery, goats and cattle, as little or no monetary aid has been available. Sponsorship in the initial stages has mainly taken the form of the granting of land at a nominal price, and the provision of administration and guidance. Nearly all of these settlements have been sponsored by either Christian missions or by Indian organizations and their officials, working for the benefit of their fellow-countrymen. Official sponsorship in this instance has

---

[1] Among those interviewed by the writer early in 1966 was Pongaivanam, son of the *kangani* in charge of the first pre-war settlers.

amounted to the blessings of the Agriculture and Labour Departments and the supervision of health.

The best examples of this type of settlement are the Mission d'Etrangérers' St. Joseph's Tamil Mission Settlement or, as it is more popularly known, Kg. Padri or Samyar Kampong, at Bagan Serai, Perak, and the Ramapuram Indian settlement at Chuah, Negri Sembilan (fig. 41).

Kg. Padri, originally known as Soosay Paleam or St. Joseph's Camp, was begun in January 1882, for the settlement principally of Tamil and other South Indian labourers on the land. The original settlers were given holdings of up to 5 acres of land each as their own property on which to live and plant *padi* and coconuts and other crops; as others arrived, they too were given similar concessions.[1]

In 1937, there were about 400 persons living in this settlement of nearly 700 acres, compared with some 430 on 450 acres 48 years earlier.[2] In 1966, the population was about 1,000 persons; but not all of them were Indians, as by this time a number of Chinese and Malay families had also moved into the area to take up plots mortgaged, abandoned or sold by former Indian settlers. The Indian population alone was estimated to be in the region of 600 persons, all of them locally born. According to several of these people interviewed by the writer in 1966, almost all the Indian settlers tilled and lived on their land and only when they were in need of ready cash did they seek work elsewhere and then, too, only for a limited time.[3]

The Ramapuram or Ramanathpuram Indian settlement, four miles from the village of Chuah in the Port Dickson district of Negri Sembilan (fig. 41), occupies an area of 243 acres of a flat coastal plain. Although this settlement was not formally established until 1932,[4] a number of Indian labourers, either employed on estates close by or squatters in neighbouring Malay Reservations and *kampongs*, had moved into the area by 1927 and had begun clearing plots for themselves under the

[1] *FFRB*; *PLCSS*, 1893, paper no. 6, British Resident, Perak, to Colonial Secretary, Straits Settlements, 5 April 1892; Assistant Indian Immigration Agent, Taiping, to Secretary to Government, Perak, 6 February 1892; *SSAR*, 1890, p. 207.

[2] *FFRB*; *MAJ*, xxvi (1938), 454.

[3] The resident Indian population of this settlement seems to have remained fairly constant since the 1890s. In 1892, for example, it was about 550 while almost three-quarters of a century later it is estimated to have been no more than some 600 persons. This stability in the Indian numbers appears to have been maintained largely on account of a fairly high death rate, especially in the earlier pioneering stages, and through a steady movement of younger people out of the settlement to schools, jobs and domicile elsewhere, including as far afield as Singapore (*PLCSS*, 1893, paper no. 6, British Resident, Perak, to Colonial Secretary, Straits Settlements, 5 April 1892; personal interviews with the Rev. Father Manikam, the parish priest, and the Headman, Kg. Padri).

[4] *DOPD:CISF*, 7, Agent of the government of India to District Officer, Port Dickson, 6.8.1932.

leadership of S. Suppiah, the present-day 'Elder Spokesman' of the settlement, and the late V. A. Muthiah.[1] With the onset of the Great Depression, and the attendant widespread unemployment amongst Indian estate labourers (Parts 1, 2) the need to provide such people with land for farming purposes became even more pressing. In the Port Dickson district this was fully appreciated by the local government officials and others concerned with Indian affairs as a whole. In the case of the Chuah area the efforts of such people finally bore fruit in August 1932, when sixty-nine settlers, all of whom had been in Malaya 'for more than a decade or two', led by S. Suppiah, were given land on temporary occupation licences, in the first instance with the proviso that permanent titles would be granted when the owners had paid the premium, survey fees and rent. The fees amounted to about $10 per acre with an annual quit rent of $2 per acre and the titles stipulated that no rubber trees be cultivated. The land was parcelled out into lots of 4, 3, 2 and $1\frac{1}{2}$ acres and the total acreage of land given to each settler was not uniform, the final award being largely determined by the size of the individual settler's family. Of the initial group of sixty-nine settlers, for example, thirty-nine were given 4 acres each, fourteen 3 acres each and the remainder 2 acres each.[2]

The overall organization of the settlement was placed in the hands of the Malayan Cooperative Department, through the Indian Cooperative Officer, Negri Sembilan. The settlers were informed that permanent alienation of land (as opposed to temporary occupation licences) would be granted in the first instance to a group of settlers and not to individual members of such a group. Accordingly some of the settlers got together and formed a cooperative society, the Chuah Indian Settlers' General Purposes Cooperative Society Ltd., which was given legal status by being registered. One of the conditions of admission into this society was that only selected settlers could join it and that they had to act in accordance with the orders of the committee of the Society. Failure to do so entailed expulsion from the settlement.[3] In connection with this it should be remembered that several of the settlers had little knowledge of the type of work that lay before them and almost all of them were without adequate capital, vital for any successful pioneering. No financial assistance was forthcoming from the government and in these

[1] *DOPD:CISF*, 8, copy of enclosure no. 3 in Negri Sembilan Government 783/32; personal interview with Mr S. Suppiah of Ramapuram.
[2] *DOPD:CISF*, 6, inspection report on the Indian settlement at Chuah by the Health Officer, Seremban, 20.12.1935; 5, District Officer, Port Dickson, to Secretary to the Resident, Negri Sembilan, 16.11.1941; *MAJ*, xxvi (1938), 452.
[3] *DOPD:CISF*, 3, copy of no. 5 in Negri Sembilan Co-operation 85/45; 1, memorandum by the District Officer, Port Dickson, on the Chuah Indian settlement, 4.11.1947; *MAJ*, xxvi (1938), 452.

circumstances the settlers were forced to raise whatever capital they could through the pawning or sale of family possessions. The advantages of working together were soon apparent, the whole area being felled at one time and adequate drainage carried out at an early date. Once the felling was done, temporary structures of bark and wood were erected and the settlers began to house themselves. Shortly after the foundation a Tamil school and a temple were built while some land was set aside as common grazing land and as a reserve for a burial ground.[1]

The settlement filled up rapidly and, by the time of the Japanese invasion in 1941, sixty-two houses had been erected and the total resident population is reputed to have exceeded 500 persons. By this time, it had also been decided by the society that, unlike Kg. Padri, for example,[2] the settlers of Ramapuram were not to be allowed to mortgage, sell or otherwise dispose of their plots to anyone without the written permission of the committee of the Society.[3] This in practice ensured that Ramapuram remained homogeneously Indian—a situation which, apart from a couple of Chinese tenants, has not changed to this day.

Ramapuram survived the Japanese occupation but at some sacrifice to its former prosperity. Several of the houses in the settlement were abandoned and the fields neglected on account of the occupants deserting the settlement. Rehabilitation in the post-war period was a slow process but in 1953 permanent titles were issued to all the settlers[4] and certainly by 1958, if not earlier, Ramapuram had largely recovered much of its pre-war well-being and patterns of livelihood. A field survey conducted by the writer in 1958 showed that the settlement then had forty-seven homes holding a population of 357. With the exception of about thirty people who worked as tappers on neighbouring rubber estates, the settlers were all farmers growing mainly tapioca and coconuts. In addition, nearly all the farmers raised livestock of one kind or another, particularly pigs (for sale to nearby Chinese settlers), goats, cows and poultry. A few of the settlers had so prospered that they could afford to support two wives each.

A visit in 1966 revealed that the position in Ramapuram had not

---

[1] *DOPD:CISF*, 8, copy of enclosure no. 3 in Negri Sembilan Government 783/32; *MAJ*, xxvi (1938), 452.

[2] See p. 267 above.

[3] Personal interview with Mr S. Suppiah of Ramapuram; *DOPD:CISF*, 5, District Officer, Port Dickson, to Secretary to the Resident, Negri Sembilan, 16.11.1941; 1, memorandum by the District Officer, Port Dickson, on the Chuah Indian settlement, 4.11.1947.

[4] Personal interview with Mr S. Suppiah of Ramapuram; *DOPD:CISF*, 1, memorandum by the District Officer, Port Dickson, on the Chuah Indian settlement, 4.11.1947.

changed very much over the preceding eight years apart from the following main developments. In the first place, the number of houses had grown to seventy-one and the resident population to over 400 persons. Secondly, with improvement in wages on rubber estates and in other avenues of employment, the proportion in the total gainfully occupied population of settlers who were not full-time farmers had increased to over 40 per cent compared with less than 20 per cent in 1958. Thirdly, beginning in 1959, the leasing of coconut groves, at the rate of $2 per palm per month, for toddy tapping had become a profitable undertaking. Finally, the intrepid Suppiah had interplanted his plot of coconuts with oil palm. He expected his example to be followed by the others shortly.

The final category of sponsored Indian farm settlement in Malaya has been that directly or indirectly undertaken by the government. For example, besides the Bengal farmers brought by Francis Light to Penang in 1790, and given four acres of land each (Part 1), there were also two other government-sponsored schemes designed exclusively for Indian settlers. The first of these, for the cultivation of *padi*, was at Telok Anson, Perak. It was designed for 100 Indian families, who were to be selected in India and assisted to migrate. Each family was to be given 3 acres of land, tools, assistance in felling and clearing, and building materials for a house. All this assistance was in the form of a recoverable loan, with the exception of the passage money.

The scheme began in 1885 with an intake of twenty-four families. The others were to follow later. However, the scheme had hardly been initiated before it was abandoned, largely it appears because there was no support from the central Malayan authorities and because of the attractions of cash wages on adjoining plantations and government projects.[1]

The second venture, principally for the cultivation of coffee, was at Kajang in Selangor. It began in the same year as the Telok Anson scheme and, before the end of 1886, contained fifty Tamil settlers.[2] The subsequent history of this scheme is unknown as it ceases to feature in official records thereafter, but what is certain is that it, too, did not take permanent root.[3]

The foregoing are the only known instances of government-sponsored land-settlement schemes designed exclusively for Indians. There have, however, been several government-sponsored schemes which have

[1] *SSSF*, 1886, Misc. 970/86; *SSAR*, 1890, p. 207; *PLCSS*, 1893, paper no. 6, Superintendent, Lower Perak, to Secretary to Government, Perak, 10 October 1892.
[2] *SAR*, 1886, pp. 209–10.
[3] Personal communication from District Office, Kajang.

catered for all the different people inhabiting Malaya, and Indians have been eligible for entry into such schemes as a group or as individuals.[1] In these schemes, as for example in the Tanjong Karang Padi Scheme of Selangor (fig. 41),[2] more often than not each of the three main communities of Malaya—Malays, Chinese and Indians—has been given separate portions of the new land where its members can live among their own kind, but under a single overall system.

Government-sponsored land-settlement schemes for Malays existed before the Japanese occupation, but the inclusion of immigrant Chinese and Indians in such schemes has been almost wholly a post-World War II phenomenon. These post-war schemes have been designed to:

(i) make the maximum use of land, thereby creating the 'economic basis...for maximum wealth';

(ii) relieve pressure on developed areas and open up virgin territory, particularly in eastern Malaya;

(iii) diversify the agricultural economy of the country by encouraging the cultivation of new crops in self-contained units; and

(iv) give the immigrant communities a stake in the country.[3]

To implement these aims, each state instituted Land Development Boards or Corporations, while a federal organization, the Federal Land Development Authority, was created in 1956 to coordinate the work of all these boards and in general give whatever aid it could to the individual state boards, in addition to undertaking schemes on its own.[4]

By the end of 1965 the total number of Federal Land Development Authority schemes, completed or in progress, numbered sixty-two. Once these schemes are completed some 100,000 people would have been settled on new land. How many of these will be Indians is unknown; up

---

[1] Department of Information, 1953.

[2] The preliminary work on the Tanjong Karang Padi Scheme commenced in 1932–3 and within two years 300 Malay cultivators had moved into it. Although not officially allowed into it until 1946, Indians also began to take up plots in the scheme, particularly during the Japanese occupation. At the end of the war there were about 200 Indians growing *padi* in Tanjong Karang and following negotiations between the Malayan government and the Malayan Indian Relief Committee, set up by Pandit Nehru, they were given official permission to remain. Moreover, it was also agreed that other Indians too, albeit in small numbers, would be allowed into the scheme (*Federated Malay States: Report on the progress of schemes for the improvement and extension of rice cultivation*, Kuala Lumpur, 1935, p. 8; *H*, 13.7.1946).

A field survey conducted by the writer in 1966 showed that by this time there were some 120 Indian dwellings, housing about 600 persons, in Tanjong Karang and that these Indians owned about 900 acres of *padi* land.

[3] *FLDAAR*, 1958–59, pp. 38–40.

[4] For a useful and penetrating summary of the formation and functions of the Federal Land Development Authority see, for example, Wikkramatileke, 1965, pp. 377 ff. and Ho, 1965, pp. 1–15.

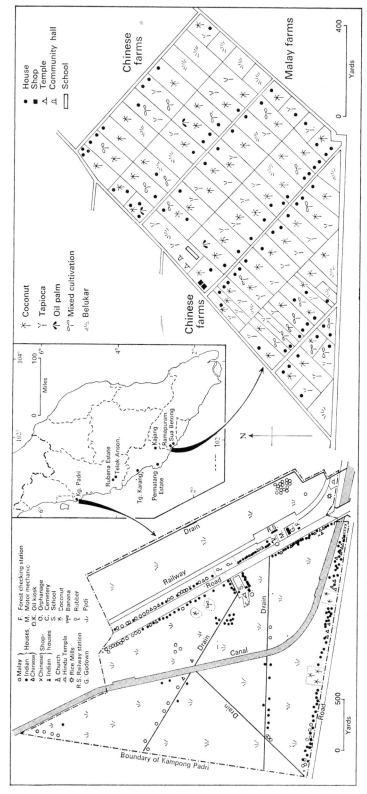

Legend (Chinese/Malay farms inset):

House ●
Shop ■
Temple △
Community hall ⌂
School ▭

Coconut
Tapioca
Oil palm
Mixed cultivation
Belukar

Chinese farms
Chinese farms
Malay farms

400
0
Yards

N

104°   100
6°
4°
102°   102

Miles
0   100

Kg. Padri
Rubana Estate
Telok Anson.
Tg. Karang
Permatang
Estate
Kajang
Ramapuram
Sua Betong

2°

Legend (Kg. Padri map):

○ Malay) Houses.
● Indian)
▲ Chinese)
× Chinese) Shop-
I Indian) houses
▲ Church
⌂ Hindu Temple
R.S. Railway station
G. Godown

F. Forest checking station
M. Motor mechanic
O.K. Oil kiosk
O. Orphanage
C. Cemetery
S. School
✳ Coconut
⌇ Banana
Q Rubber
⅄ Padi

Drain
Railway
Road
Drain
Canal
Drain
Road
Boundary of Kampong Padri

500
0
Yards

Fig. 41. Kg. Padri and Ramapuram: two examples of Indian pioneer land-settlement schemes in Malaya, 1966.

to mid-1966 only 225 Indian families, numbering some 1,350 persons, had entered such schemes.[1]

Despite these various schemes to settle Indian labourers and other workers, and despite the fact that the community's participation in smallholding agriculture dates from almost the beginning of British rule in Penang (Part 1), Indians never became significant in this sector of the Malayan economy. It has remained dominated very largely by Malays and to a lesser extent Chinese. For example, even as late as 1965, there were estimated to be less than 20,000 Indian farmers in the country compared with some 600,000 Malays and 150,000 Chinese.

There are several reasons for this limited Indian participation in smallholding agriculture. In the first place, apart from individual schemes designed mainly to meet particular exigencies, and despite public statements to the effect that the government accepted the principle that settlement of Indian labourers on land in Malaya was desirable, there was never any sustained or countrywide effort on the part of the British Malayan government to settle Indians on land. Indeed, if anything, certainly by the 1920s if not earlier, the government was not keen 'to see a bigger proportion of Chinese and Indians induced to settle in Malaya than (was) necessary to carry on (the) vital industries'. Some senior British officials even went to the extent of stating quite categorically that they looked on Indians as 'birds of passage and would discourage them from doing anything but living and working on rubber estates'. Tied up with this, as noted earlier on,[2] was the fear that '...it is at least possible that those who would take up land under large-scale schemes, while they might act as a reservoir for estate labour, might come to eschew employment as wage earners and take up small farming for their own profit...'[3] Secondly, from 1913 the government enacted legislation from time to time setting aside large areas of the country as Malay Reservations, in which only Malays could settle and own land.[4] By the 1930s, these Malay Reservations covered about a quarter of the total area of Malaya and, together with the large areas alienated to estates, left little easily accessible and suitable agricultural land for occupation by non-Malay smallholders. Thirdly, in the scramble for the limited agricultural land available to non-Malays,

[1] Personal communication from the Federal Land Development Authority, Kuala Lumpur; *FLDAAR*, 1960–1, pp. 43–5; Federal Land Development Authority, 1966, pp. 1–2.
[2] See p. 259 above.
[3] *NAI:EP*, 1933, file no. 84–2/33—L & O; 1936, confidential file no. 227/36—L & O 1936B.
[4] The purpose of these enactments was to protect the existing and future Malay ownership of land against the encroachment of financially stronger non-Malay interests.

Indians have faced stiff competition from the more versatile and enter-prising Chinese farmers who have enjoyed the added advantage of better credit and marketing facilities; the trading channels have for long been largely Chinese-dominated. Fourthly, the vast majority of Indian immigrants into Malaya have been labourers, tradesmen, clerks or professional men, who came into the country not as colonists but as wage-earners intending to stay only long enough to make sufficient money for retirement to their village hearth in India. Fifthly, nearly all the potential settlers have been, and still are, labourers, principally from estates, where they have enjoyed such amenities as free housing and medical care for their dependants. Most of the land-settlement schemes, particularly those of the post-war period, have been located in new areas, away from the existing places of work. Settlement in these areas has thus entailed a wholesale shift of dwellings, a move about which the Indian labourer has not been enthusiastic, except in circum-stances of dire need. Sixthly, almost all of the Indian labourers came into the country virtually penniless to take up generally low-income jobs and their continued lack of capital has been a major impediment to successful land settlement. It often takes about two years before a settler can get any return from his land and this can easily discourage a potential settler, especially if he has been engaged in temporary casual labour and has not saved enough even for an initial working capital, let alone money to see him through the two years. Seventhly, there has been the Indian preference, both on the part of labourers and other workers, for the security of permanent wages as opposed to, for example, the Chinese propensity for private enterprise, no matter how arduous or insecure. Finally, the Indians have tended to be too particular, or as the *Straits Times* puts it, 'they want land at their doorstep'.[1] There appears to be much truth in this statement and in similar feelings expressed by government officials, for numbers of Indians interviewed by the writer on estates in 1958 and 1966 wanted land close to the estates, so that they could till it in their spare time and in the event of permanent settlement could still be close to their original home and relatives. In view of the present prosperity of the country, generally improving wages and service conditions on estates and the lack of pressure to settle on land, it seems almost impossible to reconcile the Indian labourer's desire for land close to his existing employment and the present-day government's policy of opening up the virgin lands of comparatively underdeveloped eastern Malaya. The desire for the type of land that the Indian labourer wants can only be satisfied if the estates, the largest employers of Indian labour, are prepared to give

[1] *ST*, 20.5.1958.

land to their employees on a much larger scale than the present niggardly allotments of one-sixteenth of an acre. This, however, appears to be unlikely and thus large-scale Indian settlement on land will have to wait for a change either in circumstance or in attitudes towards land settlement in general.

The total land holdings of the Indian smallholders in Malaya in 1938 amounted to some 235,000 acres or less than 8 per cent of all land in smallholdings.[1] No comparable official data are available for the post-war period but the oral testimony of several Indians interviewed and the field surveys carried out by the writer in 1961–2 and 1965–6 leave little doubt that the Indian-held acreage increased during this period. In terms of Indian farmer-settlers, however, this increase does not appear to have been really significant since there does not seem to have been any marked change in the attitude of Indians to settlement on the land. Then much of the increase since the end of World War II appears to have been in rubber lands as well; but here again the acquisitions seem to have been made more on a speculative basis than with a view to permanent settlement, in the sense that they were acquired not so much to be worked by the new owners but more with the idea of quick sale the moment there was a favourable appreciation of prices.

Mixed farming, the raising of livestock, particularly for milk, *padi* planting and rubber cultivation have been the most important occupations of the few thousand Indian farmers. In the 1950s and early 1960s more than three-quarters of these farmers were estimated to have been in these four categories.

Mixed agriculture has been an important activity in Malaya; but it has been dominated by the Chinese, and the Indians have played an insignificant role. For example, in 1957 there were only about 1,140 Indian market-gardeners (compared with 61,500 Chinese) out of a total of 87,000.[2] Vegetables, fruits, *sireh* and flowers have been the most important crops cultivated on the Indian mixed-farms, which have been usually on the fringes of the larger urban centres which have constituted their principal markets.

Livestock farming has been concerned principally with the keeping of milch animals, chiefly cows and water-buffaloes. To a lesser extent, goats have also been kept for the same purpose, and were frequently taken from door to door so that the milk could be supplied directly to the person who wanted it. The milch animals have been raised and kept close to large urban centres, particularly Singapore and Kuala Lumpur, which are the chief consumers of milk.

[1] *SSAR*, 1938, pp. 524–6; *NAI:EP*, 1940, file no. 51–7/40—Os.
[2] Fell, 1960, table 11; Chua, 1964, table 84.

Apart from goats and poultry, few Indians have raised livestock for meat. This has been largely because the majority of the livestock farmers have either been Hindus or Sikhs, whose religious scruples forbade the slaughter, consumption or sale of cattle and buffaloes for such purposes.

Padi cultivation in Malaya has been predominantly a Malay activity. *Padi* has been cultivated by Malays from very early times but Malaya has rarely been an exporter of rice, the cultivators growing only sufficient rice to meet their domestic needs. This state of affairs has resulted not because of a lack of markets or land, but rather the availability of more profitable pursuits such as the cultivation of rubber or, where available, the mining of tin. It was estimated in 1956 that an acre of land containing tin deposits produced a gross value of $69,700 per year compared with $1,000 for rubber, and only $340 for *padi*.[1] Thus it has not been surprising that in a number of places in Malaya rubber trees have grown knee-deep in water on land more suitable for *padi* cultivation!

The total number of full-time *padi* planters in Malaya in 1957 was 398,300 of whom 381,600 were Malays and only 508 were Indians.[2] Although the non-Malays have never been totally excluded from *padi* planting they began officially to be discouraged from about the end of the nineteenth century, principally for fear that their participation might deprive the Malays of what was subsequently termed 'the only forte in their existence as a race in Malaya'.[3] This state of affairs continued till the late 1930s, when the pro-Malay *padi* land policy was relaxed as part of the government's efforts to increase rice production.[4] However, this plan was not implemented till after the war and even then was limited in practice to the inclusion of small numbers of Chinese and Indian *padi* planters in government-sponsored schemes, principally in Perak and Selangor. This general discouragement of non-Malays from the *padi* lands, together with the greater attractiveness of other economic pursuits, like wage-earning and rubber cultivation, largely explains the small numbers of Indian *padi* planters.

Smallholding rubber cultivation has been essentially a Malay and Chinese undertaking. In 1952, for example, compared with the 46·8 and 41·7 per cent shares of the Malays and Chinese, respectively, Indians owned only 7·7 per cent of the approximately 1,624,000 acres under smallholding rubber then.[5] No comparable data are available for

---

[1] Federation of Malaya, 1958, p. 15.
[2] Fell, 1960, table 11; Chua 1964, table 84.
[3] *SSSF*, 1920, 2438/1920; *FMSRRCC 1930*, II, 48; *ST*, 6.8.1939; Tan, 1963, pp. 15–35.　　　　　　　　　　　　　　[4] *JSSF*, G.A. 350/1939; *ST*, 5.8.1939.
[5] Department of Statistics, 1953, tables 28, 45; *MSB*, Dec. 1966, p. 17; Jackson, 1964, pp. 249–52.

the 1960s, but it is reasonably safe to assume that the foregoing pattern of ethnic ownership in the smallholding rubber industry of the country has not undergone any major change up to today.

The actual number of Indian cultivators of rubber has been limited, because many of the Indian rubber smallholdings have been worked by Chinese family labour on a *bagi-dua* or share-basis. Indian owner-cultivators numbered less than 2,000 in 1957.[1]

Forestry

Forestry and fishing are the other main primary agricultural industries of Malaya, besides farming and the estate economy. The forest industry has supplied Malaya's domestic requirements and a small amount of timber for export. In spite of the very large forest area of Malaya only a very small part has been commercially exploited, mainly it appears because access and exploitation is difficult and the forests are dominated by no particular tree species so that the quality of timber is low.

The logging, milling and marketing operations of this industry have been predominantly in Chinese hands, while the majority of the forest rangers have been Malays: Indians have had little to do with forestry. In 1957, for example, Indians formed less than 1 per cent of the 19,244 persons in forestry occupations in Malaya.[2]

Fishing

The fishing industry of Malaya consists of freshwater and off-shore fishing. The latter, extending along most of Malaya's coastline, has been the more important, contributing substantially to food supply and employment. Almost all the fish caught have been locally consumed.

Indians played a prominent role in the fishing industry of Malaya in the nineteenth century. Besides featuring prominently as fishermen, in some places even to the extent of exercising a virtual monopoly of all fishing, Indians were also the main middlemen and financiers, particularly for the Malay fishermen. A government inquiry into the fishing industry in 1896 revealed that, quite apart from its direct participation, there was 'a very large' amount of Indian capital indirectly connected with the fishing industry. In Penang, for instance, the Indian middlemen appeared to be an indispensable link between the Malay fishermen and the consumer. The proceeds of the Malay fishing stakes in Penang were almost invariably distributed among Indian fish-kings who often made loans to Malay and other fishermen to enable them to construct and

---

[1] Fell, 1960, table 12; personal communication from the Superintendent of Census, Singapore.
[2] Fell, 1960, table 11; Chua, 1964, table 84.

maintain their stakes and other fishing equipment. They recouped themselves by buying the catch at favourable rates. Indians were also prominent as fish-retailers, especially in Penang, where they numbered between a quarter and a third fewer than the Chinese in 1896.[1]

In the ensuing years, however, they lost their commanding position as financiers and middlemen to the Chinese. Their role as retailers and fishermen also declined considerably. No evidence has come to light to explain this change in their fortunes, but stiffer and more effective Chinese competition and the growth of the rival attraction of plantation, particularly rubber, agriculture would in all probability have been contributory factors. Whatever the reasons, there were only about 450 Indians in a total of some 66,000 people, mainly Malays and Chinese, in the fishing industry in Malaya in 1957, compared with more than 1,500 in 1896.[2] By 1965 the number of Indians engaged in fishing activities had further slumped to less than 200 in a total of 71,971.[3] Moreover, nearly all these Indians were small-scale entrepreneurs, or employees of such, who used small boats and limited their activities to coastal fishing.

MINING AND QUARRYING

Production of tin has been Malaya's most important mining industry. The only other minerals worked on any substantial scale have been iron-ore, coal and, to a lesser extent, bauxite, gold, ilmenite, manganese and granite for building.

Tin was being exported from Malaya as early as the first millennium A.D. (Part 1). However, large-scale production did not begin till after the Industrial Revolution and the immigration of Chinese miners. In the ensuing years tin became second only to rubber in commercial and financial significance in the Malayan economy. In 1957, for example, the gross value of tin exported was 20 per cent of the total value of Malaya's exports ($4,171,000,000), while direct tax receipts from tin mining contributed nearly 10 per cent of the Federation's revenues. The value of other minerals exported was in all only about 12 per cent that of tin in 1957.[4]

The tin rush and the influx of Chinese immigrants in substantial numbers did not begin till the 1880s when the fabulously rich tin fields of the Kinta valley of Perak began to be mined (figs. 4, 38). Under the

[1] *PLCSS*, 1899, pp. C14–37.
[2] *PLCSS*, 1899, pp. C14–76; Fell, 1960, tables 11, 14; Chua, 1964, table 84.
[3] Ministry of Agriculture and Co-operatives, Malaysia, 1965, app. x; *SYB*, 1965, p. 125.
[4] International Bank of Reconstruction and Development, 1955, pp. 9–17 *et seq.*; *FMAR*, 1957, pp. 115–29, 230–8; *CSAR*, 1957, pp. 98–107.

diligent enterprise of the Chinese miners, tin production in Malaya rose from an estimated few hundred tons at the beginning of British rule to 26,000 tons in 1889 and 51,730 tons by 1904.[1] Until 1910 tin mining was principally undertaken by Chinese, who controlled more than three-quarters of the output. After this date, with the introduction of mechanized and highly capitalized mining, the Chinese 'monopoly' was gradually undermined, and by 1927 about 68 per cent of tin production was from European, chiefly British, owned mines. Following upon mechanization, the labour force in mining gradually decreased in numbers from a record of more than 200,000 in 1913 to some 34,000 in 1957 (table 18). Malaya's production, however, increased to over 80,000 tons in 1940. The post-war production has generally been in the region of 50,000 to 60,000 tons per annum, which has represented about a third of the world's known output.[2]

It is often stated that 'tin made the Federated Malay States'. In 1957 more than 90 per cent of Malaya's production of tin came from these states, principally Perak. Revenues from tin enabled expansion to be carried out in other industries, such as rubber, and tin attracted thousands of Chinese immigrants, who played an important role in the creation of modern Malaya. It also laid the foundations of the present road and railway network of the country, besides introducing an important new modern industry, tin smelting, in the 1880s.[3] A smelter was established at Singapore and another at Butterworth, Penang, in 1902, and these smelted all the tin produced in Malaya, and also a substantial portion of the tin ore from the rest of Southeast Asia. The tin-smelting industry employed more than 1,000 labourers in 1957, many of them Indians.

Besides being employed in smelting, Indians have been prominent in tin mining as *jagas* or watchmen; virtually every *jaga* on both Chinese and European mines has been a Sikh or some other North Indian. A number of Sikhs have also been employed as labourers as they have been considered particularly good for heavy work, such as carrying stones or *karang*. But the most numerous Indian mining labourers, certainly after the beginning of the present century, have not been Sikhs but mainly South Indians. On the whole, however, participation by Indians, of whatever origin, in tin mining has been very limited, the industry being almost completely controlled by European and Chinese capital and employing almost exclusively Chinese labour (table 18).[4]

---

[1] Mills, 1942, p. 179.
[2] International Bank of Reconstruction and Development, 1955, pp. 66–7; Fisher, 1964, p. 615; *FMAR*, 1957, p. 231.   [3] *MM*, 5.9.1935.
[4] Wong, 1965, pp. 17 ff.; *MCECLFMS*, pp. 15 *et seq.*; Puthucheary, pp. 81–95; Chou, 1966, pp. 164–8.

*Table 18: Racial composition of the labour force employed
in tin mining in Malaya, 1901–1957*

year	total labour force	percentage			
		Chinese	Indians	Malays	others
1901	158700	97·0	0·3	2·6	0·1
1913	200000	96·0	3·0	1·0	—
1914	171800	95·4	3·4	1·0	0·2
1936	80700	82·4	11·1	4·9	1·6
1957	34000	67·7	15·0	15·6	1·7

Source: Compiled from Wong, 1965, p. 219; *MCECLFMS*, p. 13; Department of
Labour and Industrial Relations, 1958, table 3; International Bank for Reconstruction and Development, 1955, pp. 66–7.

This dominance of the Chinese and the insignificance of Indians in
tin-mining operations arose largely because Indians were attracted to
Malaya chiefly by wages in the plantation economy or government
services, while the Chinese were the independent entrepreneurs of the
modern tin-mining industry. Later on, when Indians did venture into
this industry, the Chinese were already too well entrenched. In fact,
had it not been for the advent of European capital and modern
machinery, it is doubtful if the Indians would have been able to play
even their contemporary minor role.

Until 1900, with the exception of a few Sikhs, tin-mining operations
in Malaya were a Chinese monopoly, but Indians began to be employed
as engine drivers, firemen, greasers, winchmen and as labourers in the
actual work of mining, following the introduction of machinery at the
turn of the present century. The employment of non-Sikh Indian labour
in actual mining was the result of the introduction of winding gear and
tracks-on-rails in the mining operations, which considerably lessened the
drudgery of mining work. Until this time, only the hardy Chinese and
Sikhs could stand up to the lifting of *karang*. After the introduction of
this new machinery, many Europeans in fact preferred Indian, particularly Tamil, labourers because they carried their loads on their heads
and thus could transfer their loads direct to the waiting conveyance. In
contrast, the Chinese carried their loads on their shoulders and, when
loading, needed staging platforms, ladders and such like which had
continuously to be shifted owing to the temporary character of tin
mining. Furthermore, through the engagement of Indian labour, the
European miners found that not only were they cheaper and more
manageable, but they also enabled the Europeans to break the Chinese

monopoly of tin-mining labour, thereby bringing operating costs down. Thus expansion of European-controlled mining led to greater employment of Indians but, though their absolute numbers declined following increasing mechanization, the long-established Chinese never lost their position as the dominant tin-mining labour group of the country (table 18).

Other mining

As in the tin industry, Indians have played a minor role in other forms of mining, with the exception of coal and stone quarrying.

Malaya's coal production totalled 152,311 tons in 1957,[1] and Indians were then prominent in this industry, forming 53 per cent of the 800 labourers employed in the industry and also a substantial portion of the technical and administrative staff. But the demand for the poor-quality Malayan coal had been declining in the post-war years following the switch to oil by the Malayan railways, the chief users of local coal. The coal mines were finally closed in January 1960.[2]

Stone and earth quarrying operations have also been Indian-dominated in the government quarries since the days of the Indian convicts (Part 1). The private quarries, however, have largely been a monopoly of the Chinese.

MANUFACTURING

The development of manufacturing in Malaya in 1957 was fairly advanced by Asian standards, being exceeded only by Japan, India, Hong Kong and China. What was more significant was the fact that industrialization, especially during the post-war period, was steadily increasing. Thus, while less than 10 per cent of the gainfully occupied in Malaya in 1947 were in manufacturing,[3] the figure for 1957 was 13 per cent[4] and today would in all likelihood exceed 15 per cent of the gainfully employed population.

Malayan manufacturing has included substantial engineering and boat-building works, but the typical industrial enterprises of the country have been the small-scale secondary manufacturing activities such as the processing of rubber, tin and foodstuffs; the manufacture of food preparations, drinks and tobacco; and the production of a variety of miscellaneous consumer goods such as rubber goods, clothing, furniture and jewellery.[5]

[1] *FMAR*, 1957, p. 233.
[2] Department of Labour and Industrial Relations, 1958, table 3; *FMOYB*, 1961, p. 268.
[3] del Tufo, 1949, table 88, p. 102.
[4] Fell, 1960, table 11; Chua 1964, table 84.
[5] Department of Statistics, 1961, pp. 1 ff.

Manufacturing, like tin mining, has been predominantly an activity of the Chinese who formed more than 67 per cent of the 312,000 persons engaged in industrial pursuits in 1957. Indians formed less than 15 per cent of the total numbers then engaged. In the ensuing years the Chinese appear to have further consolidated their position, largely it seems at the expense of the Indians, and, by 1965, they formed an estimated 70 per cent of those engaged in manufacturing (table 15).

For the most part Indian industrial workers have been small-scale independent entrepreneurs. Metal work, dress-making and tailoring, food processing and cigar-rolling have been some of their more conspicuous occupations. For example, in 1957, nearly 45 per cent of the Indians in manufacturing were engaged in tailoring and dress-making and metal work of one sort or another.[1]

[1] Fell, 1960, table 11; Chua, 1964, table 84.

11

COMMUNICATIONS AND COMMERCE

Much of the present-day excellent transport and communications system of Malaya is less than seventy years old. At the time of the British intervention in the Malay States there were no railways or roads there. The principal means of inland communication were rivers, and movement between the different states was possible only with great difficulty along rivers or footpaths through forests. One of the first duties of the British administration was to connect these states with the ports. At first short roads and railway lines were made to a convenient place on the coast where small steamers, like those of an inter-Straits Settlements steamship concern, founded by a group of Malacca Chinese in the 1860s, and its successor, the Straits Settlements Steamship Company, a joint European–Straits Chinese venture inaugurated in 1890,[1] could collect tin and other produce and land supplies. Few short railways had been built by the time the Federated Malay States were created in 1896. Under the unifying policy of the Federated Malay States, these different railways were placed under a single management—The Federated Malay States (subsequently, Malayan) Railways Department—and the task of linking them into a single system that would eventually include the rest of the country began immediately. Before World War I railways had penetrated all the west coast states, and the tin-mining regions and rubber areas were directly connected with the ports of Singapore and Penang. This happened just at the time when the cultivation of rubber was spreading rapidly and helped to bring about the prosperity of the western coast states during the first two decades of the present century.

The east coast states had to wait till 1931 before being linked with the rest of the country and Thailand, and even then Trengganu was left out of the rail system. This later and incomplete development of rail transport in eastern Malaya doubtless contributed to its comparatively slow and late development (figs. 38, 39, 42).

The first important roads in the country were also constructed in the same more developed western coastal region. By 1890 there were skeletal road networks in each unit of the Straits Settlements and some of the

---

[1] Oversea-Chinese Association, India, 1944, p. 8; Tregonning, 1965*b*, pp. 280–9.

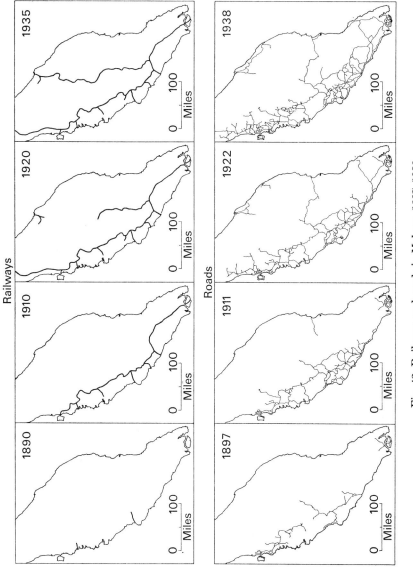

Fig. 42. Railways and roads in Malaya, 1887–1938.

284

Malay states. In the latter roads were chiefly feeders to the railway lines. From about the second decade of this century, however, motor-cars, buses and trucks began to play an ever-increasing part in Malaya's transport system. Among other requirements this led to a great programme of road construction. The older bridle paths and several discrete networks of roads and feeder tracks of the west coast were linked and developed into a north–south trunk road, following closely the railway line. Concurrently, a system of secondary macadamized roads was also developed in the western zone and linked with the laterite roads constructed and maintained by estates (fig. 42). By 1957 the east coast states had also been provided with a road network, though roads in this region were still few compared with western Malaya. However, Malaya's system of some 6,000 miles of metalled main roads and several hundred miles of tertiary roads, at the time of *Merdeka*, made it easily the best equipped country in Southeast Asia in terms of road transport.

In addition to the roads and 1,000 miles of rail-lines, Malaya had an excellent internal and external system of shipping, telecommunications, postal services, air services and wireless communications (fig. 43).

Indians played a prominent, often dominant, role in almost every phase of development of the modern transport and communication system, particularly the rail, road and telecommunication networks. In these, not only were they the principal labourers but also, together with the Ceylon Tamils, formed the bulk of the clerical, administrative and technical staff.[1]

The affiliation of organized Indian labour to Malayan railways goes back to the early 1880s. Construction, which began in 1882, on the Taiping–Port Weld line of Perak was soon halted for want of labour.[2] The project was saved from abandonment only by the timely aid of the government of Ceylon, which lent two divisions of South-Indian composed Ceylon Pioneer Corps. In the meantime, however, the government had adopted and begun to implement plans to import Indian labourers on a substantial scale to prevent any similar mishap. By 1900 almost all railway work was done by Tamil labour.[3]

The subordinate technical, administrative and clerical spheres of the railway system were also staffed predominantly by Tamils, but this time mainly by those from Ceylon. The railway police, on the other hand, were Indians—almost totally Sikhs and Muslims and Hindus from the Punjab.

The roads of Malaya had a similar history for, from as early as the convict days (Part 1), almost the whole of public-works staff was made up of Indians.

[1] Coomaraswamy, 1946, pp. 3 ff.   [2] *CPMS*, 1882, serial no. 1, p. 1.
[3] *MM*, 2.7.1901; *RIIFMS*, pp. 1–54.

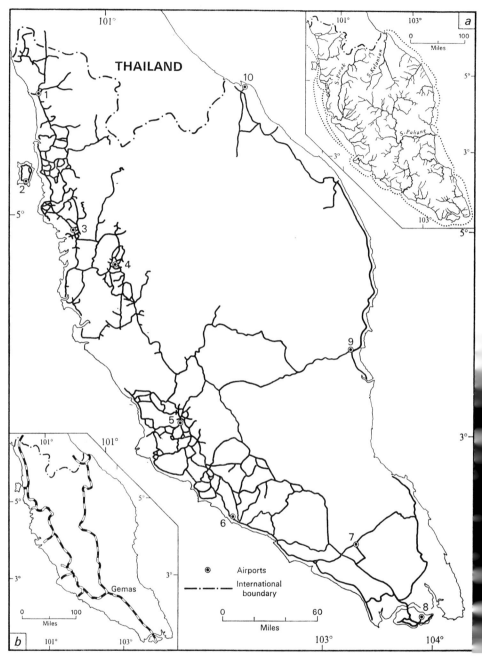

Fig. 43. Communications in Malaya, 1957. 1, Alor Star. 2, Penang. 3, Taiping. 4, Ipoh. 5, Kuala Lumpur. 6, Malacca. 7, Kluang. 8, Singapore. 9, Kuantan. 10, Kota Bharu. *Insert a:* Rivers and coastal shipping. *Insert b:* Railways.

286

Communications and commerce

Telecommunications were also dominated by Indians, both as labourers and administrators, while they also figured substantially in the harbour installations, coastal shipping and road transport, both as owners and workers. For example, in 1957, more than a quarter of the 2,500 *tongkang* or lighter workers at the harbour of Singapore were South Indians, predominantly Malabar and Madras Muslims. A century earlier South Indians had a virtual monopoly of this *tongkang* traffic and it was not until 1867 that they began to be replaced by others, predominantly Chinese, who subsequently became the dominant element amongst the lighter workers of Singapore.[1]

Beginning in the 1930s, but particularly during the post-war years, the prominent position of the Indians in the other transport and communication systems of Malaya also underwent a relative decline, following the stoppage of labour emigration by the Indian government, the large number of deaths amongst the Indian labourers in Malaya during the Japanese occupation (Part 2) and, more important, the Malayan government's policy of encouraging more Malays to enter the services. In 1957, for example, the proportion of Indian labourers in railways was some 56 per cent of the total while eight years later it was less than 50 per cent compared with their virtual monopoly in the early 1900s.[2] But as this and other figures indicate, Indians are still the largest single group among the workers in the government and quasi-government transport and communication activities.

Private transport and communications have been largely dominated by the Chinese, although the Indians, in addition to even controlling certain such services as the *tongkang* traffic of nineteenth-century Singapore, have continued to take a steady 10–15 per cent share of the total business, especially as owners and drivers of trucks, buses and taxis. In such cases the Indians have even improved their position in some parts of the country. In Negri Sembilan, for instance, almost the entire bus services of the State at present are either directly or indirectly owned or operated by a few Sikh families and their employees.

PUBLIC AND PERSONAL SERVICES

The professional, executive, public, clerical and personal services, though largely Chinese-dominated in the private sector and, since the 1930s, Malay in the government sector, have also included substantial numbers of Indians. However, Indian participation in these positions has been

[1] Ministry of Culture, Singapore, 1966, p. 203.
[2] Department of Labour and Industrial Relations, 1958, tables 1–3; 1966, apps. 12–13; personal communication from the Malayan Railways Office, Kuala Lumpur.

decreasing over the last few decades; for example, Indians formed more than 23 per cent of the 341,000 persons engaged in services in Malaya in 1947, but by 1957 this proportion had decreased to less than 16 per cent of the total of 481,000. Expressed in another form, services accounted for less than 20 per cent of the total gainfully occupied Indian population of 370,000 in 1957, compared with more than 23 per cent of 344,000 persons in 1947, a decrease of more than 13 per cent (tables 14, 15). These decreases reflect the implementation of selective emigration and immigration policies by India and Malaya respectively (Part 1); also the Malayan government's policy of encouraging more Malays to enter the services; and, finally, the continual spread of education, particularly in the 1940s and 1950s, and the increasing sophistication, desire and effort among the Indians to better themselves by getting away from lowly-paid wage-earning occupations into more profitable enterprises such as business and trade.

The largest number of Indians in these services has been in government and quasi-government, domestic, catering and clerical activities. For instance, Indians have figured prominently as clerks, administrators and technicians in the government public utilities, and more than a quarter of the approximately 200,000 labourers in government and quasi-government employment were Indians in 1957. In certain sectors, such as the municipal services, Indians have formed the single most important community. For example, 53 and 50 per cent of the municipal labour force of the country in 1957 and 1965, respectively, were Indians.[1]

There have also been a number of Indian engineers, lawyers, doctors, managers, teachers, trade unionists and members of the uniformed services. For instance, in the largely Malay-dominated police force of the country, nearly 15 per cent of the 2,629 officers in 1957 were Indians.[2]

At one stage in the early years of British rule in the Malay States, Indians, principally Sikhs, formed most of the rank and file of the force (Part 1), while even before World War II Sikh policemen were numerically second only to the Malays. But most of them left the force during and after the Japanese occupation to strike out on their own in other undertakings. In 1957 there were only 1,107 Indian policemen in the whole of Malaya, out of a total of 23,220 men, 19,362 of whom were Malays.[3] In the field of trade unions, on the other hand, Indians have continued to play a prominent role, especially as office bearers and

---

[1] Department of Labour and Industrial Relations, 1958, tables 1–3; 1966, apps. 12–13; *ARLDCS*, 1957–8, tables II–IV; *ARLDS*, table II.
FMAR, 1957, p. 316; *CSAR*, 1957, p. 197.   [3] *Ibid.*

leaders. In 1960–1, for example, while some 55–60 per cent of the membership of the employees' unions affiliated to the Malayan Trades Union Congress were Indians, almost 80 per cent of the Executive Committee of the Malayan Trades Union Congress were Indian.[1]

COMMERCE AND FINANCE

The commercial and financial sector of the Malayan economy, though largely dominated by European and Chinese capital, has also contained a substantial Indian element which has been slowly but certainly growing in stature. In 1957 Indians formed nearly 16 per cent of the 317,000 persons in commercial and financial occupations in the country compared with less than 12 per cent of the total 212,000 so engaged in 1931 (table 15). This growing role of the Indians is reflected in the increasing number of Indians switching occupations and entering the business life of the country. In 1931 only 5·6 per cent of all the gainfully occupied Indians in Malaya were listed in commercial pursuits. The percentage rose to 10·1 by 1947 and 13·4 by 1957, while at present it is probably well above 17 (table 14).

Like the Chinese and Malays, considerable numbers of the Indian business firms have been self-owned and operated. In 1957, nearly 48 per cent of all the Indians in commercial pursuits in the Federation were self-employed.[2] Comparable information is unavailable for Singapore but, if it were available, the percentage of the self-employed Indians in business in Malaya would almost certainly be much higher, as Singapore was, and still is, the headquarters of many Indian as well as other Malayan businesses. Here, as in Kuala Lumpur and Penang, the two other major centres of Indian commercial enterprise, the Indian business-men have had their own chambers of commerce and trade guilds.

The exact amount of Indian investment in Malaya up to 1957 or today is unknown, although it has certainly been of considerable magnitude. In 1951, S. O. K. Ubaidulla,[3] then President of the Associated Indian Chamber of Commerce in Malaya, estimated it to be about $666,000,000 of which 75 per cent was owned by Chettiars.[4] This invest-ment is estimated to have amounted to more than 9 per cent of the country's total gross national income of $7,145,000,000 in 1951. In

---

[1] The Malayan Trades Union Congress, 1961, p. vi.   [2] Fell, 1960, table 12.
[3] *ST*, 19.6.1951.
[4] The *Hindu*, a Madras daily (7.4.1946), Nanjudan (1950, p. 36) and Kondapi (1951, p. 301) quote figures ranging from 170,000,000 to 300,000,000 rupees, or between $110,000,000 and $192,000,000, for the Chettiar investment in Malaya. These, however, are estimates based on figures supplied by Chettiars themselves who would almost certainly have grossly understated their wealth.

addition, Indian capital in Malaya, bearing in mind their traditional affinity for gold and liquid assets, in the form of bank deposits, jewellery and cash, must have been very large despite a constant flow of cash remittances to India. During the years 1935–40 and 1946–7 alone, the total remittance to India by the Indians in Malaya amounted to 140,000,000 rupees or some $91,000,000 at an average of more than $11,000,000 a year.[1] When conditions were unsettled in Malaya in the 1950s, because of the Emergency and the agitation for *Merdeka*, the flow of remittances to India was even higher. In 1951, for instance, a figure of $29,000,000 a year was quoted by S. O. K. Ubaidulla.[2] Reliable or complete data for the subsequent period are lacking but knowledgeable people feel that the flow of money to India has been steadily decreasing in recent years, following Independence, the easing and finally the end of the Emergency, and the increasing tendency among Indians in Malaya to settle permanently in the country.[3]

Lately some Indians have been working their way into the complex network of directorships, holding companies and inter-company investments of the European agency houses (Part 1), which between them have controlled a lion's share of the Malayan economy for the past several decades.[4] But on the whole direct participation of Indians or Indian capital in this large-scale agency-house business is still insignificant, partly because opportunities for Asian penetration are limited, and partly because there is intensely keen competition from the generally richer, more enterprising and commercially better placed Chinese, and, since *Merdeka*, from the politically well-connected Malays, for such openings as are available.

A large proportion of the Indian investment in Malaya has been in land but substantial amounts have also been found in wholesale, retail and other small-scale enterprises. In 1957, for example, there were 4,817 Indians in the total of 39,032 wholesalers in Malaya.[5] The majority of these Indians and the main retailers were in the textile, piece-goods, grain, spice, copra and jute import-export and retail trades. In Singapore, out of the 300 Indian firms listed as members of the Singapore Indian Chamber of Commerce on 1.1.1954, there were 155 retailing piece-goods and 78 in the import-export business.[6] The wholesale Asian textile trade of post-war Malaya appears to have been largely controlled by the

---

[1] *MYB*, 1936, p. 154; *MYB*, 1939, p. 162; *ARPSDM*, 1947, p. 9; Nanjudan, 1950, p. 38.
[2] *ST*, 19.6.1951.
[3] See, for example, *SM*, 8.10.1961; *MM*, 27.2.1963.
[4] Bauer, 1948, pp. 8–12 *et seq.*; Puthucheary, 1960, pp. 23–95; Chou, 1966, pp. 82–3, 145–72.
[5] Fell, 1960, table 11; Chua, 1964, table 84.   [6] *ARICCS*, 1953, pp. 1–8.

Singapore Indian textile merchants, particularly by the Sindhis and Sikhs.

However, the largest numbers of Indians involved in commercial enterprises have been mostly salesmen, hawkers and street vendors. These three categories accounted for 29,000 or more than 58 per cent of the total 49,600 Indians engaged in commercial and financial occupations in Malaya in 1957.[1]

Insurance, banking and moneylending, particularly the last, have been the important financial occupations of the Indians. For example, Indians formed almost 62 per cent of the 974 registered moneylenders and pawnbrokers of Malaya in 1947.[2] No comparable data are available for the later period but it is unlikely that the prominence of the Indians in the registered moneylending business has been any less than that in 1947. For instance, in 1963, out of the 104 registered moneylenders in Singapore some 80 per cent were Indians.[3] Comparable information on the number of unregistered Indian moneylenders, principally small-scale operators such as *kanganis, jagas* and shopkeepers, in Singapore and the rest of the country then or in 1947 is unavailable but it is estimated that they were at least two or three times as numerous as their legally registered countrymen.

The most important moneylenders among the Indians have been the Chettiars, though the Sikhs have also carried on a substantial moneylending business. The Naattukkoottai Chettiars or Nakarattaars, more popularly known simply as Chettiars or Chetties, are one of the principal banking, moneylending and trading communities of India. They are particularly prominent in South India, their homeland, and Southeast Asia with which they have had commercial contacts from very early times (Part 1). In the first instance most of the Chettiars in Malaya appear to have been merely agents for principals (also Chettiars), for as a rule Chettiars only do business with Chettiar capital, based in the homeland. They were provided with a certain amount of capital to start a business in Malaya and were paid a salary, and also given a bonus or a share in the profits. An account was maintained between the agent in Malaya and the head of the firm in India and if need arose for more capital the agent was allowed to draw upon this account. The usual tenure of an agency was about three years. A few months before an agent's term expired his successor was sent to take charge of his (the outgoing agent's) outstanding business at a mutually agreed valuation. On relief the agent returned to the *Ceṭṭinaaṭu*, the Chettiar homeland in Madras State, settled accounts and after such rest as he thought proper

---

[1] Fell, 1960, table 11; Chua, 1964, table 84. [2] del Tufo, 1949, table 88.
[3] *MM*, 27.2.1963.

usually sought re-employment. In the course of time some of these agents appear to have put together sufficient wealth to start in business on their own.[1]

Information on this point is far from complete, but the oral testimony of a number of Chettiars interviewed by the writer in 1960 and 1966 seems to leave little doubt that much of the present-day Chettiar capital in Malaya is owned and managed by locally-domiciled members of the community. They and their ancestors, in addition to being the principal Indian landowners of the country, were the main source of medium and long term credit in Malaya until the advent of the modern banks and the growth of the cooperative movement, the latter only from the 1930s.[2] They have had numerous firms in Malaya and their clientele has included European proprietary planters, Chinese miners and businessmen, Malay royalty and peasants, and Indian traders and contractors. A survey by the writer of fifteen Chettiar firms, chosen for convenience, in Singapore and Segamat (Johore) in 1960, revealed that a number of local Chinese businessmen were owing money to these Chettiar firms. This was not totally surprising as it is well-known in Malaya that many a successful Chinese *towkay* began his climb on a loan from a Chettiar.

The credit requirements of the estate labourers have usually been met by the *kanganis*, *keranis* and Chinese pawnbrokers while in the urban centres it has been the North Indian watchman-cum-money-lender, generally a Sikh, who has provided the necessary loans to labourers, clerks and small shopkeepers, usually at usurious, though not unrealistic (given the social context), interest rates.

To summarize, it can be said that the conclusion of British rule in Malaya found the Indians in almost every walk of Malayan economic life, their economic hierarchy ranging from cabinet ministers and wealthy financiers to countryside bread-sellers and toddy-tappers. However, the majority of them were still labourers, principally in plantation agriculture that formed the main economic enterprise of the country. But subsequent to the stoppage of labour immigration just before the Japanese occupation, and the spread of education, particularly in the post-war period, the proportion of labourers in the Indian population of Malaya steadily declined and it is estimated that at present less than three-fifths of the gainfully occupied Indians are labourers. Indian female participation in the work force of the country has also been declining, primarily, it appears, on account of the decreasing

[1] Madras, 1930, I, 29–30; III, 1101–92; V. Krishnan, *Indigenous banking in South India* (Bombay, 1959), pp. 29–35.

[2] T. B. Lim, *The co-operative movement in Malaya* (Cambridge, 1950), pp. 13 *et seq.*; *SJ*, IV (1896), 101; Ooi, 1959, pp. 176–82; *FMSRRCC 1930*, I, 40.

proportion of Indians living on plantations and increasing urbanization. However, although it has yet to be seen, there is a distinct possibility that, with increasing and better education and a growing freedom from social restrictions associated with their place in the family and society, there will be a significant increase in work-participation amongst the urban Indian females in the foreseeable future.

EPILOGUE

APPENDICES

BIBLIOGRAPHY

INDEX

EPILOGUE

It will be remembered that the aim of this work is to make a study of some aspects of Indian overseas migration to, and settlement in, Malaya with special reference to the period of British rule. The size of the Indian population in Malaya, the wide historical and spatial scope of the subject, coupled with the limitations of data and the availability of time and space, dictated concentration on the barest essentials of the topic. The purpose of this concluding chapter is to review the general characteristics of the Indians in Malaya and to summarize some of the more salient tendencies apparent within the community.

The situation of Malaya, astride Asian lines of commerce and communication, makes it the focal point of Southeast Asia. Thus control of Malaya was essential to any power aspiring to dominance in Southeast Asia. This fact was recognized not only by the early Indianized and Malay empires but also by the Portuguese, Dutch, English and Japanese who followed them. Consequently external influences, particularly Indian, British and Chinese, have figured prominently in the political and economic evolution of the country, giving it a civilization and an economy that is essentially foreign.

Malaya's contacts with India go back to the pre-Christian era, when commercial motives, it appears, first brought Indian traders to its shores. These occasional trading voyages soon became firm commercial and social ties and, through intermarriage and cultural assimilation, gave rise to a number of city-states and an indigenous civilization which bears the stamp of Indian influence in almost every aspect. These were the halcyon days of Indian influence in Malaya, for with the rise of the Malacca Sultanate and the arrival of European powers, particularly the British, the whole position was altered. In contrast to their earlier countrymen who represented a powerful and respected commercial, economic and political force, the Indians who now flocked into Malaya were chiefly illiterate labourers.

This transformation took place as British power was established in both India and Malaya and the economies of the two countries subordinated to imperial needs, which in practice entailed, *inter alia*, the curbing of large-scale Indian enterprise in India on the one hand and the encouragement of large numbers of cheap, docile Indian labour to work the Malayan plantations and government projects on the other.

Epilogue

This labour movement was perhaps unique, in that it incorporated adaptations of both the indentured system of Indian labour recruitment prevalent in the Caribbean, Fiji, Mauritius and southern Africa, and the basic ingredients of the *kangani, maistry* and garden *sirdar* system of labour recruitment of Ceylon, Burma and Assam respectively. In addition it included such other methods of formal and informal recruitment as assisted voluntary and free immigrants and a variation of the Chinese credit-ticket system of immigration.

With the possible exception of events in Burma and southeast Africa, the non-labour movement of Indians into Malaya was the largest single exodus out of India. These immigrants came as shopkeepers, tradesmen, clerks, professional élites and potential policemen or militiamen. They sought to cater for the special needs of their countrymen or hoped to find opportunities in the expanding economy of the country. This latter movement continued long after labour immigration was stopped by the Indian government just before World War II, but in a gradually decreasing volume following immigration restrictions imposed by the Malayan government in the post-war period. It was this section of the Indian immigrants which appears to have first sunk its roots in Malaya, thus beginning the stabilization of the local Indian population. In contrast, until only recently the vast majority of labourers formed a transitory floating population which has been coming and going since the beginnings of modern Indian migration, the volume of the movement depending principally on the economic conditions in Malaya.

The Indian population increased steadily, through immigration, until the 1930s and later through natural increase, following the improvement in the sex-ratio and the general stabilization of the community. Most of the Indians in Malaya are now locally born and are multiplying at a fast rate. If the present trend continues their numbers are expected to pass the 2,000,000 mark by 1987.

With stabilization, changes have also taken place in their occupational structure, urban–rural ratios and settlement patterns. Following the Indian government's ban on unskilled labour emigration and the spread of education in Malaya, the proportion of labourers in the Indian population has been steadily declining. For example, it is estimated that less than 60 per cent of the economically active Indians were labourers at the beginning of 1967, compared with more than 80 per cent in the 1920s. This trend will probably continue as the majority of the younger-generation Indians appear to prefer clerical, technical, commercial and professional occupations.

Until 1947 little more than a third of the Indians were urban dwellers, but by 1957 more than 47 per cent were living in urban centres of 1,000 or more persons. Today, the proportion of such urban dwellers in the total Indian population is estimated to be well above 50 per cent. If this rapid rate of urbanization is maintained, and there is no reason to believe that it will not be, Indians might well rival the Chinese as the community with the highest ratio of urban dwellers.

The social and cultural status of the Indians has undergone a marked change, particularly in the post-war years. Improved labour legislation has provided better housing and other social facilities for the labourers while the generally increasing prosperity of the community as a whole, and the decision of many members of the community to make Malaya their home, has made more money available for better schools, clubs, *āśramas*, temples and other public buildings. The settlements, too, have changed, not so much in basic pattern but in *degree* of nucleation. The already high degree of concentration of pre-war days was accentuated by the regroupment and relocation programmes of the Emergency in post-war Malaya. Although the Emergency has officially ended this pattern is not likely to change because the existing New Villages and larger regroupment units already form the nuclei of future urban centres.

The role and character of Indian participation in the political life of Malaya has also undergone some remarkable changes. Indians have for quite some time taken a part in local politics out of all proportion to their numbers. This has been particularly so since World War II. Prior to this they had little political interest in Malaya, their activities being largely oriented towards their mother country, with which they retained strong economic, political and sentimental links. Consequently most of their political organizations were just pale reflections of the Indian National Congress. This India-orientation of the Indians in Malaya was strengthened by periodic visits of Indian leaders such as Pandit Nehru, Rabindranath Tagore and Srinivasa Sastri. It was finally brought into the open with the establishment of an Indian National Army (I.N.A.)[1] in Malaya, following the defeat of the British by the Japanese in the Malayan campaign.

Between 1942 and 1945 thousands of Indians volunteered to join the Indian National Army, under the command of Subhas Chandra Bose

[1] Only a brief account is possible here of the Indian National Army and its allied organizations that sprang up in Malaya and the rest of Southeast Asia during the Japanese occupation. What follows is based largely on Desai (1946), Singh (1946), Khan (1946), J. S. Jessey ('The Indian Army of Independence, 1942–1945', B.A. Honours Academic Exercise, History Department, University of Malaya, Singapore, 1958), Office of Strategic Services (*R. & A. No. 1595: Indian minorities in Southeast Asia: The background of the Indian Independence Movement outside India*, mimeo., Washington, D.C., 1944), Toye (1959) and Mahajani (1960), who between them give a fairly detailed account of the subject.

for the purpose of fighting for the independence of India. In addition, Indian Independence League organizations were established in all leading centres in Southeast Asia to recruit men, collect funds, and generally coordinate the independence movement.

Men and money poured into the independence movement on an unprecedented scale from all over Southeast Asia, particularly from Malaya, the headquarters of the movement. Although it is true that some of the volunteers joined the independence movement for safety, better rations or for want of something better to do, the majority appear to have been genuinely inspired and patriotic. They regarded themselves as the vanguard of the liberation movement and Subhas Chandra Bose as the veritable Messiah come to lead them, with Japanese help, to the completion of the Indian struggle for freedom from Britain.

Many regiments of the Indian National Army fought bravely and with distinction on the Burma Front while the Tricolour was formally hoisted on Indian soil, at Madawk, in eastern Chittagong, in May 1944. These successes, however, were short-lived. The whole independence movement collapsed following the surrenders of the Indian National Army and the Japanese and the death of Subhas Chandra Bose in 1945. Shortlived though the Indian independence movement was in Malaya and the rest of Southeast Asia, its repercussions were nevertheless far-reaching in both India and Malaya.

In India members of the Indian National Army were acclaimed as national heroes. The Indian National Army became the rallying point of the Indian people and the Congress and helped to precipitate the final surrender of British power in India on 15 August 1947.

In Malaya, the independence movement, particularly as manifested in the Indian National Army and its achievements, fired the imagination of Indians and wrought a tremendous psychological revolution in their minds. Down to the humblest labourer they felt confident of themselves and proud of being Indians.

However, over the last two decades the position of Indians in Malaya has undergone a number of fundamental changes. In the first place, it will be recalled, there has been a stabilization of the Indian population, more than two-thirds of which is at present estimated to be Malayan-born. Secondly, though many Indians still retain their emotional ties with India, actual contact with the country has been diminishing. This has been illustrated by the decreasing frequency of visits of 'Malayan' Indians to India, a tendency accentuated by the disruption of shipping during the war and the large increase in the deck-passage fare (more than double) between Malaya and India since the Japanese occupation. Thirdly, many Indians in Malaya, following the independence of India, were hoping to acquire dual Indian and Malayan citizenship so as to enjoy the benefits of both. This idea was condemned not only by Pandit Nehru but also by the Indian government, which made it quite clear that all Indians outside India must decide either to remain Indian citizens or become citizens of the country where they lived, preferably the latter, and that no dual citizenship would be allowed. Faced with the alternative of remaining aliens in an independent Malaya, most of the Indians have decided to become Malayan citizens, an opportunity opened to them following the liberalization of the country's citizenship laws in 1952 and 1957 which allowed non-Malays to become citizens of Malaya provided they fulfilled certain requirements. As Malayan citizens, they now occupy a position that seems to be increasing in importance in the political life of the country.

The Indians form an important minority in a plural society pre-dominantly Malay and Chinese. The political role of the Indians appears to be assuming increased importance, as they are wooed both by the Chinese and Malay leaders in their bid for political power. The 4,480,000 Malays are citizens of the country by law. Only about three-quarters of the 4,520,000 Chinese are estimated to be citizens at present. The position of the more than 1,000,000 Indians in this respect is virtually the same as that of the Chinese in that about three-quarters of their number are Malayan citizens today. The Indians, however, are increasing at a faster rate than the Chinese, thereby increasing their relative voting strength and future representation in the government.

The distribution pattern of the Indian population and its economic concentration in plantation agriculture, Malaya's chief industry, also have important political implications. The large Indian concentrations on estates, lying as they often do between the major rural and urban concentrations of Malay and Chinese populations respectively, may have the power to act either as unifying or separating agents or to remain neutral. In the economic sphere, through their strong position on estates as administrators and labourers, now organized into powerful trade unions, they have the means to make or mar the country's economy through its major primary product and chief item of export.

Since 1946, the Indians have had their own communal political party, the Malayan Indian Congress (M.I.C.). In conjunction with the United Malays' National Organisation (U.M.N.O.) and the Malayan Chinese Association (M.C.A.) it forms the Alliance Party, which not only successfully led the Independence movement in the Federation (States) of Malaya but also is the present (1967) governing party of that country. In addition, Indians provide the top echelons, and the bulk too, of the trade-union leadership of Malaya while they are also members of the important non-communal, multi-racial political parties of the country; for example, the Labour Party on the mainland, and the Peoples Action Party and the Barisan Sosialis in Singapore. It appears that, in contrast to their earlier role as birds of passage in temporary exile from their village hearth, the Indians are becoming increasingly Malayanized, and it seems likely that as they tend to identify their interests with the future of the country they will assume an even greater role in its politico-economic development.

It remains now to summarize briefly the manifold ways in which the Indians, directly or indirectly, have influenced the adaptation and moulding of the overall Malayan environment.

The fact that Malay culture bears the indelible imprint of the Hindu and Buddhist era of the first millennium A.D. has been sufficiently stressed and need not be repeated here except to state that it was during this period that there evolved the *nāgara*, the city-state focused on a new feature of the Malayan landscape, the town, from which subsequently were to develop the territorial states and thalassocracies whose conflicting interests comprise the main theme of pre-European Southeast Asian history. Under the Indianizing influences, local society and landscape underwent a remarkable change, succinctly summarized by Paul Wheatley as

...the change from tribal chief to god-king, from gerontocracy to sultanism, from consensus to hereditary charismatic authority inherent in manifest divinity, from *pawang* to 'brāhmaṇ', from head-hunter to *kṣatriya*, from primitive tribesman to peasant, from kampong to *nāgara*, from spirit house to temple, from reciprocity to redistribution, in short from culture to civilization ...[1]

There is little direct evidence in the present-day Malayan landscape of the Hindu and Buddhist era of its history. However, the indirect evidence as manifest in the Malay cultural landscape and way of life is abundantly clear.

The passing of the Hindu–Buddhist millennium and the emergence of a new force, Islam, stimulated further changes in the landscape. The new faith proved a powerful factor in the moulding of the cultural landscape. To every *kampong* and town it gave a mosque or *surau* and the *sekolah ugama*, and into nearly every Malay holding it introduced a potential for subdivision and fragmentation, only checked by legislation in some states in the present century.

With the advent of the British, the role of the Indians as catalysts took on a new direction and emphasis. A new genre of Indian immigrant —Ramasamy, the labourer, Tulsi Ram, the convict, Bhai Singh, the

---

[1] Wheatley, 1964*a*, pp. 42–3.

Epilogue

policeman, Maniam the technical assistant and Pillai the clerk—arrived in the country. Quite apart from seeing such uniquely Indian features as the much decorated Hindu temple, 'banana-leaf' vegetarian eating shops and *āśramas* firmly established in the Malayan landscape, they witnessed the passing of huge tracts of jungle and swamp and the emergence in their place of the softer, more regular lines of plantations; footpaths and aerial ropeways give way to bridges, railways and macadamized highways; *atap* and *kajang kampongs* and rumbustious and rowdy mining shanties give way to orderly and thriving towns and metropoles. In short, they saw the transformation of a swamp-infested, hostile, jungle sparsely populated by Malays, into a highly developed agricultural landscape of interlocking cash and subsistence economies with immigrant and indigenous peoples all linked together and served by a network of communications together with marketing and distributing points. Such transformation is almost without parallel. Nearly all this change took place in the course of less than a hundred years and much of it through manual labour. Virtually nowhere else in tropical pioneering has such a feat been accomplished through such methods and on such a scale and in so short a time.

In this metamorphosis the Indians played an important role. They were the principal labourers and security guards and, together with the Tamils from Ceylon, the main administrative and technical assistants. At the same time Indian financiers and entrepreneurs, quite apart from their own direct contributions, were the saviours and grub-stakers of many a latter-day Chinese millionaire, successful British planter and Malay aristocrat. Perhaps the most eloquent memorial to the pioneering efforts of the Indian, Chinese and other immigrants in Malaya is the country's present position as one of the best developed and richest independent nations of Asia.

APPENDICES

Appendix 1: Indian labour immigration into Malaya, 1844–1941

year	assisted	non-assisted	TOTAL
1844	1 800	N	1 800
1845	1 800	N	1 800
1846	1 800	N	1 800
1847	1 800	N	1 800
1848	1 800	N	1 800
1849	1 800	N	1 800
1850	1 800	N	1 800
1851	2 000	N	2 000
1852	2 000	N	2 000
1853	2 000	N	2 000
1854	2 000	N	2 000
1855	2 500	N	2 500
1856	2 500	N	2 500
1857	2 500	N	2 500
1858	2 500	N	2 500
1859	3 800	N	3 800
1860	4 000	N	4 000
1861	4 000	N	4 000
1862	4 000	N	4 000
1863	4 000	N	4 000
1864	4 000	N	4 000
1865	6 000	N	6 000
1866	6 617	N	6 617
1867	5 294	1 000	6 294
1868	5 849	1 000	6 849
1869	8 013	1 000	9 013
1870	4 000	1 000	5 000
1871	4 000	1 000	5 000
1872	5 000	1 000	6 000
1873	4 500	1 000	5 500
1874	4 500	1 000	5 500
1875	4 700	1 000	5 700
1876	4 700	1 000	5 700
1877	4 700	1 000	5 700
1878	4 675	1 000	5 675
1879	4 353	500	4 853
1880	4 691	200	4 891
1881	3 679	2 000	5 679
1882	4 252	3 800	8 052
1883	4 250	4 500	8 750
1884	5 039	8 800	13 839
1885	5 442	12 000	17 442
1886	6 548	10 000	16 548
1887	8 536	6 600	15 136
1888	8 484	9 000	17 484
1889	6 547	8 700	15 247
1890	6 760	8 700	15 460
1891	5 443	16 000	21 443

year	assisted	non-assisted	TOTAL
1892	3628	10000	13628
1893	4106	10000	14106
1894	3688	8000	11688
1895	3549	8800	12349
1896	4652	11000	15652
1897	4405	12000	16405
1898	4424	10000	14424
1899	7894	7000	14894
1900	15667	13000	28667
1901	6761	10000	16761
1902	4525	11000	15525
1903	3052	15000	18052
1904	6697	16000	22697
1905	13009	17000	30009
1906	24389	18000	42389
1907	29120	19000	48120
1908	26005	17000	43005
1909	24908	15000	39908
1910	59025	17000	76025
1911	78356	18000	96356
1912	73671	20000	93671
1913	91236	17000	108236
1914	36905	8500	45405
1915	54881	12000	66881
1916	72091	16942	89033
1917	78407	7985	86392
1918	55583	6193	61776
1919	88021	7780	95801
1920	78855	8812	87667
1921	15413	16000	31413
1922	38336	12630	50966
1923	30234	10608	40842
1924	43147	11935	55082
1925	70198	13209	83407
1926	149414	15963	165377
1927	123826	21349	145175
1928	27240	25566	52806
1929	82188	22825	105013
1930	42771	19463	62234
1931	111	12003	12114
1932	17	6518	6535
1933	20	9222	9242
1934	45469	27306	72775
1935	20771	25625	46396
1936	3754	24104	27858
1937	54849	50128	104977
1938	4580	16332	20912
TOTAL	1910820	811598	2722418
1939	—	2166	2166
1940	—	833	833
1941	—	500	500
TOTAL	1910820	815097	2725917

Source: As for Appendix 3.

Appendix 2: Types and numbers of Indian assisted labour arrivals in Malaya, 1844–1938

year	(1) indentured recruits			(2) kangani recruits		(3) voluntary immigrants	(4) dependants of (1), (2) and (3) and other immigrants	(5) TOTAL	(6) percentage female of total
	written contracts	verbal contracts	total	number of licences issued	number of labourers				
1844	N	N	1800	N	N	—	N	1800	N
1845	N	N	1800	N	N	—	N	1800	N
1846	N	N	1800	N	N	—	N	1800	N
1847	N	N	1800	N	N	—	N	1800	N
1848	N	N	1800	N	N	—	N	1800	N
1849	N	N	1800	N	N	—	N	1800	N
1850	N	N	1800	N	N	—	N	1800	N
1851	N	N	2000	N	N	—	N	2000	N
1852	N	N	2000	N	N	—	N	2000	N
1853	N	N	2000	N	N	—	N	2000	N
1854	N	N	2000	N	N	—	N	2000	N
1855	N	N	2500	N	N	—	N	2500	N
1856	N	N	2500	N	N	—	N	2500	N
1857	N	N	2500	N	N	—	N	2500	N
1858	N	N	2500	N	N	—	N	2500	N
1859	N	N	3800	N	N	—	N	3800	N
1860	N	N	4000	N	N	—	N	4000	N
1861	N	N	4000	N	N	—	N	4000	N
1862	N	N	4000	N	N	—	N	4000	N
1863	N	N	4000	N	N	—	N	4000	N
1864	N	N	4000	N	N	—	N	4000	N
1865	N	N	5000	N	1000	—	N	6000	N
1866	N	N	5617	N	1000	—	N	6617	8
1867	N	N	4294	N	1000	—	N	5294	11

Appendix 2 (cont.)

year	(1) indentured recruits			(2) kangani recruits		(3) voluntary immigrants	(4) dependants of (1), (2) and (3) and other immigrants	(5) TOTAL	(6) percentage female of total
	written contracts	verbal contracts	total	number of licences issued	number of labourers				
1868	N	N	4849	N	1000	—	N	5849	13
1869	N	N	7013	N	1000	—	N	8013	15
1870	500	2500	3000	N	1000	—	N	4000	N
1871	0	3000	3000	N	1000	—	N	4000	N
1872	500	3500	4000	N	1000	—	N	5000	N
1873	1000	2500	3500	N	1000	—	N	4500	N
1874	1000	2500	3500	N	1000	—	N	4500	N
1875	1200	2500	3700	N	1000	—	N	4700	N
1876	1200	2500	3700	N	1000	—	N	4700	N
1877	1200	2500	3700	N	1000	—	N	4700	N
1878	1175	2500	3675	N	1000	—	N	4675	13
1879	853	2500	3353	N	1000	—	N	4353	19
1880	1191	2500	3691	N	1000	—	N	4691	19
1881	879	1800	2679	N	1000	—	N	3679	21
1882	1452	1800	3252	N	1000	—	N	4252	N
1883	1450	1800	3250	N	1000	—	N	4250	20
1884	1539	2500	4039	N	1000	—	N	5039	N
1885	1642	2800	4442	N	1000	—	N	5442	N
1886	2748	2800	5548	N	1000	—	N	6548	20
1887	4736	2800	7536	N	1000	—	N	8536	21
1888	4684	2800	7484	N	1000	—	N	8484	N
1889	2747	2800	5547	N	1000	—	N	6547	N
1890	2960	2800	5760	N	1000	—	N	6760	N
1891	3443	1000	4443	N	1000	—	N	5443	N
1892	1628	1000	2628	N	1000	—	N	3628	N

Appendix 2 (cont.)

year	(1) indentured recruits			(2) kangani recruits		(3)	(4)	(5)	(6)
	written contracts	verbal contracts	total	number of licences issued	number of labourers	voluntary immigrants	dependants of (1), (2) and (3) and other immigrants	TOTAL	percentage female of total
1893	2106	1000	3106	N	1000	—	N	4106	N
1894	1688	1000	2688	N	1000	—	N	3688	N
1895	1549	1000	2549	N	1000	—	N	3549	N
1896	2652	1000	3652	N	1000	—	N	4652	N
1897	2405	1000	3405	N	1000	—	N	4405	N
1898	2989	1000	3989	N	435	—	N	4424	N
1899	4677	1000	5677	N	2217	—	N	7894	N
1900	7615	1000	8615	N	2000	—	5052	15667	N
1901	2785	500	3285	N	2000	6	1470	6761	22
1902	2430	500	2930	N	1474	19	102	4525	13
1903	572	500	1072	N	1858	51	71	3052	15
1904	2670	500	3170	280	3375	113	39	6697	12
1905	4823	500	5323	N	7429	257	0	13009	19
1906	3674	500	4174	938	19177	758	280	24389	15
1907	5499	500	5999	N	21260	856	1005	29120	13
1908	5456	500	5956	1225	16293	572	3184	26005	15
1909	4119	500	4619	1914	15888	1500	2901	24908	15
1910	2523	500	3023	N	52440	1327	2235	59025	17
1911	—	—	—	9248	74898	2187	1271	78356	17
1912	—	—	—	10145	71266	1467	938	73671	18
1913	—	—	—	10806	80528	2750	7958	91236	19
1914	—	—	—	5732	31140	2170	3595	36905	18
1915	—	—	—	5436	50000	4800	81	54881	21
1916	—	—	—	9007	61260	3918	6918	72091	21
1917	—	—	—	11410	65260	6691	6456	78407	19

Appendix 2 (cont.)

year	(1) indentured recruits			(2) *kangani* recruits		(3) voluntary immigrants	(4) dependants of (1), (2) and (3) and other immigrants	(5) TOTAL	(6) percentage female of total
	written contracts	verbal contracts	total	number of licences issued	number of labourers				
1918	—	—	—	6735	42658	7036	5889	55583	24
1919	—	—	—	8447	67247	11663	9111	88021	27
1920	—	—	—	9441	61889	8625	8341	78855	20
1921	—	—	—	1555	12651	1935	827	15413	16
1922	—	—	—	3632	30966	4488	2882	38336	19
1923	—	—	—	3316	20011	7462	2761	30234	22
1924	—	—	—	3005	28363	9641	5143	43147	25
1925	—	—	—	6561	43021	18797	8380	70198	23
1926	—	—	—	10962	102155	28618	18641	149414	23
1927	—	—	—	7882	75820	32302	15704	123826	26
1928	—	—	—	2913	13253	10980	3007	27240	35
1929	—	—	—	5312	44314	28917	8957	82188	26
1930	—	—	—	2234	21148	21623	—	42771	26
1931	—	—	—	—	—	111	—	111	38
1932	—	—	—	—	—	17	—	17	40
1933	—	—	—	—	—	20	—	20	90
1934	—	—	—	N	2067	20000	23402	45469	33
1935	—	—	—	42	1862	18909	N	20771	29
1936	—	—	—	N	669	3085	N	3754	30
1937	—	—	—	N	5337	26894	22618	54849	31
1938	—	—	—	N	88	2000	2492	4580	35
TOTAL	181132	68700	249832	137138	1186717	292560	181711	1910820	24

N = No information available.
Source: As for Appendix 3.

Appendix 3: Total Indian arrivals in Malaya, 1786–1957

The figures in this appendix have limited reliability, several of them being little more than estimates. However, they have been checked with the governments of India and Malaya where possible. The same applies to figures in the other appendices.

		non-labourers				
year	labourers	North Indians	South Indians	total	percentage female of total	GRAND TOTAL
1786	N	N	N	N	N	N
1787	N	N	N	N	N	N
1788	N	N	N	N	N	N
1789	N	N	N	N	N	N
1790	N	N	N	N	N	1500
1791	N	N	N	N	N	1500
1792	N	N	N	N	N	1500
1793	N	N	N	N	N	1500
1794	N	N	N	N	N	1500
1795	N	N	N	N	N	1500
1796	N	N	N	N	N	1500
1797	N	N	N	N	N	1500
1798	N	N	N	N	N	1500
1799	N	N	N	N	N	1500
1800	N	N	N	N	N	1500
1801	N	N	N	N	N	2000
1802	N	N	N	N	N	2000
1803	N	N	N	N	N	2000
1804	N	N	N	N	N	2000
1805	N	N	N	N	N	2000
1806	N	N	N	N	N	2000
1807	N	N	N	N	N	2000
1808	N	N	N	N	N	2000
1809	N	N	N	N	N	2000
1810	N	N	N	N	N	2000
1811	N	N	N	N	N	2000
1812	N	N	N	N	N	2000
1813	N	N	N	N	N	2000
1814	N	N	N	N	N	2000
1815	N	N	N	N	N	2000
1816	N	N	N	N	N	2000
1817	N	N	N	N	N	2000
1818	N	N	N	N	N	2000
1819	N	N	N	N	N	2000
1820	N	N	N	N	N	2000
1821	N	N	N	N	N	2000
1822	N	N	N	N	N	2000
1823	N	N	N	N	N	2000
1824	N	N	N	N	N	2000
1825	N	N	N	N	N	2000
1826	N	N	N	N	N	2000
1827	N	N	N	N	N	2000

Appendix 3

		non-labourers				
year	labourers	North Indians	South Indians	total	percentage female of total	GRAND TOTAL
1828	N	N	N	N	N	2 000
1829	N	N	N	N	N	2 000
1830	N	N	N	N	N	2 000
1831	N	N	N	N	N	2 000
1832	N	N	N	N	N	2 000
1833	N	N	N	N	N	2 000
1834	N	N	N	N	N	2 000
1835	N	N	N	N	N	2 000
1836	N	N	N	N	N	2 000
1837	N	N	N	N	N	2 000
1838	N	N	N	N	N	2 000
1839	N	N	N	N	N	2 000
1840	N	N	N	N	N	2 000
1841	N	N	N	N	N	3 000
1842	N	N	N	N	N	3 000
1843	N	N	N	N	N	3 000
1844	1 800	N	N	1 200	N	3 000
1845	1 800	N	N	1 200	N	3 000
1846	1 800	N	N	1 200	N	3 000
1847	1 800	N	N	1 200	N	3 000
1848	1 800	N	N	1 200	N	3 000
1849	1 800	N	N	1 200	N	3 000
1850	1 800	N	N	1 200	N	3 000
1851	2 000	N	N	1 800	N	3 800
1852	2 000	N	N	1 800	N	3 800
1853	2 000	N	N	1 800	N	3 800
1854	2 000	N	N	1 800	N	3 800
1855	2 500	N	N	2 300	N	4 800
1856	2 500	N	N	2 300	N	4 800
1857	2 500	N	N	2 300	N	4 800
1858	2 500	N	N	2 300	N	4 800
1959	3 800	N	N	2 500	N	6 300
1860	4 000	N	N	3 000	N	7 000
1861	4 000	N	N	3 000	N	7 000
1862	4 000	N	N	3 000	N	7 000
1863	4 000	N	N	3 000	N	7 000
1864	4 000	N	N	3 000	N	7 000
1865	6 000	N	N	3 500	N	9 500
1866	6 617	N	N	3 000	N	9 617
1867	6 294	N	N	2 403	11	8 697
1868	6 849	N	N	1 834	13	8 683
1869	9 013	N	N	1 255	15	10 268
1870	5 000	N	N	2 000	N	7 000
1871	5 000	N	N	2 500	N	7 500
1872	6 000	N	N	2 500	N	8 500
1873	5 500	N	N	2 500	N	8 000
1874	5 500	N	N	2 500	N	8 000

Appendix 3

Appendix 3 (cont.)

| year | labourers | non-labourers | | | | GRAND TOTAL |
		North Indians	South Indians	total	percentage female of total	
1875	5700	N	N	3000	N	8700
1876	5700	N	N	3500	N	9200
1877	5700	N	N	3500	N	9200
1878	5675	N	N	2348	N	8023
1879	4853	N	N	1578	N	6431
1880	4891	N	N	1755	N	6646
1881	5679	N	N	1969	N	7648
1882	8052	N	N	2676	N	10728
1883	8750	N	N	2679	N	11429
1884	13839	N	N	3765	N	17604
1885	17442	N	N	6019	N	23461
1886	16548	N	N	5516	N	22064
1887	15136	N	N	3756	N	18892
1888	17484	N	N	5012	N	22496
1889	15247	N	N	4785	N	20032
1890	15460	1905	4841	6746	N	22206
1891	21443	2000	9446	11446	N	32889
1892	13628	2000	5370	7370	N	20998
1893	14106	2000	4877	6877	N	20983
1894	11688	2000	4155	6155	N	17843
1895	12349	2000	4613	6613	N	18962
1896	15652	2500	5498	7998	N	23650
1897	16405	2500	6000	8500	N	24905
1898	14424	2500	4828	7328	N	21752
1899	14894	2500	4087	6587	N	21481
1900	28667	3000	6684	9684	N	38351
1901	16761	3000	8596	11596	9	28357
1902	15525	3000	2017	5017	11	20542
1903	18052	3000	4478	7478	8	25530
1904	22697	3000	8004	11004	N	33701
1905	30009	3000	9530	12530	N	42539
1906	42389	3500	9652	13152	N	55541
1907	48120	3500	12422	15922	N	64042
1908	43005	3500	11517	15017	N	58022
1909	39908	3500	9909	13409	N	53317
1910	76025	4000	11698	15698	N	91723
1911	96356	4000	13115	17115	N	113471
1912	93671	4000	13257	17257	23	110928
1913	108236	4000	10347	14347	6	122583
1914	45405	2000	5812	7812	N	53217
1915	66881	1000	8442	9442	N	76323
1916	89033	1000	6533	7533	7	96566
1917	86392	1000	3685	4685	7	91077
1918	61776	1317	3515	4832	7	66608
1919	95801	4097	5632	9729	12	105530
1920	87667	4254	7553	11807	12	99474
1921	31413	7439	14260	21699	9	53112

Appendix 3

Appendix 3 (cont.)

| year | labourers | non-labourers | | | | GRAND TOTAL |
		North Indians	South Indians	total	percentage female of total	
1922	50966	6376	7708	14084	9	65050
1923	40842	7119	8660	15779	8	56621
1924	55082	7406	6970	14376	9	69458
1925	83407	6451	7301	13752	9	97159
1926	165377	10260	9418	19678	9	185055
1927	145175	10133	12316	22449	10	167624
1928	52806	8935	10949	19884	8	72690
1929	105013	18352	10244	28596	6	133609
1930	62234	15835	8085	23918	8	86152
1931	12114	11695	8620	20315	8	32429
1932	6535	8879	12102	20981	N	27516
1933	9242	10744	21191	31935	10	41177
1934	72775	13421	18631	32052	11	104827
1935	46396	15000	19954	34954	13	81350
1936	27858	11678	40512	52190	12	80048
1937	104977	15623	18755	34378	12	139355
1938	20912	13398	24127	37525	9	58437
TOTAL	2722418	283517	603864	887381	10	3715299
1939	2166	14000	28287	42287	N	44453
1940	833	12000	19227	31227	N	32060
1941	500	10000	21500	31500	N	32000
TOTAL	2725917	319517	672878	992395	10	3823812
1942 1943 1944 1945	Period of Japanese occupation					
1946	N	N	N	N	N	5500
1947	N	N	N	N	N	31000
1948	N	N	N	N	N	25000
1949	N	N	N	N	N	31000
1950	N	N	N	N	N	39000
1951	N	N	N	N	N	40000
1952	N	N	N	N	N	50000
1953	N	N	N	N	N	47752
1954	N	N	N	N	N	27379
1955	N	N	N	N	N	35147
1956	N	N	N	N	N	43400
1957	N	N	N	N	N	47000
TOTAL	2725917	319517	672878	992395	10	4245990

N = No information available.

Source: Compiled from *SSFR*, 6 (1794), 25.1.1794; *GMPPD*, 1870, 40–4 of 13.9.1870; *IO:EP*, 69 (1872); *GRAPM*, 1855–6—1956–7; *MAREI*, 1908–41; *ARAGIBM*, 1925–40; *SSG*, 1880–6; *IICMM*, 1907–41; *MUAR*, 1946–7; *FMAR*, 1948–57; *CSAR*, 1946–57; *ARSILFB*, 1959–60; O'Sullivan, 1913, pp. 185–6; del Tufo, 1949, p. 597; *SABI*, 1911–41.

Appendix 4: Total Indian departures from Malaya, 1786–1957

year	repatriates	other departures	TOTAL	net immigration
1786	—	N	—	—
1787	—	N	—	—
1788	—	N	—	—
1789	—	N	—	—
1790	—	1 200	1 200	300
1791	—	1 200	1 200	300
1792	—	1 200	1 200	300
1793	—	1 200	1 200	300
1794	—	1 200	1 200	300
1795	—	1 200	1 200	300
1796	—	1 200	1 200	300
1797	—	1 200	1 200	300
1798	—	1 200	1 200	300
1799	—	1 200	1 200	300
1800	—	1 200	1 200	300
1801	—	1 600	1 600	400
1802	—	1 600	1 600	400
1803	—	1 600	1 600	400
1804	—	1 600	1 600	400
1805	—	1 600	1 600	400
1806	—	1 600	1 600	400
1807	—	1 600	1 600	400
1808	—	1 600	1 600	400
1809	—	1 600	1 600	400
1810	—	1 600	1 600	400
1811	—	1 600	1 600	400
1812	—	1 600	1 600	400
1813	—	1 600	1 600	400
1814	—	1 600	1 600	340
1815	—	1 600	1 600	400
1816	—	1 600	1 600	400
1817	—	1 600	1 600	400
1818	—	1 600	1 600	400
1819	—	1 600	1 600	400
1820	—	1 600	1 600	400
1821	—	1 600	1 600	400
1822	—	1 600	1 600	400
1823	—	1 600	1 600	400
1824	—	1 600	1 600	400
1825	—	1 600	1 600	400
1826	—	1 600	1 600	400
1827	—	1 600	1 600	400
1828	—	1 600	1 600	400
1829	—	1 600	1 600	400
1830	—	1 600	1 600	400
1831	—	1 600	1 600	400
1832	—	1 600	1 600	400
1833	—	1 600	1 600	400
1834	—	1 600	1 600	400

Appendix 4

year	repatriates	other departures	TOTAL	net immigration
1835	—	1 600	1 600	400
1836	—	1 600	1 600	400
1837	—	1 600	1 600	400
1838	—	1 600	1 600	400
1839	—	1 600	1 600	400
1840	—	1 600	1 600	400
1841	—	2 400	2 400	600
1842	—	2 400	2 400	600
1843	—	2 400	2 400	600
1844	—	2 500	2 500	500
1845	—	2 500	2 500	500
1846	—	2 500	2 500	500
1847	—	2 500	2 500	500
1848	—	2 500	2 500	500
1849	—	2 500	2 500	500
1850	—	2 500	2 500	500
1851	—	3 000	3 000	800
1852	—	3 000	3 000	800
1853	—	3 000	3 000	800
1854	—	3 000	3 000	800
1855	—	3 500	3 500	1 300
1856	—	3 500	3 500	1 300
1857	—	3 500	3 500	1 300
1858	—	3 500	3 500	1 300
1859	—	5 400	5 400	900
1860	—	5 600	5 600	1 400
1861	—	5 600	5 600	1 400
1862	—	5 600	5 600	1 400
1863	—	5 600	5 600	1 400
1864	—	5 600	5 600	1 400
1865	—	7 500	7 500	2 000
1866	—	7 700	7 700	1 917
1867	—	7 000	7 000	1 697
1868	—	6 900	6 900	1 783
1869	—	8 200	8 200	2 068
1870	—	5 600	5 600	1 400
1871	—	6 000	6 000	1 500
1872	—	6 800	6 800	1 700
1873	—	6 400	6 400	1 600
1874	—	6 400	6 400	1 600
1875	—	7 000	7 000	1 700
1876	—	8 300	8 300	900
1877	—	8 300	8 300	900
1878	—	6 400	6 400	1 623
1879	—	5 100	5 100	1 331
1880	—	5 300	5 300	1 346
1881	—	5 269	5 269	2 379
1882	—	5 947	5 947	4 781
1883	—	9 041	9 041	2 388
1884	—	10 749	10 749	6 855

year	repatriates	other departures	TOTAL	net immigration
1885	—	13417	13417	10044
1886	—	18105	18105	3959
1887	—	12596	12596	6296
1888	—	13190	13190	9306
1889	—	14099	14099	5933
1890	—	16055	16055	6151
1891	—	23912	23912	8977
1892	—	17722	17722	3276
1893	—	14044	14044	6939
1894	—	13537	13537	4306
1895	—	15962	15962	3000
1896	—	12997	12997	10653
1897	—	14530	14530	10375
1898	—	11500	11500	10252
1899	—	10766	10766	10715
1900	—	10995	10995	27356
1901	—	16204	16204	12153
1902	—	18183	18183	2359
1903	—	17832	17832	7698
1904	—	19550	19550	14151
1905	—	19754	19754	22785
1906	—	21879	21879	33662
1907	—	30522	30522	33520
1908	—	30920	30920	27102
1909	—	31374	31374	21943
1910	—	39080	39080	52643
1911	—	48103	48103	65368
1912	—	63885	63885	47043
1913	593	69497	70090	52493
1914	N	N	63073	—9856
1915	1096	49224	50320	26003
1916	980	53499	54479	42087
1917	N	N	57583	33494
1918	N	N	52132	14476
1919	N	N	46767	58763
1920	N	N	55481	43993
1921	5977	55574	61551	—8439
1922	N	N	45733	19317
1923	814	41964	42778	13843
1924	N	N	37326	32132
1925	2271	40873	43144	54015
1926	3205	62581	65786	119269
1927	9607	83415	93022	74602
1928	18147	73283	91430	—18740
1929	6731	70123	76854	56755
1930	77761	74470	152231	—66079
1931	56119	45971	102090	—69661
1932	56476	28575	85051	—57535
1933	9338	23953	33291	7886
1934	1959	26508	28467	76360

year	repatriates	other departures	TOTAL	net immigration
1935	6185	32684	38869	42481
1936	8629	31928	40557	39491
1937	6566	38601	45167	94188
1938	29043	47156	76199	−17762
TOTAL	301497	2278293	2579790	1135509
1939	10775	31949	42724	1729
1940	5872	34128	40000	−7940
1941	N	N	40000	−8000
TOTAL	318144	2344370	2662514	1161298
1942 1943 1944 1945		Period of Japanese occupation		
1946	N	N	11000	−5500
1947	N	N	27400	3600
1948	3293	20896	24189	811
1949	3107	21893	25000	6000
1950	2564	35330	37894	1106
1951	1100	37900	39000	1000
1952	925	43657	44582	5418
1953	819	37518	38337	9415
1954	1197	23090	24287	3092
1955	1320	26583	27903	7244
1956	1201	38799	40000	3400
1957	1476	46524	48000	−1000
TOTAL	335146	2676560	3011706	1234284

N = No information available.
Source: As for Appendix 3.

SELECT BIBLIOGRAPHY

ABBREVIATIONS

CHM   *Cahiers d'Histoire Mondiale* (*Journal of World history*) (Paris).
EHR   *Economic History Review* (London).
EI   *Epigraphia Indica* (Calcutta).
JASB   *Journal of the Asiatic Society of Bengal* (Calcutta).
JGIS   *Journal of the Greater India Society* (Calcutta).
JMBRAS   *Journal of the Malayan Branch of the Royal Asiatic Society* (Singapore, Kuala Lumpur).
JRAS   *Journal of the Royal Asiatic Society of Great Britain and Ireland* (London).
JSBRAS   *Journal of the Straits Branch of the Royal Asiatic Society* (Singapore).
JSEAH   *Journal of Southeast Asian History* (Singapore).
(M)JTG   (*Malayan*) *Journal of Tropical Geography* (Singapore, Kuala Lumpur).
MAJ   *Malayan Agricultural Journal* (Kuala Lumpur).
MER   *Malayan Economic Review* (Singapore).
MHJ   *Malayan Historical Journal* (Kuala Lumpur).
PRCI   *Proceedings of the Royal Colonial Institute* (London).
SAMSJV   *Sir Asutosh Mookerjee Silver Jubilee Volumes* (Calcutta).

UNPUBLISHED SOURCES

Annual report of the Agent of the Government of India in British Malaya, 1923–1924 (Madras).

Annual report of the Labour Department of Singapore for the year 1965 (Singapore).

Birch papers. Private papers of J. W. W. Birch, British Resident, Perak (1874–5) and his son, E. W. Birch, British Resident, Perak (1904–11) (London).

British Museum: Broughton papers. Correspondence of Sir J. C. Hobhouse, afterwards Baron Broughton, as President of the Board of Control, with George Eden, Earl of Auckland, Governor-General of India, 1835–41 (London).

Central Indian Association of Malaya: Minutes of meetings, 27th January, 1936–7th October, 1941 (Kuala Lumpur).

Central Indian Association of Malaya: Report of the Council of Management for the year ending 31st December, 1941 (Kuala Lumpur).

Chinese Secretariat, Singapore: Monthly review of Chinese affairs, June 1938 (Singapore).

C.O.273 Series: The Colonial Office's Straits Settlements original correspondence, 1838–1922 (London).

318

Select bibliography

C.O.537 Series: The Colonial Office's Straits Settlements supplementary original correspondence, 1873–1898 (London).

Conference of Residents, Federated Malay States: Abstract of proceedings, 1922–1931 (Singapore).

District Office, Port Dickson: Chuah Indian settlement file (Port Dickson).

Early Indonesian commerce and the origin of Sri Vijaya, a thesis submitted by O. W. Wolters for the degree of Doctor of Philosophy, University of London, 1960 (London).

Father Fée's record book on the founding of St. Joseph's Tamil Settlement, Bagan Serai (Singapore).

Federated Malay States: Proceedings of Durbars held in 1897, 1903 and 1927 (Kuala Lumpur).

F.O.17 Series: The Foreign Office's general correspondence relating to China, 1895 (London).

F.O.69 Series: The Foreign Office's general correspondence relating to Siam, 1891–1895 (London).

Government of Madras (Emigration) proceedings in the Public Department, 1870–1916 (Madras).

Government of Madras (Emigration) proceedings of the Board of Revenue (Separate Revenue Department), 1898–1923 (Madras).

Government of Madras (Emigration) proceedings in the Judicial (Law [General]) Department, 1921–1926 (Madras).

Government of Madras (Emigration) proceedings in the Public Works and Labour Department, 1926–1936 (Madras).

Government of Madras (Emigration) proceedings in the Development Department, 1936–1940 (Madras).

Hamilton collection of the India Office Library (London).

High Commissioner's (including the Secretary to High Commissioner's) Office files, 1898–1926, 1928–1941 (Kuala Lumpur).

Index of decisions of Residents' conferences (Federated Malay States), 1897–1928 (Singapore).

India Office: Parliamentary (Parliamentary Branch) papers collection of the Government of India, 1795–1891 (London).

India Office: Public, Post Office, and Ecclesiastical letters of the Government of India, 1857–1876 (London).

India Office: Revenue, Judicial and Legislative Committee (of the Board of Control): Miscellaneous papers, 1857 (London).

India Office: Emigration proceedings of the Government of India, 1871–1922 (London).

India Office: Public despatches to India (Original drafts), 1871 (London).

India Office: Home correspondence (Public Department) of the Government of India, 1871–1878 (London).

India Office: Foreign proceedings of the Government of India, 1873–1875 (London).

India Office: Emigration letters from India and Bengal, 1880–1910 (London).

India Office: Judicial proceedings of the Government of India, 1854, 1880–1910 (London).

Indian Immigration Committee: Minutes of meetings, 1907–1941 (Kuala Lumpur).

Select bibliography

Indian Immigration Committee: Report of a meeting of the General Labour Committee, British Malaya, held at 12, Market Street, Kuala Lumpur, on May 31st, 1920 (Kuala Lumpur).

Indian Immigration Committee: Reprint of the official verbatim report of meeting of the Indian Immigration Committee held on February 9th, 1924 (Kuala Lumpur).

Indian Immigration Committee: Official verbatim report of meetings of the Indian Immigration Committee held on August 10th and October 25th, 1925 (Kuala Lumpur).

Indian Immigration Committee: Official verbatim report of meetings of the Indian Immigration Committee held on March 9th, 1927 (Kuala Lumpur).

Indian Immigration Committee: Official verbatim report of meeting of the Indian Immigration Committee held on May 9th, 1927 (Kuala Lumpur).

Indian Immigration Committee: Memorandum compiled by the Klang, Kuala Langat and Kuala Selangor District Planters' Associations to be read at the meeting of the Indian Immigration Committee called at Klang on October 29th, 1928 to fix a standard rate of wages for the above Districts (Kuala Lumpur).

Indian Immigration Committee: Official verbatim report of meetings of the Indian Immigration Committee held on July 16th, 1930 and July 31st, 1930 (Kuala Lumpur).

Innes, J., *Letter book and Note book kept by James Innes, Collector of Revenue and Magistrate, Langat, Selangor, 14th February, 1876–23rd February, 1881* (London).

Johore State Secretariat files, 1910–1914 (Johore Bahru).

Labour Department, Malaya, Miscellaneous files, 1937–1942 (Kuala Lumpur).

Maxwell papers. Private papers of Sir George Maxwell, Chief Secretary, Federated Malay States (1920–6) (London).

Methods and conditions of employment of Chinese labour in the Federated Malay States, 1938, by W. L. Blythe (Kuala Lumpur).

Minutes of meetings of the Executive Council of the Straits Settlements, 1867–1914 (London).

National Archives of India: Consultations of the Emigration Branch of the Home Department of the Government of India, 1830–1859 (New Delhi).

National Archives of India: Foreign political proceedings of the Government of India, 1850–1860 (New Delhi).

National Archives of India: Emigration proceedings of the Government of India, 1871–1941 (New Delhi).

National Archives of India: Revenue and Agriculture Department (Survey) proceedings of the Government of India, 1884 (New Delhi).

National Archives of India: Home Department political proceedings of the Government of India, 1914–1918 (New Delhi).

National Archives of Malaysia: Original correspondence between the Colonial Office (London) and the High Commissioner for the Malay States, 1897–1942 (Kuala Lumpur).

Notes on the historical geography of the Malay Peninsula (mainly before 1900) prepared at the Centre for Southeast Asian Studies, University of California, Berkeley, for the Regional Conference of Southeast Asian Geographers,

Select bibliography

Kuala Lumpur, Malaya, 2–23 April, 1962, by Paul Wheatley (Kuala Lumpur).

Origin and growth of the Malay States Guides, an Academic Exercise submitted by A. K. Bagoo in partial fulfilment of the requirements for a Bachelor of Arts (Honours) degree of the University of Malaya, Singapore, 1956 (Singapore).

Papers of Penang Sugar Estate, 1897–1900 (Singapore).

(United) Planters' Association of Malaya: Circulars to members, 1924–1941, 1946 (Kuala Lumpur).

(United) Planters' Association of Malaya: Minutes of meetings, 1909, 1911–1918, 1920–1923 (Kuala Lumpur).

Principal Medical Officer, Johore, *Memorandum on the collection by cess from employers of labour of dues for hospital treatment, 1938* (Johore Bahru).

Proceedings of the Government of Madras Board of Revenue, 1839–1869 (Madras).

Report of the committee set up to enquire and investigate the causes, extent and results of the sub-division of estates in the Federation of Malaya, 1957 (Kuala Lumpur).

Report on the proceedings of a commission appointed to consider the question of the encouragement of Indian immigration to the Federated Malay States, 1900 (Kuala Lumpur).

Royal Commonwealth Society: British Association of Malaysia historical collection, being the reminiscences, letters and other papers of members of the Association and their friends (London).

Selangor State Secretariat files, 1875–1941 (Kuala Lumpur).

Singapore National Library: Original correspondence between the Colonial Office (London) and the Governor of the Straits Settlements, 1867–1916 (Singapore).

Statistical information concerning New Villages in the Federation of Malaya, 1952 (Kuala Lumpur).

Straits Settlements factory records, 1769–1830 (London).

Straits Settlements records, 1800–1867 (Singapore).

PUBLISHED SOURCES

(A): Books, parts of books, pamphlets, articles and maps

Aiyangar, S. K. (1921). *South India and her Muhammadan invaders* (Oxford).

al-Attas, S. N. (1963). *Some aspects of Ṣūfism* (Singapore).

All Malayan Estates Staff Union: Biennial report 1962–1964 and connected papers (Kuala Lumpur, 1964).

Anderson, J. (1824). *Political and commercial considerations relative to the Malayan Peninsula and the British settlements in the Straits of Malacca* (Penang).

Andrew, E. J. L. (1933). *Indian labour in Rangoon* (Oxford).

Andrews, C. F. (1930). 'India's emigration problem', *Foreign affairs* (New York), VIII, 430–41.

Annual report of the Agent of the Government of India in British Malaya, 1925–40 (Calcutta, New Delhi).

Annual report of the Indian Chamber of Commerce, Singapore, 1936–8, 1953 (Singapore).

Annual report of the Labour Department of the Colony (State) of Singapore, 1946–58 (Singapore).

Annual report of the Labour Department of the Federation of Malaya, 1948–57 (Kuala Lumpur).

Annual report of the Labour Department of Malaya, 1912–40 (Kuala Lumpur).

Annual report of the Postal Services Department, Malaya, 1946–9 (Kuala Lumpur, Singapore).

Annual report of the South Indian Labour Fund Board, 1959–64 (Kuala Lumpur).

Appadorai, A. (1936). *Economic conditions in Southern India, c. 1000–1500 A.D.,* 2 vols. (Madras).

Arasaratnam, S. (1965–66). 'Social reform among Malayan Indians: The temperance movement', *Tamil Oli: Journal of the Tamil Language Society, University of Malaya* (Kuala Lumpur), v, 86–92.

Asian Relations Organisations, 1948. *The Asian relations conference, 1947* (New Delhi).

Aspinall, A. (1931). *Cornwallis in Bengal* (Manchester).

A.W.S. (1910). *Rubber estate values* (Singapore).

Aziz, U. (1962). *Sub-division of estates in Malaya, 1951–60,* 3 vols. (Kuala Lumpur).

Bannerjea, P. (1951). *A study of Indian economics* (Calcutta).

Bassett, D. K. (1960). 'European influence in the Malay Peninsula, 1511–1786', *JMBRAS,* xxxiii, iii, pp. 9–35.

(1963). 'European influence in Southeast Asia, c. 1500–1600', *JSEAH,* iv, ii, pp. 134–65.

(1964). 'The historical background, 1500–1815', in *Malaysia: A survey,* G. W. Wang, ed. (Singapore), pp. 113–27.

Battacharya, S. (1954). *The East India Company and the economy of Bengal from 1704 to 1740* (London).

Bauer, P. T. (1948). *The rubber industry* (London).

Baxter, J. (1941). *Report on Indian immigration* (Rangoon).

Bhatia, B. M. (1963). *Famines in India* (London).

Blythe, W. L. (1947). 'A historical sketch of Chinese labour in Malaya', *JMBRAS,* xx, i, pp. 64–114.

Boulger, D. C. (1897). *The life of Sir Stamford Raffles* (London).

Bosch, F. D. K. (1952). ' 'Local genius' en oud-Javaanse kunst', *Mededeelingen der Koninklijke Nederlandsche Akademie van Wetenschappen* (Amsterdam), Nieuwe reeks, xv, i, pp. 1–25.

(1961). *Selected studies in Indonesian archaeology* (The Hague).

Bowrey, T. (1905). *A geographical account of the countries round the Bay of Bengal* (London).

Braddell, R. (1935–41). 'An introduction to the study of ancient times in the Malay Peninsula', *JMBRAS,* xiii, ii, pp. 70–109; xiv, iii, pp. 10–71; xv, iii, pp. 64–126; xvii, i, pp. 146–212; xix, i, pp. 21–74.

(1947–51). 'Notes on ancient times in Malaya', *JMBRAS,* xx, i, pp. 161–86; xx, ii, pp. 1–19; xxii, i, pp. 1–24; xxiii, i, pp. 1–36; xxiii, iii, pp. 1–35; xxiv, i, pp. 1–27.

(1950). 'Lung-ya-men and Tan-ma-hsi', *JMBRAS,* xxiii, i, pp. 37–51.

(1956). 'Malayadvipa', *(M)JTG*, ix, 1–20.

(1958). 'Most ancient Kedah', *Malaya in history* (Kuala Lumpur), iv, ii, pp. 18–40.

Braddell, T. (1861). *Statistics of the population, commerce, agriculture, revenue and government establishments of the British settlements in the Straits of Malacca* (Penang).

Bremmer, M. J. (1927). 'Report of Governor Balthasar Bort on Malacca, 1678', *JMBRAS*, v, i, pp. 9–205.

Briggs, L. P. (1951). 'The ancient Khmer empire', *Transactions of the American Philosophical Society* (Philadelphia), New Series, xli, i, pp. 1–273.

British Guiana (1916). *Court of Policy first session, 1916: Despatch from Secretary of State for the Colonies (with enclosures) on the subject of the total abolition of indentured migration from India, Court of Policy No. 860/1916* (Georgetown).

Brown, C. C. (1952). 'Sĕjarah Mĕlayu or "Malay Annals"', *JMBRAS*, xxv, ii, iii, pp. 5–276.

Brown, M. (1944). *India need not starve!* (London).

Brown, M. B. (1963). *After imperialism* (London).

Buckley, C. B. (1902). *An anecdotal history of old times in Singapore*, 2 vols. (Singapore).

Cameron, J. (1865). *Our tropical possessions in Malayan India* (London). (Reprinted, Kuala Lumpur, 1965.)

Cameron, W. (1883). 'On the Patani', *JSBRAS*, xi, 123–42.

Cardon, R. E. (1934). 'Portuguese Malacca', *JMBRAS*, xii, ii, pp. 1–23.

Carey, E. V. (1895). 'Recruiting Tamil labour', *The Selangor journal* (Kuala Lumpur), iii, 409–15.

Carr-Saunders, A. M. (1936). *World population* (Oxford).

Cavendish, A. (1911). *Report on the census of Kedah and Perlis A. H. 1329 (A.D. 1911)* (Penang).

Central Indian Association of Malaya (1937). *Memorandum on 'Toddy in Malaya' submitted to the Agent of the Government of India by the Central Indian Association of Malaya* (Kuala Lumpur).

Ceylon (1908). *Ceylon: The labour commission, 1908* (Colombo).

Chai, H. C. (1964). *The development of British Malaya, 1896–1909* (Kuala Lumpur).

Chanda, R. (1922). 'Early Indian seamen', *SAMSJV*, iii, i, pp. 105–24.

Chang, T. T. (1934). *Sino-Portuguese trade from 1514 to 1644* (Leiden).

Chaudhari, S. (1952). *Jātakamālā Ārya Śūra Jātaka 1–20 mulasamskrita aura Hindi anuvada: sampadaka aura anuvadaka (True translation into Hindi of Āyra Śūra's Jātakamālā, 1–20)* (in Hindi, Kathatiya, Bihar).

Cheeseman, H. R. (1955). 'Education in Malaya, 1900–1941', *MHJ*, ii, i, pp. 30–47.

Chettur, S. K. (1948). *Malayan adventure* (Mangalore).

Chhabra, B. ch. (1935). 'Expansion of Indo-Aryan culture during Pallava rule, as evidenced by inscriptions', *JASB*, i, i, pp. 1–64.

Chin, K. O. (1946). *Malaya upside down* (Singapore).

(1953). *Ma-rai-ee* (London).

Chou, K. R. (1966). *Saving and investment in Malaya* (Hong Kong).

Select bibliography

Chua, S. C. (1964). *State of Singapore: Report on the census of population* (Singapore).

Clodd, H. P. (1948). *Malaya's first pioneer* (London).

Coedès, G. (1948). *Les états hindouises d'Indochine et d'Indonésie* (Paris).

(1962). *Les peuples de la Péninsule Indochinoise* (Paris).

Colony (State) of Singapore annual report, 1946–59 (Singapore).

Colony of Singapore annual report of the Immigration Department, 1953–7 (Singapore).

Consolidated annual report on the working of the Indian Emigration Act, 1922, 1934–40, 1944–50, 1953–7 (New Delhi).

Coomaraswamy, A. K. (1927). *History of Indian and Indonesian art* (London).

Coomaraswamy, V. (1946). *Report on the general and economic conditions, etc., of the Ceylonese in Malaya* (Colombo).

Correspondence relating to the Protected Malay States, 1874–82 (London).

Corry, W. C. S. (1954). *A general survey of the New Villages, 12th October, 1954* (Singapore).

Cortesão, A. (1944). *The Suma Oriental of Tomé Pires, an account of the East, from the Red Sea to Japan, written in Malacca and India in 1512–5, and the Book of Francisco Rodrigues, rutter of a voyage in the Red Sea, nautical rules, almanack and maps, written and drawn in the East before 1575*, 2 vols. (London).

Crawfurd, J. (1856). *A descriptive dictionary of the Indian islands and the adjacent countries* (London).

Cullin, E. G. and Zehnder, W. F. (1905). *The early history of Penang, 1592–1827* (Penang).

Cumpston, I. M. (1953). *Indians overseas in British territories, 1834–1854* (London).

Dale, W. L. (1956). 'Wind and drift currents in the South China Sea', *(M)JTG*, VIII, 1–31.

Dames, M. L. (1918–21). *The Book of Duarte Barbosa: An account of the countries bordering the Indian Ocean and their inhabitants written by Duarte Barbosa, and completed about the year 1518 A.D.*, 2 vols. (London).

Das, R. K. (1931). *Plantation labour in India* (Calcutta).

Das, S. C. (1893). 'Indian pandits in Tibet', *Journal of the Buddhist Text Society of India* (Calcutta), I, i, pp. 1–38.

Datta, K. (1961). *Survey of India's social life and economic condition in the eighteenth century (1707–1813)* (Calcutta).

Davis, K. (1951). *The population of India and Pakistan* (New Jersey).

Debates of the Council of State of India, 1921–40 (New Delhi).

Debates of the Legislative Assembly of India, 1921–40 (New Delhi).

de Gray Birch, W. (1875–84). *The commentaries of the great Afonso Dalboquerque*, 4 vols. (London).

del Tufo, M. V. (1949). *Malaya: A report on the 1947 census of population* (London).

Dennery, E. (1931). *Asia's teeming millions* (London).

Department of Information, Federation of Malaya (1953). *Federal Government press statement D. INF. 11/53/1 (Lands): 'South Indian land settle-*

ment' (*Opportunities for South Indians to settle permanently on the land in Malaya*) (Kuala Lumpur).

Department of Labour and Industrial Relations, Federation (States) of Malaya

(1958). *Employment, wage and amenity statistics for July, 1957* (Kuala Lumpur).

(1966). *Employment, wage and amenity statistics for July, 1965* (Kuala Lumpur).

Department of Statistics, Federation (States) of Malaya

(1948). *Malaya: Rubber statistics handbook, 1947* (Kuala Lumpur).

(1953). *Malaya: Rubber statistics handbook, 1952* (Kuala Lumpur).

(1958*a*). *Household budget survey of the Federation of Malaya, 1957–1958* (Kuala Lumpur).

(1958*b*). *Malaya: Rubber statistics handbook, 1957* (Kuala Lumpur).

(1961). *Census of manufacturing industries in the Federation of Malaya, 1959* (Kuala Lumpur).

(1963). *Federation of Malaya: Report on employment, unemployment and under-employment 1962* (Kuala Lumpur).

(1965). *Report on employment and unemployment in metropolitan towns States of Malaya 1965* (Kuala Lumpur).

Desai, B. J. (1946). *I.N.A. defence* (Delhi).

de Silva, G. W. (ed.) (1940). *Selected speeches by S. N. Veerasamy* (Kuala Lumpur).

Dev, D. Y. (1940). *Our countrymen abroad* (Allahabad).

Devahuti, D. (1965). *India and ancient Malaya* (Singapore).

Dew, A. T. (1887). 'Exploring expedition from Selama, Perak, over the mountains to Pong, Patani', *JSBRAS*, xix, 105–20.

Digby, W. (1901). *Prosperous India* (London).

Dobby, E. H. G. (1940). 'Singapore: Town and country', *Geographical review* (New York), xxx, 84–109.

(1950). *Southeast Asia* (London).

(1957). 'Padi landscapes of Malaya', (*M*)*JTG*, x, 3–143.

Durairajasingam, S. (1954). *India and Malaya through the ages* (Singapore).

Dutt, R. (1950). *The economic history of India under early British rule* (London).

Earl, G. W. (1846). *Enterprise in tropical Australia* (London).

(1853). *Contributions to the physical geography of Southeastern Asia and Australia* (London).

Edgar, A. T. (1937). *Manual of rubber planting (Malaya)* (Kuala Lumpur).

'Emigrant', (1924). *Indian emigration* (London).

Evans, I. H. N. (1927). *Ethnology and archaeology of the Malay Peninsula* (Cambridge, England).

Fabian Society, The (1942). *Labour in the Colonies* (London).

Fatimi, S. Q. (1963). *Islām comes to Malaysia* (Singapore).

Fabvre, P. (1849). 'A journey in Johore', *Journal of the Indian Archipelago and eastern Asia* (Singapore), iii, 50–64.

Federal Land Development Authority annual report, 1958–62 (Kuala Lumpur).

Federal Land Development Authority (1956). *No need to be poor: A policy statement* (Kuala Lumpur).

Select bibliography

Federal Land Development Authority (1966). *Land settlement in Malaya under the Federal Land Development Authority* (Kuala Lumpur).

Federated Malay States annual report, 1896–1940 (Kuala Lumpur).

Federated Malay States Police annual report, 1896–1940 (Kuala Lumpur).

Federated Malay States, 1928, *Report on the rivers in the Federated Malay States* (Kuala Lumpur).

Federated Malay States: Report of the rice cultivation committee, 1930, 2 vols. (Kuala Lumpur, 1931).

Federated Malay States Railways (1935). *Fifty years of railways in Malaya* (Kuala Lumpur).

Federation of Malaya (1949). *Report of Dr A. Morland on tuberculosis in Malaya* (Kuala Lumpur).

(1952). *The new Immigration Law* (Kuala Lumpur).

(1958). *Report of the land commission* (Kuala Lumpur).

(1959). *Immigration Ordinance, 1959* (Kuala Lumpur).

(1960). *Malayan constitutional documents* (Kuala Lumpur).

(1961). *Interim report of the subdivision of estates committee* (Kuala Lumpur).

Federation of Malaya annual report, 1948–57 (Kuala Lumpur).

Federation of Malaya government gazette, 1948–59 (Kuala Lumpur).

Federation of Malaya (Malaysia) official year book, 1961–4 (Kuala Lumpur).

Fell, H. (1960). *1957 population census of the Federation of Malaya: Report No. 14* (Kuala Lumpur).

Ferguson, D. S. (1954). 'The Sg. Manik irrigation scheme', *(M)JTG*, II, 9–16.

Ferguson, J. (1911). 'Ceylon, the Malay States and Java compared as plantation and residential colonies', *United empire* (London), new series, II, 104–15, 165–76.

Ferrand, G. (1919). 'Le K'ouen-louen et les anciennes navigations interocéaniques dans les mers du sud', *Journal Asiatique* (Paris), IIe série, XIII, 431–92; XIV, 6–68, 201–41.

Figart, D. W. (1925). *The plantation rubber industry in the Middle East* (Washington).

Financial News map of the estates of the rubber plantation companies in the Malay Peninsula, 1910, The (London).

Fisher, C. A. (1956). 'The problem of Malayan unity in its geographical setting', in R. W. Steel and C. A. Fisher (eds.), *Geographical essays on British tropical lands* (London), pp. 269–344.

(1964). *Southeast Asia: A social, economic and political geography* (London).

Freedman, M. (1957). *Chinese family and marriage in Singapore* (London).

Fryer, D. W. (1964). 'The plantation industry—The estates', in G. W. Wang (ed.), *Malaysia: A survey* (Singapore), pp. 227–45.

Gadgil, D. R. (1942). *The industrial evolution of India in recent times* (London).

(1950). *The industrial evolution of India* (London).

Gamba, C. (1962). *The National Union of Plantation Workers: A history of the plantation workers of Malaya, 1946–1958* (Singapore).

Gangulee, N. (1947). *Indians in the empire overseas* (London).

General report on the administration of the Province (Presidency) of Madras, 1855/6–1956/7 (Madras).

Geoghegan, J. (1873). *Note on emigration from India* (Calcutta).

Select bibliography

Ghosh, D. (1946). *Pressure of population and economic efficiency in India* (New Delhi).

Gillion, K. (1962). *Fiji's Indian migrants: A history to the end of indenture in 1920* (Melbourne).

Ginsburg, N. and Roberts, P. E. (1958). *Malaya* (Singapore).

Glamann, K. (1958). *Dutch-Asiatic trade, 1620–1740* (Copenhagen).

Gopinatha Rao, T. A. (1925). 'A note on Manigramattar occurring in Tamil inscriptions', *EI*, xviii, 69–73.

Gore, M. S. (1963). 'India', in R. D. Lambert and R. F. Hoselitz (eds.), *The role of savings and wealth in southern Asia and the West* (Paris), pp. 178–218.

Grist, D. (1932). *Malayan agricultural statistics* (Kuala Lumpur).

(1933). *Nationality and ownership and nature of constitution of rubber estates in Malaya* (Kuala Lumpur).

(1936). *An outline of Malayan agriculture* (Kuala Lumpur).

Groeneveldt, W. P. (1876). *Notes on the Malay Archipelago and Malacca* (Batavia).

Gullick, J. M. (1953). 'Captain Speedy of Larut', *JMBRAS*, xxvi, iii, pp. 4–103.

Hacobian, M. (1936). 'The siege and capture of Malacca from the Portuguese in 1640–41', *JMBRAS*, xiv, i, pp. 1–178.

Hall, D. G. E. (1955). *A history of South-East Asia* (London).

(1964). *A history of South-East Asia* (London).

Hansard's Official report of the (British) Parliamentary debates, 1910–12 (London).

Hare, G. T. (1902). *Federated Malay States census of the population, 1901* (London).

Harris, J. (1933). *A century of emancipation* (London).

Harrison, B. (1954). 'Malacca in the eighteenth century: Two Dutch governors' reports', *JMBRAS*, xxvi, i, pp. 24–34.

(1963). *South-east Asia: A short history* (London).

Harrison, C. W. (1929). *Some notes on the government services in British Malaya* (London).

Hervey, D. F. A. (1885). 'Valentijn's description of Malacca', *JSBRAS*, xv, 49–74.

Hill, A. H. (1961). *The coming of Islam to Southeast Asia* (Singapore).

Hinton, W. J. (1929). *Government of the Pacific dependencies: British Malaya* (Honolulu).

Ho, R. (1965). 'Land settlement projects in Malaya: An assessment of the role of the Federal Land Development Authority', *(M)JTG*, xx, 1–15.

Hodder, B. W. (1953). 'Racial groupings in Singapore', *(M)JTG*, i, 25–36.

(1959). *Man in Malaya* (London).

Hourani, G. F. (1951). *Arab seafaring in the Indian Ocean in the ancient and early medieval times* (New Jersey).

Hultzch, E. (1891–1929). *South Indian inscriptions*, 3 vols. (Madras).

Hunter, W. W. (1908). *The India of the Queen and other essays* (London).

Hutton, J. H. (1961). *Caste in India* (London).

Select bibliography

Imperial Indian Citizenship Association: The Indians abroad bulletin, nos. 1–14, 1923–5 (Bombay, 1924–6).

India (1891–4). *Census of India, 1891*, 34 vols. (Calcutta).

  (1901–5). *Census of India, 1901*, 26 vols. (Delhi, Calcutta).

  (1911–15). *Census of India, 1911*, 23 vols. (Delhi).

  (1921–4). *Census of India, 1921*, 25 vols. (Delhi).

  (1932–7). *Census of India, 1931*, 30 vols. (Delhi).

  (1935). *The Indian Emigration Act, 1922 (VII of 1922) (As modified up to the 31st March, 1935)* (Delhi).

  (1941). *Indian Emigration Rules 1923 and special rules applicable to Ceylon and Malaya (corrected up to 31st December, 1940)* (Delhi).

Indian Education Committee, Federation of Malaya (1951). *Memorandum on Indian education in the Federation of Malaya* (Kuala Lumpur).

Innes, J. R. (1901). *Report on the census of the Straits Settlements taken on the 1st March, 1901* (London).

International Bank for Reconstruction and Development (1955). *The economic development of Malaya* (Singapore).

International Labour Organisation (1950). *Basic problems of plantation labour* (Geneva, Bandung).

Jackson, E. St. J. (1938). *Report of a commission on immigration into Ceylon* (Colombo).

Jackson, J. C. (1964). 'Smallholding cultivation of cash crops', in G. W. Wang (ed.), *Malaysia: A survey* (Singapore), pp. 246–73.

  (1965). 'Chinese agricultural pioneering in Singapore and Johore, 1800–1917', *JMBRAS*, xxxviii, i, pp. 77–84.

Jackson, P. *Plan of the town of Singapore (showing the recommendations of the Town Committee of 1823)* (National Library, Singapore).

Jackson, R. N. (1961). *Immigrant labour and the development of Malaya, 1786–1920* (Kuala Lumpur).

Jagoe, R. B. (1952). ''Deli' oil palms and early introduction of *Elaeis guineensis* to Malaya', *MAJ*, xxv, i, pp. 3–10.

Jātakamālā (edited by H. Kern, Boston, 1891).

Jenks, J. W. (1920). *Report on certain economic questions in the English and Dutch colonies in the Orient* (Washington, D.C.).

Jha, G. (1922). 'Bodhayana's prayascitta for sea-voyage', *SAMSJV*, iii, i, pp. 35–6.

Johns, A. H. (1957). 'Malay Sufism', *JMBRAS*, xxx, ii, pp. 1–11.

  (1961). *Sufism as a category in Indonesian literature and history* (Singapore).

Johore annual report, 1910–40, 1948 (Singapore, Johore Bahru).

Jones, G. W. (1965a). 'The employment characteristics of small towns in Malaya', *MER*, x, i, pp. 44–72.

  (1965b). 'Female participation in the labour force in a plural economy: The Malayan example', *MER*, x, ii, pp. 61–82.

Jones, J. W. (1863). *The travels of Ludovico di Varthema* (London).

Josselin de Jong, P. E. de (1960). 'The Malacca Sultanate', *JSEAH*, i, ii, pp. 20–9.

Kanakasabhai Pillay, V. (1956). *The Tamils eighteen hundred years ago* (Madras).

Kanwar, H. I. S. (1950). 'India's link with Malaya', *United Asia* (Bombay), ii, pp. 423–5.

—— (1952). 'Indians in Malaya', *Eastern world* (London), vi, 14–15.

—— (1953). 'Indians in Malaya', *Eastern world* (London), vii, 19.

—— (1954). 'Malaya's cultural contacts with India', *Asia* (Saigon), iii, 536–44.

Kathāsaritsāgara (edited by P. Durga Prasad and K. P. Parab, Bombay, 1889).

Kelantan (annual) administrative report, 1909–40 (Kota Bharu).

Kennaway, M. J. (1912). *Some investigations of Straits Settlements and Federated Malay States recruiting in the Madras Presidency* (Kuala Lumpur).

Khan, S. N. (1946). *I.N.A. and its Netaji* (Delhi).

Kodanda Rao, P. (1946). 'Indians overseas: The position in Malaya', *India quarterly* (New Delhi), ii, 150–62.

—— (1963). *The Right Honourable V. S. Srinivasa Sastri: A political biography* (New York).

Kondapi, C. (1951). *Indians overseas, 1838–1949* (New Delhi).

Krishnan, R. B. (1936). *The Indians in Malaya: A pageant of Greater India* (Singapore).

Krishnaswami, S. Y. (1947). *Rural problems in Madras* (Madras).

Kumar, D. (1965). *Land and caste in South India* (Cambridge, England).

Kumaran, K. K. (1964a). *History of wage negotiations in the planting industry* (Kuala Lumpur).

—— (1964b). *National Union of Plantation Workers: Collective bargaining 1963–1964* (Kuala Lumpur).

Labour Research Department (1926). *British imperialism in Malaya* (London).

Laidlay, J. W. (1948). 'Notes on the inscriptions from Singapore and Province Wellesley', *JASB*, xvii, ii, pp. 66–72.

Lake, H. W., and Kelsall, H. J. (1894). 'A journey on the Sembrong River from Kuala Indau to Batu Pahat', *JSBRAS*, xxvi, 1–15.

Lamb, A. (1961). 'Miscellaneous papers on early Hindu and Buddhist settlements in northern Malaya and southern Thailand', *Federated Museums journal* (Kuala Lumpur), vi, 1–90.

Lamb, H. B. (1955). 'The "State" and economic development in India', in S. Kuznets *et al.* (eds.), *Economic growth: Brazil, India, Japan* (Durham, U.S.A.), pp. 464–95.

Law, B. C. (1954). *Historical geography of ancient India* (Paris).

Law, C. R. (1877). *History of the Indian navy, 1613–1863*, 2 vols. (London).

League of Nations (1937). *Migration problems* (Geneva).

Lee, H. L. (1960). 'The pattern of savings of households of Government employees in the State capitals', in K. R. Chou (ed.), *Savings in the Malayan economy* (Singapore), chap. 8, pp. 1–75.

Legge, J. (1886). *A record of Buddhistic kingdoms* (Oxford).

LeMay, R. (1954). *The culture of South-East Asia* (London).

Leur, J. C. van (1955). *Indonesian trade and society: Essays in Asian social and economic history* (The Hague).

Lim, C. Y. (1967). *Economic development of modern Malaya* (Kuala Lumpur).

Loewenstein, J. and Sieveking, G. de G. (1956). 'Papers on the Malayan Metal Age', *JMBRAS*, xxix, ii, pp. 5–138.

329

Select bibliography

Lohuizen-de Leeuw, J. E. van (1954). 'India and its cultural empire', in D. Sinor (ed.), *Orientalism and its history* (Cambridge, England).

Lovat, A. (1914). *Life of Sir Fredrick Weld* (London).

Low, J. (1836). *A dissertation on the soil and agriculture of the British settlement of Penang in the Straits of Malacca: including Province Wellesley on the Malayan Peninsula. With brief references to the settlements of Singapore and Malacca, and accompanied by incidental observations on various subjects of local interest in these Straits* (Singapore).

— (1848). 'An account of several inscriptions found in Province Wellesley, on the Peninsula of Malacca', *JASB*, xvii, ii, pp. 62–6.

— (1849). 'On an inscription from Kedah', *JASB*, xviii, i, pp. 247–9.

Low, J. (1908). *The Kedah Annals* (Bangkok).

Luce, G. H. (1925). 'Countries neighbouring Burma', *Journal of the Burma Research Society* (Rangoon), xiv, ii, pp. 138–205.

Macalister, N. (1803). *Historical memoir relative to the Prince of Wales Island* (London).

Macgregor, I. (1955). 'Notes on the Portuguese in Malacca', *JMBRAS*, xxxviii, ii, pp. 5–47.

McNair, J. F. A. (1899). *Prisoners their own warders* (Westminster).

McNeil, J. and Lal, C. (1915). *Report to the Government of India on the conditions of Indian immigrants in four British colonies and Surinam*, 2 pts. (London).

Madras annual report on emigration and immigration, 1881–1941 (Madras).

Madras (1930). *Report of the Madras Provincial banking committee, 1929*, 6 vols. (Calcutta).

Mahajani, U. (1960). *The role of Indian minorities in Burma and Malaya* (Bombay).

Major, R. H. (1857). *India in the fifteenth century: Being a collection of narratives of voyages to India in the century preceding the Portuguese discovery of the Cape of Good Hope, from Latin, Persian, Russian and Italian sources*, 4 pts. (New York).

Majumdar, N. (1960). *Justice and police in Bengal, 1765–1793* (Calcutta).

Majumdar, N. G. (1926). 'Nalanda copper-plate of Devapaladeva', *Monographs of the Varendra Research Society* (Rajshahi).

Majumdar, R. C. (1927). *Champa*, 2 pts. (Lahore).

— (1937). *Suvarnadvipa. Part I, political history* (Dacca).

— (1951–60). *History and culture of the Indian people*, 6 vols. (London, Bombay).

— (1955). *Ancient Indian colonization in South-East Asia* (Baroda).

— (1963). *Hindu colonies in the Far East* (Calcutta).

Makepeace, W. (ed.) (1921). *One hundred years of Singapore*, 2 vols. (London).

Malay States Guides annual report, 1898–1913 (Kuala Lumpur).

Malayan Trades Union Congress (1961). *Annual report 1960–1961 and connected papers* (Kuala Lumpur).

Malayan Union annual report, 1946–7 (Kuala Lumpur).

Malayan Union annual report of the Labour Department, 1946–7 (Kuala Lumpur).

Malayan year book, 1936–9 (Singapore).

Malaysia (1965). *First Malaysian Plan 1966–1970* (Kuala Lumpur).

Select bibliography

Manual of statistics relating to the Federated Malay States, 1910–33 (Kuala Lumpur).

Marjoribanks, N. E. and Marakkayar, A. R. (1917). *Report on Indian labour emigration to Ceylon and Malaya* (Madras).

Marrison, G. E. (1951). 'The coming of Islam to the East Indies', *JMBRAS*, XXIV, i, pp. 28–37.

(1955). 'Persian influences on Malay life (1280–1650)', *JMBRAS*, XXVIII, i, pp. 52–69.

Marriot, H. (1911*a*). *Report on the census of the State of Johore taken on 10th March, 1911* (Singapore).

(1911*b*). *Report on the census of the Straits Settlements taken on the 10th March, 1911* (Singapore).

Maxwell, G. (1911). 'Barretto de Resende's account of Malacca', *JSBRAS*, LX, 1–24.

(1945). 'The Malays and the Malayans', *Nineteenth century and after* (London), CXXXVII, 276–85.

Maxwell, W. E. (1882). 'A journey on foot to the Patani frontier, 1876', *JSBRAS*, IX, 1–67.

(1891–2). 'The Malay Peninsula: Its resources and prospects', *PRCI*, XXIII, 3–46.

Meilink-Roelofsz, M. A. P. (1962). *Asian trade and European influence in the Indonesian Archipelago between 1500 and about 1630* (The Hague).

Memorandum presented to the Rt. Hon. V. S. Srinivasa Sastri, P.C., C.H., on deputation to Malaya, on behalf of the Selangor Indian Association, Kuala Lumpur, the Young Men's Indian Association, Sentul, the Coastal Indian Association, Klang (Kuala Lumpur, 1937).

Merewether, E. M. (1892). *Report on the census of the Straits Settlements taken on the 5th April, 1891* (Singapore).

Mills, J. V. (1930). 'Emanuel Godinho de Eredia's "Declaram de Malacca e India Meridional com o Cathay"', *JMBRAS*, XXXIII, iii, pp. 1–288.

Mills, L. A. (1942). *British rule in eastern Asia* (London).

(1960). 'British Malaya, 1824–67', *JMBRAS*, XXXIII, iii, pp. 5–326.

Ministry of Agriculture and Co-operatives, Malaysia (1965). *Kementerian Pertanian dan Sharikat Kerjasama: Bahagian perikanan perangkaan tahunan 1965. Ministry of Agriculture and Co-operatives: Fisheries Division annual report, 1965* (Kuala Lumpur).

Ministry of Culture, Singapore (1966). *Singapore Guide and Street Directory* (Singapore).

Minutes and Council papers of the Federal Legislative Council, 1948–56 (Kuala Lumpur).

Misra, B. (1932). *Economic survey of a village (Maswanpur) in Cawnpore district (U.P.)* (Allahabad).

Monthly digest of statistics, 1962–January 1967 (Singapore).

Monthly statistical bulletin of the Federation (States) of Malaya, 1952–66 (Kuala Lumpur).

Mookerji, R. (1957). *A history of Indian shipping and maritime activity* (Bombay).

Moothedan, A. V. (1932). *Our countrymen in Malaya* (Trivandrum).

Select bibliography

Moraes, F. (ed.) (1952). *The Indian and Pakistani year book and who's who, 1951* (Bombay).

Moreland, W. H. (1920*a*). *India at the death of Akbar: An Economic History* (London).

(1920*b*). 'The shahbandar in the eastern seas', *JRAS*, pp. 517–33.

(1923). *From Akbar to Aurangzeb: A study in Indian economic history* (London).

Moreland, W. H. and Geyl, P. (translators) (1925). *Jahangir's India: The 'Remonstrantie' of Francisco Pelsaert* (Cambridge, England).

Morris, M. D. (1960). 'Caste and the evolution of the industrial work force in India', *Proceedings of the American Philosophical Society* (Philadelphia), 104, 2, pp. 124–33.

(1963). 'Towards a re-interpretation of nineteenth century Indian economic history', *The journal of economic history* (New York), XXXIII, iv, pp. 606–18.

(1965). *The emergence of an industrial labour force in India* (Berkeley, U.S.A.).

(1966). 'Economic change and agriculture in nineteenth century India', *The Indian economic and social history review* (New Delhi), III, ii, pp. 185–209.

Mukerjee, R. (1936). *Migrant Asia* (Rome).

Mukherjee, K. M. (1954). *Our countrymen abroad* (New Delhi).

Mukherjee, R. (ed) (1939–41). *Economic problems of modern India*, 2 vols. (London).

Mukhtyar, G. C. (1930). *Life and labour in a south Gujarat village* (Calcutta).

Nagam Aiya, Y. (1894). *Report on the census of Travancore, 1891* (Madras).

Nair, M. N. (1937). *The Indians in Malaya* (Kodnayur Printing Works, India).

Nair, V. G. (1960). *Swami Satyananda and cultural relations between India and Malaya* (Kuala Lumpur).

Nanavati, M. B. and Anjaria, J. J. (1944). *Indian rural problems* (Bombay).

Nanjudan, S. (1950). *Indians in Malayan economy* (New Delhi).

Nanporia, N. J. (1965). *The Times of India directory and year book including who's who, 1964–65* (Bombay).

Natarajan, B. (1938–9). 'Influence of classical theories on interest regulations in India, 1800–55', *EHR*, IX, 186–92.

Nathan, J. E. (1922). *The census of British Malaya, 1921* (London).

National Land Finance Co-operative Society Limited (1962). *Chenderamata Ladang Rinching* (Kuala Lumpur).

National Union of Plantation Workers (1965). *General report 1962–1965* (Kuala Lumpur).

Negri Sembilan annual report, 1888–1939 (Kuala Lumpur, Seremban).

Neelakandha Aiyer, K. A. (1938). *Indian problems in Malaya* (Kuala Lumpur).

Nehru, S. S. (1932). *Caste and credit in the rural areas* (London).

Netto, G. (1961). *Indians in Malaya: Historical facts and figures* (Singapore).

Newbold, T. J. (1839). *Political and statistical account of the British settlements in the Straits of Malacca*, 2 vols. (London).

Nilakanta Sastri, K. A. (1938). 'The beginnings of intercourse between India and China', *Indian historical quarterly* (Calcutta), XIV, 380–7.

(1949 a). *South Indian influences in the Far East* (Bombay).

(1949 b). 'Takuapa and its Tamil inscription', *JMBRAS*, xxii, i, pp. 25–30.

(1954). 'Ancient contacts between India and South-East Asia', *MHJ*, i, i, pp. 11–15.

(1955). *The Cōḷas* (Madras).

(1959). *Cultural expansion of India* (Gauhati).

Office of the Honorary Commissioner for Depressed Classes, Straits Settlements (1927). *Commissioner's report on Malaya, 1926* (Singapore).

(1928). *Report of the Honorary Commissioner for Depressed Classes, Straits Settlements and Federated Malay States, on traffic between South Indian ports and Malaya, 1928* (Cidambaram).

O'Malley, L. S. S. (ed.) (1941). *Modern India and the West* (London).

Onraet, R. (1947). *Singapore—A police background* (London).

Ooi, J. B. (1959). 'Rural development in tropical areas, with special reference to Malaya', *(M)JTG*, xii, 1–222.

(1963). *Land, people and economy in Malaya* (London).

O'Sullivan, A. W. S. (1913). 'The relations between South India and the Straits Settlements', in the Straits Philosophical Society, Singapore, *Noctes Orientales: Being a selection of essays read before the Straits Philosophical Society between the years 1893 and 1910* (Singapore), pp. 165–87.

Oversea-Chinese Association, India (1944). *Memorandum on the future of Malaya* (Bangalore).

Pahang annual report, 1888–1939 (Kuala Lumpur, Kuala Lipis).

Papers of the Indian National Congress, 1885–1946 (New Delhi, London).

Parliamentary papers, 1810–1937 (London).

Parmer, J. N. (1960). *Colonial labor policy and administration* (New York).

Parr, C. W. C. (1910). *Report of the commission appointed to enquire into the conditions of indentured labour in the Federated Malay States* (Kuala Lumpur).

Patel, S. J. (1952). *Agricultural labourers in modern India and Pakistan* (Bombay).

Pearson, A. C. (1914). *Report on the working of various departments of the Federated Malay States Government and the Philippine Forest Bureau* (London).

Pelliot, P. (1903). 'Le Fou-nan', *Bulletin de l'Ecole Française d'Extrême-Orient* (Hanoi), iii, 248–330.

Perak annual report, 1888–1939 (Taiping, Kuala Lumpur, Ipoh).

Perak government gazette, 1888–1909 (Taiping, Kuala Lumpur).

Perlis annual report, 1909–40 (Penang, Alor Star).

(United) Planters' Association of Malaya annual report, 1910, 1913–40 (Kuala Lumpur).

(United) Planters' Association of Malaya (1919). *Papers on Tamil immigration presented at 12th annual meeting of the Planters' Association of Malaya, April 30th, 1919* (Kuala Lumpur).

(1928). *Interim report of the special labour committee on matters relating to wages for Indian estate labourers* (Kuala Lumpur).

Select bibliography

1957 Population census of the Federation of Malaya, Reports nos 1–14 (Kuala Lumpur).

Pountney, A. M. (1911). *The census of the Federated Malay States, 1911* (London).

Proceedings of the Council of the Governor-General of India, 1862–1920 (Calcutta, New Delhi).

Proceedings of the Federal Council, 1909–40 (Kuala Lumpur).

Proceedings of the Legislative Council of India, 1854–61 (Calcutta).

Proceedings of the Legislative Council of the Straits Settlements, 1867–1941 (Singapore).

Public Relations Department, Singapore (1953). *Press Statement A.P. 53/190 dated April 24th, 1953* (Singapore).

Punjab (1930). *Report of the Punjab Provincial banking committee, 1929*, 3 vols. (Calcutta).

Purbatjaraka, P. (1961). *Sjahabhandars in the Archipelago* (Singapore).

Purcell, V. (1948). *The Chinese in Malaya* (London).

Puri, B. N. (1956). 'Some aspects of social life in ancient Kambujadesa', *JGIS*, xv, 85–92.

Puthucheary, J. J. (1960). *Ownership and control in the Malayan economy* (Singapore).

Raghavaiyangar, S. S. (1892). *Memorandum on the progress of the Madras Presidency during the last forty years of British administration* (Madras).

Raghavan, N. (1954). *India and Malaya: A study* (Bombay).

Rai, A. (1914a). *The Indian coolie in British Malaya* (Madras).

(1914b). 'The Indian cooly in British Malaya', *The Indian review* (Madras), xv, 452–60.

Raju, A. S. (1941). *Economic conditions in the Madras Presidency, 1800–1860* (Madras).

Raman Rao, A. V. (1958). *Economic development of Andhra Pradesh, 1766–1957* (Bombay).

Rama Sastry, C. S. (1947). *Congress mission to Malaya* (Tenali, Madras).

Ramaswamy, T. N. (1946). *Economic stabilization of Indian agriculture* (Benares).

Rao, V. K. R. V. (1944). 'National income of India', *Annals of the American Academy of Political and Social Sciences* (Philadelphia), ccxxxiii, 99–105.

Raychaudhuri, T. (1962). *Jan Company in Coromandel 1605–1690* (The Hague).

Report of the commission appointed to enquire into certain matters affecting the health of estates in the Federated Malay States, 1924 (Singapore, 1924).

Report of the commission appointed to enquire into the question of Indian immigration, 1896 (Singapore, 1896).

Report of the commissioners appointed to enquire into the state of labour in the Straits Settlements and the Protected Native States, 1890 (Singapore, 1891).

Rubber Growers' Association (annual) report of the Council to members of the Association, 1909–13, 1920–39 (London).

Ruhomon, P. (1939). *Centenary history of the East Indians in British Guiana, 1838–1938* (Georgetown).

Sachau, E. (ed.) (1910). *Alberuni's India, an account of the religions, philosophy,* literature, geography, chronology, astrology, customs, laws and astronomy of India, about A.D. 1030, 2 vols. (London).

Sanderson, Lord (1910). *Emigration from India to the Crown Colonies and Protectorates*, 3 pts. (London).

Sandhu, K. S. (1961a). 'Chinese colonization of Malacca', (*M)JTG*, xv, 1–26.

(1961b). 'The population of Malaya: Some changes in the pattern of distribution between 1947 and 1957', (*M)JTG*, xv, 82–96.

(1964a). 'Emergency resettlement in Malaya', (*M)JTG*, xviii, 157–83.

(1964b). 'The saga of the "squatter" in Malaya: A preliminary survey of the causes, characteristics and consequences of the resettlement of rural dwellers during the Emergency between 1948 and 1960', *JSEAH*, v, i, pp. 143–77.

Sastri, H. (1924). 'The Nalanda copper-plate of Deva-paladeva', *EI*, xviii, vii, pp. 310–27.

Saw, S. H. (1964). 'A note on the under-registration of births in Malaya during the intercensal period 1947–1957', *Population studies* (London), xviii, 35–52.

Scott, W. D. (1912). *Translation of census (taken in Malay) of the State of Trengganu taken in 1329=1911* (Kuala Trengganu).

Schrieke, B. (1955–7). *Indonesian sociological studies*, 2 pts. (The Hague).

Sějarah Mělayu (edited by R. O. Winstedt, 1938, *JMBRAS*, xvi, iii, pp. 1–226).

Selangor annual report, 1886–1939 (Kuala Lumpur).

Selangor government gazette, 1890–1909 (Kuala Lumpur).

Sendut, H. (1962). 'Pattern of urbanization in Malaya', (*M)JTG*, xvi, 114–30.

Sheehan, J. J. (1934). 'Seventeenth century visitors to the Malay Peninsula', *JMBRAS*, xii, ii, pp. 71–107.

Silcock, T. H. and Fisk, E. K. (eds.) (1966). *The political economy of independent Malaya* (Singapore).

Singapore Department of Social Welfare (1948). *Social survey of Singapore, 1947* (Singapore).

Singapore (1955–6). *The revised edition of the laws in Singapore, 1955*, 8 vols. (Singapore).

(1959). *The Immigration (Amendment) Ordinance, 1959* (Singapore).

Singapore year book, 1964–5 (Singapore).

Singh, D. (1946). *Formation and growth of the Indian National Army* (Lahore).

Singh, S. K. and Ahluwalia, M. L. (1963). *Punjab's pioneer freedom fighters* (Calcutta).

Sinha, N. C. (1946). *Studies in Indo-British economy a hundred years ago* (Calcutta).

Smith, T. E. (1952). *Population growth in Malaya: An analysis of recent trends* (London).

Sovani, N. V. (1954a). 'British impact on India after 1850–57', *CHM*, ii, i, pp. 77–105.

(1954b). 'British impact on India before 1850–57', *CHM*, i, iv, pp. 857–82.

Speyer, J. S. (1895). *The Jātakamālā or garland of birth stories* (London).

Select bibliography

Srinivas, M. N. and Shah, A. M. (1960). 'The myth of self-sufficiency of the Indian village', *The economic weekly* (Bombay), XII, xxxvii, pp. 1375–8.

Srinivasa Sastri, V. S. (1937). *Report on conditions of Indian labour in Malaya* (reprint, Kuala Lumpur).

State of Kelantan (1911). *The total population of the State of Kelantan distributed in the various districts in accordance with census taken in 1329 = 1911* (Kota Bharu).

State of Perak (1894). *Perak handbook, 1893* (Taiping).

State of Singapore annual report of the Immigration Department, 1958–62 (Singapore).

Statement exhibiting the moral and material progress and condition of India, 1860/1–1934/5 (Calcutta, New Delhi, London).

Statistical abstracts for British India, 1840–1941 (Calcutta, New Delhi, London).

Straits Settlements annual report, 1855/6–1858/9, 1865/6–1867/8, 1886–1940 (Calcutta, Singapore).

Straits Settlements blue book, 1867–1920 (Singapore).

Straits Settlements government gazette, 1867–1938 (Singapore).

Strachey, J. (1937). *India, its administration and progress* (London).

Subramaniam, S. (1945). *Statistical summary of the social and economic trends in India* (Washington, D.C.).

Subrahmanya Aiyar, K. V. (1934). 'The Larger Leiden plates (of Rajaraja I)', *EI*, XXII, iv, pp. 213–60.

Sundaram, L. (1930). *International aspects of Indian emigration* (London).

Swettenham, F. A. (1885). 'Journal kept during a journey across the Malay Peninsula', *JSBRAS*, XV, 1–37.

(1895–6). 'British rule in Malaya', *PRCI*, XXVII, 273–312.

Tan, D. E. (1963). *The rice industry in Malaya, 1920–1940* (Singapore).

Tawney, C. H. (1925). *The ocean of story*, 10 vols. (London).

Thomas, P. J. and Natarajan, B. (1936–7). 'Economic depression in the Madras Presidency (1825–54)', *EHR*, VII, 67–75.

Thomas, P. J. (ed.) (1940). *Some South Indian villages* (Madras).

Thorburn, S. S. (1886). *Musalmans and moneylenders in the Punjab* (Edinburgh).

Thorner, D. (1955). 'Long-term trends in output in India', in S. Kuznets *et al.* (eds.), *Economic growth: Brazil, India, Japan* (Durham, U.S.A.), pp. 103–28.

Thorner, D. and Thorner, A. (1962). *Land and labour in India* (Bombay).

Tibbetts, G. R. (1956). 'The Malay Peninsula as known to the Arab geographers', *(M)JTG*, IX, 21–60.

Tilman, R. O. (1964). *Bureaucratic transition in Malaya* (Durham, U.S.A.).

Ton That Thien (1963). *India and South East Asia, 1947–1960* (Geneva).

Toye, H. (1959). *The springing tiger* (London).

Trengganu annual report, 1910–40 (Kuala Trengganu, Kota Bharu).

Tregonning, K. G. (1958). 'Factors in the founding of Penang', *JGIS*, XVIII, 23–32.

(1965a). *The British in Malaya: The first forty years 1786–1826* (Tucson, U.S.A.).

Select bibliography

(1965 b). 'The origin of the Straits Steamship Company in 1890', *JMBRAS*, xxxviii, ii, pp. 274–89.

Tweedie, M. W. F. (1953). 'The stone age in Malaya', *JMBRAS*, xxvi, ii, pp. 1–190.

United Kingdom (1880–5). *Report of the Indian famine commission, 1878,* 3 vols. (London).

(1918). *Imperial war conference, 1918: Extracts from minutes of proceedings and papers laid before the conference* (London).

(1921). *Conference of Prime Ministers and Representatives of the United Kingdom, the Dominions and India, held in June, July and August, 1921: Summary of transactions* (London).

(1923). *Imperial conference, 1923* (London).

(1927–8). *Report of the Royal Commission on agriculture in India,* 14 vols. (London).

(1931). *Report of the Royal Commission on labour in India* (London).

United Nations (1962). 'Evaluation of the population data of Malaya', *Economic bulletin for Asia and the Far East* (New York), xiii, ii, pp. 23–44.

Venkatasubbiah, N. (1920). *The structural basis of India's economy* (London).

Vermont, J. M. (1888). 'Immigration from India to the Straits Settlements', *Straits Settlements pamphlets* (Colonial Office, London), i, x, pp. 1–60.

Vlieland, C. A. (1932). *British Malaya: A report on the 1931 census* (London).

(1934). 'The population of the Malay Peninsula', *Geographical review* (New York), xxiv, 61–78.

Vogel, J. Ph. (1925). *The relation between the art of India and Java* (London).

Wales, H. G. Q. (1935). 'A recently explored route of ancient Indian cultural expansion', *Indian art and letters* (London), new series, ix, i, pp. 1–31.

(1937). *Towards Angkor: In the footsteps of the Indian invaders* (London).

(1940). 'Archaeological researches in ancient Indian colonization in Malaya', *JMBRAS*, xviii, i, pp. 1–85.

(1948). 'Culture change in Greater India', *JRAS*, pp. 2–32.

(1961). *The making of Greater India* (London).

Wang, G. W. (ed.) (1964). *Malaysia: A survey* (Singapore).

Warmington, E. H. (1928). *The commerce between the Roman empire and India* (Cambridge, England).

Weber, M. (1950). *The Hindu social system* (Minneapolis).

Weld, F. (1883–4). 'The Straits Settlements and British Malaya', *PRCI*, xv, 266–311.

Wheatley, P. (1954). 'Land use in the vicinity of Singapore in the eighteen-thirties', *(M)JTG*, ii, 63–6.

(1961). *The Golden Khersonese* (Kuala Lumpur).

(1964 a). 'Desultory remarks on the ancient history of the Malay Peninsula', in J. Bastin and R. Roolvink (eds.), *Malayan and Indonesian studies: Essays presented to Sir Ronald Winstedt on his eighty-fifth birthday* (London), pp. 33–75.

(1964 b). *Impressions of the Malay Peninsula in ancient times* (Singapore).

Wikkramatileke, R. (1965). 'State aided rural land colonization in Malaya:

Select bibliography

An appraisal of the F.L.D.A. program', *Annals of the Association of American Geographers* (Washington, D.C.), LV, iii, pp. 377–403.

Wilkinson, R. J. (1908). *Papers on Malay subjects* (Kuala Lumpur).

(1935). 'The Malacca Sultanate', *JMBRAS*, XIII, ii, pp. 22–67.

Wilson, T. B. (1961). *Census of agriculture Federation of Malaya: Preliminary report number three: Type, tenure and fragmentation of farms* (Kuala Lumpur).

Winstedt, R. O. (1923). *Malaya* (London).

(1925). *Shaman, Saiva and Sufi: a study of the evolution of Malay magic* (London).

(1932). 'History of Johore', *JMBRAS*, X, iii, pp. 1–167.

(1935). 'A history of Malaya', *JMBRAS*, XIII, i, pp. 1–270.

(1938). 'The Malay Annals or Sĕjarah Mĕlayu', *JMBRAS*, XVI, iii, pp. 1–226.

(1942). 'Malaysia', in A. J. Arberry and R. Landau (eds.), *Islam to-day* (London), pp. 211–26.

(1944). 'Indian influence in the Malay World', *JRAS*, pp. 186–96.

(1947). *The Malays: A cultural history* (London).

(1958). *The Malays: A cultural history* (London).

Wong, L. K. (1965). *The Malayan tin industry to 1914* (Tucson, U.S.A.).

Wright, A. (1908). *Twentieth century impressions of British Malaya* (London).

Yearly (annual) report on the State of Kedah, 1905–6, 1909–40 (Penang, Alor Star).

(B): Newspapers

Amrita bazar patrika (Calcutta), 1912–16.

Daily digest of non-English press (Singapore), 1952–66.

Eastern Sun, The (Singapore), 1966–mid-1967.

Hindu, The (Madras), 1910–57 (various years).

Hindustan Times, The (New Delhi), 1937–8.

Indian, The (Kuala Lumpur), 1935–41.

Indian Daily Mail, The (Singapore), 1946–9.

Indian Pioneer, The (Kuala Lumpur), 1926–30.

Malay Mail, The (Kuala Lumpur), 1896–1941, 1946–mid-1967 (various years).

Malaya Tribune (Kuala Lumpur), 1925–6.

Penang Gazette, The (Penang), 1852–7.

Prince of Wales Island Gazette, The (Penang), 1806–27 (various years).

Singapore Daily Times, The (Singapore), 1881.

Singapore Free Press, The (Singapore), 1835–1940, 1952–62 (various years).

Straits Budget, The (Singapore), 1890–1940 (various years).

Straits Times, The (Singapore), 1858–1941, 1946–mid-1967 (various years).

Sunday Mail, The (Kuala Lumpur), 1960–6.

Syonan shimbun (Singapore), 1942–5.

Times, The (London), 1884, 1902, 1909.

Select bibliography

(C): Periodicals

British Malaya (*Malaya*) (London), 1926–57 (various years).

Grenier's rubber news (Kuala Lumpur), 1909–20 (various years).

Indian, The (Singapore), 1925–32.

Indian emigrant, The (Madras), 1914–19.

Indian Association bulletin, The (Penang), 1932–3.

Indian review, The (Madras), 1905–40 (various years).

Indo-Malayan review, The (Ipoh), 1933–4.

Journal of the Indian Archipelago and eastern Asia (Singapore), 1847–59.

Kew Gardens bulletin, The (London), 1897–1900.

Malayan agricultural journal, The (Kuala Lumpur), 1930–40, 1950–2.

Malayan Police magazine, The (Kuala Lumpur), 1928–40 (various years).

Modern review, The (Calcutta), 1909–40 (various years).

Monthly record of migration (Geneva), 1926–8.

Planter, The (Kuala Lumpur), 1920–41 (various years).

Rubber statistical bulletin, The (London), 1959–65.

Selangor journal, The (Kuala Lumpur), 1893–7.

Servant of India, The (Poona), 1918–37.

Union herald: Monthly organ of the N.U.P.W. (*National Union of Plantation Workers*) (Kuala Lumpur), 1958–66.

INDEX

Acheh, 118
Adamson, McTaggart & Co., 80
Adi-dravidas, 40, 57, 99
adimai, 40
agriculture, 10, 26, 34, 36–41, 49, 77, 200, 217, 230, 245 ff.; Malay Peninsula Association, 87; plantation, 249–54, 301; settlements, 263–77
Ahmedabad, 119
Aldworth, J. R. O., 93
Allahabad, 120
Alor Star, 179
America (Miriken), 126–7, 157
Amrita Bazar Patrika, 101, 109
Amritsar, 119
Anak Bukit, 179
Andamans, 133, 140; prisoners, 136
Andhra Pradesh, 99, 162, 239
Andrews, C. F., 108
Anglo-Dutch treaty (1824), 4, 133
Anti-Slavery Society, 86
Arabs, 28
āśramas, 233, 303
Assam, 90, 298
Australia, 68, 126, 182
Avadi, 64, 92–3, 95, 104
Azamgarh, 120

babu, 42
Balestier, J., 77
Bangkok, 119, 122
Barisan Sosialis (Singapore), 302
Beaumont, J., 76
Belgaum, 129
Benares, 120, 136
Bencoolen, 133–4
Bengal, 26, 82, 88, 119, 123, 129–31; convicts, 132, 136; farmers, 270
beri-beri, 60
Bhai Singh, 302–3
Bihar, 131
Bikaner, 119, 120
Binny & Co., 92
Birch, J. W. W., 180
Blundell, Colonel, 139
Bombay, 88, 119, 120, 129, 222
Borneo, 6, 118
Bose, Subhas Chandra, 300

brāhmaṇas, 23–4, 57
British Colonial Development Corporation, Ltd., 190
British India Steamship Navigation Co., 61–2, 92–3
British Malaya, 4–6, 10, 15, 17, 27, 31, 43, 177, 180, 205, 297; Agent, 15, 17; Indian Army, 74; Military Administration, 14
Buddhists, 22–6, 233, 235, 302
buildings, 232–5
Burma, 61, 156–7, 235, 298; rice, 90, 182; Front, 300

Calcutta, 78, 119, 120, 123, 125, 130, 140, 222
camp-followers, 130–1
Canada (Kaneida), 126–7, 157
caṅkams, 233
Carey, E. V., 64
Caribbean, 298
caste, 39–40
Caturvargacintāmani, 23
Ceṭṭinaaṭu, 118
Ceylon, 10, 11, 57, 68–9, 97, 141, 156–7, 298; coffee and tea, 90–1; Jaffna Tamils, 69, 123, 261, 303; Pioneer Corps, 285; wages, 61
Chamars, 58, 99
Chamberlain, Joseph, 49
Chettiars, 121, 136, 220; moneylenders and financiers, 191–2
Chinese, 1, 9, 10, 16, 44, 68, 73, 127, 182, 205–6, 219, 220–2, 225, 230–1, 235, 256, 258, 271, 297; communists, 148; compared with Indians, 260–1; farming, 274; fishing, 278; forestry, 277; labour, 54–8, 148, 189, 217; Malayan Association, 301; numbers, 153, 301, 215–16; problems of, 70–1; rubber, 261–2; squatters, 188; tea, 253; tin, 280; women, 247
Chingleput, 41, 99, 105
Chittagong, 119, 300
cholera, 107, 181
Christians, 167, 234; numbers, 233
Chuah, 267–8; Indian Settlers' Co-operative Society, 268

341

Index

Index

301; Co-operative Department, 268; Department of Labour, 46, 106; Indian Congress, 256, 301; Labour Party, 302; Trades Union Congress, 289
mandurs, 114
Maniam, 303
mantras, 25
manufacturing, 282
Marwaris, 119–20
masok Melaya, 167
Mauritius, 76, 78, 298
medical facilities, 170–1, 184
Melpakkam, 64
Merdeka, 167, 255, 285, 290
metals, 26; from mining, 278–82
Midnapore, 119
military forces, 70–3, 240
mirasdars, 41, 105
Mission d'Etrangérers, 267
moneylenders, 291
Montagu-Chelmsford reforms, 109
Mughals, 23, 27, 30
mukim, 6
mulada, 40
munsif, 100
musafirkhanas, 120
Muslims, 23–7, 44, 117–18, 162, 167, 302; Muharram celebrations, 139; number, 233; of South India, 119–23, 129, 225, 234
Muthiah, V. A., 268

Nachodar Gianty, 29
nāgara, 2, 22, 302
Nagore, 80, 82, 119
Nakarattaars, 119, 291
narakam, 66
nationalism: India, 34–5, 44, 144–5; Malaya, 149
Negapatam, 61, 64, 80, 92–3, 95, 99, 103–5, 119, 156
Negri Sembilan, 4, 9, 24, 83, 177, 179, 188–9, 197, 252; bus service, 287; Indian population, 200, 210, 217; Settlement, 267–8
Nehru, Jawaharlal, 299, 301
New Villages, 216, 230–1
New Zealand, 68
Norfolk Island, 137
North Arcot, 99, 161

oil palm, 10, 50, 52, 123, 181, 212, 217, 249, 257–8, history, 250–2
Ordinance I (1876), 80; *VII (1897)*, 88; *Immigration (1953)*, 150

Oriyas, 88
O'Sullivan, A. W. S., 78
outcastes, 41

padiyal, 40
Pahang, 4, 9, 136, 179, 188–9
paisa, 33, 125
Pakistan: partition, 121
Pallas, 57–8, 99
pannaiyal, 40–1, 105
Papakovil, 64
Pariahs, 57–8, 99
Parmer, J. N., 112
Parsis, 119, 121, 136, 178
Pathans, 63, 123, 127, 129
Penang, 9, 47, 61, 64, 82, 88, 92, 107, 118, 134, 167, 179–80, 188, 193, 221, 225, 236, 253, 270, 289; convicts, 132–3, 139; fishing, 277; foundation of, 4, 12, 15, 31, 43, 129–30, 131, 177; Indian population, 177–8, 197, 210–11, 217; port of entry, 95; schools, 67; tin, 279–80; walking-sticks, 138
Peoples Action Party (Singapore), 302
pepper, 26, 49, 249
Perak, 4, 9, 61, 73, 83, 99, 124, 131, 165, 177, 179–80, 188–9, 197, 230–1, 237, 239, 240, 249, 252; guardian genies, 24; Gula estate, 85; Indian population, 210, 212, 217; Mission Settlement, 267; railway, 285; rice, 276
Perlis, 118, 188, 190
Permatang Estate Settlement, 265–6
Persekutuan Tanah Melayu, 6
Pillai, 303
pineapples, 10, 258; history, 253
Planters' Association (Malaya), 93, 100, 102, 112–13, 259
Polak, 108
police, 70–3, 240, 288; railway, 285
Pondicherry, 80, 82, 119
population, 9–13, 16, 31, 81–2; growth, 35, 37, 175 ff.
Port Dickson, 267–8; Indian population, 212
Porto Novo, 82, 119
Port Swettenham, 64, 95, 107
Portuguese, 2–4, 26, 28–9, 177, 297
Prai, 118
prices, 41–2
Puddukkottai, 118
pukka nawkri, 69, 74, 124
Punjabis, 63, 88, 119, 122–3, 125, 127, 129, 154, 162, 240, 285
Purāṇas, 22
puthal-surats, 106–7

344

Index